Microsoft® Official Academic Course

Microsoft® .NET Framework Application Development Foundation, Exam 70–536

Credits

EXECUTIVE EDITOR	John Kane
DIRECTOR OF SALES	Mitchell Beaton
EXECUTIVE MARKETING MANAGER	Chris Ruel
MICROSOFT SENIOR PRODUCT MANAGER	Merrick Van Dongen of Microsoft Learning
EDITORIAL PROGRAM ASSISTANT	Jennifer Lartz
PRODUCTION MANAGER	Micheline Frederick
PRODUCTION EDITOR	Kerry Weinstein
CREATIVE DIRECTOR	Harry Nolan
COVER DESIGNER	Jim O'Shea
TECHNOLOGY AND MEDIA	Tom Kulesa/Wendy Ashenberg

This book was set in Garamond by Aptara, Inc. and printed and bound by Bind Rite Graphics. The cover was printed by Phoenix Color.

ISBN 978-0-470-18369-4

Printed in the United States of America

10 9 8 7 6 5 4 3 2 1

Foreword from the Publisher

Wiley's publishing vision for the Microsoft Official Academic Course series is to provide students and instructors with the skills and knowledge they need to use Microsoft technology effectively in all aspects of their personal and professional lives. Quality instruction is required to help both educators and students get the most from Microsoft's software tools and to become more productive. Thus our mission is to make our instructional programs trusted educational companions for life.

To accomplish this mission, Wiley and Microsoft have partnered to develop the highest quality educational programs for Information Workers, IT Professionals, and Developers. Materials created by this partnership carry the brand name "Microsoft Official Academic Course," assuring instructors and students alike that the content of these textbooks is fully endorsed by Microsoft, and that they provide the highest quality information and instruction on Microsoft products. The Microsoft Official Academic Course textbooks are "Official" in still one more way—they are the officially sanctioned courseware for Microsoft IT Academy members.

The Microsoft Official Academic Course series focuses on *workforce development*. These programs are aimed at those students seeking to enter the workforce, change jobs, or embark on new careers as information workers, IT professionals, and developers. Microsoft Official Academic Course programs address their needs by emphasizing authentic workplace scenarios with an abundance of projects, exercises, cases, and assessments.

The Microsoft Official Academic Courses are mapped to Microsoft's extensive research and job-task analysis, the same research and analysis used to create the Microsoft Certified Technology Specialist (MCTS) exam. The textbooks focus on real skills for real jobs. As students work through the projects and exercises in the textbooks they enhance their level of knowledge and their ability to apply the latest Microsoft technology to everyday tasks. These students also gain resume-building credentials that can assist them in finding a job, keeping their current job, or in furthering their education.

The concept of life-long learning is today an utmost necessity. Job roles, and even whole job categories, are changing so quickly that none of us can stay competitive and productive without continuously updating our skills and capabilities. The Microsoft Official Academic Course offerings, and their focus on Microsoft certification exam preparation, provide a means for people to acquire and effectively update their skills and knowledge. Wiley supports students in this endeavor through the development and distribution of these courses as Microsoft's official academic publisher.

Today educational publishing requires attention to providing quality print and robust electronic content. By integrating Microsoft Official Academic Course products, *WileyPLUS*, and Microsoft certifications, we are better able to deliver efficient learning solutions for students and teachers alike.

Bonnie Lieberman

General Manager and Senior Vice President

Preface

Welcome to the Microsoft Official Academic Course (MOAC) program for Microsoft .NET Framework Application Development Foundation. MOAC represents the collaboration between Microsoft Learning and John Wiley & Sons, Inc. publishing company. Microsoft and Wiley teamed up to produce a series of textbooks that deliver compelling and innovative teaching solutions to instructors and superior learning experiences for students. Infused and informed by in-depth knowledge from the creators of Microsoft .NET Framwork, and crafted by a publisher known worldwide for the pedagogical quality of its products, these textbooks maximize skills transfer in minimum time. Students are challenged to reach their potential by using their new technical skills as highly productive members of the workforce.

Because this knowledgebase comes directly from Microsoft, architect of the Microsoft .NET Framework and creator of the Microsoft Certified Technology Specialist and Microsoft Certified Professional exams (www.microsoft.com/learning/mcp/mcts), you are sure to receive the topical coverage that is most relevant to students' personal and professional success. Microsoft's direct participation not only assures you that MOAC textbook content is accurate and current; it also means that students will receive the best instruction possible to enable their success on certification exams and in the workplace.

■ The Microsoft Official Academic Course Program

The *Microsoft Official Academic Course* series is a complete program for instructors and institutions to prepare and deliver great courses on Microsoft software technologies. With MOAC, we recognize that, because of the rapid pace of change in the technology and curriculum developed by Microsoft, there is an ongoing set of needs beyond classroom instruction tools for an instructor to be ready to teach the course. The MOAC program endeavors to provide solutions for all these needs in a systematic manner in order to ensure a successful and rewarding course experience for both instructor and student—technical and curriculum training for instructor readiness with new software releases; the software itself for student use at home for building hands-on skills, assessment, and validation of skill development; and a great set of tools for delivering instruction in the classroom and lab. All are important to the smooth delivery of an interesting course on Microsoft software, and all are provided with the MOAC program. We think about the model below as a gauge for ensuring that we completely support you in your goal of teaching a great course. As you evaluate your instructional materials options, you may wish to use the model for comparison purposes with available products.

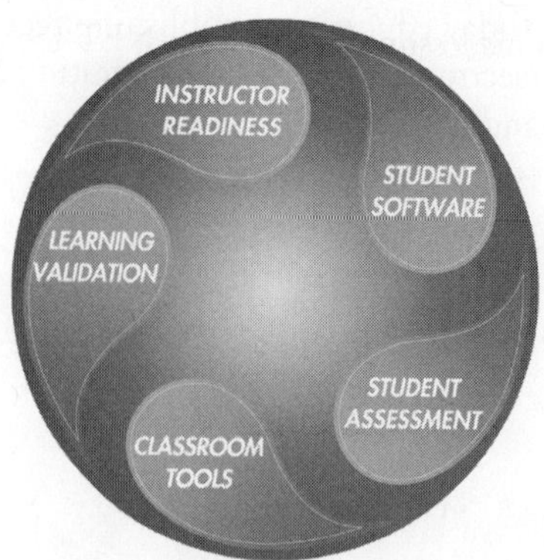

What should I know to read this book?

MOAC 70-536, Microsoft .NET Framework Application Development Foundation, serves as a foundation course for a Visual Studio ASP.NET curriculum. This book includes coverage of the objectives of the Microsoft certification exam 70-536, which is a Technology Specialist level exam.

To make the most of this course, students should have fundamental knowledge on the C# programming language. This book assumes that the students will have working knowledge in the following topics:

- Structure of a program, assemblies, and namespaces
- Basic data types such int, char, and double
- Scope of variables and access modifiers
- Operators, expressions, declarations, statements
- Arrays, structures, unions
- Exception handling
- Classes, methods, and interfaces
- Inheritance
- Overloading and overriding
- Events and delegates

Students should also know the basics of XML and SOAP as these topics are prerequisites for XML Serialization and Serialization using SOAP Formatters.

What is in this book?

This textbook covers the .NET Framework Application Development Foundation course in twelve lessons.

Lesson 1: Exploring .NET Fundamentals

This lesson focuses on the fundamentals of the .NET Framework such as:

- Value types
- Reference types
- Conversion between the types
- Basics of class creation

Lesson 2: Working with Collections, Dictionaries, and Generics

This lesson discusses on .NET techniques to handle collections of data effectively such as:

- Generics
- Collections
- Dictionaries
- Specialized and Generic Collections

Lesson 3: Working with File System I/O

This lesson explains the various file handling mechanisms such as:

- Streams
- System.IO namespace

- Compression of data streams
- Isolated data storage

Lesson 4: Creating Graphic Applications

This lesson describes the ways in which you can create graphical applications that include:

- Graphic objects
- Shapes and Sizes
- Images
- Text

Lesson 5: Serializing .NET Applications

This lesson covers the techniques in serializing .NET applications such as:

- Serializing objects
- XML Serialization
- Custom Serialization

Lesson 6: Creating Application Domains and Windows Services

This lesson deals with .NET techniques to enhance application personalization such as:

- Application domains
- Windows Services

Lesson 7: Using Threading and Reflection

This lesson describes how to create .NET applications that include:

- Multithreading
- Reflection

Lesson 8: Monitoring Application Performance

This lesson explains how to monitor application performance using mechanisms such as:

- Management Events
- Events Logs
- Performance Counters

Lesson 9: Securing Applications, Users, and Data in .NET

This lesson deals with various ways to secure application, data and user in .NET such as:

- Code Access Security
- Declarative Security
- Imperative Security
- Authentication
- Authorization
- Access Control Lists
- Data Encryption

Lesson 10: Extending Capabilities of .NET Applications

This lesson discusses how to include the following facilities in .NET applications:

- E-mail
- Globalization

- Pattern Matching
- Text Encoding and Decoding

Lesson 11: Programming .NET Interoperability

This lesson covers the various techniques that facilitate .NET and COM interoperability to:

- Call COM components in ,NET applications
- Use .NET types in COM components
- Control marshalling of data

Lesson 12: Configuring and Installing .NET Applications

This lesson focuses on concepts to deploy applications such as:

- Configuration
- Creation of Custom Installers

Illustrated Book Tour

■ Pedagogical Features

The MOAC textbook for .NET Framework Application Development Foundation is designed to cover all the learning objectives for that MCTS exam, which is referred to as its "objective domain." The Microsoft Certified Technology Specialist (MCTS) exam objectives are highlighted throughout the textbook. Many pedagogical features have been developed specifically for *Microsoft Official Academic Course* programs.

Presenting the extensive procedural information and technical concepts woven throughout the textbook raises challenges for the student and instructor alike. The Illustrated Book Tour that follows provides a guide to the rich features contributing to *Microsoft Official Academic Course* program's pedagogical plan. Following is a list of key features in each lesson designed to prepare students for success on the certification exams and in the workplace:

- Each lesson begins with an **Objective Domain**. More than a standard list of learning objectives, the Domain Matrix correlates each software skill covered in the lesson to the specific exam objective domain.
- Concise and frequent Step-by-Step instructions teach students new features and provide an opportunity for hands-on practice. Numbered steps give detailed step-by-step instructions to help students learn software skills. The steps also show results and screen images to match what students should see on their computer screens.
- **Illustrations:** Screen images provide visual feedback as students work through the exercises. The images reinforce key concepts, provide visual clues about the steps, and allow students to check their progress.
- **Key Terms:** Important technical vocabulary is listed at the beginning of the lesson. When these terms are used later in the lesson, they appear in bold italic type and are defined.
- Engaging point-of-use **Reader aids**, located throughout the lessons, tell students why this topic is relevant (*The Bottom Line*), provide students with helpful hints (*Take Note*), or show alternate ways to accomplish tasks (*Another Way*). Reader aids also provide additional relevant or background information that adds value to the lesson.
- **Certification Ready?** features throughout the text signal students where a specific certification objective is covered. They provide students with a chance to check their understanding of that particular MCTS exam objective and, if necessary, review the section of the lesson where it is covered.
- **Knowledge Assessments** provide progressively more challenging lesson-ending activities, including practice exercises and case scenarios.
- A Lab Manual accompanies this textbook package. The Lab Manual contains hands-on lab work corresponding to each of the lessons within the textbook. Numbered steps give detailed, step-by-step instructions to help students learn workplace skills associated with Microsoft's .NET Framework. The labs are constructed using real-world scenarios to mimic the tasks students will see in the workplace.

■ Lesson Features

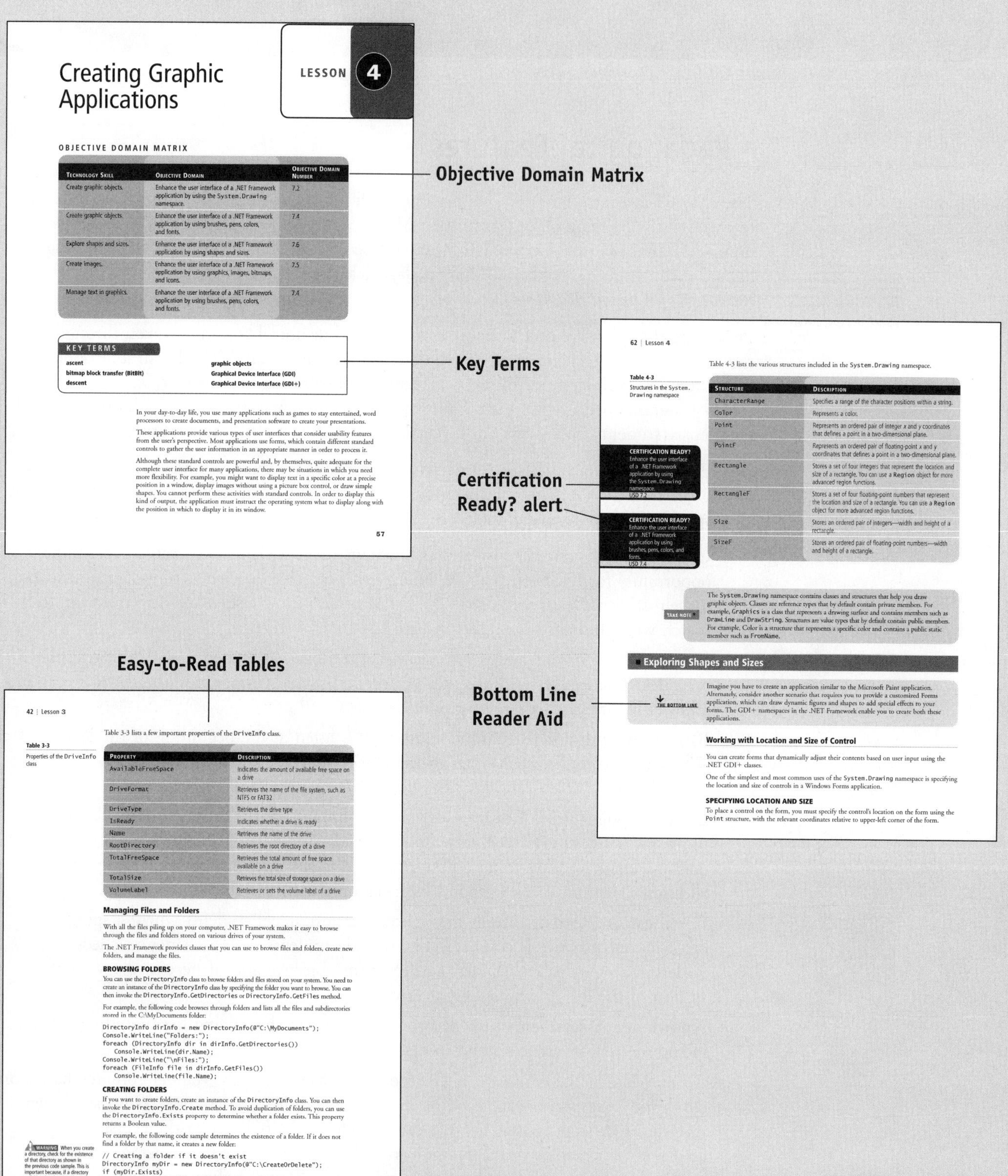

www.wiley.com/college/microsoft *or*
call the MOAC Toll-Free Number: 1+(888) 764-7001 (U.S. & Canada only)

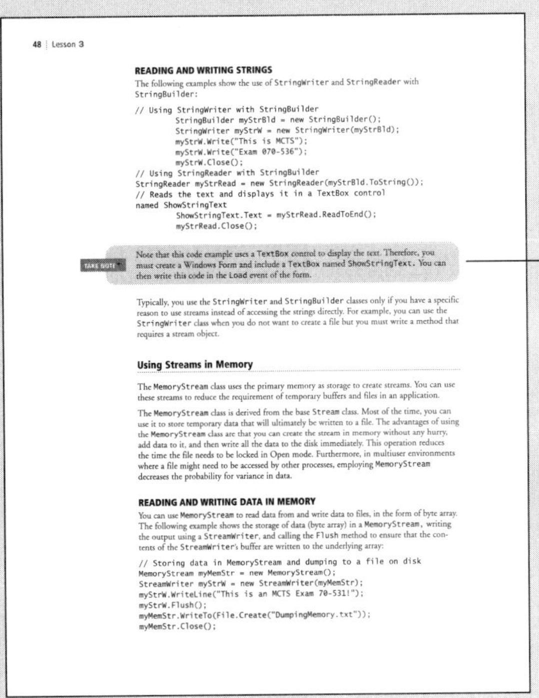

48 | Lesson 3

READING AND WRITING STRINGS

The following examples show the use of StringWriter and StringReader with StringBuilder:

```
// Using StringWriter with StringBuilder
        StringBuilder myStrBld = new StringBuilder();
        StringWriter myStrW = new StringWriter(myStrBld);
        myStrW.Write("This is MCTS");
        myStrW.Write("Exam 070-536");
        myStrW.Close();
// Using StringReader with StringBuilder
StringReader myStrRead = new StringReader(myStrBld.ToString());
// Reads the text and displays it in a TextBox control
named ShowStringText
        ShowStringText.Text = myStrRead.ReadToEnd();
        myStrRead.Close();
```

TAKE NOTE* Note that this code example uses a TextBox control to display the text. Therefore, you must create a Windows Form and include a TextBox named ShowStringText. You can then write this code in the Load event of the form.

Typically, you use the StringWriter and StringBuilder classes only if you have a specific reason to use streams instead of accessing the strings directly. For example, you can use the StringWriter class when you do not want to create a file but you must write a method that requires a stream object.

Using Streams in Memory

The MemoryStream class uses the primary memory as storage to create streams. You can use these streams to reduce the requirement of temporary buffers and files in an application.

The MemoryStream class is derived from the base Stream class. Most of the time, you can use it to store temporary data that will ultimately be written to a file. The advantages of using the MemoryStream class are that you can create the stream in memory without any hurry, add data to it, and then write all the data to the disk immediately. This operation reduces the time the file needs to be locked in Open mode. Furthermore, in multiuser environments where a file might need to be accessed by other processes, employing MemoryStream decreases the probability for variance in data.

READING AND WRITING DATA IN MEMORY

You can use MemoryStream to read data from and write data to files, in the form of byte array. The following example shows the storage of data (byte array) in a MemoryStream, writing the output using a StreamWriter, and calling the Flush method to ensure that the contents of the StreamWriter's buffer are written to the underlying array:

```
// Storing data in MemoryStream and dumping to a file on disk
MemoryStream myMemStr = new MemoryStream();
StreamWriter myStrW = new StreamWriter(myMemStr);
myStrW.WriteLine("This is an MCTS Exam 70-531!");
myStrW.Flush();
myMemStr.WriteTo(File.Create("DumpingMemory.txt"));
myMemStr.Close();
```

Take Note Reader Aid

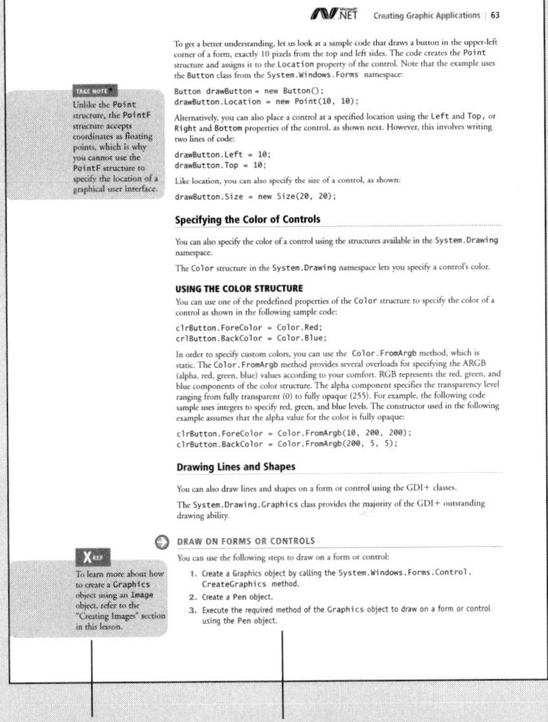

.NET Creating Graphic Applications | 63

To get a better understanding, let us look at a sample code that draws a button in the upper-left corner of a form, exactly 10 pixels from the top and left sides. The code creates the Point structure and assigns it to the Location property of the control. Note that the example uses the Button class from the System.Windows.Forms namespace:

```
Button drawButton = new Button();
drawButton.Location = new Point(10, 10);
```

TAKE NOTE* Unlike the Point structure, the PointF structure accepts coordinates as floating points, which is why you cannot use the PointF structure to specify the location of a graphical user interface.

Alternatively, you can also place a control at a specified location using the Left and Top, or Right and Bottom properties of the control, as shown next. However, this involves writing two lines of code:

```
drawButton.Left = 10;
drawButton.Top = 10;
```

Like location, you can also specify the size of a control, as shown:

```
drawButton.Size = new Size(20, 20);
```

Specifying the Color of Controls

You can also specify the color of a control using the structures available in the System.Drawing namespace.

The Color structure in the System.Drawing namespace lets you specify a control's color.

USING THE COLOR STRUCTURE

You can use one of the predefined properties of the Color structure to specify the color of a control as shown in the following sample code:

```
clrButton.ForeColor = Color.Red;
crlButton.BackColor = Color.Blue;
```

In order to specify custom colors, you can use the Color.FromArgb method, which is static. The Color.FromArgb method provides several overloads for specifying the ARGB (alpha, red, green, blue) values according to your comfort. RGB represents the red, green, and blue components of the color structure. The alpha component specifies the transparency level ranging from fully transparent (0) to fully opaque (255). For example, the following code sample uses integers to specify red, green, and blue levels. The constructor used in the following example assumes that the alpha value for the color is fully opaque:

```
clrButton.ForeColor = Color.FromArgb(10, 200, 200);
clrButton.BackColor = Color.FromArgb(200, 5, 5);
```

Drawing Lines and Shapes

You can also draw lines and shapes on a form or control using the GDI+ classes.

The System.Drawing.Graphics class provides the majority of the GDI+ outstanding drawing ability.

DRAW ON FORMS OR CONTROLS

You can use the following steps to draw on a form or control:

1. Create a Graphics object by calling the System.Windows.Forms.Control.CreateGraphics method.
2. Create a Pen object.
3. Execute the required method of the Graphics object to draw on a form or control using the Pen object.

X REF To learn more about how to create a Graphics object using an Image object, refer to the "Creating Images" section in this lesson.

X-Ref Reader Aid

Step-by-Step Exercises

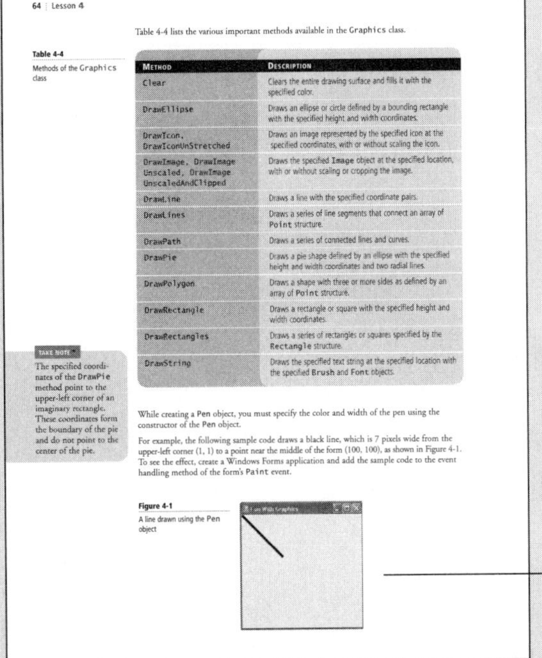

64 | Lesson 4

Table 4-4 lists the various important methods available in the Graphics class.

Table 4-4
Methods of the Graphics class

METHOD	DESCRIPTION
Clear	Clears the entire drawing surface and fills it with the specified color.
DrawEllipse	Draws an ellipse or circle defined by a bounding rectangle with the specified height and width coordinates.
DrawIcon, DrawIconUnStretched	Draws an image represented by the specified icon at the specified coordinates, with or without scaling the icon.
DrawImage, DrawImage Unscaled, DrawImage UnscaledAndClipped	Draws the specified Image object at the specified location, with or without scaling or cropping the image.
DrawLine	Draws a line with the specified coordinate pairs.
DrawLines	Draws a series of line segments that connect an array of Point structure.
DrawPath	Draws a series of connected lines and curves.
DrawPie	Draws a pie shape defined by an ellipse with the specified height and width coordinates and two radial lines.
DrawPolygon	Draws a shape with three or more sides as defined by an array of Point structure.
DrawRectangle	Draws a rectangle or square with the specified height and width coordinates.
DrawRectangles	Draws a series of rectangles or squares specified by the Rectangle structure.
DrawString	Draws the specified text string at the specified location with the specified Brush and Font objects.

TAKE NOTE* The specified coordinates of the DrawPie method point to the upper-left corner of an imaginary rectangle. These coordinates form the boundary of the pie and do not point to the center of the pie.

While creating a Pen object, you must specify the color and width of the pen using the constructor of the Pen object.

For example, the following sample code draws a black line, which is 7 pixels wide from the upper-left corner (1, 1) to a point near the middle of the form (100, 100), as shown in Figure 4-1. To see the effect, create a Windows Forms application and add the sample code to the event handling method of the form's Paint event.

Figure 4-1
A line drawn using the Pen object

Screen Image

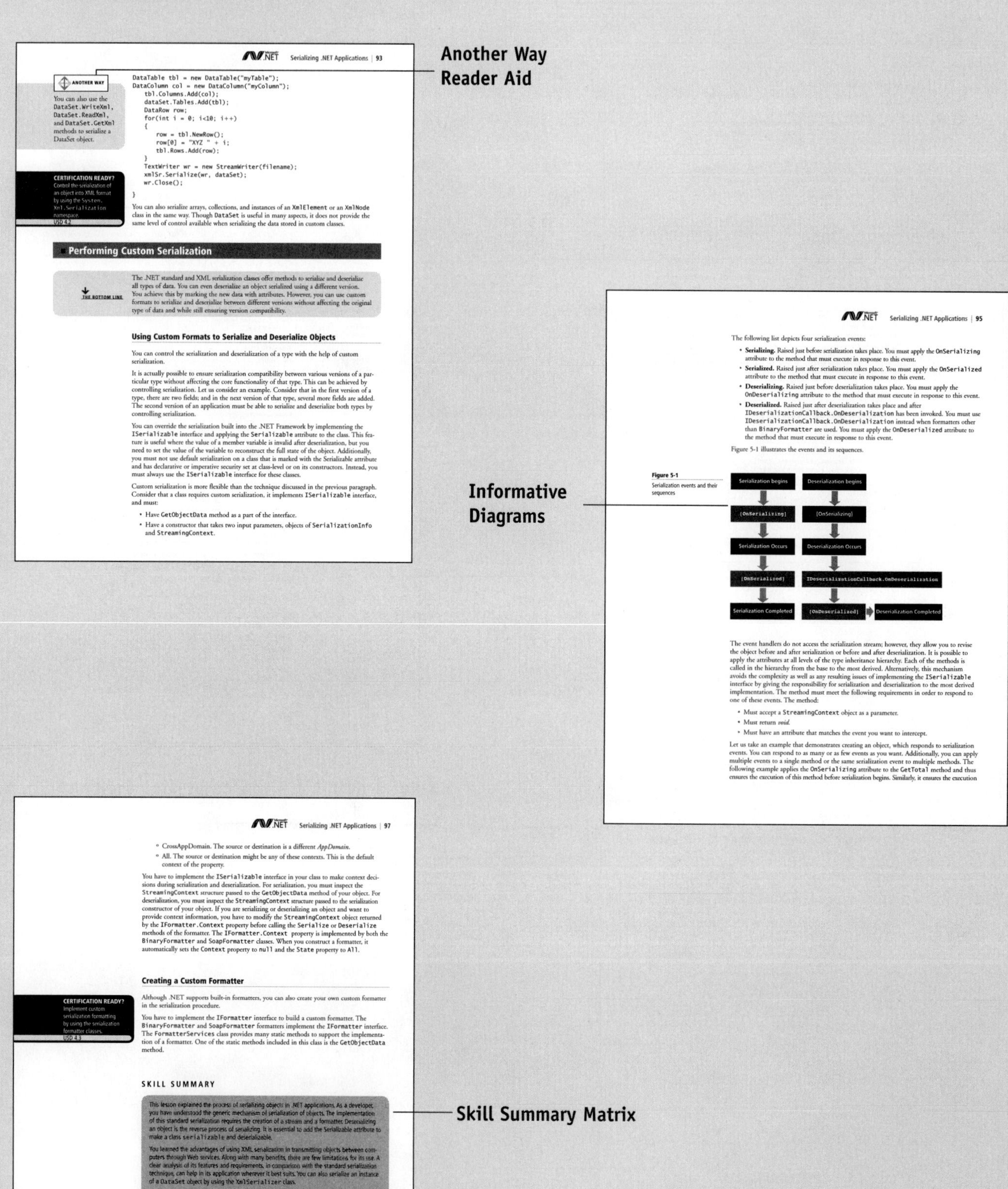

Serializing .NET Applications | 93

ANOTHER WAY

You can also use the `DataSet.WriteXml`, `DataSet.ReadXml`, and `DataSet.GetXml` methods to serialize a DataSet object.

```
DataTable tbl = new DataTable("myTable");
DataColumn col = new DataColumn("myColumn");
   tbl.Columns.Add(col);
   dataSet.Tables.Add(tbl);
   DataRow row;
   for(int i = 0; i<10; i++)
   {
      row = tbl.NewRow();
      row[0] = "XYZ " + i;
      tbl.Rows.Add(row);
   }
   TextWriter wr = new StreamWriter(filename);
   xmlSr.Serialize(wr, dataSet);
   wr.Close();
}
```

CERTIFICATION READY?
Control the serialization of an object into XML format by using the `System.Xml.Serialization` namespace.
USD 4.2

You can also serialize arrays, collections, and instances of an `XmlElement` or an `XmlNode` class in the same way. Though `DataSet` is useful in many aspects, it does not provide the same level of control available when serializing the data stored in custom classes.

Performing Custom Serialization

THE BOTTOM LINE

The .NET standard and XML serialization classes offer methods to serialize and deserialize all types of data. You can even deserialize an object serialized using a different version. You achieve this by marking the new data with attributes. However, you can use custom formats to serialize and deserialize between different versions without affecting the original type of data and while still ensuring version compatibility.

Using Custom Formats to Serialize and Deserialize Objects

You can control the serialization and deserialization of a type with the help of custom serialization.

It is actually possible to ensure serialization compatibility between various versions of a particular type without affecting the core functionality of that type. This can be achieved by controlling serialization. Let us consider an example. Consider that in the first version of a type, there are two fields; and in the next version of that type, several more fields are added. The second version of an application must be able to serialize and deserialize both types by controlling serialization.

You can override the serialization built into the .NET Framework by implementing the `ISerializable` interface and applying the `Serializable` attribute to the class. This feature is useful where the value of a member variable is invalid after deserialization, but you need to set the value of the variable to reconstruct the full state of the object. Additionally, you must not use default serialization on a class that is marked with the Serializable attribute and has declarative or imperative security set at class-level or on its constructors. Instead, you must always use the `ISerializable` interface for these classes.

Custom serialization is more flexible than the technique discussed in the previous paragraph. Consider that a class requires custom serialization, it implements `ISerializable` interface, and must:

- Have `GetObjectData` method as a part of the interface.
- Have a constructor that takes two input parameters, objects of `SerializationInfo` and `StreamingContext`.

Serializing .NET Applications | 95

The following list depicts four serialization events:

- **Serializing.** Raised just before serialization takes place. You must apply the `OnSerializing` attribute to the method that must execute in response to this event.
- **Serialized.** Raised just after serialization takes place. You must apply the `OnSerialized` attribute to the method that must execute in response to this event.
- **Deserializing.** Raised just before deserialization takes place. You must apply the `OnDeserializing` attribute to the method that must execute in response to this event.
- **Deserialized.** Raised just after deserialization takes place and after `IDeserializationCallback.OnDeserialization` has been invoked. You must use `IDeserializationCallback.OnDeserialization` instead when formatters other than `BinaryFormatter` are used. You must apply the `OnDeserialized` attribute to the method that must execute in response to this event.

Figure 5-1 illustrates the events and its sequences.

Figure 5-1
Serialization events and their sequences

The event handlers do not access the serialization stream; however, they allow you to revise the object before and after serialization or before and after deserialization. It is possible to apply the attributes at all levels of the type inheritance hierarchy. Each of the methods is called in the hierarchy from the base to the most derived. Alternatively, this mechanism avoids the complexity as well as any resulting issues of implementing the `ISerializable` interface by giving the responsibility for serialization and deserialization to the most derived implementation. The method must meet the following requirements in order to respond to one of these events. The method:

- Must accept a `StreamingContext` object as a parameter.
- Must return *void*.
- Must have an attribute that matches the event you want to intercept.

Let us take an example that demonstrates creating an object, which responds to serialization events. You can respond to as many or as few events as you want. Additionally, you can apply multiple events to a single method or the same serialization event to multiple methods. The following example applies the `OnSerializing` attribute to the `GetTotal` method and thus ensures the execution of this method before serialization begins. Similarly, it ensures the execution

Serializing .NET Applications | 97

- CrossAppDomain. The source or destination is a different *AppDomain*.
- All. The source or destination might be any of these contexts. This is the default context of the property.

You have to implement the `ISerializable` interface in your class to make context decisions during serialization and deserialization. For serialization, you must inspect the `StreamingContext` structure passed to the `GetObjectData` method of your object. For deserialization, you must inspect the `StreamingContext` structure passed to the serialization constructor of your object. If you are serializing or deserializing an object and want to provide context information, you have to modify the `StreamingContext` object returned by the `IFormatter.Context` property before calling the `Serialize` or `Deserialize` methods of the formatter. The `IFormatter.Context` property is implemented by both the `BinaryFormatter` and `SoapFormatter` classes. When you construct a formatter, it automatically sets the `Context` property to `null` and the `State` property to `All`.

Creating a Custom Formatter

CERTIFICATION READY?
Implement custom serialization formatting by using the serialization formatter classes.
USD 4.3

Although .NET supports built-in formatters, you can also create your own custom formatter in the serialization procedure.

You have to implement the `IFormatter` interface to build a custom formatter. The `BinaryFormatter` and `SoapFormatter` formatters implement the `IFormatter` interface. The `FormatterServices` class provides many static methods to support the implementation of a formatter. One of the static methods included in this class is the `GetObjectData` method.

SKILL SUMMARY

This lesson explained the process of serializing objects in .NET applications. As a developer, you have understood the generic mechanism of serialization of objects. The implementation of this standard serialization requires the creation of a stream and a formatter. Deserializing an object is the reverse process of serializing. It is essential to add the Serializable attribute to make a class `serializable` and deserializable.

You learned the advantages of using XML serialization in transmitting objects between computers through Web services. Along with many benefits, there are few limitations for its use. A clear analysis of its features and requirements, in comparison with the standard serialization technique, can help in its application wherever it best suits. You can also serialize an instance of a `DataSet` object by using the `XmlSerializer` class.

You also learned how to use custom formats to serialize and deserialize objects. A custom formatter is created by implementing the `IFormatter` interface. Custom serialization helps to control the serialization and the deserialization of a type.

For the certification examination:

- Know how to apply runtime serialization on objects.
- Understand the requirements to use XML serialization and its applications.
- Know how to control serialization by implementing your own serialization classes.

www.wiley.com/college/microsoft *or*
call the MOAC Toll-Free Number: 1+(888) 764-7001 (U.S. & Canada only)

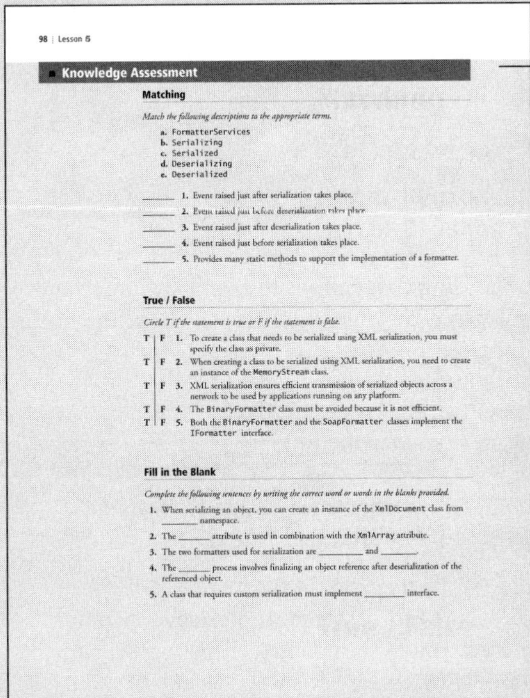

98 | Lesson 5

■ Knowledge Assessment

Matching

Match the following descriptions to the appropriate terms.

a. `FormatterServices`
b. `Serializing`
c. `Serialized`
d. `Deserializing`
e. `Deserialized`

_______ 1. Event raised just after serialization takes place.
_______ 2. Event raised just before deserialization takes place.
_______ 3. Event raised just after deserialization takes place.
_______ 4. Event raised just before serialization takes place.
_______ 5. Provides many static methods to support the implementation of a formatter.

True / False

Circle T if the statement is true or F if the statement is false.

T | F 1. To create a class that needs to be serialized using XML serialization, you must specify the class as private.
T | F 2. When creating a class to be serialized using XML serialization, you need to create an instance of the `MemoryStream` class.
T | F 3. XML serialization ensures efficient transmission of serialized objects across a network to be used by applications running on any platform.
T | F 4. The `BinaryFormatter` class must be avoided because it is not efficient.
T | F 5. Both the `BinaryFormatter` and the `SoapFormatter` classes implement the `IFormatter` interface.

Fill in the Blank

Complete the following sentences by writing the correct word or words in the blanks provided.

1. When serializing an object, you can create an instance of the `XmlDocument` class from _______ namespace.
2. The _______ attribute is used in combination with the `XmlArray` attribute.
3. The two formatters used for serialization are _________ and _______.
4. The _______ process involves finalizing an object reference after deserialization of the referenced object.
5. A class that requires custom serialization must implement _________ interface.

Knowledge Assessment

Serializing .NET Applications | 99

Multiple Choice

Circle the letter or letters that correspond to the best answer or answers.

1. Which of these elements can be serialized using XML serialization?
   a. Objects
   b. Object graphs
   c. Public data
   d. Private data
2. During deserializing an object, which namespace will you use to create an instance of the `StringReader` class?
   a. `System.IO`
   b. `System.Xml`
   c. `System.Xml.Serialization`
   d. None of the above
3. Which of the following is the process of reconstructing a data object to its original state?
   a. Serialization
   b. Deserialization
   c. Formatting
   d. Initiation
4. Which of the following, along with a stream, is required for the process of serialization?
   a. Formatter
   b. Deformatter
   c. Attribute
   d. Custom Object
5. Which method does the runtime call during custom serialization?
   a. `GetObjectData`
   b. `SerializationInfo`
   c. `BinaryFormatter.Serialize`
   d. `AddInfo`

Review Questions

1. What happens when the ObjectManager identifies that a particular object has not been deserialized before?
2. What must you do to optimize the size of the object to be serialized?

Case Scenarios

■ Case Scenarios

Scenario 5-1: Choosing the Appropriate Serialization

In your movie Web site, you have a class named `Movie`. This class contains information about a movie such as its name, release date, director, lead actors, and number of prints released. You must share this object with other movie Web sites.

Select the type of serialization that you must choose if you want to transport this object through network to different movie sites and application.

Scenario 5-2: Creating Serialized Objects

Create a program to serialize the `Movie` object using the standard serialization mechanism. Mention whether the output you create is usable by a Java-based program.

Workplace Ready

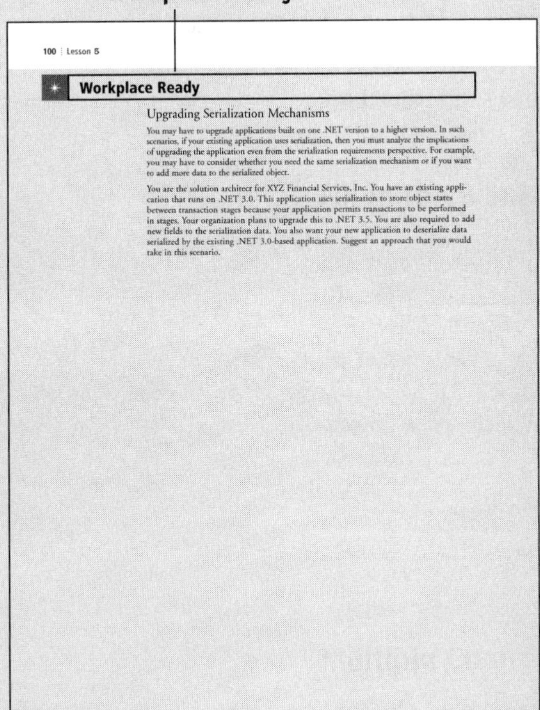

100 | Lesson 5

Workplace Ready

Upgrading Serialization Mechanisms

You may have to upgrade applications built on one .NET version to a higher version. In such scenarios, if your existing application uses serialization, then you must analyze the implications of upgrading the application even from the serialization requirements perspective. For example, you may have to consider whether you need the same serialization mechanism or if you want to add more data to the serialized object.

You are the solution architect for XYZ Financial Services, Inc. You have an existing application that runs on .NET 3.0. This application uses serialization to store object states between transaction stages because your application permits transactions to be performed in stages. Your organization plans to upgrade this to .NET 3.5. You are also required to add new fields to the serialization data. You also want your new application to deserialize data serialized by the existing .NET 3.0-based application. Suggest an approach that you would take in this scenario.

Conventions and Features Used in This Book

This book uses particular fonts, symbols, and heading conventions to highlight important information or to call your attention to special steps. For more information about the features in each lesson, refer to the Illustrated Book Tour section.

CONVENTION	MEANING
↓ THE BOTTOM LINE	This feature provides a brief summary of the material to be covered in the section that follows.
CERTIFICATION READY?	This feature signals the point in the text where a specific certification objective is covered. It provides you with a chance to check your understanding of that particular MCTS objective and, if necessary, review the section of the lesson where it is covered.
TAKE NOTE*	Reader aids appear in shaded boxes found in your text. *Take Note* provides helpful hints related to particular tasks or topics.
ANOTHER WAY	*Another Way* provides an alternative procedure for accomplishing a particular task.
XREF	These notes provide pointers to information discussed elsewhere in the textbook or describe interesting features of Microsoft .NET Framwork that are not directly addressed in the current topic or exercise.
A ***shared printer*** can be used by many individuals on a network.	Key terms appear in bold italic.
Click **OK**.	Any button on the screen you are supposed to click on or select will also appear in color.

Instructor Support Program

The *Microsoft Official Academic Course* programs are accompanied by a rich array of resources that incorporate the extensive textbook visuals to form a pedagogically cohesive package. These resources provide all the materials instructors need to deploy and deliver their courses. Resources available online for download include:

- The **MSDN Academic Alliance** is designed to provide the easiest and most inexpensive developer tools, products, and technologies available to faculty and students in labs, classrooms, and on student PCs. A free 3-year membership is available to qualified MOAC adopters.

  Note: Microsoft Visual Studio and Microsoft Expression can be downloaded from MSDN AA for use by students in this course.
- The **Instructor's Guide** contains Solutions to all the textbook exercises as well as chapter summaries and lecture notes. The Instructor's Guide and Syllabi for various term lengths are available from the Book Companion site (www.wiley.com/college/microsoft).
- The **Test Bank** contains hundreds of questions orgainzed by lesson in multiple-choice, true-false, short answer, and essay formats and is available to download from the Instructor's Book Companion site (www.wiley.com/college/microsoft). A complete answer key is provided.
- **PowerPoint Presentations and Images.** A complete set of PowerPoint presentations is available on the Instructor's Book Companion site (www.wiley.com/college/microsoft) to enhance classroom presentations. Tailored to the text's topical coverage and Skills Matrix, these presentations are designed to convey key Microsoft .NET Framwork concepts addressed in the text.

  All figures from the text are on the Instructor's Book Companion site (www.wiley.com/college/microsoft). You can incorporate them into your PowerPoint presentations, or create your own overhead transparencies and handouts.

  By using these visuals in class discussions, you can help focus students' attention on key elements of Windows Server and help them understand how to use it effectively in the workplace.
- When it comes to improving the classroom experience, there is no better source of ideas and inspiration than your fellow colleagues. The **Wiley Faculty Network** connects teachers with technology, facilitates the exchange of best practices, and helps to enhance instructional efficiency and effectiveness. Faculty Network activities include technology training and tutorials, virtual seminars, peer-to-peer exchanges of experiences and ideas, personal consulting, and sharing of resources. For details visit www.WhereFacultyConnect.com.

MSDN ACADEMIC ALLIANCE—FREE 3-YEAR MEMBERSHIP AVAILABLE TO QUALIFIED ADOPTERS!

The Microsoft Developer Network Academic Alliance (MSDN AA) is designed to provide the easiest and most inexpensive way for universities to make the latest Microsoft developer tools, products, and technologies available in labs, classrooms, and on student PCs. MSDN AA is an annual membership program for departments teaching Science, Technology, Engineering, and Mathematics (STEM) courses. The membership provides a complete solution to keep academic labs, faculty, and students on the leading edge of technology.

Software available in the MSDN AA program is provided at no charge to adopting departments through the Wiley and Microsoft publishing partnership.

As a bonus to this free offer, faculty will be introduced to Microsoft's Faculty Connection and Academic Resource Center. It takes time and preparation to keep students engaged while giving them a fundamental understanding of theory, and the Microsoft Faculty Connection is designed to help STEM professors with this preparation by providing articles, curriculum, and tools that professors can use to engage and inspire today's technology students.

Contact your Wiley rep for details.

For more information about the MSDN Academic Alliance program, go to:

msdn.microsoft.com/academic/

Note: Microsoft Visual Studio and Microsoft Expression can be downloaded from MSDN AA for use by students in this course.

Important Web Addresses and Phone Numbers

To locate the Wiley Higher Education Rep in your area, go to the following Web address and click on the "*Who's My Rep?*" link at the top of the page.

www.wiley.com/college

Or Call the MOAC Toll Free Number: 1 + (888) 764-7001 (U.S. & Canada only).

To learn more about becoming a Microsoft Certified Professional and exam availability, visit www.microsoft.com/learning/mcp.

Student Support Program

Book Companion Web Site (www.wiley.com/college/microsoft)

The students' book companion site for the MOAC series includes any resources, exercise files, and Web links that will be used in conjunction with this course.

Wiley Desktop Editions

Wiley MOAC Desktop Editions are innovative, electronic versions of printed textbooks. Students buy the desktop version for 50% off the U.S. price of the printed text, and get the added value of permanence and portability. Wiley Desktop Editions provide students with numerous additional benefits that are not available with other e-text solutions.

Wiley Desktop Editions are NOT subscriptions; students download the Wiley Desktop Edition to their computer desktops. Students own the content they buy to keep for as long as they want. Once a Wiley Desktop Edition is downloaded to the computer desktop, students have instant access to all of the content without being online. Students can also print out the sections they prefer to read in hard copy. Students also have access to fully integrated resources within their Wiley Desktop Edition. From highlighting their e-text to taking and sharing notes, students can easily personalize their Wiley Desktop Edition as they are reading or following along in class.

Microsoft Software

As an adopter of a MOAC textbook, your school's department is eligible for a free three-year membership to the MSDN Academic Alliance (MSDN AA). Through MSDN AA, full versions of Microsoft Visual Studio and Microsoft Expression are available for your use with this course. See your Wiley rep for details.

Preparing to Take the Microsoft Certified Technology Specialist (MCTS) Exam

The Microsoft Certified Technology Specialist (MCTS) certifications enable professionals to target specific technologies and to distinguish themselves by demonstrating in-depth knowledge and expertise in their specialized technologies. Microsoft Certified Technology Specialists are consistently capable of implementing, building, troubleshooting, and debugging a particular Microsoft Technology.

For organizations the new generation of Microsoft certifications provides better skills verification tools that help with assessing not only in-demand skills on Microsoft .NET Framework, but also the ability to quickly complete on-the-job tasks. Individuals will find it easier to identify and work toward the certification credential that meets their personal and professional goals.

To learn more about becoming a Microsoft Certified Professional and exam availability, visit www.microsoft.com/learning/mcp.

Microsoft Certified Technology Specialist

The new Microsoft Certified Technology Specialist (MCTS) credential highlights your skills using a specific Microsoft technology. You can demonstrate your abilities as an IT professional or developer with in-depth knowledge of the Microsoft technology that you use today or are planning to deploy.

The MCTS certifications enable professionals to target specific technologies and to distinguish themselves by demonstrating in-depth knowledge and expertise in their specialized technologies. Microsoft Certified Technology Specialists are consistently capable of implementing, building, troubleshooting, and debugging a particular Microsoft technology.

You can learn more about the MCTS program at www.microsoft.com/learning/mcp/mcts.

Microsoft Certified Professional Developer

The Microsoft Certified Professional Developer (MCPD) credential validates a comprehensive set of skills that are necessary to deploy, build, optimize, and operate applications successfully by using Microsoft Visual Studio and the Microsoft .NET Framework. This credential is designed to provide hiring managers with a strong indicator of potential job success.

MCPD certification will help you validate your skill and ability to develop applications by using Visual Studio 2008 and the Microsoft .NET Framework 3.5. Certification candidates should have two to three years of experience using the underlying technologies that are covered in the exam. The available certification paths include the following:

- ASP.NET Developer 3.5 for developers who build interactive, data-driven ASP.NET applications by using ASP.NET 3.5 for both intranet and Internet uses.
- Windows Developer 3.5 for developers who build rich client applications for the Windows Forms platform by using the Microsoft .NET Framework 3.5.
- Enterprise Application Developer 3.5 for developers who build distributed solutions that focus on ASP.NET and Windows Forms rich-client experiences.

You can learn more about the MCTS program at www.microsoft.com/learning/mcp/mcpd.

Preparing to Take an Exam

Unless you are a very experienced user, you will need to use a test preparation course to prepare to complete the test correctly and within the time allowed. The *Microsoft Official Academic Course* series is designed to prepare you with a strong knowledge of all exam topics, and with some additional review and practice on your own, you should feel confident in your ability to pass the appropriate exam.

After you decide which exam to take, review the list of objectives for the exam. You can easily identify tasks that are included in the objective list by locating the Lesson Skill Matrix at the start of each lesson and the Certification Ready sidebars in the margin of the lessons in this book.

To take the MCTS test, visit www.microsoft.com/learning/mcp to locate your nearest testing center. Then call the testing center directly to schedule your test. The amount of advance notice you should provide will vary for different testing centers, and it typically depends on the number of computers available at the testing center, the number of other testers who have already been scheduled for the day on which you want to take the test, and the number of times per week that the testing center offers MCTS testing. In general, you should call to schedule your test at least two weeks prior to the date on which you want to take the test.

When you arrive at the testing center, you might be asked for proof of identity. A driver's license or passport is an acceptable form of identification. If you do not have either of these items of documentation, call your testing center and ask what alternative forms of identification will be accepted. If you are retaking a test, bring your MCTS identification number, which will have been given to you when you previously took the test. If you have not prepaid or if your organization has not already arranged to make payment for you, you will need to pay the test-taking fee when you arrive.

Student CD

The CD-ROM included with this book contains practice exams that will help you hone your knowledge before you take the Microsoft .NET Framework Application Development Foundation (Exam 70-536) certification examination. The exams are meant to provide practice for your certification exam and are also good reinforcement of the material covered in the course.

The enclosed Student CD will run automatically. Upon accepting the license agreement, you will proceed directly to the exams. The exams also can be accessed through the Assets folder located within the CD files.

Acknowledgments

MOAC Instructor Advisory Board

We thank our Instructor Advisory Board, an elite group of educators who has assisted us every step of the way in building these products. Advisory Board members have acted as our sounding board on key pedagogical and design decisions leading to the development of these compelling and innovative textbooks for future Information Workers. Their dedication to technology education is truly appreciated.

Charles DeSassure, Tarrant County College

Charles DeSassure is Department Chair and Instructor of Computer Science & Information Technology at Tarrant County College Southeast Campus, Arlington, Texas. He has had experience as a MIS Manager, system analyst, field technology analyst, LAN Administrator, microcomputer specialist, and public school teacher in South Carolina. DeSassure has worked in higher education for more than ten years and received the Excellence Award in Teaching from the National Institute for Staff and Organizational Development (NISOD). He currently serves on the Educational Testing Service (ETS) iSkills National Advisory Committee and chaired the Tarrant County College District Student Assessment Committee. He has written proposals and makes presentations at major educational conferences nationwide. DeSassure has served as a textbook reviewer for John Wiley & Sons and Prentice Hall. He teaches courses in information security, networking, distance learning, and computer literacy. DeSassure holds a master's degree in Computer Resources & Information Management from Webster University.

Kim Ehlert, Waukesha County Technical College

Kim Ehlert is the Microsoft Program Coordinator and a Network Specialist instructor at Waukesha County Technical College, teaching the full range of MCSE and networking courses for the past nine years. Prior to joining WCTC, Kim was a professor at the Milwaukee School of Engineering for five years where she oversaw the Novell Academic Education and the Microsoft IT Academy programs. She has a wide variety of industry experience including network design and management for Johnson Controls, local city fire departments, police departments, large church congregations, health departments, and accounting firms. Kim holds many industry certifications including MCDST, MCSE, Security+, Network+, Server+, MCT, and CNE.

Kim has a bachelor's degree in Information Systems and a master's degree in Business Administration from the University of Wisconsin Milwaukee. When she is not busy teaching, she enjoys spending time with her husband Gregg and their two children—Alex and Courtney.

Penny Gudgeon, Corinthian Colleges, Inc.

Penny Gudgeon is the Program Manager for IT curriculum at Corinthian Colleges, Inc. Previously, she was responsible for computer programming and web curriculum for twenty-seven campuses in Corinthian's Canadian division, CDI College of Business, Technology and Health Care. Penny joined CDI College in 1997 as a computer programming instructor at one of the campuses outside of Toronto. Prior to joining CDI College, Penny taught productivity software at another Canadian college, the Academy of Learning, for four years. Penny has experience in helping students achieve their goals through various learning models from instructor-led to self-directed to online.

Before embarking on a career in education, Penny worked in the fields of advertising, marketing/sales, mechanical and electronic engineering technology, and computer programming. When not working from her home office or indulging her passion for lifelong learning, Penny likes to read mysteries, garden, and relax at home in Hamilton, Ontario, with her Shih-Tzu, Gracie.

Margaret Leary, Northern Virginia Community College

Margaret Leary is Professor of IST at Northern Virginia Community College, teaching Networking and Network Security Courses for the past ten years. She is the co-Principal Investigator on the CyberWATCH initiative, an NSF-funded regional consortium of higher education institutions and businesses working together to increase the number of network security personnel in the workforce. She also serves as a Senior Security Policy Manager and Research Analyst at Nortel Government Solutions and holds a CISSP certification.

Margaret holds a B.S.B.A. and MBA/Technology Management from the University of Phoenix, and is pursuing her Ph.D. in Organization and Management with an IT Specialization at Capella University. Her dissertation is titled "Quantifying the Discoverability of Identity Attributes in Internet-Based Public Records: Impact on Identity Theft and Knowledge-based Authentication." She has several other published articles in various government and industry magazines, notably on identity management and network security.

Wen Liu, ITT Educational Services, Inc.

Wen Liu is Director of Corporate Curriculum Development at ITT Educational Services, Inc. He joined the ITT corporate headquarters in 1998 as a Senior Network Analyst to plan and deploy the corporate WAN infrastructure. A year later he assumed the position of Corporate Curriculum Manager supervising the curriculum development of all IT programs. After he was promoted to the current position three years ago, he continued to manage the curriculum research and development for all the programs offered in the School of Information Technology in addition to supervising the curriculum development in other areas (such as Schools of Drafting and Design and Schools of Electronics Technology). Prior to his employment with ITT Educational Services, Liu was a Telecommunications Analyst at the state government of Indiana working on the state backbone project that provided Internet and telecommunications services to the public users such as K-12 and higher education institutions, government agencies, libraries, and healthcare facilities.

Wen Liu has an M.A. in Student Personnel Administration in Higher Education and an M.S. in Information and Communications Sciences from Ball State University, Indiana. He used to be the director of special projects on the board of directors of the Indiana Telecommunications User Association, and used to serve on Course Technology's IT Advisory Board. He is currently a member of the IEEE and its Computer Society.

Jared Spencer, Westwood College Online

Jared Spencer has been the Lead Faculty for Networking at Westwood College Online since 2006. He began teaching in 2001 and has taught both on-ground and online for a variety of institutions, including Robert Morris University and Point Park University. In addition to his academic background, he has more than fifteen years of industry experience working for companies including the Thomson Corporation and IBM.

Jared has a master's degree in Internet Information Systems and is currently ABD and pursuing his doctorate in Information Systems at Nova Southeastern University. He has authored several papers that have been presented at conferences and appeared in publications such as the Journal of Internet Commerce and the Journal of Information Privacy and Security (JIPC). He holds a number of industry certifications, including AIX (UNIX), A+, Network+, Security+, MCSA on Windows 2000, and MCSA on Windows 2003 Server.

We thank Colin Archibald from Valencia Community College, Igor Belagorudsky, and Jeff Riley for their diligent review and for providing invaluable feedback in the service of quality instructional materials.

Focus Group and Survey Participants

Finally, we thank the hundreds of instructors who participated in our focus groups and surveys to ensure that the Microsoft Official Academic Courses best met the needs of our customers.

Jean Aguilar, Mt. Hood Community College
Konrad Akens, Zane State College
Michael Albers, University of Memphis
Diana Anderson, Big Sandy Community & Technical College
Phyllis Anderson, Delaware County Community College
Judith Andrews, Feather River College
Damon Antos, American River College
Bridget Archer, Oakton Community College
Linda Arnold, Harrisburg Area Community College–Lebanon Campus
Neha Arya, Fullerton College
Mohammad Bajwa, Katharine Gibbs School–New York
Virginia Baker, University of Alaska Fairbanks
Carla Bannick, Pima Community College
Rita Barkley, Northeast Alabama Community College
Elsa Barr, Central Community College–Hastings
Ronald W. Barry, Ventura County Community College District
Elizabeth Bastedo, Central Carolina Technical College
Karen Baston, Waubonsee Community College
Karen Bean, Blinn College
Scott Beckstrand, Community College of Southern Nevada
Paulette Bell, Santa Rosa Junior College
Liz Bennett, Southeast Technical Institute
Nancy Bermea, Olympic College
Lucy Betz, Milwaukee Area Technical College
Meral Binbasioglu, Hofstra University
Catherine Binder, Strayer University & Katharine Gibbs School–Philadelphia
Terrel Blair, El Centro College
Ruth Blalock, Alamance Community College
Beverly Bohner, Reading Area Community College
Henry Bojack, Farmingdale State University
Matthew Bowie, Luna Community College
Julie Boyles, Portland Community College
Karen Brandt, College of the Albemarle
Stephen Brown, College of San Mateo
Jared Bruckner, Southern Adventist University
Pam Brune, Chattanooga State Technical Community College
Sue Buchholz, Georgia Perimeter College
Roberta Buczyna, Edison College
Angela Butler, Mississippi Gulf Coast Community College
Rebecca Byrd, Augusta Technical College
Kristen Callahan, Mercer County Community College
Judy Cameron, Spokane Community College
Dianne Campbell, Athens Technical College
Gena Casas, Florida Community College at Jacksonville
Jesus Castrejon, Latin Technologies
Gail Chambers, Southwest Tennessee Community College
Jacques Chansavang, Indiana University–Purdue University Fort Wayne
Nancy Chapko, Milwaukee Area Technical College
Rebecca Chavez, Yavapai College
Sanjiv Chopra, Thomas Nelson Community College
Greg Clements, Midland Lutheran College
Dayna Coker, Southwestern Oklahoma State University–Sayre Campus
Tamra Collins, Otero Junior College
Janet Conrey, Gavilan Community College
Carol Cornforth, West Virginia Northern Community College
Gary Cotton, American River College
Edie Cox, Chattahoochee Technical College
Rollie Cox, Madison Area Technical College
David Crawford, Northwestern Michigan College
J.K. Crowley, Victor Valley College
Rosalyn Culver, Washtenaw Community College
Sharon Custer, Huntington University
Sandra Daniels, New River Community College
Anila Das, Cedar Valley College
Brad Davis, Santa Rosa Junior College
Susan Davis, Green River Community College
Mark Dawdy, Lincoln Land Community College
Jennifer Day, Sinclair Community College
Carol Deane, Eastern Idaho Technical College
Julie DeBuhr, Lewis-Clark State College
Janis DeHaven, Central Community College
Drew Dekreon, University of Alaska–Anchorage
Joy DePover, Central Lakes College
Salli DiBartolo, Brevard Community College
Melissa Diegnau, Riverland Community College
Al Dillard, Lansdale School of Business
Marjorie Duffy, Cosumnes River College

Sarah Dunn, Southwest Tennessee Community College
Shahla Durany, Tarrant County College–South Campus
Kay Durden, University of Tennessee at Martin
Dineen Ebert, St. Louis Community College–Meramec
Donna Ehrhart, State University of New York–Brockport
Larry Elias, Montgomery County Community College
Glenda Elser, New Mexico State University at Alamogordo
Angela Evangelinos, Monroe County Community College
Angie Evans, Ivy Tech Community College of Indiana
Linda Farrington, Indian Hills Community College
Dana Fladhammer, Phoenix College
Richard Flores, Citrus College
Connie Fox, Community and Technical College at Institute of Technology West Virginia University
Wanda Freeman, Okefenokee Technical College
Brenda Freeman, Augusta Technical College
Susan Fry, Boise State University
Roger Fulk, Wright State University–Lake Campus
Sue Furnas, Collin County Community College District
Sandy Gabel, Vernon College
Laura Galvan, Fayetteville Technical Community College
Candace Garrod, Red Rocks Community College
Sherrie Geitgey, Northwest State Community College
Chris Gerig, Chattahoochee Technical College
Barb Gillespie, Cuyamaca College
Jessica Gilmore, Highline Community College
Pamela Gilmore, Reedley College
Debbie Glinert, Queensborough Community College
Steven Goldman, Polk Community College
Bettie Goodman, C.S. Mott Community College
Mike Grabill, Katharine Gibbs School–Philadelphia
Francis Green, Penn State University
Walter Griffin, Blinn College
Fillmore Guinn, Odessa College
Helen Haasch, Milwaukee Area Technical College
John Habal, Ventura College
Joy Haerens, Chaffey College
Norman Hahn, Thomas Nelson Community College
Kathy Hall, Alamance Community College
Teri Harbacheck, Boise State University
Linda Harper, Richland Community College
Maureen Harper, Indian Hills Community College
Steve Harris, Katharine Gibbs School–New York
Robyn Hart, Fresno City College
Darien Hartman, Boise State University
Gina Hatcher, Tacoma Community College
Winona T. Hatcher, Aiken Technical College
BJ Hathaway, Northeast Wisconsin Tech College
Cynthia Hauki, West Hills College–Coalinga
Mary L. Haynes, Wayne County Community College
Marcie Hawkins, Zane State College
Steve Hebrock, Ohio State University Agricultural Technical Institute
Sue Heistand, Iowa Central Community College
Heith Hennel, Valencia Community College
Donna Hendricks, South Arkansas Community College
Judy Hendrix, Dyersburg State Community College
Gloria Hensel, Matanuska-Susitna College University of Alaska Anchorage
Gwendolyn Hester, Richland College
Tammarra Holmes, Laramie County Community College
Dee Hobson, Richland College
Keith Hoell, Katharine Gibbs School–New York
Pashia Hogan, Northeast State Technical Community College
Susan Hoggard, Tulsa Community College
Kathleen Holliman, Wallace Community College Selma
Chastity Honchul, Brown Mackie College/Wright State University
Christie Hovey, Lincoln Land Community College
Peggy Hughes, Allegany College of Maryland
Sandra Hume, Chippewa Valley Technical College
John Hutson, Aims Community College
Celia Ing, Sacramento City College
Joan Ivey, Lanier Technical College
Barbara Jaffari, College of the Redwoods
Penny Jakes, University of Montana College of Technology
Eduardo Jaramillo, Peninsula College
Barbara Jauken, Southeast Community College
Susan Jennings, Stephen F. Austin State University
Leslie Jernberg, Eastern Idaho Technical College
Linda Johns, Georgia Perimeter College
Brent Johnson, Okefenokee Technical College
Mary Johnson, Mt. San Antonio College
Shirley Johnson, Trinidad State Junior College–Valley Campus
Sandra M. Jolley, Tarrant County College
Teresa Jolly, South Georgia Technical College
Dr. Deborah Jones, South Georgia Technical College
Margie Jones, Central Virginia Community College
Randall Jones, Marshall Community and Technical College
Diane Karlsbraaten, Lake Region State College
Teresa Keller, Ivy Tech Community College of Indiana
Charles Kemnitz, Pennsylvania College of Technology
Sandra Kinghorn, Ventura College

Bill Klein, Katharine Gibbs School–Philadelphia
Bea Knaapen, Fresno City College
Kit Kofoed, Western Wyoming Community College
Maria Kolatis, County College of Morris
Barry Kolb, Ocean County College
Karen Kuralt, University of Arkansas at Little Rock
Belva-Carole Lamb, Rogue Community College
Betty Lambert, Des Moines Area Community College
Anita Lande, Cabrillo College
Junnae Landry, Pratt Community College
Karen Lankisch, UC Clermont
David Lanzilla, Central Florida Community College
Nora Laredo, Cerritos Community College
Jennifer Larrabee, Chippewa Valley Technical College
Debra Larson, Idaho State University
Barb Lave, Portland Community College
Audrey Lawrence, Tidewater Community College
Deborah Layton, Eastern Oklahoma State College
Larry LeBlanc, Owen Graduate School–Vanderbilt University
Philip Lee, Nashville State Community College
Michael Lehrfeld, Brevard Community College
Vasant Limaye, Southwest Collegiate Institute for the Deaf – Howard College
Anne C. Lewis, Edgecombe Community College
Stephen Linkin, Houston Community College
Peggy Linston, Athens Technical College
Hugh Lofton, Moultrie Technical College
Donna Lohn, Lakeland Community College
Jackie Lou, Lake Tahoe Community College
Donna Love, Gaston College
Curt Lynch, Ozarks Technical Community College
Sheilah Lynn, Florida Community College–Jacksonville
Pat R. Lyon, Tomball College
Bill Madden, Bergen Community College
Heather Madden, Delaware Technical & Community College
Donna Madsen, Kirkwood Community College
Jane Maringer-Cantu, Gavilan College
Suzanne Marks, Bellevue Community College
Carol Martin, Louisiana State University–Alexandria
Cheryl Martucci, Diablo Valley College
Roberta Marvel, Eastern Wyoming College
Tom Mason, Brookdale Community College
Mindy Mass, Santa Barbara City College
Dixie Massaro, Irvine Valley College
Rebekah May, Ashland Community & Technical College
Emma Mays-Reynolds, Dyersburg State Community College
Timothy Mayes, Metropolitan State College of Denver
Reggie McCarthy, Central Lakes College
Matt McCaskill, Brevard Community College
Kevin McFarlane, Front Range Community College
Donna McGill, Yuba Community College
Terri McKeever, Ozarks Technical Community College
Patricia McMahon, South Suburban College
Sally McMillin, Katharine Gibbs School–Philadelphia
Charles McNerney, Bergen Community College
Lisa Mears, Palm Beach Community College
Imran Mehmood, ITT Technical Institute–King of Prussia Campus
Virginia Melvin, Southwest Tennessee Community College
Jeanne Mercer, Texas State Technical College
Denise Merrell, Jefferson Community & Technical College
Catherine Merrikin, Pearl River Community College
Diane D. Mickey, Northern Virginia Community College
Darrelyn Miller, Grays Harbor College
Sue Mitchell, Calhoun Community College
Jacquie Moldenhauer, Front Range Community College
Linda Motonaga, Los Angeles City College
Sam Mryyan, Allen County Community College
Cindy Murphy, Southeastern Community College
Ryan Murphy, Sinclair Community College
Sharon E. Nastav, Johnson County Community College
Christine Naylor, Kent State University Ashtabula
Haji Nazarian, Seattle Central Community College
Nancy Noe, Linn-Benton Community College
Jennie Noriega, San Joaquin Delta College
Linda Nutter, Peninsula College
Thomas Omerza, Middle Bucks Institute of Technology
Edith Orozco, St. Philip's College
Dona Orr, Boise State University
Joanne Osgood, Chaffey College
Janice Owens, Kishwaukee College
Tatyana Pashnyak, Bainbridge College
John Partacz, College of DuPage
Tim Paul, Montana State University–Great Falls
Joseph Perez, South Texas College
Mike Peterson, Chemeketa Community College
Dr. Karen R. Petitto, West Virginia Wesleyan College
Terry Pierce, Onandaga Community College
Ashlee Pieris, Raritan Valley Community College
Jamie Pinchot, Thiel College
Michelle Poertner, Northwestern Michigan College
Betty Posta, University of Toledo
Deborah Powell, West Central Technical College
Mark Pranger, Rogers State University
Carolyn Rainey, Southeast Missouri State University
Linda Raskovich, Hibbing Community College

Leslie Ratliff, Griffin Technical College
Mar-Sue Ratzke, Rio Hondo Community College
Roxy Reissen, Southeastern Community College
Silvio Reyes, Technical Career Institutes
Patricia Rishavy, Anoka Technical College
Jean Robbins, Southeast Technical Institute
Carol Roberts, Eastern Maine Community College and University of Maine
Teresa Roberts, Wilson Technical Community College
Vicki Robertson, Southwest Tennessee Community College
Betty Rogge, Ohio State Agricultural Technical Institute
Lynne Rusley, Missouri Southern State University
Claude Russo, Brevard Community College
Ginger Sabine, Northwestern Technical College
Steven Sachs, Los Angeles Valley College
Joanne Salas, Olympic College
Lloyd Sandmann, Pima Community College–Desert Vista Campus
Beverly Santillo, Georgia Perimeter College
Theresa Savarese, San Diego City College
Sharolyn Sayers, Milwaukee Area Technical College
Judith Scheeren, Westmoreland County Community College
Adolph Scheiwe, Joliet Junior College
Marilyn Schmid, Asheville-Buncombe Technical Community College
Janet Sebesy, Cuyahoga Community College
Phyllis T. Shafer, Brookdale Community College
Ralph Shafer, Truckee Meadows Community College
Anne Marie Shanley, County College of Morris
Shelia Shelton, Surry Community College
Merilyn Shepherd, Danville Area Community College
Susan Sinele, Aims Community College
Beth Sindt, Hawkeye Community College
Andrew Smith, Marian College
Brenda Smith, Southwest Tennessee Community College
Lynne Smith, State University of New York–Delhi
Rob Smith, Katharine Gibbs School–Philadelphia
Tonya Smith, Arkansas State University–Mountain Home
Del Spencer – Trinity Valley Community College
Jeri Spinner, Idaho State University
Eric Stadnik, Santa Rosa Junior College
Karen Stanton, Los Medanos College
Meg Stoner, Santa Rosa Junior College
Beverly Stowers, Ivy Tech Community College of Indiana
Marcia Stranix, Yuba College
Kim Styles, Tri-County Technical College
Sylvia Summers, Tacoma Community College
Beverly Swann, Delaware Technical & Community College
Ann Taff, Tulsa Community College
Mike Theiss, University of Wisconsin–Marathon Campus
Romy Thiele, Cañada College
Sharron Thompson, Portland Community College
Ingrid Thompson-Sellers, Georgia Perimeter College
Barbara Tietsort, University of Cincinnati–Raymond Walters College
Janine Tiffany, Reading Area Community College
Denise Tillery, University of Nevada Las Vegas
Susan Trebelhorn, Normandale Community College
Noel Trout, Santiago Canyon College
Cheryl Turgeon, Asnuntuck Community College
Steve Turner, Ventura College
Sylvia Unwin, Bellevue Community College
Lilly Vigil, Colorado Mountain College
Sabrina Vincent, College of the Mainland
Mary Vitrano, Palm Beach Community College
Brad Vogt, Northeast Community College
Cozell Wagner, Southeastern Community College
Carolyn Walker, Tri-County Technical College
Sherry Walker, Tulsa Community College
Qi Wang, Tacoma Community College
Betty Wanielista, Valencia Community College
Marge Warber, Lanier Technical College–Forsyth Campus
Marjorie Webster, Bergen Community College
Linda Wenn, Central Community College
Mark Westlund, Olympic College
Carolyn Whited, Roane State Community College
Winona Whited, Richland College
Jerry Wilkerson, Scott Community College
Joel Willenbring, Fullerton College
Barbara Williams, WITC Superior
Charlotte Williams, Jones County Junior College
Bonnie Willy, Ivy Tech Community College of Indiana
Diane Wilson, J. Sargeant Reynolds Community College
James Wolfe, Metropolitan Community College
Marjory Wooten, Lanier Technical College
Mark Yanko, Hocking College
Alexis Yusov, Pace University
Naeem Zaman, San Joaquin Delta College
Kathleen Zimmerman, Des Moines Area Community College

We also thank Lutz Ziob, Merrick Van Dongen, Jim LeValley, Bruce Curling, Joe Wilson, Rob Linsky, Jim Clark, Jim Palmeri, Scott Serna, Ben Watson, and David Bramble at Microsoft for their encouragement and support in making the Microsoft Official Academic Course programs the finest instructional materials for mastering the newest Microsoft technologies for both students and instructors.

Brief Contents

Contents

Lesson 4: Creating Graphic Applications 57

Lesson 5: Serializing .NET Applications 79

Lesson 6: Creating Application Domains and Windows Services 101

Lesson 7: Using Threading and Reflection 118

Exploring .NET Fundamentals

LESSON 1

OBJECTIVE DOMAIN MATRIX

Technology Skill	Objective Domain	Objective Domain Number
Understand value types.	Manage data in a .NET Framework application by using .NET Framework system types.	1.1
Understand reference types.	Manage data in a .NET Framework application by using .NET Framework system types.	1.1
Create classes.	Manage data in a .NET Framework application by using .NET Framework system types.	1.1
Create classes.	Implement .NET Framework interfaces to cause components to comply with standard contracts.	1.5
Create classes.	Control interactions between .NET Framework application components by using events and delegates.	1.6
Convert between types.	Manage data in a .NET Framework application by using .NET Framework system types.	1.1

KEY TERMS

attributes
boxing
built-in type
enumerations
events
explicit
implicit
interface
namespace
narrowing
unboxing
user-defined type
value type
widening

Our lives are filled with all kinds of forms, like job applications, driver's license forms, passport applications, and tax forms to report our earnings at tax time.

These forms serve a specific purpose. They collect information from you and help process the information to get you an appointment letter, a driver's license, a passport, or to help you file your taxes. Usually, you are required to enter your information in a specific format. For example, spell your name in the NAME field, enter your date of birth in a specific format, such as mm-dd-yy or mmm-dd-yyyy, and so on. The .NET Framework calls these specifications ***value types***.

The .NET Framework implements the Common Type System (CTS), a standard that defines how the computer memory stores the information. Standards such as CTS enable the .NET Framework to exchange information seamlessly across platforms.

■ Understanding Value Types

Data can either be simple, such as a person's gender, or complex, such as a person's educational qualifications. Simple data is directly stored in memory locations, and complex data is stored in multiple locations with reference pointers. Value types are useful to store simple data.

Introducing Value Types

A value type, as the name suggests, directly stores a value such as your nine-digit bank account number.

You can create instances of a value type where actual data is stored in a value type. The value type resides on a stack in the memory. This provides easy access at runtime. When a program contains a value type instance, the scope of the instance ends when the program completes its execution.

The .NET Framework supports three kinds of value types:

- Base .NET Framework types (built-in)
- User-defined value types (structure types)
- Enumerations

These three value types are derived from the `System.Value` base type.

Working with Built-In Value Types

Base .NET Framework types are the primitive or base types provided with the .NET Framework. Other types can be created from any of these base types. There are two kinds of built-in value types: numeric and nonnumeric.

Built-in types are base types provided within the .NET Framework on which you can build other value types. All numeric types are built-in value types. You choose a numeric type based on the kind of value you expect to store in that value type based on the data's size and precision. For example, the value type for your Social Security Number (SSN) should be an integer, not a floating number. Built-in value types can be numeric such as int, float, or decimal; or nonnumeric datatypes such as char, Boolean, or date.

Table 1-1 lists the various built-in value types that the .NET Framework supports.

Table 1-1

Numeric value types

Value Type (C# Type)	Bytes	Value Range	Used For
`System.SByte` (`sbyte`)	1	–128 to 127	Signed byte values
`System.Byte` (`byte`)	1	0 to 255	Unsigned byte values
`System.Int16` (`short`)	2	–32768 to 32767	Signed integer values
`System.Int32` (`int`)	4	–2147483648 to 2147483647	Whole numbers and counters
`System.UInt32` (`uint`)	4	0 to 4294967295	Positive whole numbers and counters
`System.Int64` (`long`)	8	–9223372036854775808 to 9223372036854775807	Large whole numbers
`System.Single` (`float`)	4	–3.402823E+38 to 3.402823E+38	Floating point numbers
`System.Double` (`double`)	8	–1.79769313486232E+308 to 1.79769313486232E+308	Precise or large floating point numbers
`System.Decimal` (`decimal`)	16	–79228162514264337593543950335 to 79228162514264337593543950335	Financial and scientific calculations that require great precision

TAKE NOTE* The Value Type column in Table 1-1 describes the .NET Framework type. In addition, it contains the C# type in parentheses.

The built-in value types support certain nonnumeric value types to store characters, strings, and Boolean values. Table 1-2 lists the various nonnumeric built-in value types supported by the .NET Framework.

Table 1-2

Nonnumeric value types

.NET Framework	Bytes	Value Range	Used For . . .
`System.Char` (`Char/char`)	2	0 to 65535 or hexadecimal 0x0000 to 0xFFFF	Single unicode characters
`System.Boolean` (`Boolean/bool`)	1	True or false	Options with a true-false value
`System.IntPtr`	Platform-dependent	(None)	Pointers to a memory address
`System.DateTime` (`Date/date`)	8	1/1/0001 12:00:00 AM to 12/31/9999 11:59:59 PM	Date and time specifications

DECLARING AND INITIALIZING VALUE TYPES

The method of declaring and initializing a variable varies depending on the kind of programming language you are using. For example, in C#, it is mandatory to initialize a variable before it is used anywhere in your application:

```
// Declaring a variable in C#
int age;
```

Note that you have declared the variable age, but you have not yet assigned a value to it. To initialize, you can use the default constructor new():

```
// Invoke default constructor
age = new int();
```

In this syntax, the program invokes the default constructor new() and assigns its value to the age variable. There are two ways to assign a value to the variable. First:

```
// Assign an initial value 0
age = 0;
```

Alternatively, you can use a single statement to declare and initialize the variable:

```
// Declaration and initialization in the single statement
int age = new int();
```

Another, and by far the easiest, way to initialize a variable is to directly assign the value at the time of declaring the variable.

```
int age = 0;
```

Using versions .NET Framework 2.0 and beyond, you can create nullable datatypes. A nullable type represents all the values of its underlying type, including a null value. For example, a nullable System.Boolean can contain a true-false or a null value. This is useful when working with applications based on relational databases. In C#, you can use the nullable type to represent a numerical data point with undefined value or no value. You can use the question mark to define a nullable variable type. Note that this is significant to value types alone and does not work with reference types, including strings, and returns a compile-time error.

The following code explains how the nullable value types are used:

```
// Nullable value types using a question mark '?'
int? nullableInt = 11;
double? nullableDouble = 1.25;
bool? nullableBool = null;
char? nullableChar = 'M';
int?[] arrayOfNullableInts = new int?[5];
// Reference types are not nullable
string? nullableString = "This returns a compile-time error!"
```

The question mark symbol is used to create an instance of the System.Nullable <T> structure type as shown next:

```
// Define nullable value types using Nullable<T>
Nullable<int> nullableInt = 11;
Nullable<double> nullableDouble = 1.25;
Nullable<bool> nullableBool = null;
Nullable<char> nullableChar = 'M';
Nullable<int>[] arrayOfNullableInts = new int?[5];
```

CERTIFICATION READY?
Manage data in a .NET Framework application by using .NET Framework system types.
USD 1.1

When you declare a variable nullable, it enables the `HasValue` and `Value` members. To detect whether a value has been set, use `HasValue` as follows:

```
// Reading nullable type value with HasValue
if (nullableBool.HasValue)
  Console.WriteLine("nullableBool is {0}.", nullableBool.Value);
else
  Console.WriteLine("nullableBool is not set.");
```

Working with User-Defined Value Types

Using the .NET Framework, you can create your own value types to suit your program. These ***user-defined value types*** are also known as structures or structs, depending on the programming language you are working with. These value types are derived from `System.ValueType`.

Structure types behave as lightweight class types; that is, structures are implicitly sealed in nature, and so they cannot be used to build an inheritance hierarchy. Though they do not support inheritance, structures can have constructors and methods, just like a proper class.

Structures hold related data together. For example, to open a bank account you would need to have, among other things, your name, last name, and SSN handy. You can create a structure called NewCustomer with FirstName, LastName, and SSN attributes. Notice that the FirstName and LastName attributes hold characters whereas the SSN attribute holds numeric values. Therefore, structures can contain other types, making it easier to work with the set of related attributes irrespective of their types.

For example:

```
struct XyPoint
{
  public int xPoint, yPoint;
  // Structures can contain parameterized constructors
  public XyPoint(int x, int y)
  {
    xPoint = x;
    yPoint = y;
  }
  // Structures may define methods
  public void Display()
  {
    Console.WriteLine("({0}, {1}", xPoint, yPoint);
  }
}
```

CERTIFICATION READY?
Manage data in a .NET Framework application by using .NET Framework system types.
USD 1.1

User-defined value types and their instances also reside on the memory stack.

Working with Enumerations

You use ***enumerations*** or enum (a C# programming construct) when you want to provide a list of options while defining a class, for example, the different types of accounts that you can open in a bank—checking account, savings account, or a money market deposit account (MMDA). Grouping these value pairs simplifies the readability of the code. Also, note that these values are fixed.

CERTIFICATION READY?
Manage data in a .NET Framework application by using .NET Framework system types.
USD 1.1

Enumerations store a set of related constant values together. All enumeration types are derived from a base class called `System.Enum`. Enumerations simplify the readability of the code by assigning meaningful symbols instead of numeric values. It is a desirable programming practice to use enumerations to avoid programming errors. For example, to create an enumeration for the different types of bank accounts a customer can open, the syntax is:

```
// C# enumeration type
enum AccountType
{
  Checking,
  Savings,
  MoneyMarket
}
```

Understanding Reference Types

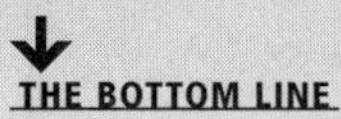

One of the categories of types supported by the .NET Framework is the reference type. A reference type stores only the reference (that is, the memory address) of the variable, not the original value of the variable. The .NET Framework supports various kinds of reference types.

Introducing Reference Types

In a reference type, the original value of the variable resides in a section of memory called heap. The reference type contains only the pointer or address in which the variable value resides on a stack.

The .NET Framework's garbage collector manages the heap where the reference type variable value resides. The garbage collector runs as a low priority thread in the background process and periodically releases unused variable values from the memory. That is, when the reference type no longer contains the pointer in the stack, the garbage collector removes the variable data from the heap.

When assigning a reference type variable, say a, to another reference type variable, say b, only the address in which the variable value resides is assigned. Therefore, both the reference type variables a and b point to the modified data if the value of the variable changes in the referenced address.

Introducing the Built-In Reference Types

The .NET Framework provides a variety of built-in reference types.

Table 1-3 lists the most commonly used built-in reference types of .NET Framework.

Table 1-3

Built-in reference types

TYPE	DESCRIPTION
`System.Object`	The root of the type hierarchy and the base class for all classes in the .NET Framework. Therefore, it is possible to convert any type to this type. In addition, all types inherit the `ToString`, `GetType`, and `Equals` members inherited from this type.
`System.String`	Represents fixed-text data.
`System.Text.StringBuilder`	Represents variable string of characters.
`System.Array`	Represents an array of data and serves as the base class for all arrays.
`System.IO.Stream`	The abstract base class that represents different types of input/output for file, device, or network. Any task-specific classes, such as `FileStream`, that read and write to a file derive from this class.
`System.Exception`	Represents both the system-defined and user-defined application-specific errors that occur when the application executes.

CERTIFICATION READY?
Manage data in a .NET Framework application by using .NET Framework system types.
USD 1.1

Exploring Strings

Strings play a vital role in the development of any application. The .NET Framework provides classes to support text data.

CREATING IMMUTABLE TEXT

The `System.String` class in the .NET Framework represents an immutable set of characters. In other words, any `System.String` type object contains text, whose initial value once assigned is not modifiable. Trying to modify the initial value only disposes the original `String` object and creates a new `String` object with the modified value.

The following example shows how the .NET Framework's runtime creates a new instance of the `String` object `straddress` when trying to add additional string values to the `straddress` object:

```
string straddress;
straddress = "Lamplighter Park ";
straddress += "15501 NE 10th ST ";
straddress += "Seattle WA USA ";
Console.WriteLine(straddress);
```

TAKE NOTE*

A method that modifies the value of a `String` object actually returns only a new instance of the `String` object with the modified value.

When executing the previous code, each time the `straddress` object is appended with a string, the runtime creates a new instance of `straddress` and the garbage collector disposes of the old instance of the `straddress` object. Finally, the runtime creates a new instance of `straddress` that has a reference to the value Lamplighter Park 15501 NE 10th ST Seattle WA USA.

Trying to modify the value of a `String` object with temporary strings, as in the previous example, forces garbage collection, which, in turn, decreases performance. Therefore, using the methods such as `Concat`, `Join`, or `Format` provided by the `System.String` class for any modification to the value of a `String` object avoids the use of temporary string, thus, improving performance.

The `System.String` class supports properties and methods that are used to manipulate strings, such as finding the length of a given string, converting the given string to uppercase or lowercase, or concatenating strings.

Table 1-4 and Table 1-5 list some of the key members of `System.String` class.

Table 1-4

`String` class properties

PROPERTY	DESCRIPTION
`Length`	Returns the number of characters present in the current String object.
`Char`	Returns the character at the specified position from the current String object.

Table 1-5

`String` class methods

METHOD	DESCRIPTION
`Compare`	Compares two given strings.
`Contains`	Determines whether the current String object contains the specified string.
`Equals`	Determines whether two String objects contain identical character data.
`Format`	Formats a string using primitives such as numerical data, other strings, and using {0} notation.
`Insert`	Inserts the specified string within the current String object at the specified position.
`PadLeft`	Pads the beginning of the string with specified characters.
`PadRight`	Pads the ending of the string with specified characters.
`Remove`	Removes the specified number of characters from the current String object.
`Split`	Returns a string array containing the substrings of the current object, delimited by elements of a specified character or string array.
`Trim`	Removes all occurrences of a set of specified characters from the beginning and end of the String object.
`ToUpper`	Creates a copy of the String object in uppercase.
`ToLower`	Creates a copy of the String object in lowercase.

CERTIFICATION READY?
Manage data in a .NET Framework application by using .NET Framework system types.
USD 1.1

CREATING MUTABLE TEXT

The `System.Text.StringBuilder` class in the .NET Framework represents mutable text. That is, you can modify the value of the `StringBuilder` object by adding, deleting, or replacing characters at runtime.

The `StringBuilder` object can increase its capacity to store the number of characters needed when the length of the value of a `StringBuilder` object increases.

The minimum default capacity of a `StringBuilder` object is a 16-byte buffer. It is also possible to increase or decrease the capacity of the `StringBuilder` object through the `Capacity` property or `EnsureCapacity` method.

The following example shows the manipulation of string by using `StringBuilder` class. The code creates the `StringBuilder` object `aptAddress` with the initial capacity of 50. The `Append` method appends the specified string to the instance of the `StringBuilder` object `aptAddress` and returns the reference to the same instance of the `aptAddress` object.

```
StringBuilder aptAddress = new System.Text.StringBuilder(50);
aptAddress.Append("Lamplighter Park ");
aptAddress.Append("15501 NE 10th ST ");
aptAddress.Append("Seattle WA USA ");
Console.WriteLine(aptAddress);
```

Using Arrays

MORE INFORMATION

For more information on arrays, refer to the article on arrays in the MSDN Library.

An array is a set of adjacent data items of the same type. Arrays are accessed by using a numerical index. The `System.Array` class in the .NET Framework serves as the base class for all arrays.

CREATING AND SORTING ARRAYS

In C#, arrays are declared by using square brackets `[ ]` as part of the variable declaration.

Here is a code sample that declares and initializes an array with numeric values. The code sorts the elements of arrnum by using the `Array.Sort` method:

```
int[] arrnum = {13,21,12,1,5};
Array.Sort(arrnum);
```

Performing Input/Output Services

The .NET Framework provides the `System.IO` namespace that contains types to support all file-based and memory-based input/output services.

Recall that a ***namespace*** can be defined as an abstract container or environment that holds a logical grouping of classes, structures, interfaces, enumerators, and delegates. This conceptual container ensures that there are no naming conflicts of classes, functions, variables, etc. inside a project.

The `System.IO` namespace provides the majority of types for the programmatic manipulation of physical directories and files. However, the `System.IO` namespace also provides additional types that support read-write operations on string buffers and raw memory locations.

CLASSIFYING STREAMS

Streams are the most common type provided by the `System.IO` namespace. Streams involve read-write operations to disk and communication across the network. `System.IO.Stream` is the abstract base class for all stream types.

Table 1-6 lists some of the most commonly used stream types.

Table 1-6

Stream types

Type	Description
`FileStream`	Creates a base stream that supports read-write operations on a file.
`MemoryStream`	Creates a base stream that supports read-write operations on memory.
`StreamReader`	Reads data from a text file.
`StreamWriter`	Writes data to a text file.

In addition to these stream types, network streams and encrypted streams are available in the `System.Network.Sockets` and `System.Security.Cryptography` namespaces, respectively.

READING AND WRITING INTO TEXT FILES

`StreamReader` and `StreamWriter` are the simplest stream classes that enable reading and writing to text files.

The following example demonstrates how to read and write to a text file. The code requires importing `System.IO` namespace for it to work.

TAKE NOTE*

It is always a good practice to close streams after working with them to enable the release of underlying resources such as file handlers.

In the example code, both the `StreamWriter` and `StreamReader` constructors accept a file name to open as an argument. The example code also calls the `Close` method to ensure that the file does not remain locked:

```
StreamWriter swFile = new StreamWriter("Chapter1.txt");
swFile.WriteLine("Working with Streams!");
swFile.Close();
StreamReader srFile = new StreamReader("Chapter1.txt");
Console.WriteLine(srFile.ReadToEnd());
srFile.Close();
```

Handling Exceptions

The .NET Framework provides a standard technique known as Structured Exception Handling (SEH) to raise and catch runtime errors.

The SEH technique enables the developer to follow a unified approach to error handling, which is common to all languages in the .NET platform. Therefore, the way a C# programmer handles an error is syntactically similar to the way a VB.NET programmer and a C++ programmer handle the error using managed extensions.

PROGRAMMING STRUCTURED EXCEPTIONS

Programming with structured exceptions involves the combination of four interrelated entities that include:

- A class type that represents the details of the exception
- A member that throws an instance of the exception class to the caller
- A block of code on the caller's side that invokes the exception-prone member
- A block of code on the caller's side that will process (or catch) the exception if it occurs

The following example shows a simple structured error handler using try-catch block:

```
try
{
  StreamReader srFile = new StreamReader("Chapter1.txt");
  Console.WriteLine(srFile.ReadToEnd());
}
catch (Exception ex)
{
  Console.WriteLine("Error reading file: " + ex.Message);
}
```

In the example code, when an error such as `FileNotFoundException` or insufficient privileges occurs during the reading of the file, the runtime stops executing the additional lines of code in the `try` block. The control then transfers to the `catch` block and executes the exception handling code within the `catch` block. If no error occurs, the runtime just skips the `catch` block.

USING SYSTEM.EXCEPTION CLASS

All the user-defined and system-defined exceptions derive ultimately from the `System.Exception` class, which in turn inherits from the `System.Object` class. The `System.Exception` class includes the `Message` property that describes the error. In addition, the `System.Exception` class also contains other properties that help in locating the code that caused the error, the reason for the exception, and so on.

TAKE NOTE*
You cannot set the value of the StackTrace property manually because the compiler generates this value automatically.

For example, the StackTrace property allows you to identify the series of calls that resulted in the exception. The StackTrace property returns a string that contains the sequence of calls that caused the current exception. The lowest line number of the returned string identifies the first call in the sequence; the topmost line number identifies the exact location of the code that caused the exception.

The information obtained from the StackTrace property is quite helpful when debugging an application. The StrackTrace property enables you to follow the flow of the error's origin in an application.

Two main types of exceptions in the .NET Framework include:

- System-defined exceptions that derive from the System.SystemException class
- User-defined application exceptions that derive from the System.ApplicationException class

Both System.SystemException and System.ApplicationException inherit from the System.Exception class.

CATCHING MULTIPLE EXCEPTIONS

By specifying multiple catch blocks, it is possible to handle multiple errors that may occur during the execution of an application. Each catch block handles a specific error.

TAKE NOTE*
You must order the catch blocks according to the exception type, from the most specific to the most general. Otherwise, you get compilation errors. In addition, to handle any unexpected errors that may occur during application execution, add a catch block that handles exceptions of type System.Exception at the end of all other catch blocks.

The following code shows how to handle different errors by using multiple catch blocks. When an error occurs, the runtime transfers control to the first catch block with the matching exception type and ignores the other catch blocks. The code uses a finally block to close the StreamReader irrespective of the occurrence of an error. Note that you must add reference to the System and System.IO namespaces for the following code snippet to compile without errors:

TAKE NOTE*
The runtime executes the finally block after executing the try block and any catch block, regardless of whether an exception occurs.

CERTIFICATION READY?
Manage data in a .NET Framework application by using .NET Framework system types.
USD 1.1

```
StreamReader srFile = new StreamReader("Chapter1.txt");
try
{
  Console.WriteLine(srFile.ReadToEnd());
}
catch (FileNotFoundException ex)
{
  Console.WriteLine("The file could not be found." + ex.Message);
}
catch (UnauthorizedAccessException ex)
{
  Console.WriteLine("You do not have sufficient permissions." +
ex.Message);
}
catch (Exception ex)

{
  Console.WriteLine("Error reading file: " + ex.Message);
}
finally
{
  srFile.Close();
}
```

■ Creating Classes

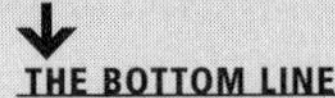

All .NET languages support class types, which is the base pillar of Object Oriented Programming. The classes in the .NET Framework provide much functionality.

All .NET applications can take advantage of the functionality provided by the .NET Framework classes to accomplish application specific tasks. For example, an ASP.NET application uses the `Control` class in the `System.Web.UI` namespace to create controls in a web forms page.

Defining a Class and an Object

A class is a definition or blueprint of a ***user-defined type*** (UDT).

A class provides an abstract definition of an object that has attributes, properties, events, and methods. An object defines a specific instance of the class. Each object has its own set of states, separated from each other. In other words, an object is an instance of a particular class in memory.

DECLARING CLASSES IN C#

In C#, classes are declared using the `class` keyword. The following example shows how to declare a class. The code declares the myCalc class using the `class` keyword. The myCalc class defines a method sum that returns the sum of two integer variables:

```
class myCalc
{
  public int Sum(int x, int y)
  {
    return x + y;
  }
}
```

DECLARING OBJECTS IN C#

WARNING It is always necessary to create objects of a particular class by using the new keyword before accessing the member of that class. Trying to access a member of a class without creating an instance of that class causes a compilation error.

An object is instantiated using the `new` keyword. The `new` keyword allocates memory for the object. The following code demonstrates how to instantiate an object by using the `new` keyword.

The code creates an object calc1 of type myCalc and calls the method sum for the newCalc object:

```
myCalc newCalc = new myCalc();

newCalc.Sum(1,2);
```

Defining an Interface

CERTIFICATION READY?
Manage data in a .NET Framework application by using .NET Framework system types.
USD 1.1

You interact with your computer through your keyboard and the monitor. Similarly, methods help the objects interface with the outside world. Interface defines the methods for a class without their actual implementation.

Interfaces are a named collection of abstract member definitions. A class or a structure may implement an interface. Interfaces are also known as contracts.

An interface defines a set of members. The class that implements the interface can take advantage of the interface members.

For example, the `IEquatable` interface defines the `Equals` method. The `Equals` method enables you to compare two instances of a class for equality. Both the custom classes and the built-in classes in the .NET Framework, which implement the IEquatable interface, can compare the instances of the class for equality.

EXPLORING TYPES OF INTERFACES

Table 1-7 lists the common types of interfaces provided by the .NET Framework.

Table 1-7
Interfaces

INTERFACE	DESCRIPTION
IComparable	Provides a type-specific comparison method that enables sorting. Types, whose values can be ordered or sorted, implement the IComparable interface. For example, all numeric and string classes implement this interface.
IDisposable	Provides for the disposal of unmanaged objects such as an open file. Large objects such as a database that consumes considerable resources can implement the IDisposable interface to dispose of resources that are no longer used.
IConvertible	Enables the conversion of a class to a base type such as Boolean, Byte, Double, or String.
ICloneable	Enables the creation of a copy of the current instance of a class.
IEquatable	Allows you to compare instances of a class for equality. For example, classes that implement the IEquatable interface can compare two instances of their class for equality of a string value or a numerical value.
IFormattable	Provides the ToString method that enables you to convert the value of an object into a specially formatted string. The ToString method of IFormattable interface provides greater flexibility than the base ToString method.

CERTIFICATION READY?
Implement .NET Framework interfaces to cause components to comply with standard contracts.
USD 1.5

The following example shows how to implement a built-in interface by a custom defined class. The custom PlainClass in the code implements the IDisposable interface.

```
// Class PlainClass implements IDisposable
{
  private FileStream _fileResource;
  // Constructor receives a FileStream object to be
disposed
  public PlainClass(FileStream myfile)
 {
    _fileResource = myFile;
 }
 // Implement the Dispose method of the IDisposable
interface
  public void Dispose()
 {
    Dispose(true);
 }
 public void DisposeFile()
 {
   // Dispose the FileStream object
   _fileResource.Dispose();
 }
}
```

TAKE NOTE*

.NET allows you to create partly developed executable code called assemblies that are compiled completely when required during runtime. You can use the `IDisposable` interface to free unused resources in the assemblies. The `Dispose` method of the `IDisposable` interface enables assemblies that create an instance of a class to free up any resource that the instance has consumed.

TAKE NOTE*

A C# interface usually has a public scope, which enables the types in other assemblies to implement the interface's behavior.

CREATING INTERFACES

In .NET Framework, the interfaces do not derive from a base interface such as the `IUnknown` interface, like the interfaces in COM. In C#, the interface types are defined using the `interface` keyword. The following example shows how to define an interface. The `IDraw` interface in the code defines a method `Draw`:

```
public interface IDraw
{
  void Draw();
}
```

The following example defines a custom interface, `IName`, which defines two `String` type member variables, FirstName and LastName, with the `get` and `set` methods. The custom class `Person` in the example code implements the custom interface `IName`:

```
public interface IName
{
  string firstName { get; set; }
  string lastName { get; set; }
}
class Person : IName
{
  public string firstName
  {
    get
    {
      throw new Exception("First name can't be read");
    }
    set
    {
      throw new Exception("First name is not specified");
    }
  }
  public string lastName
  {
    get
    {
      throw new Exception("Last name can't be read");
    }
    set
    {
     throw new Exception("Last name is not specified");
    }
  }
}
```

Understanding Partial Types

It is possible to define classes, structures, and interfaces using the partial modifier in C#. The partial modifier enables you to define a type across multiple `.cs` files.

In earlier versions of C#, all the code for a type resides in a single `.cs` file. A production-level C# class may involve hundreds of lines of code and therefore it would ultimately end up being a lengthy file.

CERTIFICATION READY?
Implement .NET Framework interfaces to cause components to comply with standard contracts.
USD 1.5

You can use a partial modifier to split the definition of a type across multiple `.cs` files. This allows you to keep the file size small while developing applications for large projects. In addition, partial classes help in separating the design aspects from the functionality aspects of an application. Therefore, graphic designers and solution developers can create their part of code using different tools without any problem.

Understanding Events

The .NET Framework supports events that enable responding to user actions.

MORE INFORMATION
For more information on events and delegates, refer to the section, "Events and Delegates" in the MSDN library.

Most Windows-based applications are nonlinear. For example, in Windows Presentation Foundation (WPF) applications, an application waits for a user action such as a key press or a mouse click and then responds to the action. To cite another example, consider a server application that waits for a network request. In .NET Framework, user actions generate ***events***, and an event handler responds to the generated events.

HANDLING EVENTS

Event senders are objects that trigger events. An event occurs when an action takes place, such as the user clicking a button, a method completing a calculation, or receiving a communication through networking.

Event receivers handle events through event handling methods. Because event senders do not know which method may handle the sent event, it is necessary to create a delegate. The delegate acts as a pointer to the event handler.

The following example shows the structure of an event handling method for the `Click` event of `btn_first`:

```
private void btn_first_Click(object sender, EventArgs e)
{
// Method code
}
```

CERTIFICATION READY?
Control interactions between .NET Framework application components by using events and delegates.
USD 1.6

The following example shows how to add the event handler to indicate which method should receive events. The example code adds the event handling method `btn_first_Click` for the `Click` event of the `Button` control, `btn_first`:

```
this.btn_first_Click += new

System.EventHandler(this.btn_first_Click);
```

Understanding Delegates

The .NET delegate type is a type-safe object that points to a method or list of methods to invoke at a later point in time.

.NET delegates are classes with built-in support for multitasking and asynchronous method invocation.

USING CALLBACKS

In earlier versions of Windows, the Windows API made frequent use of C-style function pointers to create entities named callback functions or simply callbacks. Using callbacks, programmers were able to configure one function to report to another function in the application. The callback approach enabled Win32 programmers to handle button clicking, mouse moving, menu selecting, and to perform general bidirectional communications between two programming entities.

The standard callback functions represent a raw address in the memory. In addition, traditional callback functions do not include any type-safe information such as number of parameters, parameter types, and the return value, if any, of the pointed method. Therefore, the traditional callback functions can be a frequent source of bugs, hard crashes, and other runtime disasters. Nevertheless, callbacks are useful entities.

In the .NET Framework, callbacks are still possible with the use of delegates. Delegates help achieve the callback functionality in a much safer and more object-oriented manner. It is possible to invoke the method pointed by the delegates at a later point in time.

CREATING DELEGATES

A delegate object contains three important pieces of information:

- The address of the method to which it makes the call
- The arguments, if any, of the called method
- The return value, if any, of the called method

The following example code shows how to create a delegate:

```
public delegate void HandleEvent(object sender, EventArgs e);
```

The following sample code creates an event object for the `HandleEvent` delegate:

```
public event HandleEvent FirstEvent;
```

This code sample shows how to invoke the delegate within a method to raise the specified event:

```
EventArgs e = new EventArgs();
if (FirstEvent != null)
{
  FirstEvent(this, e);
}
```

The following code sample shows a class that handles the `FirstEvent` event. The code assumes that the `SampleEventInitiator` is the class that fires the `FirstEvent` event, which is passed as the parameter to the `HandlerClass` constructor. The code adds the `HandleEvent` delegate, containing the function that actually handles the `FirstEvent` to the `SampleEventInitiator` class's `FirstEvent`. The `SampleHandler` function in the code sample, which actually handles the `FirstEvent`, displays the source that initiated the `FirstEvent`, which in this case is the `SampleEventInitiator` object:

CERTIFICATION READY?
Control interactions between .NET Framework application components by using events and delegates.
USD 1.6

```
class HandlerClass
{
  public HandlerClass(SampleEventInitiator s)
  {
    s.FirstEvent += new s.HandleEvent(SampleHandler)
  }
  void SampleHandler(object sender, EventArgs e)
  {
    Console.Writeline("SampleHandler called by ", sender.ToString());
  }
}
```

Understanding Attributes

Attributes provide declarative information about the objects in an application.

COMPARING COM ATTRIBUTES

COM IDL (interface definition language) provides numerous predefined attributes. COM attributes allow developers to describe the type contained within a given COM server.

However, COM attributes are little more than a set of keywords. That is, COM developers need to use a globally unique identifier (`GUID`) 128-bit number in the code to reference a custom COM attribute.

Unlike COM IDL attributes, .NET attributes are class types that extend the abstract `System.Attribute` base class. The namespaces in the .NET Framework provide many predefined attributes that come into use when developing applications. Furthermore, .NET Framework allows building user-defined custom attributes by creating a new type derived from `System.Attribute`.

X REF

For more information on reflections in this book, refer to the section, "Understanding Reflections" in Lesson 7: "Using Threading and Reflections."

EXPLORING USES OF ATTRIBUTES

Attributes describe a type, method, or property in a way that can be queried programmatically by using a technique called *reflection*. For example, attributes may be used to:

- Specify the required security privileges for a class
- Specify the security privileges to reduce security risk
- Declare capabilities, such as supporting serialization
- Describe the assembly by providing a title, description, and copyright notice

ADDING ASSEMBLY ATTRIBUTES

Attribute types derive from the `System.Attribute` base class. In C#, attributes are specified by using the `[ ]` notation.

The following code sample, which requires `System.Reflection` namespace, demonstrates how to add assembly attributes. You can add assembly attributes to the AssemblyInfo.cs file. When you create a project in Visual Studio, it adds the AssemblyInfo.cs file automatically to your project. This file contains details about your assembly such as name, version, culture, and producer.

```
// C# - AssemblyInfo.cs
[assembly: AssemblyTitle("ch01 MCTS C# 536")]
[assembly: AssemblyDescription("Chapter 1 Value Types")]
[assembly: AssemblyConfiguration("")]
[assembly: AssemblyCompany("Write IT Solutions")]
[assembly: AssemblyProduct("Printed Book")]
[assembly: AssemblyCopyright("Copyright © 2009")]
[assembly: AssemblyTrademark("")]
```

TAKE NOTE*

When developers create a new project, Visual Studio automatically creates some standard attributes for the assembly. Those generated attributes include a title, description, company, `GUID`, and version. You need to edit the automatically generated attributes for every newly created project because the default attributes do not include important information such as the description.

Understanding Type Forwarding

Type forwarding allows you to move a type from one assembly to another assembly without recompiling the applications that use the source assembly.

The `TypeForwardedTo` attribute enables the implementation of type forwarding. Type forwarding gives you the ability to move a type from a source component (assembly) to another assembly, even when the client applications may have started using the source component. Type forwarding also allows you to ship the updated component along with any additional assemblies, without requiring you to recompile the client applications that use the source component (assembly).

ANALYZING THE STEPS FOR TYPE FORWARDING

Only the components referenced by existing applications can use type forwarding. When an application is being rebuilt, the necessary assembly references for any types used in the application must be present.

MOVE A TYPE TO ANOTHER CLASS LIBRARY

The steps involved to move a type from one class library to another include:

1. Adding a TypeForwardedTo attribute to the source class library assembly
2. Removing the type definition from the source class library
3. Adding the removed type definition into the destination class library
4. Rebuilding both the libraries

The following example shows the attribute declaration used to move a type definition to a destination library. The code moves `TypeA` to the destination library `DestLib`.

```
using System.Runtime.CompilerServices;
[assembly:TypeForwardedTo(typeof(DestLib.TypeA))]
```

■ Converting between Types

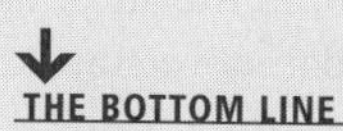

At times, when working with different types of data, you might need to store integers in a more compact format and later convert to a format that enables operations that are more complex. Alternatively, you might need to display a character as an integer. This is where type conversion comes to your rescue. It helps you convert one value type into another and take advantage of certain features of type hierarchies.

Introducing Type Conversion

Type conversion is the method of changing the entity of one value type into another.

The .NET platform supports value types and reference types. Given that two major categories of types are defined, you may need to represent a variable of one category as a variable of the other category. Such conversions can be:

- ***Implicit.*** The conversion happens automatically where the value is converted to the required type without explicit specifications.
- ***Explicit.*** The conversion happens only if specified explicitly.
- ***Narrowing.*** The conversion of data happens from a larger type to a smaller type.
- ***Widening.*** The conversion of data happens from a smaller type to a larger type.

BOXING

Boxing is a very simple mechanism provided in C# that is used to convert a value type to a reference type. Boxing may be implicit or explicit; the next example demonstrates implicit boxing.

Assume that you have created a variable of type `short`:

```
// Make a short value type
short shts = 25;
```

Now, when your application runs, you might wish to represent this value type as a reference type. So, you would box the value as follows:

```
// Box the value into an object reference
object objShort = shts;
```

CERTIFICATION READY?
Manage data in a .NET Framework application by using .NET Framework system types.
USD 1.1

Boxing is the process of explicitly converting a value type into a corresponding reference type by storing the variable in `System.Object`. When you box a value, the Common Language Runtime (CLR) allocates a new object on the heap and copies the value of the value type—in this case, 25—into that instance. After this, the CLR returns a reference to the newly allocated object. This technique facilitates developers working with the .NET Framework so that they need not use a set of wrapper classes, which are usually used to treat stack data temporarily as heap-allocated objects.

UNBOXING

Similar to boxing, you may have to convert a reference type to a value type. ***Unboxing*** is the process of converting the value held in the object reference back into a corresponding value type on the stack.

In an unboxing operation, the CLR verifies the receiving datatype to be equivalent to the boxed type. Upon verification, the CLR copies the value back into a local stack-based variable. For example, the following unboxing operation works successfully when the underlying type of objShort is indeed a `short`:

```
// Unbox the reference back into a corresponding short
short shtanotherShort = (short)objShort;
```

You must always unbox into an appropriate datatype. The following unboxing logic generates an `InvalidCastException`:

```
// Illegal unboxing
static void Main(string[] args)
{
  short shts = 25;
  object objShort = shts;
  try
  {
   // The type contained in the box is NOT an int, but a short!
    int inti = (int)objShort;
  }
  catch(InvalidCastException e)
  {
    Console.WriteLine("OOPS!\n{0} ", e.ToString());
  }
}
```

CERTIFICATION READY?
Manage data in a .NET Framework application by using .NET Framework system types.
USD 1.1

BOXING ADVANTAGES

Many developers think of boxing or unboxing as a theoretical language feature rather than a practical solution. This feature helps us to assume and treat everything as a `System.Object`. The advantage of boxing is that you can pass, say, an integer around as an object.

MORE INFORMATION
For more information on stack-heap memory, refer to the article on stack-heap memory in the MSDN library.

Understanding Performance Issues with Boxing Operations

Although boxing and unboxing are very convenient from a programmer's point of view, this simplified approach to stack-heap memory transfer comes with a baggage of performance issues (in speed of execution and code size) and a lack of type safety.

UNBOX A SIMPLE INTEGER

To better comprehend the performance issues, consider the steps that need to take place for boxing and unboxing a simple integer:

1. The CLR must allocate a new object on the managed heap.
2. The CLR must transfer the value of the stack-based data into that memory location.

3. When unboxed, the CLR must transfer the value stored on the heap-based object back to the stack.
4. The now unused objects on the heap are eventually garbage collected.

Although you would not experience any major bottleneck with codes handling a small amount of data, you would certainly feel the impact if your program were to manipulate, on a regular basis, an ArrayList that contained thousands of integers.

Converting Custom Types

Similar to built-in types, you may need to convert built-in types to custom types. In such situations, choose a type conversion method that best suits your conversion requirement.

There are several ways to define conversions for types. You may define conversion operators to assign directly from a value type to your custom type. While conversion operators simplify narrowing and widening conversions between numeric types, for greater precision, you need the `narrowing/explicit` keyword.

For example, the following structure defines operators that allow assignment to and from integer values. Note that this conversion uses the "operator overloading" mechanism for cast operators:

```
struct TypeA
{
  public int Value;
  // Allows implicit conversion from an integer to TypeA
  public static implicit operator TypeA(int arg)
  {
    TypeA res = new TypeA();
    res.Value = arg;
    return res;
  }
  // Allows explicit conversion to an integer
  public static explicit operator int(TypeA arg)
  {
    return arg.Value;
  }
  // Provides string conversion (avoids boxing)
  public override string ToString()
  {
    return this.Value.ToString();
  }
}
```

The preceding type also overrides the `ToString` method to perform the string conversion without boxing. Because the `ToString` method is part of the class itself, the value is used directly from the stack and therefore boxing is not required. You can assign integers to a variable of this type directly, as shown next:

```
TypeA a; int i;
// Widening conversion is OK implicit
a = 42; // Rather than a.Value = 42
// Narrowing conversion must be explicit in C#
i = (int)a; // Rather than i = a.Value
Console.WriteLine("a = {0}, i = {1}", a.ToString(),
inti.ToString());
```

To implement the `System.IConvertible` interface, add the `IConvertible` interface to the type definition.

TAKE NOTE*

With Visual Studio, you don't need to implement every method. The interface is implemented automatically because Visual Studio inserts member declarations for 17 methods, including `GetTypeCode`, `ChangeType`, and `ToType` methods for each base type. While invalid methods throw an exception in C#, Visual Studio automatically adds code to throw an exception for any conversion methods that you don't implement.

After you implement the `IConvertible` interface, the custom type can be converted by using the standard `System.Convert` class, as shown next:

```
TypeA a; bool b;
a = 42;
// Convert using ToBoolean
b = Convert.ToBoolean(a);
Console.WriteLine("a = {0}, b = {1}", a.ToString(), b.ToString());
```

CERTIFICATION READY?
Manage data in a .NET Framework application by using .NET Framework system types.
USD 1.1

Always select a data conversion technique based on the type of conversion required. For example, you would override the `ToString` method to provide conversion to strings, and override the `Parse` method to provide conversion from strings. For culture-specific conversions, implement the `System.IConvertible` interface to enable conversion through the `System.Convert` class.

SKILL SUMMARY

This lesson introduced you to the concepts of value types in the .NET Framework. If you had been wondering about the use of forms that you were completing, you now know the significance and the purpose behind such information collection. If you are a developer, you have now learned the different kinds of variables you can declare and interpret during the course of your application development. The .NET Framework introduces two types of data: value types and reference types.

A value type directly stores its value. There are three kinds of value types supported in .NET Framework: built-in value types, user-defined value types, and enumerations. You can have built-in datatypes that can store both numeric and nonnumeric values. Depending on the requirement of your application, you can use user-defined value types or structures to store related data irrespective of their type. You can group information pairs in enumerations, and you learned how this grouping improves the readability of your code.

A reference type stores only the reference of the variable, not the original value of the variable. The .NET Framework provides a variety of built-in reference types such as string, object, array, and exception. The .NET Framework provides classes to support text data. The `System.String` class supports properties and methods that are used to manipulate strings, such as finding the length of the given string, converting the given string to uppercase or lowercase, or concatenating strings. The `System.Text.StringBuilder` class in the .NET Framework represents mutable text. An array is a set of adjacent data items of the same type. Arrays are accessed by using a numerical index. The `System.Array` class in the .NET Framework serves as the base class for all arrays. The .NET Framework provides a standard technique known as Structured Exception Handling (SEH) to raise and catch runtime errors.

All .NET languages support class types, which is the base pillar of Object Oriented Programming. The classes in the .NET Framework provide much functionality. Methods help the objects interface with the outside world. Interface defines the methods for a class without their actual implementation. It is possible to define classes, structures, and interfaces using the partial modifier in C#. The partial modifier enables you to define a type across multiple .cs files.

The .NET Framework supports events that enable a response to user actions. The .NET delegate type is a type-safe object that points to a method or list of methods to invoke at a later point in time.

Attributes provide declarative information about the objects in an application.

Type forwarding allows you to move type from one assembly to another assembly, without the need to recompile the applications that use the source assembly.

Type conversion is the method of changing the entity of one value type into another. Boxing is a very simple mechanism provided in C# that is used to convert a value type to a reference type. Unboxing is the process of converting the value stored in the object reference back into a corresponding value type on the stack. When converting built-in types to custom types, you must choose a type conversion method that best suits your conversion requirement.

For the certification examination:

- Know how to manage data in a .NET Framework application by using the .NET Framework system types.
- Understand how each type works.
- Implement .NET Framework interfaces so that components comply with standard contracts.
- Control interactions between .NET Framework application components by using events and delegates.
- Convert data between the .NET types.

■ Knowledge Assessment

Matching

Match the following descriptions to the appropriate terms.

a. Streams
b. System.Attribute
c. Explicit Operator
d. Delegate Object
e. Attributes

_______ **1.** Contains the address of the event handler method

_______ **2.** Defines narrowing conversions

_______ **3.** Supports read-write operations to disk

_______ **4.** Base class for all the custom attributes

_______ **5.** Are specified using [ ] notation in C#

True / False

Circle T if the statement is true or F if the statement is false.

T | F 1. Multiple catch blocks need to be ordered according to the exception from the least specific to the most specific.

T | F 2. `StackTrace` property of the `System.Exception` class contains the description of the error message.

T | F 3. `System.Attribute` class is the base class for all the custom attributes.

T | F 4. All arrays derive explicitly from the `System.Array` class.

T | F 5. Boxing converts a reference type to a value type.

Fill in the Blank

Complete the following sentences by writing the correct word or words in the blanks provided.

1. The ____________ type represents a fixed set of characters.
2. __________ provide declarative information about the objects in an application.
3. A question mark is used to define a __________ variable type.
4. __________ allow you to assign constant values to a list of options that are contained in a value type.
5. ____________ mechanisms that involve stack-heap memory transfer affect execution speed and type safety.

Multiple Choice

Circle the letter or letters that correspond to the best answer or answers.

1. Select all that is true about the reference type variable.
   a. The value of the reference type variable resides in the memory called heap.
   b. The reference type holds the address of the variable in a stack.
   c. Assigning a reference type variable, say A, to another reference type variable, say B, copies the value of variable A to variable B.
   d. The reference type variable forces garbage collection.
2. Which interface provides a method to allow comparing instances of a class for equality?
   a. `IComparable`
   b. `IEquatable`
   c. `IConvertible`
   d. `IFormattable`
3. Which of the following statements about enumerations is not true?
   a. It is a set of related constants.
   b. The value within an enumeration can change during execution.
   c. Enumerations improve readability of the code.
   d. All enumeration types derive from the `System.Enum` base class.
4. Which of the following statements about structures is not true?
   a. Structures support inheritance.
   b. Structures can have constructors and methods.
   c. Structures hold related data together.
   d. Structures can contain other types within them.
5. Select all the statements that are true about conversion operators.
   a. Conversion operators allow assigning value types directly to custom types.
   b. Conversion operators allow conversions between numeric types with or without precision types.
   c. Conversion operators allow conversions to strings.
   d. Conversion operators allow only explicit conversions.

Review Questions

1. What is the difference between value and reference type?
2. What are the various types of conversions and why do you need them?

Case Scenarios

Scenario 1-1: Using the Right Type of Data

You are an employee of Fantasy Integrated Applications, Inc. Your team bags a project to program an online movie ticket reservation Web site. Make a decision about the type of data you will use to store ticket information.

Scenario 1-2: Using Enumerations

The reservation Web site that you develop caters to multiplexes that have different rates for different days, say weekdays and weekends. You need to record the reservation information in different tables for weekdays and weekends.

Hint: Use enum.

Workplace Ready

Importance of Data Handling

In today's world, software applications play an important role in achieving most of the business solutions. Software applications are based on events, and with proper user inputs, these applications can perform appropriate actions.

Consider banking applications where if you do not provide the correct password, you will be prompted with an error to provide one. These kinds of situations are handled by events based on user input. Thus, all applications are data dependent, and applications must be equipped to handle data correctly.

You are the solution architect for ABC Bank. The bank wants to create a .NET-based application to facilitate its operations. The bank offers two types of accounts—savings and current accounts. Customers can have one or more accounts of these types. Suggest the design approach that you will use to model this application.

Working with Collections, Dictionaries, and Generics

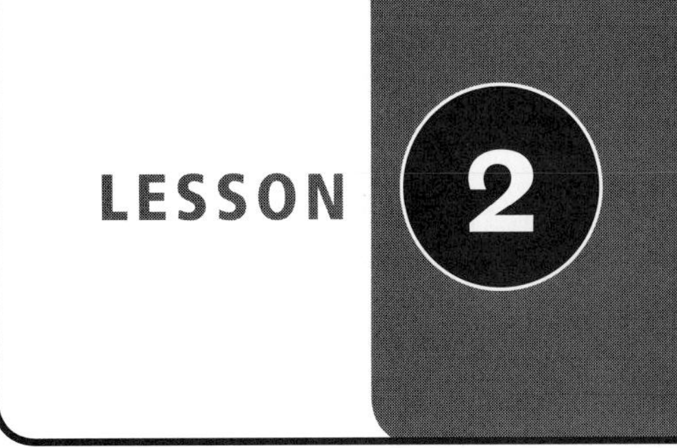

OBJECTIVE DOMAIN MATRIX

TECHNOLOGY SKILL	OBJECTIVE DOMAIN	OBJECTIVE DOMAIN NUMBER
Understand collections.	Manage a group of associated data in a .NET Framework application by using collections.	1.2
Understand dictionaries.	Manage a group of associated data in a .NET Framework application by using collections.	1.2
Explore generics.	Manage data in a .NET Framework application by using .NET Framework system types.	1.1
Use specialized and generic collections.	Manage data in a .NET Framework application by using specialized collections.	1.3
Use specialized and generic collections.	Improve type safety and application performance in a .NET Framework application by using generic collections.	1.4

KEY TERMS

ArrayList
collections
dictionaries
first in, first out (FIFO)
generics
last in, first out (LIFO)
queue
stack

Assume that a state tourism department wants to store information about the tourist attractions available in the state. This information will include place names, locations, special features, and a list of hotels with addresses and phone numbers. As a developer, you must first organize this information and make it available for easy retrieval. The structure must be such that you can add, remove, insert, and sort the available information. You can make use of collections, dictionaries, and generics as needed to perform such tasks.

You require ***collections*** to assemble the various pieces of information, ***dictionaries*** to represent a refined data structure that makes access possible based on a certain key, and ***generics*** to create type-safe collections during compiling to avoid errors.

Understanding Collections

A collection refers to accumulation. As a developer, you will work with various types of data, so organizing the data is an important step. You can use collections to group different types of objects together for better results. The `System.Collections` and `System.Collections.Specialized` namespaces contain the classes and methods to work with collections. `ArrayList`, `Stack`, `Queue`, `StringCollection`, and `BitArray` are the main classes of the `System.Collection` namespace.

Working with the ArrayList Class

You can use the ***ArrayList*** class to collect items with a single data value. It overcomes the limitations of using arrays for your work.

The `ArrayList` class:

- Is defined in the `System.Collections` namespace
- Represents a dynamically sized array of objects
- Allows you to add, remove, insert, and sort items
- Contains items in the order of addition
- Consists of an index identifier assigned to its items
- Enables you to retrieve items in any order by means of their associated index numbers

USING THE ARRAYLIST CLASS

You can perform several operations with the items in the `ArrayList` class. Along with the common operations such as adding, removing, inserting, and sorting, you can instantiate an `ArrayList` by indicating the initial capacity that you want.

The following examples exhibit the various operations of the `ArrayList` class:

```
    // Instantiating an ArrayList
ArrayList address = new ArrayList(10);

    // Creating an ArrayList named languages
ArrayList languages = new ArrayList();
    // Adding elements to the ArrayList
             languages.Add("C#");
             languages.Add("VB6");
             languages.Add("VB.NET");
    // Inserting a new item in between in an array at 3rd position
             languages.Insert(2, "070 - 536");
    // Removing an element from the ArrayList
             languages.Remove("VB6");
    // Sorting an entire ArrayList
             languages.Sort();
    // Reading all the elements from ArrayList

    foreach (Object obj in languages)
    {
             Console.WriteLine(obj.ToString());
             Console.ReadLine();
             }
```

TAKE NOTE*

The `ArrayList` class supports a default size of 16 elements when you do not specify the initial size as in

```
ArrayList address =
new ArrayList();
```

This list holds zero elements and has its capacity property set to 0. However, when you add elements to the list, the capacity is automatically increased. You can explicitly modify the capacity of a list by setting the capacity property.

TAKE NOTE*

Note that the indexes in the `ArrayList` collection are zero-based.

Implementing Methods in the ArrayList Class

You can also implement several methods on the items of the array list for specific results. Some of these methods allow you to compare, sort, and search data from an array list.

The following examples exhibit the use of the methods implemented by the ArrayList class for specific functions:

- You can create your own custom IComparer implementations to control sort order.
  - The IComparable.CompareTo method controls the default sort order for a class.
  - The IComparer.Compare method can be used to provide custom sort orders, as shown in the following example of a simple class that only implements IComparer:

```
    public class SortDesc: IComparer
{
    int IComparer.Compare(Object a, Object b)
    {
return ((new CaseInsensitiveComparer()).Compare(a, b));
        }
    }
```

- You can pass an instance of the SortDesc class to the ArrayList.Sort method. The following example demonstrates the inclusion of the ArrayList.AddRange method that adds each element of an array as a separate element to the instance of ArrayList. This is an indirect approach:

```
    ArrayList languages = new ArrayList();
    languages.AddRange(new string[] {"C#", "VB", "Ada", "Pearl",
"Java", "SQL"});
    languages.Sort(new SortDesc());
    foreach (Object lang in languages)
Console.WriteLine(lang.ToString());
```

- You can also utilize the Reverse method, which is the inbuilt feature of the ArrayList class, to achieve the same functionality as shown in the previous example:

```
languages.Reverse();
```

- ArrayList also makes it simple to locate a zero-based index of an item by implementing the BinarySearch method. You must sort an ArrayList before using the BinarySearch method to search on it because an ArrayList is not a sorted collection. The BinarySearch method accepts an instance of the object for which you are searching. The following example creates a collection of computer languages and uses the BinarySearch method to search for a particular language:

```
ArrayList languages = new ArrayList();
    languages.AddRange(new string[]
{"C#", "VB", "Ada", "Pearl", "Java", "SQL"});
    languages.Sort();

Console.WriteLine(languages.BinarySearch("VB"));
    // Returns 5 because VB is at index 5 after you sort the
array as in Ada, C#, Java, Pearl, SQL, VB
```

- Similarly, the ArrayList.Contains method returns "True," if the ArrayList instance contains the specified object, or "False," if it does not contain the object, as shown in the following example:

```
    ArrayList languages = new ArrayList();
    languages.AddRange(new string[] {"C#", "VB", "Ada", "Pearl",
"Java", "SQL"});
Console.WriteLine(languages.Contains("XAML"));
    // Returns "False" as this language is not specified in the
    provided ArrayList
```

MORE INFORMATION
To know more about array lists, refer to the section on ArrayLists in the MSDN Library.

Understanding the Queue Class

Consider a set of email messages that are ready in your outbox. The mail server sends the messages in the order in which you composed them. Queues help you program such applications.

The ***Queue*** class, located in the `System.Collections` namespace, fulfills the requirement of accessing the first added object from the collected items. It offers various benefits and allows various operations through specific methods. The `Queue` class has the following advantages. It:

- Ensures that the items are accessed using a ***first in, first out (FIFO)*** sequence
- Helps handle the items on a first come, first served basis in a business scenario

USING THE QUEUE CLASS

You can perform several operations with the items in a queue, such as adding more items and reading them. Before using these functions, you must first define the queue.

The following examples demonstrate the various operations of the `Queue` class. The examples collectively create a queue containing strings and display the items in the queue:

TAKE NOTE*
The `Queue.Peek` method allows you to access an object without removing it from the queue. On the other hand, the `Queue.Clear` method allows you to remove all the objects from the queue.

```
// Defining a Queue
          Queue language = new Queue();
// Adding items to the Queue
          language.Enqueue("C# 1.0");
          language.Enqueue("C# 2.0");
          language.Enqueue("C# 3.0");
          language.Enqueue("C# 4.0");
          Console.WriteLine("Queue of Languages");
// Reading items through the Queue
          for (int i = 1; i <= 4; i++)
          Console.WriteLine(language.Dequeue());
          Console.ReadLine();
```

Exploring the Stack Class

Consider a pile of plates stacked for a dinner buffet. The last plate on the pile would be the first one to be removed. Similarly, while programming, you may want to remove the latest added item from its collection. The ***`Stack`*** class helps you do just that.

The `Stack` class:

- Is located in the `System.Collections` namespace
- Represents a collection of items that can be accessed using a ***last in, first out (LIFO)*** sequence
- Defines a member named `Push` to place items on the stack
- Defines a member named `Pop` to remove items from the stack
- Uses the `Stack.Peek` method to access an object without removing it from the stack
- Uses the `Stack.Clear` method to remove all the objects from the stack

USING THE STACK CLASS

Using the `Stack` class, you can add or read items. Before using these functions, you must first define a stack. The following examples demonstrate the various operations of the `Stack` class. The examples collectively create a stack containing strings and display the items in the stack:

```
// Defining a Stack
          Stack language = new Stack();
```

```
// Adding items to the Stack
          language.Push("C# 1.0");
          language.Push("C# 2.0");
          language.Push("C# 3.0");
          language.Push("C# 4.0");
          Console.WriteLine("Stack of Languages");
// Reading items through the Stack
          for (int i = 1; i <= 4; i++)
Console.WriteLine(language.Pop().ToString());
          Console.ReadLine();
```

Differentiating BitArray from BitVector32

Consider that you have ten printers in your network and you have to allot print jobs to these printers from a common priority-based queue. You can use a 10-bit mask to assign a specific print job to a specific printer. `BitArray` and `BitVector32` are important entities in .NET Framework that allow you to create and manipulate bit arrays.

The `BitArray` class is located in the `System.Collections` namespace. It represents an array of bit values, wherein each of its items is either true (1) or false (0). You can use `BitArray` class when you want to deal with bit arrays that are larger than 32 bits in size.

The following examples demonstrate the various operations of the `BitArray` class. The examples collectively create a bit array and display the items in the bit array:

```
   // Create and initialize a BitArray. The constructor used takes
the size and the initial value of the BitArray as parameters
BitArray myBA = new BitArray(3, true);
   // Display the number of elements in the BitArray
Console.WriteLine("BitArray");
Console.WriteLine("Count: {0}", myBA.Count);
   // Display the values of the BitArray
Console.WriteLine("Values:");
foreach (Object obj in myBA)
{
   Console.Write("{0}", obj);
}
   // The output will be:
// BitArray
// Count: 3
// Values:
// true true true
```

The `BitVector32` structure is located in the `System.Collections.Specialized` namespace. This structure represents a string of 32 bits where each bit can either be 0 or 1. You can use the `BitVector32` structure to store small integers (up to 32 bits) and Boolean values.

The `BitArray` class varies from the `BitVector32` structure in the following characteristics:

- **Size.** `BitArray` can have unlimited size, whereas `BitVector32` (a structure) is 32 bits precisely. Therefore, you can use `BitArray` to store Boolean values of more than 32 items, whereas, you can use `BitVector32` only for items with Boolean values of 32 or less.
- **Representation.** `BitArray` is a class as well as a reference type. Therefore, it uses heap to store values and references. `BitVector32` is a structure as well as a value type that uses stack to store values.

CERTIFICATION READY?
Manage a group of associated data in a.NET Framework application by using collections.
USD 1.2

`BitVector32` is a much more efficient structure when compared to the `BitArray` class. Because the size of `BitVector32` is only 32 bits, manipulation of this bit array is easy and can be accomplished as a single operation. Even without any values, a `BitArray` might require 8 bytes of space in memory. In addition, because the size of a `BitArray` is unlimited, it becomes increasingly difficult to operate on the array as it grows. For example, consider a 500-bit array in which you want to set the bits in the 256th and 334th positions to true. You must first locate the bits and then set them. This requires more operations than the single operation of the `BitVector32` structure.

■ Understanding Dictionaries

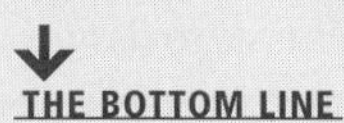

Suppose you wanted to look up the meaning of a complex word like congregate. You would thumb through the dictionary to reach the section containing words that started with the letter "c" and then flip through the pages until you reached words beginning with "con." In short, a dictionary compiles words in alphabetical order for easy retrieval of information. C# programming also uses a similar concept.

In C# programming, you can use a refined data structure to access an element based on a certain key of any datatype. These data structures are dictionaries. A dictionary consists of various classes, each of which is required for a specific purpose.

Analyzing the Features of Dictionaries

If you want to look up and associate keys with values, use the dictionary in your C# program. With ArrayLists you can store only values, but by using dictionaries you can store key-value pairs. The features available in a dictionary help perform the necessary actions. Dictionaries resemble the arrays in some features but are more powerful and are more similar to `ArrayList`.

You can refer to dictionaries also as maps or hash tables. Dictionaries include the following features:

- You can add and remove items without any restrictions or performance overheads.
- You can dynamically set the capacity of dictionaries.
- You do not need to use an integer for indexing; you can use any datatype.

WORKING WITH THE DICTIONARY CLASSES

The .NET Framework consists of several dictionary classes. Each of these classes has unique features, suitable to perform particular functions. Table 2-1 describes the key dictionary classes.

Table 2-1
Dictionary classes

DICTIONARY CLASS	DESCRIPTION
`HashTable`	A dictionary of name-value pairs that can be retrieved by name or index
`SortedList`	A dictionary of name-value pairs that is sorted automatically by the key
`StringDictionary`	A `HashTable` with name-value pairs implemented as strongly typed strings
`ListDictionary`	A dictionary optimized for a small list of objects with less than ten items
`HybridDictionary`	A dictionary that uses a `ListDictionary` for storage when the number of items is small and that automatically switches to a `HashTable` as the list increases
`NameValueCollection`	A dictionary of name-value pairs of strings that allow retrieval by name or index

FUNCTIONING OF THE DICTIONARY CLASS

The following examples exhibit the various functions performed by the various dictionary classes:

- The SortedList class, located in the System.Collections namespace, is a dictionary that consists of key-value pairs. The key and the value can be any object, and the key automatically sorts the SortedList class. The following code sample shows the creation of a SortedList instance with three key-value pairs and then displays the definition for SortedList, Stack, and Queue in that order. This is because the SortedList class sorts the entries in the order of the key:

```
// Creating a SortedList
SortedList kvp = new SortedList();
kvp.Add("Stack", "Collection of last in first out objects.");
kvp.Add("Queue", "Collection of first in first out objects.");
kvp.Add("SortedList", "Collection of key-value pairs.");
foreach (DictionaryEntry entry in kvp)
    Console.WriteLine("Key = {0}, Value = {1}", entry.Key, entry.
Value);
```

TAKE NOTE *

In this case, Queue is the first entry in the zero-based index because the SortedList instance automatically sorted the keys alphabetically.

In this example, you can infer that the SortedList is an array of DictionaryEntry objects. You can use the DictionaryEntry.Value and the DictionaryEntry.Key properties to access the objects that you originally added to the SortedList and the key, respectively.

You can also access values directly by accessing the SortedList as a collection. The following code sample (which builds on the code sample mentioned earlier) displays the definition for queue twice:

```
Console.WriteLine(kvp["Queue"]);
Console.WriteLine(kvp.GetByIndex(0));
```

- The StringDictionary class, located in the System.Collections.Specialized namespace, functions similar to the SortedList class that can accept an object of any type as its value, but only strings as keys. The differences between these two classes are that the StringDictionary class does not perform automatic sorting and requires both the keys and the values to be strings.
- The ListDictionary class, located in the System.Collections.Specialized namespace, is optimized to display better performance with lists that contain less than 10 items. Similarly, HybridDictionary, also located in the System.Collections.Specialized namespace, performs similar to the ListDictionary but shows better results on expanding the list.
- The NameValueCollection class also functions like the StringDictionary class with the exception that it allows you to use either a string or an integer index for the key. You can also store multiple string values for a single key, as shown in the following code sample, which displays two definitions for the terms Stack and Queue:

MORE INFORMATION

To know more about the dictionary classes we've discussed, refer to the System.Collections and Systems.Collections.Specialized namespaces in the MSDN Library.

```
// Creating a NameValueCollection
NameValueCollection kvp = new NameValueCollection();
kvp.Add("Stack", "Collection of last in first out objects.");
kvp.Add("Queue", "Collection of first in first out objects.");
kvp.Add("SortedList", "Collection of key-value pairs.");
kvp.Add("Stack", "Collection of objects.");
kvp.Add("Queue", "Collection of items.");
foreach (string str in kvp.GetValues(0))
    Console.WriteLine(str);
foreach (string str in kvp.GetValues("Queue"))
    Console.WriteLine(str);
```

CERTIFICATION READY?
Manage a group of associated data in a.NET Framework application by using collections.
USD 1.2

Exploring Generics

THE BOTTOM LINE

Many of the collections in the .NET Framework support adding objects of any type such as an `ArrayList`. Other collections such as `StringCollection` are strongly typed. `StringCollection` class represents a collection of strings and allows duplicate elements in the list. Type casting to the required base objects is necessary to accomplish generalization and to avoid compile time errors. ***Generics*** allow you to create collections that are type safe at compile time.

Introducing Generics

C# is a strongly typed language, and generics provide many of the benefits of strongly typed collections. Generics are a new kind of strongly typed collection that is now supported by the .NET Framework 2.0 and later.

It is easier to develop strongly typed classes because the Visual Studio designer can list and validate members automatically. In addition, it is not necessary to cast strongly typed classes to more specific types. Strongly typed classes protect the developer from casting to an inappropriate type.

Generics allow you to work with any type and provide many of the advantages of strongly typed collections. Using generic classes during development increases performance by reducing the number of required casting operations. Table 2-2 lists the most useful generic collection classes and the corresponding nongeneric collection types.

Table 2-2

Generic and nongeneric collection classes

GENERIC CLASS	NONGENERIC CLASSES	DESCRIPTION
`List<T>`	`ArrayList` `StringCollection`	A dynamically resizable list of items

`Dictionary<T,U>`	`HashTable`
	`ListDictionary`
	`HybridDictionary`
	`OrderedDictionary`
	`NameValueCollection`
	`StringDictionary`
		A generic collection of name-value pairs

`Queue<T>`	`Queue`	A generic implementation of a FIFO list
`Stack<T>`	`Stack`	A generic implementation of a LIFO list
`SortedList<T,U>`	`SortedList`	A generic implementation of a sorted list of generic name-value pairs
`Comparer<T>`	`Comparer`	Compares two generic objects for equality
`LinkedList<T>`	N/A	A generic implementation of a doubly linked list
`Collection<T>`	`CollectionBase`	Provides the basis for a generic collection
`ReadOnlyCollection<T>`	`ReadOnlyCollectionBase`	A generic implementation of a set of read-only items

TAKE NOTE*

Each of these generic collections provides better type safety and performance than non-generic collections and is much easier to use than arrays.

MORE INFORMATION

To know more about the generic collection classes we've discussed, refer to the System.Collections.Generic namespace in the MSDN Library.

Using Generics with Custom Classes

It is also possible to use generics with user-defined custom classes.

The generic classes help when working with custom classes. For example, it is possible to use the SortedList<TKey,UValue> generic class with a custom class exactly as you would use it with an integer. Note that TKey and UValue represent the type of keys and values in the collection. Consider the following custom class declaration that defines the first and last name of a person:

```
public class PersonDetails
{
    string firstName;
    string lastName;
    public PersonDetails(string _firstName, string _lastName)
    {
        firstName = _firstName;
        lastName = _lastName;
}
override public string ToString()
    {
        return firstName 1 " " 1 lastName;
    }
}
```

The following code sample demonstrates the use of SortedList<TKey,UValue> generic class with the PersonDetails custom class. The code creates a list of persons and displays the values in the list:

CERTIFICATION READY?
Manage data in a .NET Framework application by using .NET Framework system types.
USD 1.1

```
SortedList<string, PersonDetails> personList = new
SortedList<string, PersonDetails>();
personList.Add("P001", new PersonDetails("Vamika", "Agarwal"));
personList.Add("P033", new PersonDetails ("James", "Huddleston"));
personList.Add("P045", new PersonDetails ("Peter", "Bowyer"));
foreach (PersonDetails p in personList.Values)
    Console.WriteLine(p.ToString());
```

Using Specialized and Generic Collections

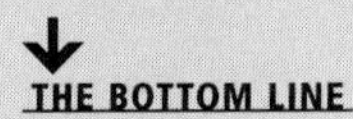

THE BOTTOM LINE

You can use several generic collection classes, such as SortedList<T,U>, Queue<T>, Stack<T>, and List<T> for specific functions. The performance of a few classes is based on certain requirements. You must remember that generic collections help you enforce type safety and specialized collections help you manage the data efficiently.

Working with Generic *SortedList<T,U>* Collection Class

Most of the standard collections have a generic implementation.

The following code sample creates a generic SortedList<T,U> that uses the strings as the keys and the integers as the values. When you type this code into the Visual Studio editor, you will observe that it prompts you to enter string and integer parameters for the SortedList.Add method because it is strongly typed. The following code uses the SortedList<T,U> generic collection to create a list and display the values in the list:

```
SortedList<string, int> dotnet = new SortedList<string, int>();
dotnet.Add(".NET 1.0", 2000);
dotnet.Add(".NET 1.1", 2002);
dotnet.Add(".NET 2.0", 2005);
foreach (int i in dotnet.Values)
   Console.WriteLine(i.ToString());
```

EXPLORING GENERIC *QUEUE<T>* AND *STACK<T>* COLLECTION CLASSES

You can use Queue<T> and Stack<T> for a generic implementation of FIFO and LIFO lists, respectively. The following code sample demonstrates using the generic versions of both queue and stack with the PersonDetails class. The code creates a queue and a stack, adds value to them, and displays their contents:

```
// Using Stack and Queue
   Queue<PersonDetails> que = new Queue<PersonDetails>();
   que.Enqueue(new PersonDetails ("Vamika", "Agarwal"));
   que.Enqueue(new PersonDetails ("James", "Huddleston"));
   que.Enqueue(new PersonDetails ("Peter", "Bowyer"));
   Console.WriteLine("Reading values from Queue");
   for (int i = 1; i <= 3; i++)
     Console.WriteLine(que.Dequeue().ToString());
   Stack<personDetails> stk = new Stack<PersonDetails>();
   stk.Push(new PersonDetails ("Vamika", "Agarwal"));
   stk.Push(new PersonDetails ("James", "Huddleston"));
   stk.Push(new PersonDetails ("Peter", "Bowyer"));
   Console.WriteLine("Reading values from Stack");
   for (int i = 1; i <= 3; i++)
     Console.WriteLine(stk.Pop().ToString());
```

UNDERSTANDING GENERIC *LIST<T>* COLLECTION CLASS

Some functions of the generic collection classes require the implementation of particular interfaces by the specified type. For example, the class that calls the List.Sort method with no parameters needs to support the IComparable interface.

The following code samples demonstrate the expansion of the PersonDetails class in order to support the IComparable interface and the requisite CompareTo method. This class further allows its items to be sorted in a List<T> generic collection:

- Implementing List<T> by adding the IComparable interface to the PersonDetails class:

```
// Implementing List<T>
public class PersonDetails: IComparable
{
string firstName;
string lastName;
        public int CompareTo(object obj)
{
 PersonDetails otherPerson = (PersonDetails)obj;
 if (this.lastName != otherPerson.lastName)
  return this.lastName.CompareTo(otherPerson.lastName);
 else
  return
this.firstName.CompareTo(otherPerson.firstName);
}
public PersonDetails(string _firstName, string _lastName)
{
```

TAKE NOTE*

After implementing the IComparable interface, you can also use the PersonDetails class as the key in a generic SortedList<T,U> or SortedDictionary <T,U> class.

CERTIFICATION READY?
Manage a group of associated data in a .NET Framework application by using specialized collections.
USD 1.3

CERTIFICATION READY?
Improve type safety and application performance in a .NET Framework application by using generic collections.
USD 1.4.

```
  firstName = _firstName;
  lastName = _lastName;
}
override public string ToString()
{
  return firstName 1 " " 1 lastName;
}
}
```

- Sorting items of the PersonDetails class in a List<T> generic collection with the person's first and last name:

```
List<personDetails> lst = new List<PersonDetails>();
lst.Add(new PersonDetails ("Vamika", "Agarwal"));
lst.Add(new PersonDetails ("James", "Huddleston"));
lst.Add(new PersonDetails ("Peter", "Bowyer"));
lst.Sort();
foreach (PersonDetails p in lst)
   Console.WriteLine(p.ToString());
```

SKILL SUMMARY

This lesson introduced you to techniques to use when managing groups of data using collections, dictionaries, specialized collections, and generics. The .NET Framework contains various namespaces that help you deal with all types of collection implementations such as stack, queue, list, and hashtable. These collections may be FIFO or LIFO implementations. Some of these collections require specific interfaces to be implemented. You must be thorough with each type of collection, the methods offered by the collection, and the prerequisites for implementing the collection.

For the certification examination:

- Know how to manage groups of data in .NET Framework using collections.
- Know how to manage groups of data in .NET Framework using dictionaries.
- Understand the importance of generics.
- Know how to manage groups of data in .NET Framework using specialized collections.

■ Knowledge Assessment

Matching

Match the following descriptions to the appropriate terms.

a. SortedList
b. ArrayList
c. StringDictionary
d. HashTable
e. StringCollection

_______ **1.** A class that holds items in the order of addition and must be sorted before using it for a binary search

_______ **2.** A dictionary of name-value pairs that can be retrieved by name or index

_______ **3.** A dynamically resizable list of items that allows duplicate values

_______ **4.** A HashTable with name-value pairs implemented as strongly typed strings

_______ **5.** A dictionary class located in the System.Collections namespace

True / False

Circle T if the statement is true or F if the statement is false.

T | F 1. Generic classes can be used with custom classes as with any base types.

T | F 2. `HybridDictionary` is a nongeneric class.

T | F 3. Generics are also referred to as maps or hashtables.

T | F 4. `ArrayList` consists of an index identifier assigned to its items.

T | F 5. `BitArray32` can be of unlimited size.

Fill in the Blank

Complete the following sentences by writing the correct word or words in the blanks provided.

1. In order to avoid compile time errors, __________ to the required base objects is essential.
2. __________ provides a base class for a generic collection.
3. The `ArrayList` class helps in the location of a zero-based index of an item through a method called ___________.
4. __________ is a dictionary of name-value pairs of strings that allow retrieval by name or index.
5. `Stack` is a class defined in the __________ namespace.

Multiple Choice

Circle the letter that corresponds to the best answer.

1. What is the function of the `Queue.Peek` method of the `Queue` class?
   a. Accesses an object without removing it from the queue
   b. Removes all objects from the queue
   c. Adds objects to the queue
   d. Reads objects through the queue
2. Which keyword will you use to add items to a queue?
   a. `Enqueue`
   b. `Dequeue`
   c. `Inqueue`
   d. `Addqueue`
3. What is the range of the Boolean values that can be stored by the `BitArray` class?
   a. More than 8 items
   b. More than 16 items
   c. More than 32 items
   d. Unlimited
4. You have been assigned to store the telephone numbers, including residence and mobile numbers, of all the employees in your organization. Further, any person should be able to retrieve the required data based on the employee name. What data structure should you use to be able to access an element based on a certain key?
   a. Collections
   b. Dictionaries
   c. Generics
   d. None of the above
5. In which namespace can you find the `StringDictionary` class?
   a. `System.Collections`
   b. `System.Collections.Specialized`
   c. `System`
   d. `System.CodeDom`

Review Questions

1. You have a list of members in your club. The list contains the name, age, height, and weight of the members. You want to perform sort and search operations on this list. One of your teammates suggests that you use the `StringCollection` class to create this list. Do you think this is the correct thing to do? Why or why not?
2. You have created a generic collection to hold product details, say `ProductDetails`. This custom class implements the `IComparable` interface. You want to sort the list of orders based on the new `ProductDetails` type that you have created. Is this possible?

■ Case Scenarios

Scenario 2-1: Using Collections and Dictionaries

In your online Web application for movie tickets, you provide a reservation number to customers who reserve tickets online. Customers also book their seats while making reservations.

Write a program that takes the reservation number of a customer as input and displays the corresponding seat numbers reserved by the customer.

Scenario 2-2: Using Specialized Collections

When reserving a movie ticket, the customer supplies number of seats, date, and time of the show. Assume that the shows in a day are numbered 1, 2, and 3 sequentially starting from the first show in the morning. Write a program that uses the `BitVector32` structure to store the show, the date, and the number of seats that the customer requires in a single variable.

Workplace Ready

Handling Groups of Data

Most of the applications that you develop may utilize collections to handle large groups of data. A few examples include reservation data, email messages, and user moves in games.

Microsoft .NET Framework offers a wide range of objects to handle groups of data. As discussed in this lesson, these include various collections, dictionaries, and specialized collections. In addition, .NET offers generic types to some of the specific collections. Generic collections offer better performance than their equivalent standard collection classes.

You must understand the correct use of each of these collections in order to use them effectively. Consider that you want to create a collection of file extensions and the corresponding program that you can use to open them. You have an ordered list of entries that you can use to populate the collection. This collection is stable—you do not want to add or delete items from it. However, you may use this collection extensively to search for item values based on the key. Suggest the best generic collection class to use to implement the required collection.

3 LESSON

Working with File System I/O

OBJECTIVE DOMAIN MATRIX

TECHNOLOGY SKILL	OBJECTIVE DOMAIN	OBJECTIVE DOMAIN NUMBER
Introduce streams.	Manage byte streams by using stream classes.	4.5
Access the file system.	Access files and folders by using file system classes.	4.4
Read and write files and streams.	Manage the .NET Framework application data by using reader and writer classes.	4.6
Implement stream compression.	Compress or decompress stream information in a .NET Framework application.	4.7
Use isolated storage.	Improve the security of application data by using isolated storage.	4.7

KEY TERMS

compressed stream
isolated storage
streams

You need storerooms, closets, and much more to store all the important things that you use in your daily life. Organizing things in separate places gives you quick accessibility, and in addition, keeps them safe and secure and easy to locate. Similarly, an application running in your computer needs to store information for various purposes in a durable storage place.

An application can store data either in a hard drive or in RAM. From your .NET applications, you can perform tasks that involve reading and writing from and to files and the system registry. In particular, you can use the .NET base classes to perform the following tasks:

- Exploring the directory structure, files, and folders and analyzing their properties
- Moving, copying, and deleting files and folders
- Reading and writing text or binary data in files
- Reading and writing keys in the registry

Microsoft has provided many intuitive object models that cover the areas discussed.

Introducing Streams

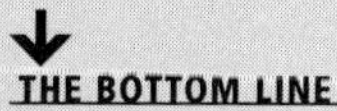
THE BOTTOM LINE

When developing applications, you will probably need to transfer data between your application and the outside world. In addition, you will want the transfer to take place independent of the destination resource, without affecting your application. The .NET Framework introduces various ***streams*** that allow your application to communicate with external devices, without bothering you about the underlying devices.

Analyzing Streams

You can use streams to transfer data either into your .NET application or out of your .NET application.

Streams, in .NET Framework, represent an abstract form of an external source of data. This abstract representation helps you develop applications that require no modifications, even if the external source of the stream changes.

A stream is a .NET object that allows data transfer in bytes. Transferring data from an external source into your application is "reading from the stream." Alternatively, transferring data from your application to an external source is "writing to the stream."

In most cases, the external source happens to be a file. However, transfer of data can also happen to and from other external sources that include reading or writing data:

- On the network share
- To a named pipe
- To system memory

INTRODUCING STREAM CLASSES

The `System.IO` namespace in the .NET Framework provides the majority of classes for file-based and stream-based operations. Figure 3-1 depicts the hierarchy of stream-related classes in the `System.IO` namespace. Table 3-1 lists the various stream classes and their uses.

Figure 3-1

Hierarchy of classes related to streams

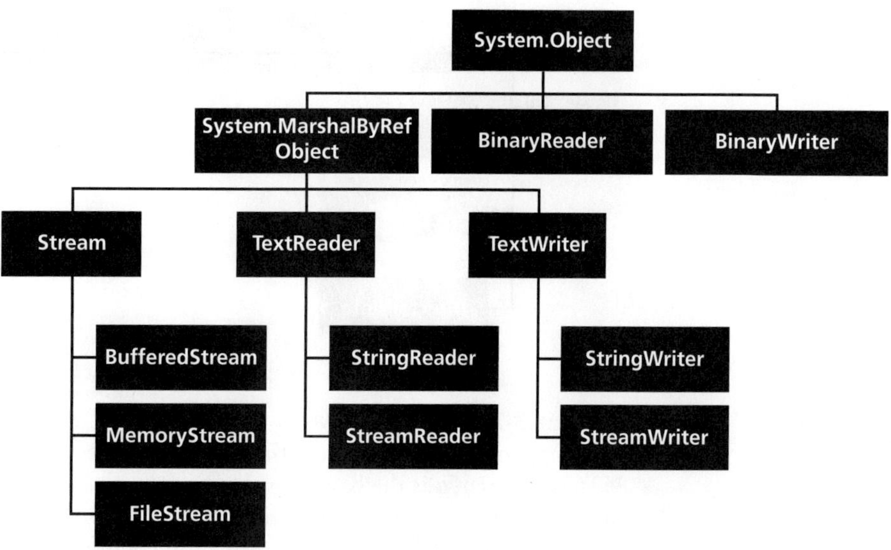

Table 3-1
Uses of stream classes

CLASS	USED TO
`FileStream`	Read and write data from and to files on a file system
`StreamReader`	Read data from text files
`StreamWriter`	Write data to text files
`MemoryStream`	Store data in the memory
`BufferedStream`	Cache data by buffering read-write operations on another stream

CERTIFICATION READY?
Manage byte streams by using stream classes.
USD 4.5

Accessing the File System

Being organized, whether in your house or workplace, makes life a whole lot easier. Organizing your hiking gear in the closet; stashing your baseball memorabilia in the attic, safely labeled in a box; and sorting your favorite photos into folders on your laptop gives you access to what you want instantly. Similarly, the .NET Framework organizes information in files and folders. The basic I/O system in the .NET Framework involves accessing and manipulating files and folders on various drives on your system.

Introducing the File System Classes

You can derive file system classes from the `System.IO` base class. You use these classes to access the specific file or folder within a directory or drive.

The `System.IO` is the parent class. Any class derived from it becomes the inherited class. This interplay of classes builds a file system class hierarchy. Figure 3-2 displays the `File System` classes and its hierarchy.

Figure 3-2
Hierarchy of file system

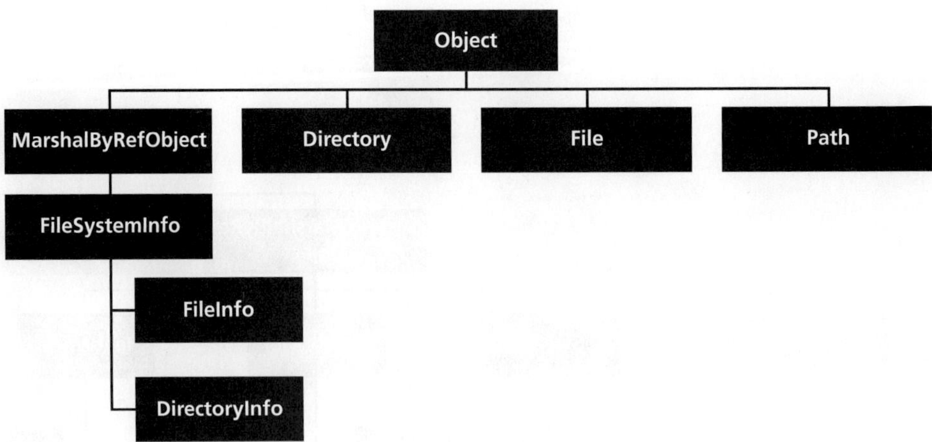

In Figure 3-2, the `System.MarshalByRefObject` class permits marshalling of data across application domains. It is the base object class for remote .NET classes. The `FileSystemInfo` is the base class that represents any file system object. The `FileInfo` and `File` classes provide information about a file on the file system. The `DirectoryInfo` and `Directory` classes provide information about a folder or a subfolder on the file system. The `Path` class contains static members used to manipulate path names.

Table 3-2 lists the various file system classes and their uses.

Table 3-2

Uses of file system classes

CLASS	PURPOSE
Directory	Provides static methods used to create, move, enumerate, and remove directories and subdirectories on a file system
DirectoryInfo	Provides instance methods used to create, move, enumerate, and remove directories and subdirectories on a file system
File	Provides static methods used to create, open, copy, move, enumerate, and delete files on a file system
FileInfo	Provides instance methods used to create, open, copy, move, enumerate, and delete files on a file system
FileSystemInfo	Provides the base class for the `FileInfo` and `DirectoryInfo` classes
Path	Allows members to operate on a string instance of a directory or file location

USING CLASSES TO ACCESS FILES AND FOLDERS

Depending on how often you access a folder or file, you can choose from the classes provided in the .NET Framework:

- **The `Directory` class and the `File` class.** These classes contain only static methods; therefore, you do not need to instantiate them. When you want to use either of these classes, simply supply the path to the appropriate file system object to invoke a member method. Because you do not instantiate them, these classes are efficient as long as you need to perform a single operation on a folder or file.
- **The `DirectoryInfo` class and the `FileInfo` class.** These classes implement the same public methods as the `Directory` class and `File` class. Additionally, they have public constructors and properties such as `Name` and `CreationTime`. The `DirectoryInfo` and `FileInfo` classes are stateful. The members of these classes are not static; therefore, you must instantiate them before you invoke them in a program. Being stateful is helpful if you are performing multiple operations using the same object. These classes read the authentication and other information for the appropriate file system only once. Once the authentication goes through, you can invoke any number of methods for each object.

ENUMERATING THROUGH SYSTEM DRIVES

If you have a computer memory partition, you can access a list of drives associated with your computer system. You can use a static `DriveInfo.GetDrives` method to retrieve a collection of `DriveInfo` objects.

The following C# syntax shows how to use the `DriveInfo` class:

```
foreach (DriveInfo drvInf in DriveInfo.GetDrives())
   Console.WriteLine("{0} ({1})", drvInf.Name, drvInf.DriveType);
```

Table 3-3 lists a few important properties of the DriveInfo class.

Table 3-3

Properties of the DriveInfo class

PROPERTY	DESCRIPTION
AvailableFreeSpace	Indicates the amount of available free space on a drive
DriveFormat	Retrieves the name of the file system, such as NTFS or FAT32
DriveType	Retrieves the drive type
IsReady	Indicates whether a drive is ready
Name	Retrieves the name of the drive
RootDirectory	Retrieves the root directory of a drive
TotalFreeSpace	Retrieves the total amount of free space available on a drive
TotalSize	Retrieves the total size of storage space on a drive
VolumeLabel	Retrieves or sets the volume label of a drive

Managing Files and Folders

With all the files piling up on your computer, .NET Framework makes it easy to browse through the files and folders stored on various drives of your system.

The .NET Framework provides classes that you can use to browse files and folders, create new folders, and manage the files.

BROWSING FOLDERS

You can use the DirectoryInfo class to browse folders and files stored on your system. You need to create an instance of the DirectoryInfo class by specifying the folder you want to browse. You can then invoke the DirectoryInfo.GetDirectories or DirectoryInfo.GetFiles method.

For example, the following code browses through folders and lists all the files and subdirectories stored in the C:\MyDocuments folder:

```
DirectoryInfo dirInfo = new DirectoryInfo(@"C:\MyDocuments");
Console.WriteLine("Folders:");
foreach (DirectoryInfo dir in dirInfo.GetDirectories())
   Console.WriteLine(dir.Name);
Console.WriteLine("\nFiles:");
foreach (FileInfo file in dirInfo.GetFiles())
   Console.WriteLine(file.Name);
```

CREATING FOLDERS

If you want to create folders, create an instance of the DirectoryInfo class. You can then invoke the DirectoryInfo.Create method. To avoid duplication of folders, you can use the DirectoryInfo.Exists property to determine whether a folder exists. This property returns a Boolean value.

For example, the following code sample determines the existence of a folder. If it does not find a folder by that name, it creates a new folder:

```
// Creating a folder if it doesn't exist
DirectoryInfo myDir = new DirectoryInfo(@"C:\CreateOrDelete");
if (myDir.Exists)
   Console.WriteLine("The folder already exists");
else
   myDir.Create();
```

WARNING When you create a directory, check for the existence of that directory as shown in the previous code sample. This is important because, if a directory or folder already exists, the CLR does not throw any exception. Additionally, the Create method would do nothing in this case.

MANAGING FILES

The .NET Framework provides various static methods, such as `File.Create`, `File.CreateText`, `File.Copy`, `File.Move`, and `File.Delete` to create, edit, copy, move, and delete files, respectively. For example, the following code sample creates a file, copies it, and then moves it to a different folder or renames the folder:

```
// Creating, Copying, Deleting, and Moving files
File.CreateText("SourceFile.txt");
File.Copy("SourceFile.txt", "TargetFile.txt");
File.Move("TargetFile.txt", "NewTargetFile.txt");
File.Delete("SourceFile.txt");
```

You can also create an instance of the `FileInfo` class that represents a specific file. By invoking the `Create`, `Create Text`, `CopyTo`, `MoveTo`, and `Delete` methods, you can create, copy, and move files. The following code sample uses the `FileInfo` class to manipulate the files:

```
// Using FileInfo Create, Copy, and Move files
// Create a new file
FileInfo myFI = new FileInfo("SourceFile.txt");
// The CreateText method returns a StreamWriter object that you can
use to add contents to that file
StreamWriter strW = myFI.CreateText();
strW.WriteLine("Include this text in the new file.");
// Copy the file
myFI.CopyTo("TargetFile.txt");
// Move the file by specifying a new name
FileInfo myFI2 = new FileInfo("TargetFile.txt");
myFI2.MoveTo("NewTargetFile.txt");
// Delete the source file
myFI.Delete();
```

Monitoring the File System

Consider a multinational company, having 5,000 associates worldwide, with each employee handling one or more files individually or simultaneously. All employees together may generate and use a large number of files. This requires constant monitoring of the file system for smooth functioning. The .NET Framework uses different classes derived out of the `System.IO` namespace to address this issue.

If you want to get notifications about the changes in your file or directory system, you can use the `FileSystemWatcher` class. For example, you can get notifications about a file update, rename, deletion, or creation of files or directories using the `FileSystemWatcher` class. To do this, you must create an instance of the `FileSystemWatcher` class. You must specify the path that needs to be monitored. You can also specify that subdirectories be monitored by configuring the properties of the `FileSystemWatcher` instance.

You can define the updates you want to track for a specified folder. You can also add an event handler method, and set the `FileSystemWatcher.EnableRaisingEvents` property to true. This event handling method alerts you whenever there are any changes to the files on the specified path.

The following code sample shows how the `FileSystemWatcher` class creates an instance and configures properties to monitor a specific path. The code also implements the handler to display the changes:

```
// Working with FileSystemWatcher
// Create an instance of FileSystemWatcher
FileSystemWatcher myFSW = new FileSystemWatcher
(Environment.GetEnvironmentVariable("USERPROFILE"));
```

```
// Set the FileSystemWatcher properties
myFSW.IncludeSubdirectories = true;
myFSW.NotifyFilter = NotifyFilters.FileName | NotifyFilters.LastWrite;
// Add the Changed event handler
myFSW.Changed += new FileSystemEventHandler(myFSW_Changed);
// Start monitoring events
myFSW.EnableRaisingEvents = true;
   // Add code to the handler method
private static void myFSW_Changed(object source, FileSystemEventArgs e)
      {
            // Display the change
            WatcherChangeTypes myWct = e.ChangeType;
            Console.WriteLine("File {0} {1}", e.FullPath,
            myWct.ToString());
      }
```

TRACKING CHANGES TO THE FILE SYSTEM

The `FileSystemWatcher` class notifies you whenever there is a change in a specified path. At the same time, the CLR invokes the `FileSystemWatcher.Changed` event handler. You can use this event handler to carry out all creations, updates, and deletions. If a user renames a file, then the CLR invokes the `FileSystemWatcher.Renamed` event handler.

The following code shows a simpler method to handle an event in C#:

```
static void myFSW_Changed(object sender, FileSystemEventArgs e)
{
   // Write the path of a changed file to the console
   Console.WriteLine(e.ChangeType + ": " + e.FullPath);
}
```

The CLR calls the `FileSystemWatcher.Changed` event handler for all changes, creations, and deletions that meet the criteria you specify. The `FileSystemEventArgs` parameter specifies the path to the updated file and specifies whether the file was changed, created, or deleted. If you want to track file renaming, you must use the `Renamed` event handler with the `RenamedEventArgs` parameter, as shown in the following code sample:

```
static void myFSW_Renamed(object sender, RenamedEventArgs e)
{
   // Write the path of a changed file to the console
   Console.WriteLine(e.ChangeType + " from " + e.OldFullPath + " to " +
   e.Name);
}
```

CONFIGURING FILE SYSTEM TRACKING

You can control the types of updates that cause the CLR to raise the `Changed` event. You can do this by setting the properties of the `FileSystemWatcher` class:

- **`Filter`.** You can use this property to configure filenames that triggers events. You can narrow your search for changed files using empty strings (" ") or wildcards ("*.*"). If you are certain about the file that you want to monitor, you can directly set the `Filter` property to the filename. For example, to track the updates for a specific file MyDoc.txt, set the property `Filter` to "MyDoc.txt". To broaden the search parameter to all text files, you can set the `Filter` property to "*.txt".
- **`NotifyFilter`.** The `NotifyFilter` property allows you to configure the types of changes that result in an event. The values that the `NotifyFilter` property can take include:
  - FileName
  - DirectoryName
  - Attributes
  - Size

  - LastWrite
  - LastAccess
  - CreationTime
  - Security

- **`Path.`** You can use the `Path` property to monitor changes to files and directories on a specific path. You can use the `FileSystemWatcher` constructor to define the path. For example, you can use the `WaitForChanged` method to monitor the renaming of text files by setting the `Filter` property of the `FileSystemWatcher` object to "*.txt" and specifying a rename value for its parameter.

CERTIFICATION READY?
Access files and folders by using File System classes.
USD 4.4

TAKE NOTE*

The `FileSystemWatcher` objects behave differently in certain Windows versions. For example, in some versions of Windows XP and Windows 2000 SP2, multiple `FileSystemWatcher` objects monitoring the same Universal Naming Convention (UNC) path, invoke an event from only one of the objects. Whereas on later versions, such as Windows XP SP1 and later, Windows 2000 running the SP3 or later, Windows Vista, or Windows Server 2008, all the objects raise specific events.

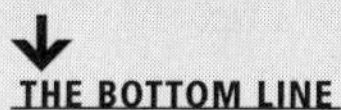

Reading and Writing Files and Streams

THE BOTTOM LINE

A stream, in .NET Framework, is a sequence of bytes. Streams support reading and writing operations of bytes, byte arrays, and strings. You can use specific stream classes to read and write data available in a text file, a binary file, and in memory.

Reading and Writing a Text File

Text files provide a common data pattern that is easy for people and programs to understand. Microsoft .NET Framework consists of classes that provide a simpler way to read data from and write data to a text file.

The `System.IO` namespace provides two classes, namely, `StreamReader` and `StreamWriter`. Both of these classes are exclusively designed to read from and write to a text file. Additionally, the `StreamReader` class derives from the `TextReader` abstract base class, and the `StreamWriter` class derives from the `TextWriter` abstract base classes. Therefore, you can also use the instances of the `TextReader` and `TextWriter` classes to read and write texts. However, as the `TextReader` and `TextWriter` are abstract base classes, you cannot directly instantiate them. Instead, you can instantiate their derived classes and assign the resultant instance to them.

READ A TEXT FILE

You can perform the following steps to read a text file:

1. Use one of the following to open a text file:
   - Create an instance of the `StreamReader` class.
   - Create an instance of the `TextReader` class by instantiating a `StreamReader` class.
   - Use the `File.OpenText` method.
2. Call the specific method of the chosen class to complete the task.

TAKE NOTE*

When using the `TextReader` class to read a text file, you can generally use the static `File.OpenText` method because this method returns a `StreamReader` object, which is the derived class of the `TextReader` class.

TAKE NOTE*

You can use the ReadLine or ReadToEnd methods of the StreamReader class to read the text files.

The following code samples exhibit the application of the StreamReader and the TextReader classes.

The code sample reads a specified text file and displays the content of the text file in a label control named ShowFileText. Note that the code may throw the FileNotFound exception if the specified file does not exist:

```
// Reading a text file using the StreamReader class
string filedata = " ";
          StreamReader myStream = new
StreamReader("C:\Windows\ReadMe.txt");
          while ((fileData = myStream.ReadLine()) != null)
ShowFileText.Text = fileData;
          myStream.Flush();
          myStream.Close();
          //Reading a text file using the TextReader class
          TextReader myText = File.OpenText("C:\Windows\ReadMe.txt");
          ShowFileText.Text = myText.ReadToEnd();
          myText.Close();
```

TAKE NOTE*

Note that the previous code example uses a Label control to display the text. Therefore, you must create a Windows Form and include a Label named ShowFileText. You can then write the code in the Load event of the form.

WRITING A TEXT FILE

You can use the StreamWriter and the TextWriter classes to write a text file. The following examples show the application of these classes:

```
// Writing a text file using the StreamWriter class
   StreamWriter myStream = new StreamWriter("C:\Windows\ReadMe.txt");
   myStream.WriteLine("This text is written to the file.");
   myText.Flush();
   myStream.Close();
   //Writing a text file using the TextWriter class
   TextWriter myText = File.CreateText("C:\windows\ReadMe.txt");
   myText.WriteLine("This text is written to the file.");
   myText.Flush();
   myText.Close();
```

WARNING Writing a file is an expansive mechanism with respect to reliability. In view of this fact, it is always important to call the Flush method to ensure that data is being written and saved on the disk to be used afterward. If not, then the data is stored in buffer, which could result in the loss of the changes if the computer shuts down suddenly.

Writing to and Reading from Binary Files

Many times, you need to program to read and write binary data. Reading and writing a binary file is a difficult task. To make things easier, .NET Framework provides you with classes that enable reading and writing data from and to binary files.

You can use the System.IO.FileStream class along with the BinaryReader and BinaryWriter classes of the System.IO namespace to read and write data in binary files.

Reading and writing to nontext or binary files involves the following steps:

1. Create an instance of the FileStream class.
2. Assign this instance to a BinaryReader or BinaryWriter class as required to read or write a binary file.

INITIATING THE PROCESS TO READ AND WRITE BINARY FILES

As a preliminary process in reading and writing binary data to a file, you must first construct a `FileStream` object, which is derived from the `Stream` base class. Its construction requires the following information:

- The **file** you want to access.
- The **mode** in which you want to open the file; for example, whether you want to create a new file or open an existing file. In the case of opening an existing file, should any write operation be interpreted as overwriting the contents of the file or appending to the file?
- The **access** type you require; for example, if you want to read or write a file.

WRITING TO A BINARY FILE

You can write to a binary file using the `BinaryWriter` class. It works in association with the `FileStream` class, as shown in this code example:

```
// Using BinaryWriter with FileStream to write the data
        FileStream myStream = new FileStream("data.bin",
FileMode.Create);
        BinaryWriter myWriter = new BinaryWriter(myStream);
myWriter.Write("Binary Data");
        myWriter.Close();
        myStream.Close();
```

READING FROM A BINARY FILE

You can read a binary file using the `BinaryReader` class. It works in association with the `FileStream` class, as shown in this code example:

```
// Using BinaryReader with FileStream to read the data
        FileStream myStream = new FileStream("data.bin",
FileMode.Open, FileAccess.Read);
        BinaryReader myReader = new BinaryReader(myStream);
        Console.WriteLine(myReader.ReadString());
        myReader.Close();
        myStream.Close();
```

READING AND WRITING STRINGS

Writing a string requires that you convert it into an array of bytes. Similarly, reading a string involves reading the bytes from an array and later converting them into a string.

The `StringBuilder` class plays an important role in reading and writing strings. It includes the following features:

- Works in association with `StringWriter` and `StringReader` classes to write to and read from the strings
- Performs a key role, similar to that of a `FileStream` when handling the `StringWriter` and `StringReader` classes

TAKE NOTE*

Usually, you use the `StringWriter` and `StringBuilder` classes only when you have a specific reason to use streams instead of accessing the strings directly. For example, you can use `StringWriter` if you have a method that requires a stream object, but you do not want to create a file.

READING AND WRITING STRINGS

The following examples show the use of `StringWriter` and `StringReader` with `StringBuilder`:

```
// Using StringWriter with StringBuilder
        StringBuilder myStrBld = new StringBuilder();
        StringWriter myStrW = new StringWriter(myStrBld);
        myStrW.Write("This is MCTS");
        myStrW.Write("Exam 070-536");
        myStrW.Close();
// Using StringReader with StringBuilder
StringReader myStrRead = new StringReader(myStrBld.ToString());
// Reads the text and displays it in a TextBox control
named ShowStringText
        ShowStringText.Text = myStrRead.ReadToEnd();
        myStrRead.Close();
```

TAKE NOTE* Note that this code example uses a `TextBox` control to display the text. Therefore, you must create a Windows Form and include a `TextBox` named `ShowStringText.` You can then write this code in the `Load` event of the form.

Typically, you use the `StringWriter` and `StringBuilder` classes only if you have a specific reason to use streams instead of accessing the strings directly. For example, you can use the `StringWriter` class when you do not want to create a file but you must write a method that requires a stream object.

Using Streams in Memory

The `MemoryStream` class uses the primary memory as storage to create streams. You can use these streams to reduce the requirement of temporary buffers and files in an application.

The `MemoryStream` class is derived from the base `Stream` class. Most of the time, you can use it to store temporary data that will ultimately be written to a file. The advantages of using the `MemoryStream` class are that you can create the stream in memory without any hurry, add data to it, and then write all the data to the disk immediately. This operation reduces the time the file needs to be locked in Open mode. Furthermore, in multiuser environments where a file might need to be accessed by other processes, employing `MemoryStream` decreases the probability for variance in data.

READING AND WRITING DATA IN MEMORY

You can use `MemoryStream` to read data from and write data to files, in the form of byte array. The following example shows the storage of data (byte array) in a `MemoryStream,` writing the output using a `StreamWriter`, and calling the `Flush` method to ensure that the contents of the `StreamWriter`'s buffer are written to the underlying array:

```
// Storing data in MemoryStream and dumping to a file on disk
MemoryStream myMemStr = new MemoryStream();
StreamWriter myStrW = new StreamWriter(myMemStr);
myStrW.WriteLine("This is an MCTS Exam 70-531!");
myStrW.Flush();
myMemStr.WriteTo(File.Create("DumpingMemory.txt"));
myMemStr.Close();
```

TAKE NOTE*

You do not need to use a `BufferedStream` with a `FileStream` object because the `FileStream` objects contain exactly the same buffering logic as the `BufferedStream` class, which means a second layer of buffering would be unnecessary and ineffective.

The previously mentioned code sample also uses the `StreamWriter` class to write a string to the `MemoryStream`. In the absence of the `StreamWriter`, a `MemoryStream` instance can only read and write bytes and byte arrays using the following methods:

- **`WriteByte` method.** To write a single byte
- **`Write` method.** To write an array of bytes
- **`ReadByte` method.** To read a single byte
- **`Read` method.** To read an array of bytes

Buffering Streams

CERTIFICATION READY?
Manage the .NET Framework application data by using Reader and Writer classes.
USD 4.6

A buffered stream acts as an intermediate data holder for another stream. When you use a buffered stream, it also enhances the process of writing to a stream.

`BufferedStream` class is derived from the base `Stream` class. You use it mainly with custom stream implementations because the stream classes built into the .NET Framework contain built-in buffering capabilities from the beginning.

You can use the `BufferedStream` class in the same way you would the `MemoryStream` class because both of these classes are only able to write bytes and byte arrays.

Implementing Stream Compression

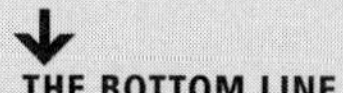

THE BOTTOM LINE

When using a personal computer, you have probably often realized the importance of valuable resources such as disk space and transmission bandwidth. Data compression techniques compress the volume of the given data to a considerably smaller size. By compressing data, you can considerably reduce the consumption of your disk space during backups; and in addition, you can transmit the data across the network with minimal bandwidth space.

Compressing Stream Data

The .NET Framework provides you with classes that help in compressing and decompressing stream data.

Generally, compression techniques work well with text files because compression results in highly compressed files. Compression in binary files results in comparatively less compressed files than text files. In addition, files that are already in a compressed format, such as music or image files, will not benefit from further compression.

In .NET Framework, the `System.IO.Compression` namespace provides the basic compression and decompression services that helps you write and read ***compressed streams***. By using the compression services provided by the .NET Framework, you can create compressed data that may invariably consume less storage space.

You can use the `GZipStream` class in the `System.IO.Compression` namespace to compress and decompress streams. The `GZipStream` class uses the `GZip` data format for file compression and decompression.

You can find more information on the MemoryStream, StreamWriter, and StreamReader classes in the "Reading and Writing Files and Streams" section covered in this lesson.

CREATING COMPRESSED STREAM

Like the `MemoryStream` class, you can read and write only individual byte arrays using the `GZipStream` class. Therefore, if you want to read and write strings from and to a compressed stream, use the `StreamReader` and `StreamWriter` classes, respectively.

The following example demonstrates how to write strings to a compressed stream. The code creates the compressed file ZipData.zip using the `GZipStream` class.

As you read the next code sample, you will notice that the `GZipStream` constructor creates an instance named `myGZStr` using the `FileStream` object and the `CompressionMode.Compress` enumeration value:

TAKE NOTE*

The `GZipStream` constructor takes a stream object as the first argument and the `CompressionMode` value as the second argument. The `CompressionMode` enumeration value indicates whether the instance of the `GZipStream` class compresses or decompresses the specified stream data.

```
// Creating a compressed stream using a new file
GZipStream myGZStr = new GZipStream(File.Create("ZipData.zip"),
CompressionMode.Compress);
// Create a StreamWriter object to allow writing strings to the
GZipStream
StreamWriter myStrW = new StreamWriter(myGZStr);
// Write data to the compressed stream, and then close it
for (int i = 1; i < 536; i++)
myStrW.Write("MCTS Exam 70-536");
// Close the stream objects
myStrW.Close();
myGZStr.Close();
```

The compressed file ZipData.zip created in the previous example consumes only 289 bytes of disk space. Whereas, if you use the `FileStream` class in the example instead of the `GZipStream` class, the resultant file created would consume 13,986 bytes of disk space.

READING COMPRESSED STREAM

You can also read data from a compressed file. The following example demonstrates how to open and read string data from a compressed file. The code decompresses the compressed file ZipData.zip using the `GZipStream` class and reads the string data from the ZipData.zip file using the `StreamReader` class.

As you read the code sample, note that the `GZipStream` constructor takes the `CompressionMode.Decompress` enumeration value in this case:

CERTIFICATION READY?
Compress or decompress stream information in a .NET Framework application.
USD 4.7

```
// Opening the created file containing the compressed data
GZipStream myGZStr = new GZipStream(File.OpenRead("ZipData.zip"),
CompressionMode.Decompress);
// Read and display the compressed data
StreamReader myStrR = new StreamReader(myGZStr);
Console.WriteLine(myStrR.ReadToEnd());
// Close the stream objects
myStrR.Close();
myGZStr.Close();
```

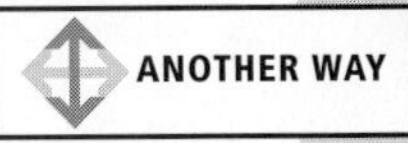

You can also use the `DeflateStream` class provided in the `System.IO.Compression` namespace to compress and decompress streams. The `DeflateStream` class uses the *Deflate* data format for compression and decompression.

Using Isolated Storage

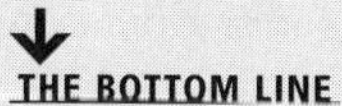

Applications may have to store user specific settings such as configuration information and preferences in a storage space that is safe and secure from hackers and other applications. The .NET Framework offers the ***isolated storage*** technique that helps your application store, read, and write application-related data from a special storage location in the hard drive.

Introducing Isolated Storage

Isolated storage is a well-opted storage medium that you can take advantage of when considering options for storing your application data.

In earlier days, programmers used .ini files to store application-specific data. However, .ini files could store only a limited amount of data because they contain plain text and are nonhierarchical in nature. Therefore, at a later stage, Windows registry became the storage medium for storing application-related information. Because of frequency of access, Windows registries are prone to corruption, and sometimes it becomes difficult to rely on them for storing application-specific data. Now the .NET Framework introduces isolated storage in which application-specific per-user information can be stored in a safe and secure manner.

ANALYZING THE BASICS OF ISOLATED STORAGE

The isolated storage mechanism enables you to store data in a safe, isolated location by providing a standardized way of associating code with the stored data. Standardization enables administrators to use tools to manipulate isolated storage just as they would any other file system folder. For example, administrators can configure file storage space, delete unused data, or even set security policies.

By using isolated storage, you do not need to specify the unique file path where you have stored the application data, which eradicates the necessity of providing the hard coded data storage location in the code.

TAKE NOTE*

Note that the physical location of isolated stores differs with each operating system. Moreover, the advantage of an isolated store is that the users need not know the exact physical location of the isolated store. However, they can still treat it as a virtual folder in their hard drive.

All the partially trusted applications such as other Web applications and downloaded components can store data in isolated storage in accordance with the computer's security policy. However, code running on the local computer, the local area network, or the Internet has the default right to use isolated storage.

MANAGING AND ISOLATING DATA

The .NET Framework manages isolated storage, which is a private file system. Like for the standard file system, you can use stream classes, such as the `StreamReader` and `StreamWriter` classes, to read and write files in isolated storage. However, writing to isolated storage requires fewer privileges than writing directly to the file system, making it useful for implementing least privilege.

As already stated, isolated storage is private and therefore, by using isolated storage, data is isolated by user, assembly, and domain. This isolation provides some additional protection, which is not possible in a conventional file system.

WARNING Although, isolated storage isolates the data, the data is not safe from the accessibility of highly trusted code, unmanaged code, or trusted users of the computer. Therefore, you should not use isolated storage to store high-value secrets, such as unencrypted keys or password.

CLASSIFYING ISOLATED STORAGE

.NET Framework offers various ways of isolating storage that include:

- **Isolation by user and assembly.** Accessibility to a file in isolated storage is always restricted to the user who creates it. In addition to isolation by user, access to the isolated storage can also be generally restricted to specific assemblies. For example, *Assembly B* cannot access files located in an isolated store, created by *Assembly A*.

- **Isolation by user, domain, and assembly.** You can also restrict access to isolated storage with respect to the application domain. That is, if a store is isolated by the application domain, the same assembly running in different application domains cannot access a single store. For example, if *Assembly A* resides in two application domains, namely *AppDomain 1* and *AppDomain 2*, then *Assembly A* of *AppDomain 1* can access the isolated storage *store X*, and *Assembly A* of *AppDomain 2* can only access another isolated storage *store Y* but not *store X*.

INTERACTING WITH ISOLATED STORAGE

The `System.IO.IsolatedStorage` namespace in the .NET Framework provides classes that you can use to interact with isolated storage. Table 3-4 lists the classes that are associated with isolated storage.

Table 3-4

Classes associated with isolated storage

CLASS	PURPOSE
IsolatedStorageFile	Provides management of isolated storage stores
IsolatedStorageFileStream	Provides access to read-write isolated storage files within stores
IsolatedStorageException	Manages exceptions relating to isolated storage

Working with Isolated Storage

You can work with the isolated storage just as you would work with standard files.

Files in isolated storage behave exactly like conventional files stored directly on a file system except that the isolated storage files exist within an isolated store. Each individual store is a separate isolated storage system that you can implement as a single file in the file system.

ACCESS ISOLATED STORAGE

You can use the following steps to access a store in isolated storage:

1. Use or import the `System.IO.IsolatedStorage` namespace in addition to the `System.IO` namespace.
2. Optionally, declare an instance of `IsolatedStorageFile` class to specify the type of isolation.
3. Construct the file system objects from classes such as the StreamReader, `StreamWriter`, and other classes in the `System.IO` namespace by using objects in the `System.IO.IsolatedStorage` namespace.

Let us look at an example that best explains how to access a store in isolated storage. The following example retrieves a user store isolated by assembly:

```
// Creating an isolated storage
// Get the store isolated by the assembly IsolatedStorageFile
myIsoStore = IsolatedStorageFile.GetUserStoreForAssembly();
  // Create the isolated storage file in the assembly
IsolatedStorageFileStream myIsoFileStr = new IsolatedStorageFileStream
("IsolatedData.txt", FileMode.Create, myIsoStore);
// Create a StreamWriter using the isolated storage file
StreamWriter myStrW = new StreamWriter(myIsoFileStr);
// Write a line of text to the file myStrW.WriteLine("This is the
sample code for using an isolated storage file.");
// Close the file myStrW.Close();
```

This code creates a file named IsolatedData.txt in the user store `myIsoStore`. In addition, the code gets the `myStrW (StreamWriter)` object using the isolated storage file object, `myIsoFileStr`. The `StreamWriter` object, `myStrW` writes a line of text to the file and then closes the underlying isolated storage file.

TAKE NOTE*

You can also access a store isolated by application domain in the same way as explained in the previous example, except that you have to change the name of the method used to retrieve the store from `IsolatedStorageFile.GetUserStoreForAssembly` to `IsolatedStorageFile.GetUserStoreForDomain`.

READING DATA FROM ISOLATED STORAGE

You can also read data stored in isolated storage. The following example illustrates how to read the contents of an isolated storage file.

The code reads the content of the isolated storage file IsolatedData.txt using the `StreamReader` class:

```
// Reading data from an isolated storage
// Get the store isolated by the assembly IsolatedStorageFile
myIsoStore = IsolatedStorageFile.GetUserStoreForAssembly();
// Open the isolated storage file in the assembly IsolatedStorageFile
Stream myIsoFile = new IsolatedStorageFileStream("IsolatedData.txt",
FileMode.Open, myIsoStore);
// Create a StreamReader using the isolated storage file
StreamReader myStr = new StreamReader(myIsoFile);
// Read a line of text from the file string filedata = myStr.
ReadLine(); Console.WriteLine(filedata);
// Close the file
myStr.Close();
```

CERTIFICATION READY?
Improve the security of application data by using isolated storage.
USD 4.7

You can also use the `IsolatedStorageFile.GetStore` method instead of `IsolatedStorageFile.GetUserStoreForAssembly` or `IsolatedStorageFile.GetUserStoreForDomain`, if both the methods are not enough to specify the specific store you need to access. You must remember these points when you choose the appropriate method to access the required isolated store:

- When you use the `IsolatedStorageFile.GetUserStoreForAssembly` method, the same assembly within different applications always uses the same isolated store.
- When you use the `IsolatedStorageFile.GetUserStoreForDomain` method, the same assembly within different applications uses different isolated stores.
- Within a single application domain, the different assemblies always use separate isolated stores.
- The `IsolatedStorageFile.GetStore` method has many overloads to access the isolated storage relevant to the given application domain, assembly evidence objects, and isolated storage scope. This method allows you to access the isolated store of a different assembly or domain by passing in the different assembly or domain evidences as parameters.

MORE INFORMATION

To create or access isolated storage, the code must have `IsolatedStorageFilePermission` granted. To know how the code can acquire this permission or how the runtime grants this permission, you can read the "Securing Isolated Storage" section from the MSDN Library.

SKILL SUMMARY

This lesson explained workings of the file system and stream classes. Working with the file I/O is most common in programming. The `System.IO` namespace consists of classes, such as `FileStream`, `MemoryStream`, `StreamWriter`, `StreamReader`, and `BufferedStream` for file-based and stream-based functions. Similarly, the `System.IO` namespace provides file system classes, such as `FileSystemInfo`, `Directory`, `File`, and `Path` to move, copy, and delete files.

You learned that you could use specific stream classes to read from and write to a text file, binary file, and memory. For example, the use of `BufferedStream` class with custom stream implementations improves writing to a stream.

You also learned about the classes that help in compression and decompression of stream data and the process of isolated storage to standardize the method used to associate code with stored data.

For the certification examination:

- Know how to manage byte streams in a .NET application by using stream classes.
- Understand how to access files and folders by using the file system classes.
- Know how to manage .NET Framework application data by using reader and writer classes.
- Compress or decompress stream data in a .NET Framework.
- Use isolated storage to improvise the security of the application data.

■ Knowledge Assessment

Matching

Match the following descriptions to the appropriate terms.

a. `IsolatedStorageFile.GetStore`
d. `Write`
c. `File.OpenText`
d. `WriteByte`
e. `ReadToEnd`

_______ 1. Method provided by the `MemoryStream` class to write an array of bytes

_______ 2. Method that returns a `StreamReader` object, which can then be assigned to an instance of the `TextReader` class to read text files

_______ 3. Method provided by the `StreamReader` and `TextReader` classes to read a text file

_______ 4. Alternative to `IsolatedStorageFile.GetUserStoreForDomain` method

_______ 5. Method provided by the `MemoryStream` class to write a single byte

True / False

Circle T if the statement is true or F if the statement is false.

T | F 1. You can only use the `BufferedStream` class to write bytes and byte arrays.

T | F 2. The `GZipStream` class uses the deflate data format for file compression and decompression.

T | F 3. To create or access isolated storage, the code must have the `IsolatedStorageFilePermission`.

T | F 4. To read a compressed stream, the `GZipStream` constructor takes the `CompressionMode.Compress` enumeration value.

T | F 5. You can use the `IsolatedStorageFile.GetStore` method instead of the `IsolatedStorageFile.GetUserStoreForAssembly` method.

Fill in the Blank

Complete the following sentences by writing the correct word or words in the blanks provided.

1. To access a store in the isolated storage, you must declare an instance of __________ class.
2. The __________ class is mainly used with custom stream implementations.
3. You do not need to use a `BufferedStream` class with a ________ object.
4. You should not use __________ to store unencrypted keys.
5. The `DeflateStream` class uses the _________ data format for compression and decompression.

Multiple Choice

Circle the letter or letters that correspond to the best answer or answers.

1. Select all the classes from the following options that inherit from `TextReader` base class.
   a. `StringReader`
   b. `BinaryReader`
   c. `GZipStream`
   d. `FileStream`
2. Which method can you use to read text files?
   a. `ReadLine`
   b. `ReadByte`
   c. `Read`
   d. None of the above
3. What are the advantages of using the compression services provided by the .NET Framework?
   a. Creates compressed data that occupies less storage space
   b. Transmits the data across the network with minimal bandwidth space
   c. Stores the data in an secluded location
   d. None of the above
4. You are the system administrator with Jack and Jill Servicing Company and want to configure file storage space for a Web application. Which mechanism should you use to perform this task?
   a. Isolated storage
   b. Compression
   c. Decompression
   d. Flush
5. Select all the classes that represent a folder on the file system.
   a. `DirectoryInfo`
   b. `Directory`
   c. `FileInfo`
   d. `DirectoryFile`

Review Questions

1. Why should you flush the data periodically when writing to files?
2. What is Isolation by Assembly?

■ Case Scenarios

Scenario 3-1: Using the Right Type of Stream Classes

You must create a text file to contain e-tickets for customers who book tickets through your Web site. Use the appropriate stream class and write the program to create a text file.

Scenario 3-2: Using Compression Classes

You are building an online movie Web site that allows users to book tickets in advance. Consider that you send a text file that contains the advanced booking data for a month in a compressed form. Write a program to read and display this data on the screen.

✳ Workplace Ready

Working with Isolated Stores

Isolated storage helps you isolate application or assembly specific data into separate stores. This store is not accessible to other processes. You must design an isolated storage mechanism for your application based on whether you need application or assembly specific isolations.

Consider that you are the design architect for XYZ Solutions, Inc. You are currently working on an assembly that must be accessible to all applications in your organization. This assembly must use the same isolated store irrespective of the application that accesses it. In addition, other assemblies must be restricted from accessing the store created by this assembly. Suggest the isolation level that you must implement. In addition, specify the method that you must use to access the isolated store in your solution.

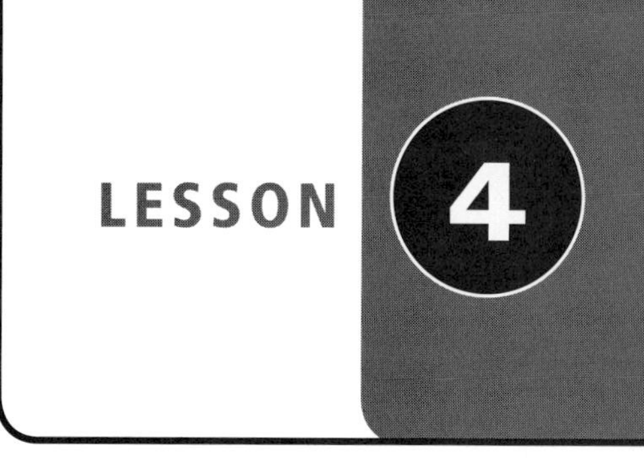

Creating Graphic Applications

OBJECTIVE DOMAIN MATRIX

TECHNOLOGY SKILL	OBJECTIVE DOMAIN	OBJECTIVE DOMAIN NUMBER
Create graphic objects.	Enhance the user interface of a .NET Framework application by using the `System.Drawing` namespace.	7.2
Create graphic objects.	Enhance the user interface of a .NET Framework application by using brushes, pens, colors, and fonts.	7.4
Explore shapes and sizes.	Enhance the user interface of a .NET Framework application by using shapes and sizes.	7.6
Create images.	Enhance the user interface of a .NET Framework application by using graphics, images, bitmaps, and icons.	7.5
Manage text in graphics.	Enhance the user interface of a .NET Framework application by using brushes, pens, colors, and fonts.	7.4

KEY TERMS

ascent
bitmap block transfer (BitBlt)
descent
graphic objects
Graphical Device Interface (GDI)
Graphical Device Interface (GDI+)

In your day-to-day life, you use many applications such as games to stay entertained, word processors to create documents, and presentation software to create your presentations.

These applications provide various types of user interfaces that consider usability features from the user's perspective. Most applications use forms, which contain different standard controls to gather the user information in an appropriate manner in order to process it.

Although these standard controls are powerful and, by themselves, quite adequate for the complete user interface for many applications, there may be situations in which you need more flexibility. For example, you might want to display text in a specific color at a precise position in a window, display images without using a picture box control, or draw simple shapes. You cannot perform these activities with standard controls. In order to display this kind of output, the application must instruct the operating system what to display along with the position in which to display it in its window.

In addition, all the applications discussed here use a variety of drawing objects such as lines, circles, and rectangles. If you want to incorporate graphical elements in your Windows-based application or Web-based application, you can use ***Graphical Device Interface (GDI+)***. The various classes in GDI+ allow you to embed and edit your images. Graphical elements can be line drawings, icons, or complex images, such as photographs stored on your desktop. You can apply various changes to your images, like zooming to a specific region or rotating and stretching to fit the space.

Knowing which fonts complement your Web application or Windows application is winning half the battle. Working with text is more complicated than graphics, especially when you are worried about how a particular font style will appear in the overall project.

Creating Graphic Objects

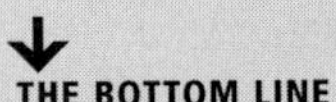

THE BOTTOM LINE

Application designers use graphics extensively in the application layouts that they design. The use of graphics makes the applications more flexible and readable. In addition, graphics enhance the presentation and usability features of an application. .NET offers various graphics classes to build graphic-rich applications.

Understanding Drawing Principles

To start drawing the ***graphic objects*** on the screen, you must understand the basic principles of graphics.

Generally, one of the strengths of the Windows operating system lies in its ability to abstract the details of particular devices without input from the developer. Let us consider an example. It is not necessary for you to understand anything about the device driver of your hard drive in order to programmatically read and write files to disk. Instead, you must simply call the appropriate methods in the relevant .NET classes. That same principle is also applicable to drawing. When drawing an object on the screen, the computer sends instructions for drawing the object to the video card. However, there are many different video cards available in the market, each having unique instruction sets and capabilities. If you consider this and write specific code for each video driver, writing any application would be an almost impossible task. To resolve this problem, Windows ***Graphical Device Interface (GDI)*** has been around since the earliest versions of Windows.

DIFFERENTIATING GDI AND GDI+

GDI provides a layer of abstraction, hiding the differences between various video cards. To perform a specific task, you simply call the Windows API function, and the GDI takes care of how to get your particular video card to perform the required task internally. If you have several display devices such as monitors and printers, GDI achieves the remarkable feat of making your printer output appear identical to the material that displays on your screen as far as your application is concerned. Suppose, you want to print something instead of displaying it on the screen, you simply instruct the system that the output device is the printer and then call the same API functions in exactly the same fashion.

The device-context (DC) object is very powerful, and under GDI, all drawing must be done through it. Device-context objects, associated with devices such as monitors or printers, store information about those devices. In GDI, any program that needs to draw an object to a device must obtain a handle to the device context of that device. Alternately, the DC is even used for operations that don't involve drawing to any device, such as updating images in memory. GDI+ has eliminated the need for a device context or a handle to device context with the introduction of the `Graphics` class. This class provides simpler methods and properties that you can use to draw graphic objects when compared to the earlier GDI device-context model.

Even though GDI exposes a relatively high-level API, it is still an API with C-style functions that is based on the old Windows API. However, in most cases, GDI+ works as a layer between GDI and your application. This feature enables GDI+ to provide an inheritance-based object model. Although GDI+ is a wrapper around GDI, the new features provided by Microsoft have been able to enhance application performance through GDI+.

Introducing GDI+ Namespaces

Because GDI+ is a vast part of the base class library in .NET, you should understand the fundamental principles required for exploring the various classes available in GDI+.

The GDI+ part of the base class library in .NET is huge. Table 4-1 lists the main various namespaces pertaining to the GDI+ base classes.

Table 4-1

GDI+ namespaces

NAMESPACE	DESCRIPTION
`System.Drawing`	Provides most of the classes, structs, enums, and delegates related to the basic functionality of drawing.
`System.Drawing.Drawing2D`	Provides classes to support advanced 2D and vector drawing, including anti-aliasing, geometric transformations, and graphics paths.
`System.Drawing.Imaging`	Provides various classes that assist in image manipulation (bitmaps, GIF files, and so on).
`System.Drawing.Printing`	Provides classes to assist when specifically targeting a printer or print preview window as the output device.
`System.Drawing.Design`	Provides some predefined dialog boxes, property sheets, and other user interface elements concerned with extending the design-time user interface.
`System.Drawing.Text`	Provides classes to perform advanced manipulation of fonts and font families.

Knowing the Basic System.Drawing Namespace

The `System.Drawing` namespace is the most basic namespace of GDI+ that allows you to draw various graphic objects. It contains classes that you can use to build objects for creating and editing images.

The .NET Framework includes the `System.Drawing` namespace. This namespace enables you to create graphics from scratch as well as modify existing images. The `System.Drawing` namespace allows you to perform the following tasks:

- Add circles, lines, and other shapes to the user interface dynamically.
- Create charts from scratch.
- Edit and resize pictures.
- Change the compression ratios of pictures stored on disk.
- Crop pictures.
- Zoom pictures.
- Add copyright logos and text to pictures.

Table 4-2 lists the most commonly used classes in the `System.Drawing` namespace.

Table 4-2

Classes in the `System.Drawing` namespace

Class	Description
`Bitmap`	Encapsulates a GDI+ bitmap, which consists of the pixel data for a graphics image and its attributes. A `Bitmap` object is an object used to work with images defined by pixel data. You can use this class when you need to load or save images.
`Brush`	Classes derived from this abstract base class define objects used to fill the interiors of graphical shapes such as rectangles, ellipses, pies, polygons, and paths.
`Brushes`	Provides brushes for all the standard colors. You cannot inherit this class. Use this class to avoid creating an instance of `Brush` class.
`ColorConverter`	Converts colors from one datatype to another. Access this class through the `TypeDescriptor` object.
`ColorTranslator`	Translates colors to and from GDI+ `Color` structures. You cannot inherit this class.
`Font`	Specifies a format for text, including font face, size, and style attributes. You cannot inherit this class.
`FontConverter`	Converts `Font` objects from one datatype to another. Access the `FontConverter` class through the `TypeDescriptor` object.
`FontFamily`	Defines a group of typefaces having a similar basic design and certain variations in styles. You cannot inherit this class.
`Graphics`	Encapsulates a GDI+ drawing surface. You cannot inherit this class. You can use this class anytime you need to draw lines, shapes, or add graphical text to a control or image.
`Icon`	Represents a Microsoft Windows icon, which is a small bitmap image used to represent an object. Icons are transparent bitmaps and the system decides their size.
`IconConverter`	Converts an `Icon` object from one datatype to another. Access this class through the `TypeDescriptor` object.
`Image`	An abstract base class that provides functionality for the `Bitmap` and `Metafile` descended classes.
`ImageAnimator`	Animates an image that has time-based frames.
`ImageConverter`	Converts `Image` objects from one datatype to another; Access this class through the `TypeDescriptor` object.
`ImageFormatConverter`	Converts colors from one datatype to another. Access this class through the `TypeDescriptor` object.
`Pen`	Defines an object used to draw lines, curves, and arrows. You cannot inherit this class.
`Pens`	Provides pens for all the standard colors. You cannot inherit this class. Use this class to avoid creating an instance of `Pen` class.

Table 4-2 (continued)

Class	Description
`PointConverter`	Converts a `Point` object from one datatype to another. Access this class through the `TypeDescriptor` object.
`RectangleConverter`	Converts rectangles from one datatype to another. Access this class through the `TypeDescriptor` object.
`Region`	Describes the interior of a graphics shape composed of rectangles and paths. You cannot inherit this class.
`SizeConverter`	Converts one datatype to another. Access this class through the `TypeDescriptor` object.
`SolidBrush`	Specifies a brush of a single color. Brushes are used to fill graphics shapes, such as rectangles, ellipses, pies, polygons, and paths. You cannot inherit this class.
`StringFormat`	Encapsulates text layout information (such as alignment and line spacing), display manipulations (such as ellipsis insertion and national digit substitution), and `OpenType` features. You cannot inherit this class.
`SystemBrushes`	Each property of the `SystemBrushes` class is a `SolidBrush` object that is the color of a Windows display element.
`SystemColors`	Each property of the `SystemColors` class is a `Color` structure that is the color of a Windows display element.
`SystemFonts`	Specifies the fonts used to display text in Windows display elements.
`SystemIcons`	Each property of the `SystemIcons` class is an `Icon` object for Windows systemwide icons. You cannot inherit this class.
`SystemPens`	Each property of the `SystemPens` class is a `Pen` object that is the color of a Windows display element and that has a width of 1.
`TextureBrush`	Each property of the `TextureBrush` class is a `Brush` object that uses an image to fill the interior of a shape. You cannot inherit this class.
`ToolboxBitmapAttribute`	You can apply a `ToolboxBitmapAttribute` to a control so that containers, such as the Form Designer in Visual Studio, can retrieve an icon that represents the control. The bitmap for the icon can be in a file by itself or can be embedded in the assembly that contains the control. The size of the bitmap that you embed in the control's assembly or store in a separate file should be 16-by-16. The `GetImage` method of a `ToolboxBitmapAttribute` object can return the small 16-by-16 image or can return a large 32-by-32 image by scaling the small image.

Table 4-3 lists the various structures included in the `System.Drawing` namespace.

Table 4-3

Structures in the `System.Drawing` namespace

STRUCTURE	DESCRIPTION
`CharacterRange`	Specifies a range of the character positions within a string.
`Color`	Represents a color.
`Point`	Represents an ordered pair of integer *x* and *y* coordinates that defines a point in a two-dimensional plane.
`PointF`	Represents an ordered pair of floating-point *x* and *y* coordinates that defines a point in a two-dimensional plane.
`Rectangle`	Stores a set of four integers that represent the location and size of a rectangle. You can use a `Region` object for more advanced region functions.
`RectangleF`	Stores a set of four floating-point numbers that represent the location and size of a rectangle. You can use a `Region` object for more advanced region functions.
`Size`	Stores an ordered pair of integers—width and height of a rectangle.
`SizeF`	Stores an ordered pair of floating-point numbers—width and height of a rectangle.

CERTIFICATION READY?
Enhance the user interface of a .NET Framework application by using the `System.Drawing` namespace.
USD 7.2

CERTIFICATION READY?
Enhance the user interface of a .NET Framework application by using brushes, pens, colors, and fonts.
USD 7.4

TAKE NOTE*

The `System.Drawing` namespace contains classes and structures that help you draw graphic objects. Classes are reference types that by default contain private members. For example, `Graphics` is a class that represents a drawing surface and contains members such as `DrawLine` and `DrawString`. Structures are value types that by default contain public members. For example, Color is a structure that represents a specific color and contains a public static member such as `FromName`.

Exploring Shapes and Sizes

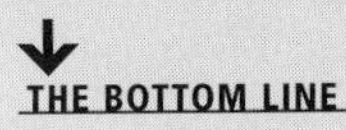

Imagine you have to create an application similar to the Microsoft Paint application. Alternately, consider another scenario that requires you to provide a customized Forms application, which can draw dynamic figures and shapes to add special effects to your forms. The GDI+ namespaces in the .NET Framework enable you to create both these applications.

Working with Location and Size of Control

You can create forms that dynamically adjust their contents based on user input using the .NET GDI+ classes.

One of the simplest and most common uses of the `System.Drawing` namespace is specifying the location and size of controls in a Windows Forms application.

SPECIFYING LOCATION AND SIZE

To place a control on the form, you must specify the control's location on the form using the `Point` structure, with the relevant coordinates relative to upper-left corner of the form.

To get a better understanding, let us look at a sample code that draws a button in the upper-left corner of a form, exactly 10 pixels from the top and left sides. The code creates the `Point` structure and assigns it to the `Location` property of the control. Note that the example uses the `Button` class from the `System.Windows.Forms` namespace:

TAKE NOTE*

Unlike the `Point` structure, the `PointF` structure accepts coordinates as floating points, which is why you cannot use the `PointF` structure to specify the location of a graphical user interface.

```
Button drawButton = new Button();
drawButton.Location = new Point(10, 10);
```

Alternatively, you can also place a control at a specified location using the `Left` and `Top`, or `Right` and `Bottom` properties of the control, as shown next. However, this involves writing two lines of code:

```
drawButton.Left = 10;
drawButton.Top = 10;
```

Like location, you can also specify the size of a control, as shown:

```
drawButton.Size = new Size(20, 20);
```

Specifying the Color of Controls

You can also specify the color of a control using the structures available in the `System.Drawing` namespace.

The `Color` structure in the `System.Drawing` namespace lets you specify a control's color.

USING THE COLOR STRUCTURE

You can use one of the predefined properties of the `Color` structure to specify the color of a control as shown in the following sample code:

```
clrButton.ForeColor = Color.Red;
crlButton.BackColor = Color.Blue;
```

In order to specify custom colors, you can use the `Color.FromArgb` method, which is static. The `Color.FromArgb` method provides several overloads for specifying the ARGB (alpha, red, green, blue) values according to your comfort. RGB represents the red, green, and blue components of the color structure. The alpha component specifies the transparency level ranging from fully transparent (0) to fully opaque (255). For example, the following code sample uses integers to specify red, green, and blue levels. The constructor used in the following example assumes that the alpha value for the color is fully opaque:

```
clrButton.ForeColor = Color.FromArgb(10, 200, 200);
clrButton.BackColor = Color.FromArgb(200, 5, 5);
```

Drawing Lines and Shapes

You can also draw lines and shapes on a form or control using the GDI+ classes.

The `System.Drawing.Graphics` class provides the majority of the GDI+ outstanding drawing ability.

DRAW ON FORMS OR CONTROLS

XREF

To learn more about how to create a `Graphics` object using an `Image` object, refer to the "Creating Images" section in this lesson.

You can use the following steps to draw on a form or control:

1. Create a Graphics object by calling the `System.Windows.Forms.Control.CreateGraphics` method.
2. Create a Pen object.
3. Execute the required method of the `Graphics` object to draw on a form or control using the `Pen` object.

Table 4-4 lists the various important methods available in the `Graphics` class.

Table 4-4

Methods of the `Graphics` class

METHOD	DESCRIPTION
`Clear`	Clears the entire drawing surface and fills it with the specified color.
`DrawEllipse`	Draws an ellipse or circle defined by a bounding rectangle with the specified height and width coordinates.
`DrawIcon`, `DrawIconUnStretched`	Draws an image represented by the specified icon at the specified coordinates, with or without scaling the icon.
`DrawImage`, `DrawImage Unscaled`, `DrawImage UnscaledAndClipped`	Draws the specified `Image` object at the specified location, with or without scaling or cropping the image.
`DrawLine`	Draws a line with the specified coordinate pairs.
`DrawLines`	Draws a series of line segments that connect an array of `Point` structure.
`DrawPath`	Draws a series of connected lines and curves.
`DrawPie`	Draws a pie shape defined by an ellipse with the specified height and width coordinates and two radial lines.
`DrawPolygon`	Draws a shape with three or more sides as defined by an array of `Point` structure.
`DrawRectangle`	Draws a rectangle or square with the specified height and width coordinates.
`DrawRectangles`	Draws a series of rectangles or squares specified by the `Rectangle` structure.
`DrawString`	Draws the specified text string at the specified location with the specified `Brush` and `Font` objects.

TAKE NOTE*

The specified coordinates of the `DrawPie` method point to the upper-left corner of an imaginary rectangle. These coordinates form the boundary of the pie and do not point to the center of the pie.

While creating a `Pen` object, you must specify the color and width of the pen using the constructor of the `Pen` object.

For example, the following sample code draws a black line, which is 7 pixels wide from the upper-left corner (1, 1) to a point near the middle of the form (100, 100), as shown in Figure 4-1. To see the effect, create a Windows Forms application and add the sample code to the event handling method of the form's `Paint` event.

Figure 4-1

A line drawn using the `Pen` object

CREATE A FORM

You can use the following steps to create a form and add the following code:

1. Create a Windows Forms application project in Visual Studio 2008.
2. Right click on the form and open its properties.
3. Scroll to the `OnPaint` event and double click that. You get the autogenerated handler for the `Paint` method of the `Form` object as shown:

   ```
   private void Form1_Paint(object sender, PaintEventArgs e)
   {
   }
   ```

4. Add the following code to this event handler:

   ```
   // Create a Graphics object
   Graphics graph = this.CreateGraphics();
   // Create a Pen object for drawing
   Pen pen = new Pen(Color.Black, 7);
   // Draw the line
   graph.DrawLine(pen, 1, 1, 100, 100);
   ```

Similarly, the following code draws a black pie shape with a 60-degree angle as shown in Figure 4-2:

```
Graphics graph = this.CreateGraphics();
Pen pen = new Pen(Color.Black, 3);
graph.DrawPie(pen, 1, 1, 100, 100, -30, 60);
```

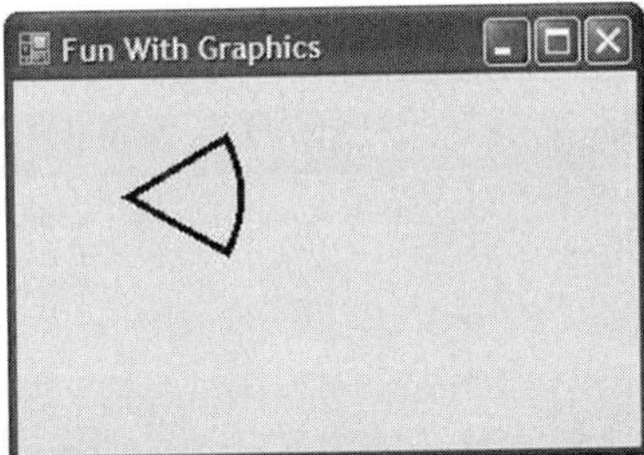

Figure 4-2

A pie drawn using the `Pen` object

You can create complex shapes, using the `Graphics.DrawLines`, `Graphics.DrawPolygon`, and `Graphics.DrawRectangles` methods that accept arrays as parameters. For example, the following code draws a black, five-sided polygon as shown in Figure 4-3:

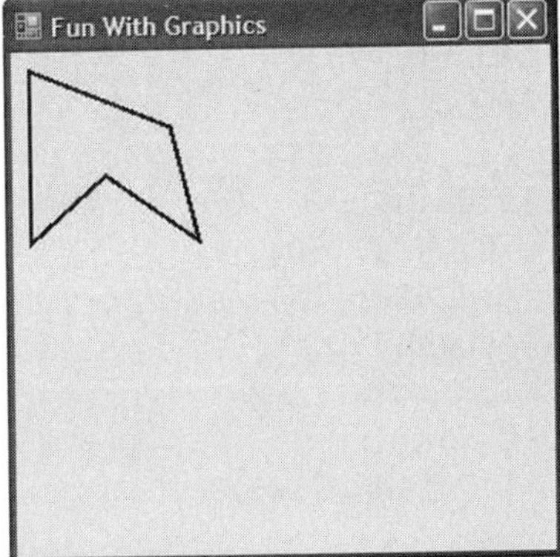

Figure 4-3

A five-sided polygon drawn using the `Pen` object

```
Graphics graph = this.CreateGraphics();
Pen pen = new Pen(Color.Black, 2);
// Create an array of points
Point[] points = new Point[]
{
    new Point(10, 10),
    new Point(10, 100),
    new Point(50, 65),
    new Point(100, 100),
    new Point(85, 40)
};
// Draw a shape defined by the array of points
graph.DrawPolygon(pen, points);
```

Customizing Pens

You can also customize the pens used to draw figures and shapes to provide an attractive and pleasant look.

The Pen class provides various properties that you can use to create different patterns and styles while drawing an image.

APPLYING STYLES AND PATTERNS

Table 4-5 lists the members of the Pen class that let you to control the pattern and the appearance of the starting and ending point of a line.

Table 4-5

Members of the Pen class

PROPERTY	DESCRIPTION
StartCap	Specifies the cap style for the beginning of a line.
EndCap	Specifies the cap style for the end of a line.
DashStyle	Specifies different styles for the dashed line that include Dash, DashDot, DashDotDot, Dot, and Solid.
DashPattern	Specifies an array of custom dashes and spaces.

TAKE NOTE*

By default, pens draw solid lines.

The following code, which requires the System.Drawing.Drawing2D namespace, demonstrates each of the pen styles and creates the result as shown in Figure 4-4:

```
Graphics graph = this.CreateGraphics();
Pen pen = new Pen(Color.Black, 7);
pen.DashStyle = DashStyle.Dot;
graph.DrawLine(pen, 50, 25, 400, 25);
pen.DashStyle = DashStyle.Dash;
graph.DrawLine(pen, 50, 50, 400, 50);
graph.DrawLine(pen, 50, 75, 400, 75);
pen.DashStyle = DashStyle.DashDotDot;
graph.DrawLine(pen, 50, 100, 400, 100);
pen.DashStyle = DashStyle.Solid;
graph.DrawLine(pen, 50, 125, 400, 125);
```

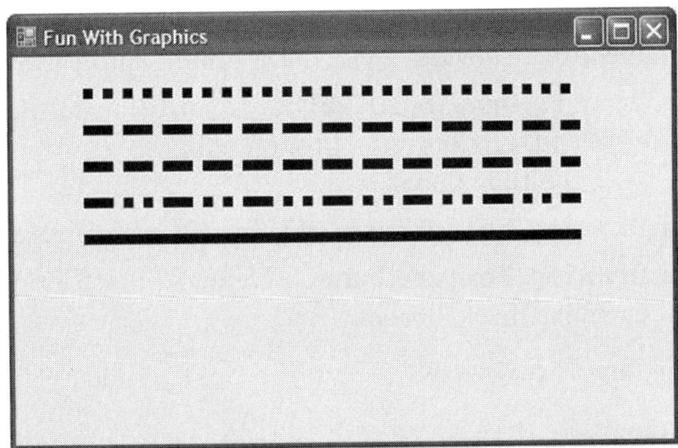

Figure 4-4

Displaying various `Pen` styles using the `DashStyle` property

You can also define custom dash patterns using the `Pen.DashOffset` and `Pen.DashPattern` methods. You can use the `LineCap` enumeration to control the end caps of a line to create special effects such as creating arrows or callouts. The following code demonstrates most of the pen cap styles and creates the result shown in Figure 4-5:

```
Graphics graph = this.CreateGraphics();
Pen pen = new Pen(Color.Black,10);
pen.StartCap = LineCap.ArrowAnchor;
pen.EndCap = LineCap.DiamondAnchor;
graph.DrawLine(pen, 50, 25, 400, 25);
pen.StartCap = LineCap.SquareAnchor;
pen.EndCap = LineCap.Triangle;
graph.DrawLine(pen, 50, 50, 400, 50);
pen.StartCap = LineCap.Flat;
pen.EndCap = LineCap.Round;
graph.DrawLine(pen, 50, 75, 400, 75);
pen.StartCap = LineCap.RoundAnchor;
pen.EndCap = LineCap.Square;
graph.DrawLine(pen, 50, 100, 400, 100);
```

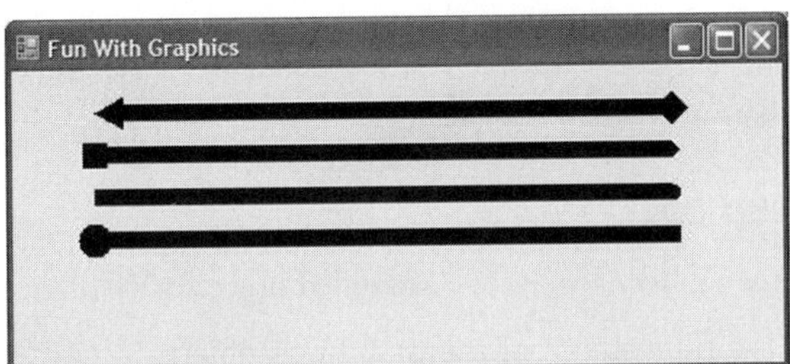

Figure 4-5

Displaying various `Pen` styles using the `LineCap` enumeration

Filling Shapes

You can also create colorful shapes by filling them with suitable colors.

Using the fill methods of the `Graphics` class, you can draw the required shape as well as fill the shape with appropriate colors.

USING THE BRUSH CLASS

The draw methods of the `Graphics` class require a `Pen` object, and the fill methods of the `Graphics` class require a `Brush` object.

Because the `Brush` class is an abstract class, you must instantiate an instance of the `Brush` class using one of the following descendant classes:

- **`System.Drawing.Drawing2D.HatchBrush`.** Defines a rectangular brush with a hatch style, a foreground color, and a background color.

- **System.Drawing.Drawing2D.LinearGradientBrush.** Encapsulates a brush with a linear gradient that provides a visually appealing, professional-looking fill.
- **System.Drawing.Drawing2D.PathGradientBrush.** Provides similar functionality like `LinearGradientBrush`. However, you can define a complex fill pattern that fades between multiple points.
- **System.Drawing.SolidBrush.** Defines a brush of a single color.
- **System.Drawing.TextureBrush.** Defines a brush made from an image that tiles across a shape like the wallpaper.

The following sample code draws a solid maroon, five-sided polygon as shown in Figure 4-6:

```
Graphics graph = this.CreateGraphics();
Brush brush = new SolidBrush(Color.Black);
Point[] points = new Point[]
{
    new Point(10, 10),
    new Point(10, 100),
    new Point(50, 65),
    new Point(100, 100),
    new Point(85, 40)
};
graph.FillPolygon(brush, points);
```

Figure 4-6

A solid five-sided polygon drawn using `Brush` object

DRAW FILLED OBJECTS

You can use the following steps to draw filled objects with an outline:

1. Call the fill methods of the `Graphics` object.
2. Call the draw methods of the `Graphics` object.

For example, the following code draws a polygon with an outline and a linear gradient fill pattern as shown in Figure 4-7:

```
Graphics graph = this.CreateGraphics();
Pen pen = new Pen(Color.Black, 2);
Brush brush = new LinearGradientBrush(new Point(1,1),
new Point(100,100), Color.White, Color.Black);
Point[] points = new Point[]
    {new Point(10, 10),
    new Point(10, 100),
    new Point(50, 65),
    new Point(100, 100),
    new Point(85, 40)};
graph.FillPolygon(brush, points);
graph.DrawPolygon(pen, points);
```

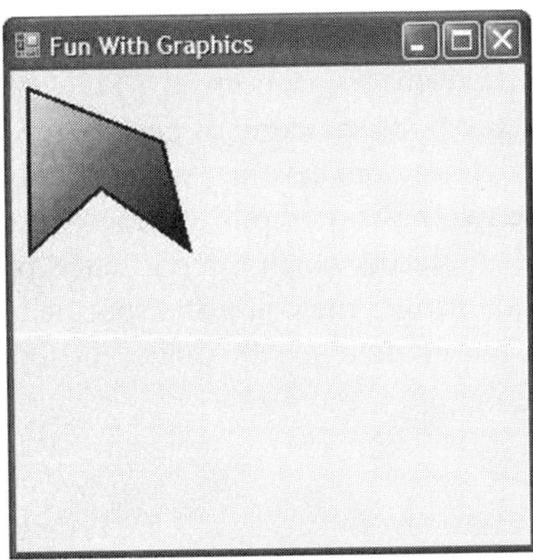

Figure 4-7

A polygon with an outline and a linear gradient fill pattern

You can use the same techniques illustrated in earlier sample codes to draw buttons or instances of the `PictureBox` class on controls.

CERTIFICATION READY?
Enhance the user interface of a .NET Framework application by using shapes and sizes.
USD 7.6

Additionally, to fill an entire graphics object with a single color, you can use the `Graphics.Clear` method as shown in this code sample:

```
Graphics graph = this.CreateGraphics();
graph.Clear(Color.Green);
```

Creating Images

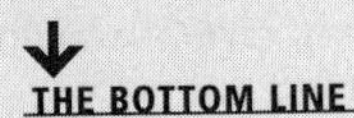

THE BOTTOM LINE .NET provides a base class, `System.Drawing.Image`, to create or apply different effects. Every instance of this class represents an image.

One of the most common things you might want to do with GDI+ is display an image that already exists in a file. Because the image is pre-drawn or already in your computer system, you need to get the GDI+ to fetch it from the location where it is saved. You can use the following syntax to read an image file:

```
Image myImage = Image.FromFile("FileName");
```

To display the image, you can use graphic instances, such as `Graphics.DrawImageUnscaled()` or `Graphics.DrawImage()`. To manipulate these images further, you can use method overloading. For example, the `DrawImage()` method can be used as follows:

```
Graphics graph = this.CreateGraphics();
graph.DrawImage(myImage, points);
```

Working with Image and Bitmap Classes

You can store an image file in various file types, such as.bmp, .jpg, .jpeg, .gif, .png, or.tif. The `System.Drawing.Image` abstract class supports multiple graphic file formatting. You can use the instance of this class to represent the graphical information in your application.

You may have to perform simple to complex edits on your images. For example, you can resize an image to fit the available space on a form, display complex information as a chart, add a watermark to images, or add copyright information.

To manipulate images, you must create instances of the `Image` class using the `Image.FromFile` method, which is a static member of the `Image` abstract class. The parameter for the `FromFile` method is the path in which the image file is stored. Alternatively, you can use the `Image.FromStream` method that accepts a `System.IO.Stream` object as a parameter.

You can use the System.Drawing.Bitmap and System.Drawing.Imaging.Metafile to work with bitmap and animated images, respectively. These classes inherit from the Image class. Bitmap formats are most often associated with new or existing images. You can use constructors to create a bitmap image from an existing image, file, or stream. The GetPixel and the SetPixel methods are the two basic methods of these classes. The GetPixel method of the Bitmap class returns a Color object, which is a particular pixel in the image—red, green, or blue. The SetPixel method changes the color of a specified pixel. For more complex image editing, you can create a Graphics object by calling the Graphics.FromImage method.

Displaying Pictures

In your .NET application, you may have to display images or photographs. You can use the PictureBox control and the Image class from the .NET Framework class library to achieve this.

You can use the Image.FromFile method to display an image stored in your computer on a .NET form. You must have an instance of the PictureBox control. You can then create an instance of the Image class and use the FromFile method to hold the image. After this, you can set the BackgroundImage property of the PictureBox control to display the image instance.

For example, consider a Windows Form with an instance of PictureBox control called *pictureBox1*. The following code displays a picture file within the form:

```
Image image = Image.FromFile(@"myImage.bmp");
pictureBox1.BackgroundImage = image;
```

Alternatively, you can use the Bitmap class to display the image file as shown next. The Bitmap class derives from the abstract base Image class. In addition, the Bitmap class is serializable making it useful to transmit images.

```
Bitmap bitmapImg = new Bitmap(@"myImage.bmp");
pictureBox1.BackgroundImage = bitmapImg;
```

SETTING THE BACKGROUND PICTURES

You can also display an image file as the background for a form by invoking the Graphics.DrawImage method. You can use the method overloads to manipulate images. For example, the following code syntax uses the Graphics.DrawImage method to set an image as a background, irrespective of its dimensions:

```
Bitmap bitmapImg = new Bitmap(@"picture.jpg");
Graphics graph = this.CreateGraphics();
graph.DrawImage(bitmapImg, 1, 1, this.Width, this.Height);
```

TAKE NOTE*

Jpeg is the most common format used for saving photographs; whereas, Gif is used to save charts, screen shots, and complex drawings.

CREATING AND SAVING PICTURES

When you want to create a new, blank picture, you need to create an instance of the Bitmap class with one of the constructors. These contructors do not need an existing image. You can use the Bitmap.SetPixel or Graphics.FromImage method to edit the image.

You can use the Bitmap.Save method to save a picture. It has several overload methods, such as System.Drawing.Imaging.ImageFormat. This method accepts the file type (Bmp, Emf, Exif, Gif, Icon, Jpeg, MemoryBmp, Png, Tiff, or Wmf) as the parameter.

The following code shows an example of creating and saving a bitmap image. It uses methods, such as `Graphics.FillPolygon` and `Graphics.DrawPolygon` to draw a shape in the blank bitmap:

```
Bitmap bmp = new Bitmap(600, 600);
Graphics graph = Graphics.FromImage(bmp);
Brush brush = new LinearGradientBrush(new Point(1, 1), new Point
(600, 600), Color.White, Color.Red);
Point[] points = new Point[]
{new Point(10, 10),
new Point(77, 500),
new Point(590, 100),
new Point(250, 590),
new Point(300, 410)};
graph.FillPolygon(brush, points);
bmp.Save("bmp.jpg", ImageFormat.Jpeg);
```

TAKE NOTE*

You can also run this code as a console application because it does not display any images. However, when running it as a console application, you need to add a reference to the `System.Drawing`, `System.Drawing.Drawing2D`, and `System.Drawing.Imaging` namespaces.

Working with Icons

Consider that you are creating an application for your organization, and you must display messages to indicate success or failure of actions, warnings, and so on. You can use the `SystemIcons` class from the .NET Framework class library to achieve this.

You can place images as icons in your application. The icons are transparent bitmaps of specific sizes that Windows uses to convey status, such as exclamation, information, and question symbols. These are represented as 40 × 40 system icons within the .NET Framework, and they are derived from the `SystemIcons` class.

The following code syntax allows you to add an icon to a form or image by calling the `Graphics.DrawIcon` or `Graphics.DrawIconUnstretched` methods:

```
Graphics graph = this.CreateGraphics();
graph.DrawIcon(SystemIcons.Question, 40, 40);
```

Figure 4-8 displays the output of this code.

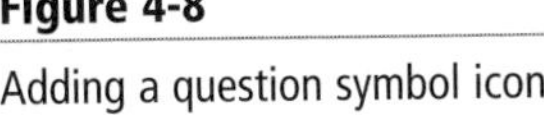

Figure 4-8

Adding a question symbol icon

TAKE NOTE*

Note that the output you receive when you execute the previous code depends on your Windows version. You can edit these system icons or use custom icons by using the constructors of the `Icon` class. You do this by creating an instance of the `Icon` class and invoking the `Icon.ToBitmap` method to create a `Bitmap` object that you can edit.

Handling Issues When Manipulating Images

> **TAKE NOTE***
> In previous versions of GDI, Windows 32 API function, `BitBlt()` was used to manipulate images. In GDI+, the GDI+ object model encapsulates the BitBlts operations.

Images can be small or large. The speed with which the system manipulates these images differs based on the representation the system uses. Treating images as rectangular blocks of pixels provides high-performance graphics.

Operating systems represent images as pixels on screen. The underlying technology in modern graphics cards copies rectangular blocks of pixels from one memory location to the other. For that, the pixels must be placed in the shape of a rectangle. This operation, referred to as ***bitmap block transfer (BitBlt),*** is very fast and is the secret behind high-performance graphics. When you call the `Graphics.DrawImageUnscaled` method, it internally uses the BitBlt technology to copy or move huge images in no time, giving an illusion of instant transfer. Most of the .NET methods use the BitBlts operations for drawing and editing images.

> **CERTIFICATION READY?**
> Enhance the user interface of a .NET Framework application by using graphics, images, bitmaps, and icons.
> USD 7.5

When the pixels of the image do not form a rectangular blocks, it is difficult to use the BitBlt technology. To copy such images, you can mark certain colors on the screen as transparent. This way, the colors in the specified areas of the source image do not overwrite the color of the corresponding pixel in the destination file. Supported by strong hardware configuration, this process too can be very fast, and you can use it to assign various effects to the images.

You can use the `DrawImage()` method to manipulate images using BitBlt. This method can handle complex forms of BitBlt to edit images, such as a specific area of an image or scaling operations.

Managing Text in Graphics

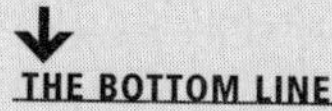

Drawing text to the screen involves a more complex process than drawing simple graphics. The screen dynamics of fonts and choosing the correct font is a crucial part of your application. To display a line or two of text, you can use the `Graphics.DrawString` method. However, if you have to display considerable amounts of text on the screen, it helps to understand fonts and their distinct characteristics. Understanding these intricacies helps you in programming your GDI+ application.

Drawing Text

Working with text involves understanding how the text needs to be placed to make optimum use of the space provided. It is also important that the text offer readability.

Similar to drawing graphics that use brushes and pens as helper objects, drawing text involves using fonts as helper objects to accomplish your task. To measure how much space a word is going to occupy, you can use the `Graphics.MeasureString` method. With text, you must also consider text wrapping and line breaks.

Understanding Fonts and Font Families

Any text processing application must take into account the text involved and its manipulation.

A font defines how the system displays a particular letter on the screen. Although there are several fonts available in any text processing application, you must apply the font that offers readability and clarity, among other things, such as aesthetics or the appearance of your text. Fonts are grouped into families, and each font family has a distinct visual style and offers several variations for you to choose from. These variations include size or effects, such as bold or italics. Some of the common variations include, bold, italic, underlined, small or CAPS, and subscript.

Another characteristic that needs to be determined is the size of the text. To measure the size of the text, you must measure its height in points, where a point is represented as 1/72 of an inch, equivalent to 0.351 mm. For example, a text made up in 10-point font is approximately

1/7" or 3.5 mm in height. To place several lines of text having this height, you must also take into account other issues, such as line spacing and word wrapping.

You cannot measure some letters by this conventional method, for example, some letters such as A or F that are taller than the others. A few other letters sometimes use ***ascent***, such as in Å or Ñ, also called the internal leading. You must also consider some letters, such as y and g have extra height below the baseline, called the ***descent***. This intricacy in fonts is what makes working with text so complicated. However, when you specify the height and font you want to use, the system takes care of all the intricacies.

Table 4-6 lists some of the features specific to font families.

Table 4-6

Features of font families

FONT FAMILY	FEATURES
`Serif`	Has little tick marks, known as serifs, that are found at the ends of many of the lines that make up the characters. For example, Times New Roman belongs to this font family.
`Sans serif`	Lacks the tick marks. Arial and Verdana are members of this family. They usually have a blunt appearance that is mostly used to emphasize important text.
`True type`	Expresses the shapes of the curves of the characters in a precise mathematical manner. Using this approach, you can draw fonts of any size within the family.

You can use two main classes to manipulate fonts: `System.Drawing.Font` and `System.Drawing.FontFamily`. You must create an instance of the `Font` class and pass it as a parameter to the `DrawString` method. This indicates the drawing of the text. You can use a `FontFamily` instance to represent all the fonts in the family. If you are sure of the font you need to use, you can use static properties, such as `GenericSerif`, `GenericSansSerif`, and `GenericMonospace`. The code syntax to specify a specific font is as follows:

```
FontFamily sansSerifFont = FontFamily.GenericSansSerif;
```

You can use the `InstalledFontCollection` class to know what fonts are available on your system. This class is available in the `System.Drawing.Text` namespace. It implements the `Families` property that stores all the fonts within an array. The following code shows an example of using the `InstalledFontCollection` class:

```
InstalledFontCollection insFont = new InstalledFontCollection();
FontFamily [] families = insFont.Families;
foreach (FontFamily family in families)
{
// Process with this font family
}
```

Creating a Font Object

To manipulate text fonts, you must first create a `Font` object.

The `Font` class has several constructors that you can use to create a `Font` object. You can create a `Font` object by specifying the font family name, size, and style attributes. The following code syntax shows the use of a constructor to create an Arial 10-point bold font:

```
Font fnt = new Font("Arial", 10, FontStyle.Bold);
```

The font style parameter is a `System.Drawing.FontStyle` enumeration value.

Alternatively, you can create a `Font` object using the `FontFamily` class, as shown in the following code, which creates an Arial 10-point font:

```
FontFamily fntfamily = new FontFamily("Arial");
Font fnt = new Font(fntfamily, 10);
```

You can use the `FontConverter` class to read the font type from a string. However, this method is not preferred because using a string to describe a font is less reliable because the compiler cannot detect errors or typos. The following example creates the Arial 10-point font:

```
FontConverter converter = new FontConverter();
Font fnt = (Font)converter.ConvertFromString("Arial, 10pt");
```

Writing Text

There are two ways to add text to a form. You can use `Label` objects or the `Graphics.DrawString` method.

The `Graphics.DrawString` method is more often used to add text to images and bitmaps as in watermarking a picture, timestamping an image, or annotating charts.

After creating a `Font` object, you can use the `Brush` object to define how the text is filled, or instead, use the `System.Drawing.Brushes` property. You can then use the `Graphics.DrawString` method to add text to images. The following code syntax draws text on a form:

```
Graphics graph = this.CreateGraphics();
Font fnt = new Font("Arial", 40, FontStyle.Bold);
graph.DrawString("Hello, World!", fnt, Brushes.Black, 10, 10);
```

Figure 4-9 displays the output for this code.

Figure 4-9

Adding text to a form

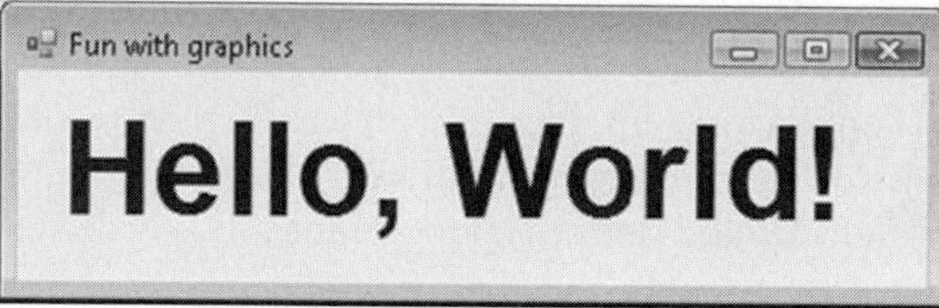

FORMATTING TEXT

You can use the `StringFormat` class to align and place text on screen. You must first create and configure a `StringFormat` object. You can pass this as a parameter to the `Graphics.DrawString` method to format texts. Table 4-7 displays some of the attributes of the `StringFormat` class.

Table 4-7

Attributes of the `StringFormat` class

Attribute	Description
`Alignment`	Aligns the text horizontally.
`StringAlignment.Center`	Centers the text horizontally.
`StringAlignment.Near`	Aligns text to the left.
`StringAlignment.Far`	Aligns text to the right.
`FormatFlags`	Applies a `StringFormatFlags` enumeration that contains formatting information.

Table 4-8 displays some of the options for `StringFormatFlags` enumeration.

Table 4-8

Attributes of `StringFormatFlags` enumeration

OPTION	DESCRIPTION
`DirectionRightToLeft`	Displays text from right to left.
`DirectionVertical`	Aligns the text vertically.
`DisplayFormatControl`	Displays control characters, such as the left-to-right mark.
`FitBlackBox`	Avoids character overhang from the string's rectangular layout.
`LineLimit`	Lays entire lines of text within the formatting rectangle.
`MeasureTrailingSpaces`	Measures the trailing spaces also at the end of each line. By default, the `MeasureString` method excludes these trailing spaces.
`NoClip`	Displays all the overhanging parts of the glyphs and unwrapped text.
`NoWrap`	Disables text wrapping.

You can also use the `StringTrimming` enumeration to trim out-of-layout characters from a string. Table 4-9 displays some of the options that you can use with the `StringTrimming` enumeration.

Table 4-9

Attributes of `StringTrimming` enumeration

OPTION	DESCRIPTION
`Character`	Returns a value that the text is trimmed to the nearest character.
`EllipsisCharacter`	Returns a value that the text is trimmed to the nearest character. Also inserts an ellipsis at the end of a trimmed line.
`EllipsisPath`	Returns a value that the center is removed from trimmed lines and replaced by an ellipsis.
`EllipsisWord`	Returns a value that text is trimmed to the nearest word. Also inserts an ellipsis at the end of a trimmed line.
`None`	Specifies that there is no trimming.
`Word`	Returns a value that text is trimmed to the nearest word.

You can use the following code to demonstrate the use of the `StringFormat` class:

```
Graphics graph = this.CreateGraphics();
// Construct a new Rectangle
Rectangle rect = new Rectangle(new Point(40, 40), new Size(80, 80));
// Construct 2 new StringFormat objects
StringFormat strfmt1 = new StringFormat(StringFormatFlags.NoClip);
StringFormat strfmt2 = new StringFormat(strfmt1);
// Set the LineAlignment and Alignment properties for
both StringFormat objects to different values
strfmt1.LineAlignment = StringAlignment.Near;
strfmt1.Alignment = StringAlignment.Center;
strfmt2.LineAlignment = StringAlignment.Center;
strfmt2.Alignment = StringAlignment.Far;
strfmt2.FormatFlags = StringFormatFlags.DirectionVertical;
```

```
// Draw the bounding rectangle and a string for each StringFormat object
graph.DrawRectangle(Pens.Black, rect);
graph.DrawString("Format1", this.Font, Brushes.Black,
(RectangleF)rect, strfmt1);
graph.DrawString("Format2", this.Font, Brushes.Black, (RectangleF)rec,
strfmt2);
```

Figure 4-10 shows the output for this code.

Figure 4-10

Adding formatted strings to a drawing object

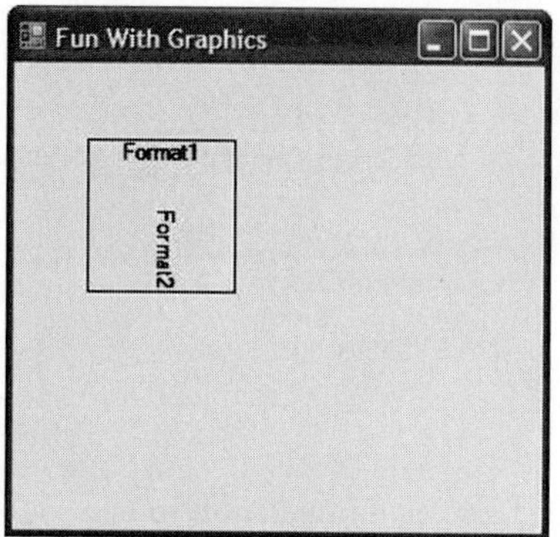

CERTIFICATION READY?
Enhance the user interface of a .NET Framework application by using brushes, pens, colors, and fonts.
USD 7.4

SKILL SUMMARY

This lesson introduced you to various graphical objects using the `Brush`, `Pen`, and `Color` classes. All these objects are part of the `System.Drawing` namespace. You can use the classes in this namespace to specify position, size, location, and color of your application's controls.

You can use GDI+ classes in the .NET Framework to draw lines and shapes. .NET provides the `System.Drawing.Image` base class for creating, modifying, and saving images. You can display images using the `FromFile` and `DrawImage` methods. You can embed images as icons in a Windows Form. Bitmap block transfer is the technique used to transfer images as rectangular blocks.

You can use the `Graphics.DrawString` method to work with text. The `System.Drawing.Font` and `System.Drawing.FontFamily` classes are used to select and apply fonts. The `Font` class provides several constructors to help you create a `Font` object which you can then use to manipulate text in graphics.

For the certification examination:

- Know how to create graphical objects using the brush, pen, and color classes.
- Learn to use the shape and size classes to enrich the user interface.
- Know how to create applications containing images, bitmaps, and icons. Learn to manage text in graphic objects using the `Font` class.

Knowledge Assessment

Matching

Match the following descriptions to the appropriate terms.

a. `Region`
b. `Brushes`
c. `Pen`
d. `Pens`
e. `SolidBrush`

_______ 1. Defines a brush of a single color
_______ 2. Describes the interior of a graphics shape composed of rectangles and paths
_______ 3. Provides brushes for all the standard colors
_______ 4. Defines an object used to draw lines, curves, and arrows
_______ 5. Provides pens for all the standard colors

True / False

Circle T if the statement is true or F if the statement is false.

T | F 1. The `System.Drawing` namespace only allows you to create graphics from scratch and does not allow you to modify them.
T | F 2. `Graphics.Clear` method clears the color filled in the entire graphics object.
T | F 3. The `PointF` method enables you to specify the location of a control on a form.
T | F 4. The `FromFile` method takes the filename as the parameter.
T | F 5. The `FormatFlags` enumeration holds formatting information.

Fill in the Blank

Complete the following sentences by writing the correct word or words in the blanks provided.

1. The _____________ namespace allows you to create graphics objects from scratch as well as modify them.
2. The _____________ class provides a facility to retrieve an icon that represents the control.
3. ____________ class provides the majority of the GDI+ drawing operations.
4. __________ methods of the `Graphics` class enable drawing and filling shapes.
5. __________ defines the way a particular text character appears on the screen.

Multiple Choice

Circle the letter or letters that correspond to the best answer or answers.

1. Which of the following namespaces contain classes to perform advanced manipulation of fonts and font families?
   a. `System.Drawing.Text`
   b. `System.Drawing`
   c. `System.Drawing.Design`
   d. `System.Drawing.Drawing2D`

2. Which of the following classes define an object used to draw lines, curves, and arrows?
   a. `Pen`
   b. `Pens`
   c. `Brush`
   d. `Brushes`

3. Select the appropriate class from which you can instantiate a `Brush` object.
   a. `System.Drawing.Graphics`
   b. `System.Drawing.Image`
   c. `System.Drawing.HatchBrush`
   d. `System.Drawing.SolidBrush`

4. Which of the following is the base class from which the `System.Drawing.Bitmap` and `System.Drawing.Imaging.Metafile` classes inherit?
   a. `File`
   b. `Drawing`
   c. `Icons`
   d. `Image`

5. Which of these methods can you use to determine the space a word occupies in the screen?
   a. `Graphics.MeasureString`
   b. `Graphics.StringLength`
   c. `Graphics.DrawString`
   d. `Graphics.Object`

Review Questions

1. You want to add the name of the employee to the employee's photograph (bmp file). How can you add the name and align it to the center of the image?
2. Consider that you are creating an image file dynamically. How can you save this image file in the jpeg format?

■ Case Scenarios

Scenario 4-1: Displaying Images

In your Windows application, you must display images about movies. You are required to handle various file types such as gif, tif, bmp, jpeg, and png. Create a program that reads an image from a file and displays it on a Windows Form.

Scenario 4-2: Drawing Texts

The Windows Form that displays the movie images files must display the movie name too. Write a program to display the movie name in different fonts so that you can decide which one that suits the image.

✳ Workplace Ready

Editing Icons at Runtime

You may have to design a graphic application that requires the user to edit graphic objects at runtime. Consider that you are a design architect at XYZ Gaming, Inc. Your organization is creating a game for kids. One part of this game requires the user to edit an icon that they choose during the game. Suggest an approach that your team should take to allow users to edit icons at runtime.

Serializing .NET Applications

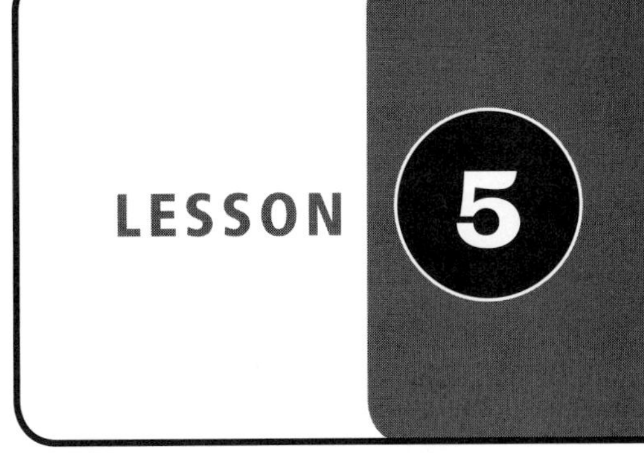

OBJECTIVE DOMAIN MATRIX

Technology Skill	Objective Domain	Objective Domain Number
Implement runtime serialization with objects.	Serialize or deserialize an object or an object graph by using runtime serialization techniques.	4.1
Perform XML serialization.	Control the serialization of an object into XML format by using the System.Xml.Serialization namespace.	4.2
Perform custom serialization.	Implement custom serialization formatting by using the Serialization Formatter classes.	4.3

KEY TERMS

backward reference
deserialization
formatters
forward reference
object graph
serialization
XML schema
XML Schema Definition tool

It is interesting to understand how information travels through networks. Information is sent across a network as instances of objects, and these objects are translated into a binary or XML-compatible format such as SOAP to transmit and retrieve with ease. This process of converting objects to a specific format is known as ***serialization***.

■ Implementing Runtime Serialization with Objects

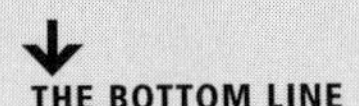

Serialization involves creating an object instance and converting it to a format that is portable across the network. ***Deserialization*** is a process where you reconstruct the object from the serialized state to its original state. The `System.Runtime.Serialization` namespace contains the classes pertaining to serialization and deserialization of objects. The classes within the `System.Runtime.Serialization.Formatters` namespace take care of the actual formatting of various datatypes encapsulated in the serialized objects.

Understanding Object Serialization

The process of serialization involves transferring an instance of an object into a stream, such as a file stream or memory. The data object includes all the information that you need to bring the object back to its original form.

X REF

Note that this section discusses the concepts of [Serializable] and [NonSerialized] attributes. An example given in the "Disabling Serialization of Specific Members" section of this lesson demonstrates the use of [Serializable] and [NonSerialized] attributes.

TAKE NOTE*

You can use SOAP formatters when you prefer to serialize your objects into XML files, because SOAP formatters are intended for text-based serialization based on the XML format.

When you save application data through serialization, that data uses fewer lines of codes. By using serialization services, you can save huge volumes of data within objects with minimal effort, irrespective of their formats.

For example, you can create a GUI-based desktop that allows users to select a custom window color, fonts, and themes. First, define a class called `CustomerChoice` that encapsulates quite a few field data. Now using `System.IO.BinaryWriter`, you can manually save each field of the `CustomerChoice` object. However, to use the data, you need to use the `System.IO.BinaryReader` and manually reconfigure a new `CustomerChoice` object.

Configuring Objects for Serialization

The .NET Framework provides attributes that you can use to configure a class for serialization.

When you want to serialize an object in .NET, you need to add each related class or structure with the `[Serializable]` attribute. Any portion of the data that you do not want to include in this process of serialization must be distinctly marked with the `[NonSerialized]` attribute. For example, you may want to exclude data, such as fixed values, random values, and transient data from the serialization process. This helps in reducing the size of the serializable data object.

Serializing an Object

The process of serialization involves creating a stream and a formatter. The stream contains bytes of serialized objects, whereas the formatter carries out the actual process of serialization.

The .NET Framework provides several built-in ***formatters***, such as the Binary and SOAP formatters. However, depending on your requirement, you can also create custom formatters. All formatters implement the `IFormatter` interface.

SERIALIZE AN OBJECT

You can use the following steps to serialize an object:

1. Create a streaming object to hold the serialized output.
2. Create a `BinaryFormatter object`. This formatter object is located in the `System.Runtime.Serialization.Formatters.Binary` namespace.
3. Invoke the `BinaryFormatter.Serialize` method to serialize the object. This output is routed to the new streaming object.

The following code shows how to serialize a string data:

```
String str = "MCTS Exams are Great!";
// Create a file to save the data
FileStream fileStrm = new FileStream("MyFile.Data", FileMode.Create);
// Create a BinaryFormatter object to perform the serialization
BinaryFormatter biFr = new BinaryFormatter();
// Use the BinaryFormatter object to serialize the data to the file
biFr.Serialize(fileStrm, str);
// Close the file
fileStrm.Close();
```

To see the output of this code, compile and run the application. Now open the MyFile.Data file using a text editor. The contents within the file are binary information. Also, note that the binary bytes preceding and following the text string that represents the data provide information for the deserializer.

> **TAKE NOTE***
> The `SerializationObjectManager` class takes care of the serialization process at runtime.

Most often, serialization is very useful when storing complex information as in the next example. The following code serializes a `DateTime` event:

```
// Create a file to save the data
FileStream fileStrm = new FileStream("SampleFile.Data", FileMode.Create);
// Create a BinaryFormatter object to perform the serialization
BinaryFormatter biFr = new BinaryFormatter();
// Use the BinaryFormatter object to serialize the data to the file
biFr.Serialize(fileStrm, System.DateTime.Now);
// Close the file
fileStrm.Close();
```

Deserializing an Object

The process of converting a serialized object to its original state is called deserialization. The serialized object also contains the information required to reconstruct the original object.

The runtime performs the deserialization process sequentially.

DESERIALIZE AN OBJECT

The process to deserialize an object involves the following steps:

1. Instantiate a stream object. This object holds the serialized output.
2. Instantiate a `BinaryFormatter` object.
3. Instantiate a new object to store the deserialized data.
4. Invoke the `BinaryFormatter.Deserialize` method.

You can use the following code to deserialize a string data:

```
// Open file from which to read the data
FileStream fileStrm = new FileStream("MyFile.Data", FileMode.Open);
// Create a BinaryFormatter object to perform the deserialization
BinaryFormatter biFr = new BinaryFormatter();
// Create the object to store the deserialized data
string str = " ";
// Use the BinaryFormatter object to deserialize the data from the file
str = (string) biFr.Deserialize(fileStrm);
// Close the file
fileStrm.Close();
// Display the deserialized string
Console.WriteLine(str);
```

You can also deserialize complex objects, such as an object involving a `DateTime` event. The following code shows how to deserialize the `DateTime` object:

```
// Open a file from which to read the data
FileStream fileStrm = new FileStream("SampleFile.Data", FileMode.Open);
// Create a BinaryFormatter object to perform the deserialization
BinaryFormatter biFr = new BinaryFormatter();
// Create the object to store the deserialized data
DateTime previousTime = new DateTime();
// Use the BinaryFormatter object to deserialize the data from the file
previousTime = (DateTime) biFr.Deserialize(fileStrm);
// Close the file
fileStrm.Close();
// Display the deserialized time
Console.WriteLine("Day: " + previousTime.DayOfWeek + ", Time: " +
previousTime.TimeOfDay.ToString());
```

Though the process of deserialization looks smooth, it gets complicated. When an object within the serializing stream points to another object, the `Formatter` queries the `ObjectManager` that keeps track of the objects as they are deserialized. If the `ObjectManager` determines that the reference points to the object that has been deserialized already, then this reference is known as ***backward reference***. However, if the `ObjectManager` determines that the reference points to an object that is not yet deserialized, then this reference is called the ***forward reference***.

In case of backward reference, the `Formatter` completes the reference. If it is a forward reference, the `Formatter` registers a process called fixup, with the `ObjectManager`. The fixup process involves finalizing an object reference after the referenced object has been deserialized. Once the fixup is complete, the `ObjectManager` completes the reference.

Creating Serializing Classes

To serialize a class, you use the `Serializable` attribute and associate it with the class. This means that you can easily store the instance of a class, or transfer the instance of a class by value, across network.

During the process of serialization, the runtime serializes all members of the class with the `Serializable` attribute. This also includes the private members of the class.

UNDERSTANDING THE GUIDELINES FOR SERIALIZATION

You must consider the following best practices when using serialization:

- **Mark classes as `Serializable`.** Even the ones you do not intend to serialize right away. Having a class marked with the `Serializable` attribute, helps you use the instance of the class anytime, reducing programming overheads.
- **Identify and mark calculated and temporary members as `NonSerialized`.** Again, this reduces programming overheads.
- **Apply the `SoapFormatter` to allow efficient portability.** `SoapFormatter` serializes objects in the SOAP format, which is a centralized standard for exchanging information in a distributed environment.
- **Apply `BinaryFormatter` for greater efficiency.** `BinaryFormatter` produces output in a binary format, which is a compact form that consumes less storage space. Moreover, computers operate on binary format.

EXPLORING THE SECURITY CONCERNS WITH SERIALIZATION

X REF

Refer to the "Performing Custom Serialization" section from this lesson to know more about the role of security permissions in serialization.

During the process of serialization, objects are exposed over the network, even those codes within the data objects that are usually not freely accessible to everyone. To avoid any security compromise, you can use the `SecurityPermission` attribute along with the `SerializationFormatter` flag. By default, the security permission is not extended to Internet-downloaded or intranet code. You can grant this permission to only that code that resides on the local computer.

When a code object is accessed, the `GetObjectData` method must explicitly ask for the `SecurityPermission` attribute with the `SerializationFormatter` flag.

DISABLING SERIALIZATION OF SPECIFIC MEMBERS

You can use serializing to improve the efficiency of classes or to meet custom requirements. However, you can exclude data, such as calculated values and temporary values from serialized data. The following code syntax shows the serialization of a `Multiplication` class:

```
[Serializable]
class Multiplication
{
   public int x;
   public int y;
   public int z;
   public Multiplication(int _x, int _y)
```

```
{
      x = _x;
      y = _y;
      z = x * y;
   }
}
```

The Multiplication class includes two members, *x* and *y*, whose values are provided at the time of object creation. The value for *z* is dynamically evaluated by multiplying the values of *x* and *y*. Because the Multiplication class has been serialized, *z* would be stored within the serialized object, costing some storage space. Therefore, to reduce the size of the serialized object, the attribute *z* can be left out of the serialization process totally by associating it with the NonSerialized attribute. The following code syntax shows how to deserialize an object element:

```
[NonSerialized] public int z;
```

Therefore, during the process of serialization, whenever you add a NonSerialized attribute to a member of an object, that member is not included in the serialization. Notice that the value of *z* has not been initialized. Therefore, it is necessary to calculate the value of *z* before the deserialized object is used. To make this process automatic, you can use the IDeserializationCallback interface and later implement the IDeserializationCallback.OnDeserialization method. Every time the class is deserialized, the runtime invokes the IDeserializationCallback.OnDeserialization method after deserialization is complete.

The following code syntax shows the modifications done to the Multiplication class to deserialize the value of *z* and automate the process of calculating the value of *z* on deserialization:

```
using System.Runtime.Serialization;
[Serializable]
class Multiplication: IDeserializationCallback
{
   public int x;
   public int y;
   [NonSerialized] public int z;
   public Multiplication(int _x, int _y)
   {
      x = _x;
      y = _y;
   }
   void IDeserializationCallback.OnDeserialization(Object sender)
   {
      // After deserialization
      z = x * y;
   }
}
```

PROVIDING VERSION COMPATIBILITY

The process of serialization also runs into the risk of version compatibility issues. For example, if you create a member within a class in one version of your application, then this new member cannot be deserialized by earlier versions. In such situations, the runtime throws an exception.

To address this issue, you can implement custom serialization or apply the OptionalField attribute to new members. Custom serialization allows you to import serialized objects from earlier versions. When you associate an OptionalField attribute to new members, the runtime logs the value of that member as null and does not throw an exception.

TAKE NOTE *

To initialize optional members, you can implement the IDeserialization Callback interface or respond to deserialization events.

The following code syntax demonstrates the use of the OptionalField attribute:

```
[Serializable]
class Multiplication: IDeserializationCallback
{
   public int x;
   public int y;
   [NonSerialized] public int z;
   [OptionalField] public int w;
}
```

UNDERSTANDING THE BEST PRACTICES FOR VERSION COMPATIBILITY

When modifying a class that may be used in different versions of your application, consider the following precautions:

- Do not remove a serialized field.
- Do not apply the NonSerialized attribute to a field if it was avoided in the previous version.
- Do not change the name or type of the serialized field.
- Apply the OptionalField attribute to new serialized object.
- Set default values for all optional fields.

Choosing a Serialization Format

To format serialized data objects, you can use the BinaryFormatter and the SoapFormatter classes.

You can use the BinaryFormatter class to format serializable objects that are read only by .NET Framework-based applications. This class is located in the System.Runtime.Serialization.Formatters.Binary namespace.

Alternatively, the SoapFormatter is an XML-based formatter that is used to format serializable objects, transmitted across a network.

USING THE XML-BASED FORMATTER FOR SOAP WEB SERVICES

Data formatted using SOAP formatters are read by non-.NET Framework applications and are mostly intended for SOAP Web services.

To use the SoapFormatter, you can add a reference to the System.Runtime.Serialization.Formatters.SOAP.dll assembly to your application. Note that by default, the BinaryFormatter adds this reference to the .NET application. The process of writing code for BinaryFormatter and SoapFormatter is quite similar, yet the output of serialized data is distinct.

The following code demonstrates the use of SoapFormatter:

```
<SOAP-ENV:Envelope xmlns:xsi="http://www.w3.org/2001/XMLSchema-
instance">
<SOAP-ENV:Body>
<a1:Multiplication id="ref-1">
<x>10.25</x>
<y>2</y>
</a1:Multiplication >
</SOAP-ENV:Body>
</SOAP-ENV:Envelope>
```

CONTROLLING SOAP SERIALIZATION

You can further format a SOAP serialized document by using several SOAP serialization attributes that are very similar to XML serialization attributes.

Table 5-1 displays a list of several SOAP serialization attributes.

Table 5-1

SOAP serialization attributes

Attribute	Description
`SoapAttribute`	Defines the class member to be serialized as an XML attribute.
`SoapDefaultValue`	Defines the default value of an XML element or attribute.
`SoapElement`	Defines that the class has to be serialized as an XML element.
`SoapEnum`	Defines the name of an enumeration member.
`SoapIgnore`	Defines the property or fields that must be ignored during the serialization of its class.
`SoapType`	Defines the schema for the XML generated during the serialization of the class.

CERTIFICATION READY?
Serialize or deserialize an object or an object graph by using runtime serialization techniques.
USD 4.1

Performing XML Serialization

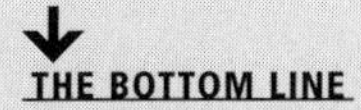

When developing .NET applications, the Hypertext Markup Language (HTML) provides a text-based standard for formatting human-readable documents. Similarly, XML provides a standard for easy processing by computers. The .NET Framework consists of several libraries for reading and writing XML files, such as `System.Xml.Serialization` namespace. You can easily transmit the serialized data, obtained by using XML serialization, over networks. XML serialization is widely used by the .NET Web services.

Analyzing the Benefits of XML Serialization

You can use XML to store all types of data, such as documents, pictures, music, binary files, and database information. The advantage of using XML serialization is that you only need to write a few lines of code to convert almost any object to a text file that can be retrieved later.

XML is a standardized, text-based document format that stores application-readable information. You can use XML serialization to transmit objects between computers through Web services even if the remote computer does not have the .NET Framework. XML serialization converts or serializes the public fields and properties of an object, or parameters, and return values of method into an XML stream. Because XML is an open standard, all applications can process the XML stream as required, irrespective of platform.

You can use XML serialization to exchange objects with applications that were not developed using .NET Framework and do not require serializing any private members.

TAKE NOTE*
The `System.Xml.Serialization` namespace provides methods for converting objects, including those based on custom classes, to and from XML files.

The benefits of using XML serialization include:

- **Better interoperability.** XML is a text-based file standard, and all modern development environments include libraries for processing XML files. Therefore, an object that is serialized using XML can be processed easily by an application written for a different operating system in a diverse development environment.
- **More administrator friendly.** You can use any text editor to view and edit objects serialized using XML. If objects are stored in XML files, administrators can view and edit those files. This can help when you are customizing your application, troubleshooting problems, and developing new applications that can interoperate with your existing application.

- **Greater forward compatibility.** Objects serialized using XML are self-describing and your applications can process them easily. Therefore, when you want to replace your application, the new application can easily process your objects that are serialized using XML without much effort and in lesser time.

You can also use XML serialization whenever you need to conform to a specific ***XML schema*** or control the encoding of an object. XML schemas are used in serialization to define the expected structure of the serialized object.

Even SoapFormatters are XML based, and offer all the benefits of XML serialization. However, as discussed earlier, SoapFormatters are primarily designed to work with SOAP-based Web services. If you require an open, standards-based document that is exposed to applications running on other platforms, then you must use XML serialization. Thus:

- If you require the serialized data to be used by your own application or any other .NET application, then you must choose binary formatter-based serialization.
- If you want to transmit serialized data over a network to be used by SOAP-based Web services, then you must choose SOAP formatter-based serialization.
- If you want applications running on any platform that recognize the standard XML format, then you must choose XML-based serialization.

Understanding the Limitations of XML Serialization

You cannot use XML serialization for all settings because XML serialization has its own restrictions.

Table 5-2 shows the utilities and the corresponding limitations for using XML serialization.

Table 5-2

Utilities and limitations of XML serialization

UTILITY	LIMITATION
`Serializes public data only`	Cannot serialize private data
`Serializes objects only`	Cannot serialize object graphs

TAKE NOTE*

An ***object graph*** represents a set of object instances with references to one another.

Using XML to Serialize an Object

You can use XML serialization on objects instead of standard serialization for better results. Serialization of an object converts its contents into XML format.

The steps to use XML serialization are similar to standard serialization.

SERIALIZE AN OBJECT IN XML

You can use the following steps to perform the XML serialization of an object:

1. Instantiate a stream, a `TextWriter`, or an `XmlWriter` object to hold the serialized output.
2. Instantiate an `XmlSerializer` object in the `System.Xml.Serialization` namespace by passing it the type of object you plan to serialize.
3. Call the `XmlSerializer.Serialize` method to serialize the object and output the results to the stream.

This console application requires the System.IO and System.Xml.Serialization namespaces to demonstrate easy serialization of an object using XML. The following code sample demonstrates the use of these steps:

```
// Create a file to save the data
FileStream fileStrm = new FileStream("SampleXmlFile.Data",
FileMode.Create);
// Create an XmlSerializer object to perform the serialization
XmlSerializer xmlFr = new XmlSerializer(typeof(DateTime));
// Use the XmlSerializer object to serialize the data to the file
xmlFr.Serialize(fileStrm, System.DateTime.Now);
// Close the file
fileStrm.Close();
```

TAKE NOTE* In comparison with the creation of a serialized DateTime object using the BinaryFormatter class, demonstrated in the "Implementing Runtime Serialization with Objects" lesson, the serialization of this object using XML results in an easily readable and editable file.

X REF You can refer to the topic, "Serializing an Object", under the "Implementing Runtime Serialization with Objects" section from this lesson to understand the standard method of serializing the DateTime object by creating a stream and a formatter.

Using XML to Deserialize an Object

Deserialization converts XML documents and streams to CLR objects.

DESERIALIZE AN OBJECT IN XML

You can use the following steps to deserialize an object using XML:

1. Instantiate a stream, a TextReader, or an XmlReader object to read the serialized input.
2. Instantiate an XmlSerializer object in the System.Xml.Serialization namespace by passing through it the type of object you plan to deserialize.
3. Call the XmlSerializer.Deserialize method to deserialize the object and cast it to the correct type.

The following code sample shows the deserialization of an XML file containing a DateTime object to exhibit the day of the week and the time:

```
// Open a file from which to read the data
FileStream fileStrm = new FileStream("MyFile.Data", FileMode.Open);
// Create an XmlSerializer object to perform the deserialization
XmlSerializer xmlFr = new XmlSerializer(typeof(DateTime));
// Use the XmlSerializer object to deserialize the data from the file
DateTime previousTime = (DateTime) xmlFr.Deserialize(fileStrm);
// Close the file
fileStrm.Close();
// Display the deserialized time
Console.WriteLine("Day: " + previousTime.DayOfWeek + ", Time: " +
previousTime.TimeOfDay.ToString());
```

Creating Classes to Be Serialized Using XML Serialization

Most of the classes in the .NET Framework are serializable. However, there are a few differences in serializing the classes using XML serialization and standard serialization.

> **TAKE NOTE***
> You can use the `System.IO`, `System.Xml`, and the `System.Xml.Serialization` namespaces to serialize and deserialize an object.

Use XML serialization to perform the following tasks to create a class that needs to be serialized:

- Specify the class as *public*.
- Specify all the members that need to be serialized as *public*.
- Create a constructor without any parameters.

In contrast with the classes that are processed using standard serialization, the classes processed with XML serialization need not have the `Serializable` attribute. Moreover, XML serialization ignores the private or the protected members.

CREATING INSTANCES OF CLASSES FOR SERIALIZATION USING XML

To serialize an object, create the instances of these built-in classes in the following order:

1. An instance of the `XmlDocument` class from `System.Xml` namespace.
2. An instance of the `XmlSerializer` class from `System.Xml.Serialization` namespace with object type as the parameter.
3. An instance of the `MemoryStream` class from `System.IO` namespace to hold the serialized data.

After creating these instances, you need to call their methods to obtain your serialized object in XML format.

The following sample code to serialize an object is a generic function, and you can use this function to pass any object type, including a collection object. The `Serialize` method returns a string, which represents the serialized object in XML format. You must add references to the `System.XML` and `System.IO` namespaces to execute the following code:

```
/// <summary>
/// Serialize an object
/// </summary>
/// <param name="obj"></param>
/// <returns></returns>
private string SerializeAnObject(object obj)
{
    XmlDocument doc = new XmlDocument();
    Serialization.XmlSerializer serializer = new Serialization.
XmlSerializer(obj.GetType());
    MemoryStream stream = new MemoryStream();
    try
    {
        serializer.Serialize(stream, obj);
        stream.Position = 0;
        doc.Load(stream);
        return doc.InnerXml;
    }
    catch
    {
    throw;
    }
    finally
    {
        stream.Close();
        stream.Dispose();
    }
}
```

You can call the previous function as shown next:

```
string xmlObject = SerializeAnObject(myClass);
```

This class appears as follows after serialization:

```
<myclass xmlns:xsi=http://www.w3.org/2001/XMLSchema-instance xmlns:
xsd="http://www.w3.org/2001/XMLSchema">
 <name> XYZ </name>
 <address> Bellevue, US</address>
</myclass>
```

CREATING INSTANCES OF CLASSES FOR DESERIALIZATION

To deserialize an object, create the instances of these classes in the following order:

1. An instance of the `StringReader` class from `System.IO` namespace to read the serialized (XML) data.
2. An instance of the `XmlReader` class from `System.Xml` namespace to read it into the `XmlReader`.
3. An instance of the `XmlSerializer` class from `System.Xml.Serialization` namespace to deserialize the object.

You can use the following code to deserialize an object. The following code example takes a string object in XML format as a parameter and deserializes it to its corresponding object type (MyClass). You must add references to the `System.XML` and `System.IO` namespaces to execute the following code:

```
/// <summary>
/// DeSerialize an object
/// </summary>
/// <param name="xmlOfAnObject"></param>
/// <returns></returns>
private object DeSerializeAnObject(string xmlOfAnObject)
{
    StringReader read = new StringReader(xmlOfAnObject);
    Serialization.XmlSerializer serializer = new Serialization.
XmlSerializer(MyClass.GetType());
    XmlReader reader = new XmlTextReader(read);
    try
    {
        return (MyClass)serializer.Deserialize(reader);
    }
    catch
    {
        throw;
    }
    finally
    {
        reader.Close();
        read.Close();
        read.Dispose();
    }
}
```

The previous code function returns an object. You must cast this object to convert it into a `MyClass` object.

You can call the previous function or apply it in the following way:

```
MyClass deSerializedClass = (MyClass) DeSerializeAnObject(xmlObject);
string name = deSerializedClass.name;
string address = deSerializedClass.address;
```

Controlling XML Serialization

There are some situations where you require more control over how you serialize your objects. You can gain this control by using specific attributes.

In scenarios where you must serialize a class without any XML serialization attributes, the runtime uses default settings to process the requirements of the user. The names of XML elements are based on class and member names and furthermore, each member is serialized as a separate XML element.

For example, consider the following simple class:

```
public class MyClass
{
   public string name = string.Empty;
   public string address = string.Empty;
}
```

You can set values for this class as shown:

```
MyClass myClass = new MyClass();
myClass.name = "XYZ";
myClass.address = "Bellevue, US";
```

When you serialize an instance of this class with sample values, you get the following XML component:

TAKE NOTE*
This code is slightly simplified for easy readability.

```
<?xml version="1.0" ?>
<myclass xmlns:xsi=http://www.w3.org/2001/XMLSchema-instance xmlns:
xsd="http://www.w3.org/2001/XMLSchema">
   <name> XYZ </name>
   <address> Bellevue, US</address>
</myclass>
```

This pattern is adequate when you define XML schema. However, if you want to create XML documents that conform to specific standards, you have to control the structuring pattern of serialization with the help of certain attributes.

Table 5-3 displays the attributes that you can use to control serialization. You can use these attributes to create a serialized class that conforms to specific XML requirements.

Table 5-3

Attributes to control XML serialization

ATTRIBUTES	APPLIES TO	FUNCTIONS
`XmlAnyAttribute`	Public fields, properties, parameters, or return values that return an array of `XmlAttribute` objects.	At the time of deserialization, `XmlAttribute` objects that represent all XML attributes unidentified by the schema, fill the array.
`XmlAnyElement`	Public fields, properties, parameters, or return values that return an array of `XmlElement` objects.	At the time of deserialization, `XmlElement` objects that represent all XML elements unidentified by the schema, fill the array.
`XmlArray`	Public fields, properties, parameters, or return values that return an array of complex objects.	Generates the members of the array as members of an XML array.
`XmlArrayItem`	Public fields, properties, parameters, or return values that return an array of complex objects.	Inserts the derived types into an array. Generally, you can use them in combination with the `XmlArray` attribute.

Table 5-3 (continued)

ATTRIBUTES	APPLIES TO	FUNCTIONS
`XmlAttribute`	Public fields, properties, parameters, or return values.	Serializes the member as an XML attribute.
`XmlChoiceIdentifier`	Public fields, properties, parameters, or return values.	Promotes the disambiguation of the member by using an enumeration.
`XmlElement`	Public fields, properties, parameters, or return values.	Serializes the field or property as an XML element.
`XmlEnum`	Public fields that are enumeration identifiers.	Displays the element name of an enumeration member.
`XmlIgnore`	Public fields and properties.	Ignores the field or property on serializing the containing class. Its function is similar to the `NonSerialized` attribute for standard serialization.
`XmlInclude`	Public-derived class declarations and return values of public methods for Web Services Description Language (WSDL) documents.	Includes the class when generating schemas (to be recognized when serialized).
`XmlRoot`	Public class declarations.	Controls XML serialization of the attribute target as an XML root element. You can use this attribute to specify the namespace and the element name.
`XmlText`	Public fields and properties.	Serializes the field or property as XML text.
`XmlType`	Public class declarations.	Specifies the name and namespace of the XML type.

Now knowing the attributes, let us make changes to the example discussed previously. You can modify the `MyClass` class with specific attributes as follows:

```
[XmlRoot ("Users")]
public class MyClass
{
    [XmlAttribute] public Int32 userId;
    public string name;
    public Int32 rank;
    [XmlIgnore] public decimal total;
    public MyClass()
    {
    }
}
```

When you serialize an instance of this class with the previously-specified attributes, you get the following XML file:

```
<?xml version="1.0" ?>
<Users userId="100">
    <name>XYZ</name>
    <rank>2</rank>
</Users>
```

TAKE NOTE*

You can control serialization by calling the `ReadXml` and `WriteXml` methods to control the `XmlReader` class that reads XML and the `XmlWriter` class that writes XML.

Though you can use attributes to meet most of the requirements of XML serialization, you can have complete control over XML serialization by implementing the `IXmlSerializable` interface in your class. For example, you can separate data into bytes instead of buffering large data sets and avoid the inflation that occurs when you encode the data using *Base64* encoding.

Conforming to XML Schema

TAKE NOTE*

An XML schema appears as the metadata that describes a certain class of XML documents.

When an XML document conforms to a specific XML schema, you can consider it as an instance of this XML schema. You can use an XML schema to build storage for the XML documents that conform to the schema and to validate these documents.

When two different applications need to exchange XML files, the developers work together to create an XML schema file that defines the structure of an XML document. There are many types of XML schemas available and whenever possible you must leverage on an existing XML schema for better results.

If you have an XML schema, you can run the ***XML Schema Definition tool*** (*Xsd.exe*) to create a set of classes that are strongly typed to the schema and annotated with attributes. On serializing an instance of such a class, the resulting XML adheres to the XML schema. This works as an easier option in comparison with using other classes in the .NET Framework, such as the `XmlReader` and `XmlWriter` classes to read from and write to an XML stream, respectively.

CREATE A CLASS THAT CONFORMS TO XML SCHEMA

You can perform the following steps to generate a class based on an XML schema:

1. Create the XML schema *.xsd* file on your computer.
2. Go to the Start menu, select Microsoft Visual Studio/Visual Studio Tools folder, and open a Visual Studio command prompt.
3. From the command prompt, type **Xsd.exe schema.xsd/classes/language:C#** and press Enter.

   For example, to create a new class based on a schema file named C:\Schema\Library.xsd, run the following command:

   ```
   xsd C:\schema\library.xsd /classes /language:CS
   ```
4. Open the newly created file (named *Schema.cs*), and add the class to your application.

TAKE NOTE*

The class file name can be library.cs matching to the schema file, library.xsd. However, the file name can also be different as shown earlier.

When you serialize this newly created class (*Schema.cs*), it automatically conforms to the XML schema. Conformance with XML schema simplifies the creation of applications to make them interoperable with standard Web services.

Serializing Datasets

The .NET Framework provides `DataSet` objects that are in-memory containers holding data in various forms, such as tables. DataSet supports various forms of serialization and is best suited for distributed application.

Apart from serializing an instance of a public class, you can also serialize an instance of a `DataSet` object. The following example shows the serialization of a `DataSet` object using the `XmlSerializer` class. Note that the code sample requires a reference to the `System.Data` namespace:

```
private void SerializeDataSet(string filename)
{
   XmlSerializer xmlSr = new  XmlSerializer(typeof(DataSet));
   // Creates a DataSet; adds a table, column, and ten rows
   DataSet dataSet = new DataSet("myDataSet");
```

You can also use the DataSet.WriteXml, DataSet.ReadXml, and DataSet.GetXml methods to serialize a DataSet object.

```
DataTable tbl = new DataTable("myTable");
DataColumn col = new DataColumn("myColumn");
    tbl.Columns.Add(col);
    dataSet.Tables.Add(tbl);
    DataRow row;
    for(int i = 0; i<10; i++)
    {
        row = tbl.NewRow();
        row[0] = "XYZ " + i;
        tbl.Rows.Add(row);
    }
    TextWriter wr = new StreamWriter(filename);
    xmlSr.Serialize(wr, dataSet);
    wr.Close();
}
```

CERTIFICATION READY?
Control the serialization of an object into XML format by using the System.Xml.Serialization namespace.
USD 4.2

You can also serialize arrays, collections, and instances of an XmlElement or an XmlNode class in the same way. Though DataSet is useful in many aspects, it does not provide the same level of control available when serializing the data stored in custom classes.

Performing Custom Serialization

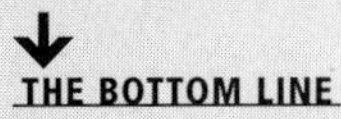

The .NET standard and XML serialization classes offer methods to serialize and deserialize all types of data. You can even deserialize an object serialized using a different version. You achieve this by marking the new data with attributes. However, you can use custom formats to serialize and deserialize between different versions without affecting the original type of data and while still ensuring version compatibility.

Using Custom Formats to Serialize and Deserialize Objects

You can control the serialization and deserialization of a type with the help of custom serialization.

It is actually possible to ensure serialization compatibility between various versions of a particular type without affecting the core functionality of that type. This can be achieved by controlling serialization. Let us consider an example. Consider that in the first version of a type, there are two fields; and in the next version of that type, several more fields are added. The second version of an application must be able to serialize and deserialize both types by controlling serialization.

You can override the serialization built into the .NET Framework by implementing the ISerializable interface and applying the Serializable attribute to the class. This feature is useful where the value of a member variable is invalid after deserialization, but you need to set the value of the variable to reconstruct the full state of the object. Additionally, you must not use default serialization on a class that is marked with the Serializable attribute and has declarative or imperative security set at class-level or on its constructors. Instead, you must always use the ISerializable interface for these classes.

Custom serialization is more flexible than the technique discussed in the previous paragraph. Consider that a class requires custom serialization, it implements ISerializable interface, and must:

- Have GetObjectData method as a part of the interface.
- Have a constructor that takes two input parameters, objects of SerializationInfo and StreamingContext.

The following sample code makes use of the System.Runtime.Serialization and System.Security.Permissions namespaces. It depicts implementation of the serialization constructor ISerializable and the GetObjectData method:

```
public class empclass: ISerializable
{ private string empname;
  private string empprofession;
  protected empclass (SerializationInfo var1, StreamingContext var2)
  {
     this.empname = var1.GetString("empname");
     this.empprofession = var1.GetString("empprofession");
  }
  void ISerializable.GetObjectData (SerializationInfo var1,
StreamingContext var2)
  {
     var1.AddValue("empname", this.empname);
     var1.AddValue("empprofession", this.empprofession);
  }
}
```

The GetObjectData object is called by the framework to indicate the serialization. The object serializes itself into the SerializationInfo object, which is then passed as a parameter to the GetObjectData. The SerializationInfo object holds the serialized object. The AddInfo method creates a name-value pair, which is ultimately serialized to the stream. You can use this method to serialize only the members that you want to serialize.

At runtime, the system calls the GetObjectData method during serialization and the serialization constructor during deserialization. In case you forget to implement the GetObjectData method, the compiler displays a related warning message. However, if you forget to implement the special constructor, then the compiler raises a serialization exception. During serialization, when the GetObjectData method is invoked, it is your task to populate the SerializationInfo object provided with the method call. To do this, you have to add the variables to be serialized as name-value pairs using the AddValue method. This method internally creates SerializationEntry structures to store the information. You can use any text as the name. You can decide which member variables must be added to the SerializationInfo object and ensure sufficient data is serialized to restore the object during deserialization. When runtime calls the serialization constructor, it is required to retrieve the values of the variables from SerializationInfo using the names used during serialization.

UNDERSTANDING THE SECURITY RISKS INVOLVED IN USING DATA VALIDATION

You must validate your data in your serialization constructor and throw a Serialization Exception in case of invalid data. This is because an attacker can use your class but provide fake serialization information in an attempt to exploit a weakness. Thus, the serialized object is at risk without proper exception handling. As a remedy to this problem, you must assume that an attacker commences any call made to your serialization constructor, and you must allow the construction only if all the data passed is valid and realistic.

Responding to Serialization Events

The serialization events are the best and easiest way to control the serialization process. The method must meet specific requirements in order to respond to the serialization events.

While using the BinaryFormatter class, the .NET Framework supports binary serialization events. The events are supported only for BinaryFormatter serialization. In case of the SoapFormatter or custom serialization, you are restricted to use the IDeserializationCallback interface. These events call the methods in your class when executing the serialization and deserialization process.

The following list depicts four serialization events:

- **Serializing.** Raised just before serialization takes place. You must apply the `OnSerializing` attribute to the method that must execute in response to this event.
- **Serialized.** Raised just after serialization takes place. You must apply the `OnSerialized` attribute to the method that must execute in response to this event.
- **Deserializing.** Raised just before deserialization takes place. You must apply the `OnDeserializing` attribute to the method that must execute in response to this event.
- **Deserialized.** Raised just after deserialization takes place and after `IDeserializationCallback.OnDeserialization` has been invoked. You must use `IDeserializationCallback.OnDeserialization` instead when formatters other than `BinaryFormatter` are used. You must apply the `OnDeserialized` attribute to the method that must execute in response to this event.

Figure 5-1 illustrates the events and its sequences.

Figure 5-1

Serialization events and their sequences

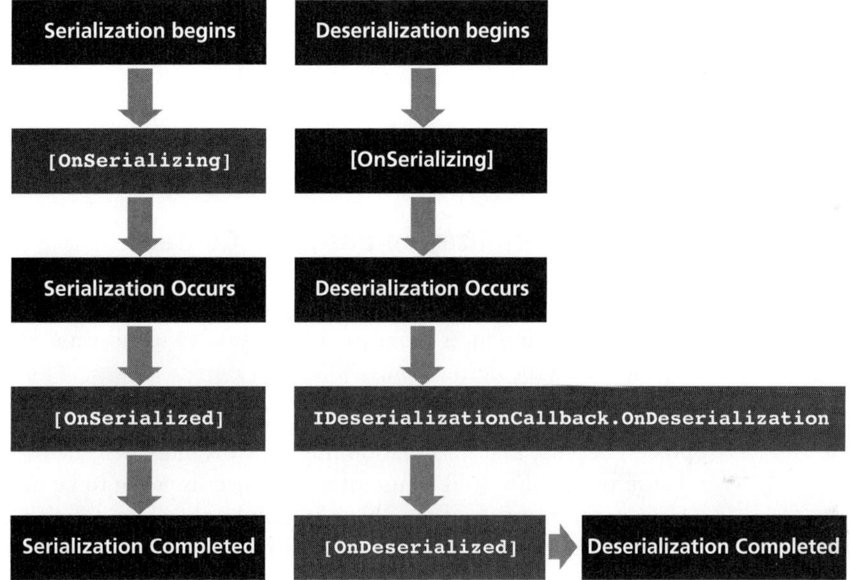

The event handlers do not access the serialization stream; however, they allow you to revise the object before and after serialization or before and after deserialization. It is possible to apply the attributes at all levels of the type inheritance hierarchy. Each of the methods is called in the hierarchy from the base to the most derived. Alternatively, this mechanism avoids the complexity as well as any resulting issues of implementing the `ISerializable` interface by giving the responsibility for serialization and deserialization to the most derived implementation. The method must meet the following requirements in order to respond to one of these events. The method:

- Must accept a `StreamingContext` object as a parameter.
- Must return *void.*
- Must have an attribute that matches the event you want to intercept.

Let us take an example that demonstrates creating an object, which responds to serialization events. You can respond to as many or as few events as you want. Additionally, you can apply multiple events to a single method or the same serialization event to multiple methods. The following example applies the `OnSerializing` attribute to the `GetTotal` method and thus ensures the execution of this method before serialization begins. Similarly, it ensures the execution of the VerifyTotal method after the deserialization process is complete by applying the OnDeserialized attribute:

```
[Serializable]
class Muliplex
{
   public int x;
   public int y;
   public int z;
   [OnSerializing]
   void GetTotal(StreamingContext strmCtext)
{
   z = x * y;
}
[OnDeserialized]
void VerifyTotal(StreamingContext strmCtext)
{
   if (z = 0)
   {
      GetTotal(strmCtext);
   }
 }
}
```

Changing Serialization Based on Context

The destination of the object is not important when you serialize an object. However, there might be some instances when you might want to serialize and deserialize an object differently depending on the destination.

Ideally, you do not need to serialize members that contain information about the current process because that information might be invalid when the object is deserialized. However, that information would be useful if the object is going to be deserialized by the same process. Alternatively, if the object is useful only when deserialized by the same process, you might decide to raise an exception, if you know that the destination process is different.

The StreamingContext structure provides information about the destination of a serialized object to classes that implement the ISerializable interface. The StreamingContext structure is passed to GetObjectData and the serialization constructor of the object. This structure has two properties:

- **Context.** Holds reference to an object that contains any user-desired context information.
- **State.** Indicates the source or destination of the object being serialized or deserialized. The following flags are set to indicate:
    - CrossProcess. The source or destination is a different process on the same machine.
    - CrossMachine. The source or destination is on a different machine.
    - File. The source or destination is a file. You must not assume that the same process deserializes the data.
    - Persistence. The source or destination is a store such as a database, file, or other. You must not assume that the same process deserializes the data.
    - Remoting. The source or destination is remoting to an unknown location. The location might be on the same machine or on another machine.
    - Other. The source or destination is unknown.
    - Clone. The object graph is being cloned. The serialization code might assume that the same process can deserialize the data, and it is therefore safe to access handles or other unmanaged resources.

- CrossAppDomain. The source or destination is a different *AppDomain*.
- All. The source or destination might be any of these contexts. This is the default context of the property.

You have to implement the `ISerializable` interface in your class to make context decisions during serialization and deserialization. For serialization, you must inspect the `StreamingContext` structure passed to the `GetObjectData` method of your object. For deserialization, you must inspect the `StreamingContext` structure passed to the serialization constructor of your object. If you are serializing or deserializing an object and want to provide context information, you have to modify the `StreamingContext` object returned by the `IFormatter.Context` property before calling the `Serialize` or `Deserialize` methods of the formatter. The `IFormatter.Context` property is implemented by both the `BinaryFormatter` and `SoapFormatter` classes. When you construct a formatter, it automatically sets the `Context` property to `null` and the `State` property to `All`.

Creating a Custom Formatter

CERTIFICATION READY?
Implement custom serialization formatting by using the serialization formatter classes.
USD 4.3

Although .NET supports built-in formatters, you can also create your own custom formatter in the serialization procedure.

You have to implement the `IFormatter` interface to build a custom formatter. The `BinaryFormatter` and `SoapFormatter` formatters implement the `IFormatter` interface. The `FormatterServices` class provides many static methods to support the implementation of a formatter. One of the static methods included in this class is the `GetObjectData` method.

SKILL SUMMARY

This lesson explained the process of serializing objects in .NET applications. As a developer, you have understood the generic mechanism of serialization of objects. The implementation of this standard serialization requires the creation of a stream and a formatter. Deserializing an object is the reverse process of serializing. It is essential to add the Serializable attribute to make a class `serializable` and deserializable.

You learned the advantages of using XML serialization in transmitting objects between computers through Web services. Along with many benefits, there are few limitations for its use. A clear analysis of its features and requirements, in comparison with the standard serialization technique, can help in its application wherever it best suits. You can also serialize an instance of a `DataSet` object by using the `XmlSerializer` class.

You also learned how to use custom formats to serialize and deserialize objects. A custom formatter is created by implementing the `IFormatter` interface. Custom serialization helps to control the serialization and the deserialization of a type.

For the certification examination:

- Know how to apply runtime serialization on objects.
- Understand the requirements to use XML serialization and its applications.
- Know how to control serialization by implementing your own serialization classes.

■ Knowledge Assessment

Matching

Match the following descriptions to the appropriate terms.

a. `FormatterServices`
b. `Serializing`
c. `Serialized`
d. `Deserializing`
e. `Deserialized`

_______ 1. Event raised just after serialization takes place.

_______ 2. Event raised just before deserialization takes place.

_______ 3. Event raised just after deserialization takes place.

_______ 4. Event raised just before serialization takes place.

_______ 5. Provides many static methods to support the implementation of a formatter.

True / False

Circle T if the statement is true or F if the statement is false.

T | F 1. To create a class that needs to be serialized using XML serialization, you must specify the class as private.

T | F 2. When creating a class to be serialized using XML serialization, you need to create an instance of the `MemoryStream` class.

T | F 3. XML serialization ensures efficient transmission of serialized objects across a network to be used by applications running on any platform.

T | F 4. The `BinaryFormatter` class must be avoided because it is not efficient.

T | F 5. Both the `BinaryFormatter` and the `SoapFormatter` classes implement the `IFormatter` interface.

Fill in the Blank

Complete the following sentences by writing the correct word or words in the blanks provided.

1. When serializing an object, you can create an instance of the `XmlDocument` class from _________ namespace.
2. The ________ attribute is used in combination with the `XmlArray` attribute.
3. The two formatters used for serialization are ___________ and _________.
4. The ________ process involves finalizing an object reference after deserialization of the referenced object.
5. A class that requires custom serialization must implement _________ interface.

Multiple Choice

Circle the letter or letters that correspond to the best answer or answers.

1. Which of these elements can be serialized using XML serialization?
   a. Objects
   b. Object graphs
   c. Public data
   d. Private data
2. During deserializing an object, which namespace will you use to create an instance of the `StringReader` class?
   a. `System.IO`
   b. `System.Xml`
   c. `System.Xml.Serialization`
   d. None of the above
3. Which of the following is the process of reconstructing a data object to its original state?
   a. Serialization
   b. Deserialization
   c. Formatting
   d. Initiation
4. Which of the following, along with a stream, is required for the process of serialization?
   a. Formatter
   b. Deformatter
   c. Attribute
   d. Custom Object
5. Which method does the runtime call during custom serialization?
   a. `GetObjectData`
   b. `SerializationInfo`
   c. `BinaryFormatter.Serialize`
   d. `AddInfo`

Review Questions

1. What happens when the ObjectManager identifies that a particular object has not been deserialized before?
2. What must you do to optimize the size of the object to be serialized?

■ Case Scenarios

Scenario 5-1: Choosing the Appropriate Serialization

In your movie Web site, you have a class named `Movie`. This class contains information about a movie such as its name, release date, director, lead actors, and number of prints released. You must share this object with other movie Web sites.

Select the type of serialization that you must choose if you want to transport this object through network to different movie sites and application.

Scenario 5-2: Creating Serialized Objects

Create a program to serialize the `Movie` object using the standard serialization mechanism. Mention whether the output you create is usable by a Java-based program.

Workplace Ready

Upgrading Serialization Mechanisms

You may have to upgrade applications built on one .NET version to a higher version. In such scenarios, if your existing application uses serialization, then you must analyze the implications of upgrading the application even from the serialization requirements perspective. For example, you may have to consider whether you need the same serialization mechanism or if you want to add more data to the serialized object.

You are the solution architect for XYZ Financial Services, Inc. You have an existing application that runs on .NET 3.0. This application uses serialization to store object states between transaction stages because your application permits transactions to be performed in stages. Your organization plans to upgrade this to .NET 3.5. You are also required to add new fields to the serialization data. You also want your new application to deserialize data serialized by the existing .NET 3.0-based application. Suggest an approach that you would take in this scenario.

Creating Application Domains and Windows Services

LESSON 6

OBJECTIVE DOMAIN MATRIX

Technology Skill	Objective Domain	Objective Domain Number
Create and unload application domains.	Create a unit of isolation for Common Language Runtime in a .NET Framework application by using application domains.	2.3
Set up application domains.	Create a unit of isolation for Common Language Runtime in a .NET Framework application by using application domains.	2.3
Create and consume Windows services.	Implement, install, and control a service.	2.1

KEY TERMS

application domain
assembly
Defense-in-Depth
Service Control Manager
Setup Project
Windows service

An ***application domain*** is a logical container that allows multiple assemblies to run within a single process but prevents them from directly accessing memory that belongs to other assemblies. In addition, application domains provide isolation from faults because unhandled exceptions do not affect other application domains.

■ Creating and Unloading Application Domains

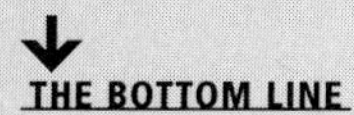

To ensure that each application executes properly without being affected by the errors in other applications, you can create application domains and make each application run in separate application domains.

Introducing Application Domains

A .NET process can contain multiple application domains, and an application domain is a way to isolate applications in the .NET Framework. Because of this isolation, an application can run in its own application domain without having an impact on the other application. When you run one application domain, the others remain unaffected. This isolation is achieved by having unique virtual address space for each application.

You can create your own application domains that host the Common Language Runtime (CLR). The CLR application domains are contained within an operating system process. You can have one or more application domains within a single process. This feature minimizes the system overheads. Having application domains confined within assemblies helps keep the process isolated without affecting other applications. Therefore, any error or exception encountered within the application domain does not affect the functioning of other applications, in any way. Each application domain within a process has its specific configuration and can have separate security access levels assigned to it.

However, if the application is executed with full trust, the application domain bypasses all security checkpoints provided within the .NET Framework. This may expose the application to unrestricted access processwide.

Figure 6-1 displays a single process that shows the relationship between application domains and assemblies.

Figure 6-1

Relationship between application domains and assemblies within a single process

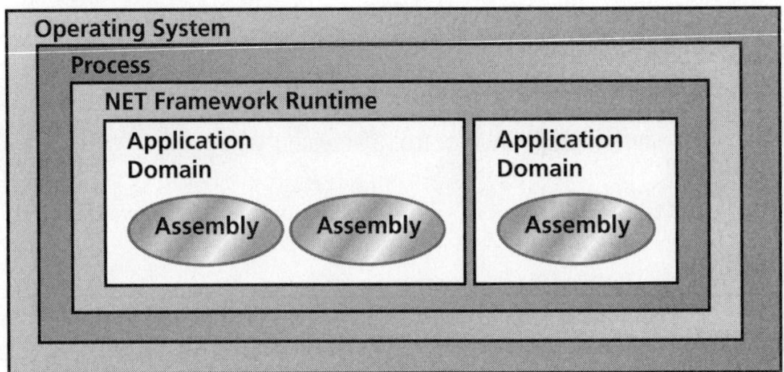

By default, the runtime hosts of Microsoft Windows such as ASP.NET, Windows Internet Explorer, and the operating system, create application domains for all assemblies. However, you can use the Internet Information Services (IIS) manager and the .NET Framework configuration tool to configure these application domains to suit your requirements. You can also create custom application domains to call assemblies, provided you are ready to take the accompanying security risks, such as exposing access to any or all resources.

Figure 6-2 displays how an ***assembly*** can host application domains. Assemblies are executables or library files that are loaded just-in-time by the CLR when your application actually needs to consume types defined in that assembly.

Figure 6-2

Assemblies hosting application domains

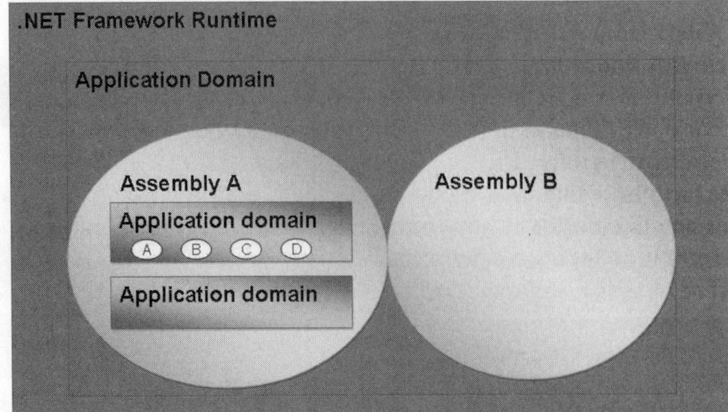

Application domains not only isolate an assembly, but also have the following advantages:

- **Application domains make the process more reliable.** And they can be used to isolate tasks that terminate a process. For example, if a task within the application domain halts for some reason, you can easily isolate it without affecting the entire process. This is specifically significant when the process is huge because that means you do not have to restart the entire process. You can also isolate data, such as addins, by running them in a separate application domain so that even if one of the addins encounters an error, it does not bring down the whole application.
- **Application domains are efficient.** For large processes, while they are running, you cannot unload the assembly. However, you can open a second application domain to load and execute the assembly. Here the assembly is unloaded along with the application domain. This saves time without affecting the other application, especially if the process involves large dynamic-link libraries (DLLs).

Working with Application Domains

You can implement application domains within the .NET Framework using the `System.AppDomain` class.

The `AppDomain` class provides several methods and properties to manage application domains. You can create an instance of the `AppDomain` class and then execute an assembly within that domain.

Table 6-1 lists several of the `AppDomain` properties.

Table 6-1

Properties of the `AppDomain` class

PROPERTY	DESCRIPTION
`ActivationContext`	Represents the activation context for the current application domain. Returns a null value if no activation context is found.
`ApplicationIdentity`	Represents the identity of the application within a manifest-based application.
`ApplicationTrust`	Specifies the security permissions granted to an application. Also specifies whether the application has a trust level to execute the application.
`BaseDirectory`	Specifies the base directory that the assembly resolver must check for assemblies.
`CurrentDomain`	Specifies the current application domain for the current thread. You can look for context or verify permissions for the current domain.
`DomainManager`	Specifies the domain manager associated with the application domain.
`DynamicDirectory`	Specifies the directory that the assembly resolver searches for dynamically created assemblies.
`Evidence`	Specifies the evidence associated with an application domain. The evidence, such as signature or location of the original code, acts as an input to the security policy.
`FriendlyName`	Represents the friendly name given to the application domain. The .NET Framework friendly name is structured as *<ProjectName>.vshost.exe*. You must specify the friendly name when you create application domains programmatically.
`Id`	Represents an integer that uniquely identifies the application domain within the process.
`RelativeSearchPath`	Specifies the path of the base directory that the assembly resolver should search for private assemblies.

(Continued)

Table 6-1 (continued)

Property	Description
SetupInformation	Specifies application domain configuration information for a particular instance.
ShadowCopyFiles	Specifies if the assemblies with application domain are shadow copied.

Table 6-2 lists the methods provided by the `AppDomain` class.

Table 6-2

Methods provided by the AppDomain class

Method	Description
ApplyPolicy	This represents the assembly display name once the policy is applied.
CreateComInstanceFrom	This method creates an instance of a particular COM type.
CreateDomain	This method has overloads that you can use to create new application domains.
CreateInstance	This method has overloads that create a new instance of a specific type for an assembly.
CreateInstanceAndUnwrap	This creates a new instance of a specific type.
CreateInstanceFrom	This creates a new instance of a specific type within a specific assembly file.
CreateInstanceFromAndWrap	This creates an instance of a specified type defined within a specified assembly file.
DefineDynamicAssembly	This specifies a dynamic assembly in the current application domain.
DoCallBack	This method runs the code in another application domain. This domain is identified by a specified delegate.
ExecuteAssembly	This method runs the assembly contained in the specified file.
ExecuteAssemblyByName	This method runs the specified assembly.
GetAssemblies	This method lists all the assemblies that are provided in the application domain context.
GetCurrentThreadId	This method specifies the current thread identifier.
GetData	This method specifies the value stored in the current application domain for the specified name.
InitializeLifetimeService	This method initializes infinite lifetime service to an AppDomain.
IsDefaultAppDomain	This method determines whether the application domain is the default application domain for the process.
IsFinalizingForUnload	This method determines whether this application domain is unloading. It also determines whether the CLR is finalizing the objects within the application domain.
Load	This method loads a specific Assembly into the application domain.
ReflectionOnlyGetAssemblies	This method determines which assemblies have been loaded into the reflection-only context of the application domain.
SetAppDomainPolicy	This method sets the security policy level for this application domain.
SetData	This method sets a value to an application domain property.
SetDynamicBase	This method sets the default directory path for storing and retrieving dynamically generated files.
SetPrincipalPolicy	This method defines the manner in which principal and identity objects are attached to a thread during execution of the application domain.
SetShadowCopyFiles	This method sets the shadow-copying feature for the application domain.

Creating an Application Domain

Though application domains are mostly used by runtime hosts, you can create your own application domains and associate them to assemblies that you want to control. The System.AppDomain class includes all the methods to create and manipulate the application domains.

To create an application domain, you can overload the CreateDomain method of the System.AppDomain base class. You can then specify the name for the new application domain. The following code syntax displays the method of creating an application domain:

TAKE NOTE*

You can use the CurrentDomain method provided within the AppDomain class to determine the assembly that runs your application domain.

```
using System;
using System.Reflection;
class AppDomain1
{
    public static void Main()
    {
        Console.WriteLine("Creating new AppDomain.");
        AppDomain domain = AppDomain.CreateDomain("MyDomain");
        Console.WriteLine("Host domain: " +
AppDomain.CurrentDomain.FriendlyName);
        Console.WriteLine("child domain: " +
domain.FriendlyName);
    }
}
```

LOADING ASSEMBLIES IN AN APPLICATION DOMAIN

When you want to load assemblies in an application domain, you must create an instance of the AppDomain class. Specify a name for the instance you created then invoke the ExecuteAssembly method. The following code displays how to load assemblies in an application domain:

```
static void Main()
{
    // Create an Application Domain:
    System.AppDomain newDomain =
System.AppDomain.CreateDomain("NewApplicationDomain");
    // Load and execute an assembly:
    newDomain.ExecuteAssembly("HelloWorld.exe");
}
```

You can also use overloads with the ExecuteAssembly method that allows you to pass command line arguments. You can either provide the entire path to the assembly or provide a reference to the assembly. Now you can use the ExecuteAssemblyByName method to run the application domain. The following code displays how to use the ExecuteAssemblyByName method.

```
static void Main()
{
    // Create an Application Domain:
    System.AppDomain newDomain =
System.AppDomain.CreateDomain("NewApplicationDomain");
    // Load and execute an assembly:
newDomain.ExecuteAssemblyByName("HelloWorld");
}
```

Unloading an Application Domain

When you load assemblies into new application domains, you can unload the application domain at any point in time and it frees up resources.

The process of unloading involves downloading both the domain and the assemblies within it. You cannot unload individual assemblies or types. To unload a domain and all assemblies that the domain contains, you must call the static `AppDomain.Unload` method, as shown in the following code:

CERTIFICATION READY?
Create a unit of isolation for Common Language Runtime in a .NET Framework application by using application domains.
USD 2.3

```
static void Main()
{
   // Create an Application Domain:
   System.AppDomain newDomain =
System.AppDomain.CreateDomain("NewApplicationDomain");
   // Load and execute an assembly:
   newDomain.ExecuteAssembly("HelloWorld.exe");
   // Unload the application domain:
   System.AppDomain.Unload(newDomain);
}
```

■ Setting Up Application Domains

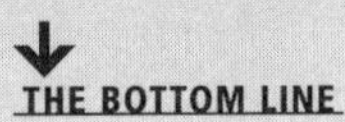

You can configure application domains when building customized environments for assemblies. The most important application of modifying the default settings for an application domain is restricting permissions to reduce the risks associated with security vulnerabilities. In case of ideal configuration, the application domain provides a unit of isolation and also limits the damage that attackers can do in an attempt to exploit an assembly.

Providing Restrictive Rights

It is advisable to provide restrictive rights for an application domain. Usually, the ***Defense-in-Depth*** principle is applied in a scenario where external code is accessed by the application. The objective of this principle is to provide multiple levels of protection so that you are still protected in the event of vulnerability.

It is a wise idea to restrict the permissions of an application domain in order to minimize the risk that an assembly you invoke will perform some malicious action. Let us consider a scenario to understand this. Consider that you purchase an assembly from a third party to communicate with a database. Now an attacker uncovers security vulnerability in the third-party assembly and makes use of it for configuring a spyware application to start automatically. The security vulnerability is the fault of the end user because the end user trusted the third-party assembly and ran it with privileges sufficient to install software.

Alternatively, consider the same scenario with an application domain having restricted privileges. An attacker in this case also uncovers security vulnerability in the third-party assembly. However, when the attacker attempts to exploit the vulnerability to write files to the local hard disk, the file input/output (I/O) request is denied because of insufficient rights. Even though the security vulnerability still exists, the restricted privileges assigned to the application domain prevent it from being exploited, thereby safeguarding it.

This example of starting assemblies with limited privileges demonstrates the Defense-in-Depth security principle. This principle is particularly important in a scenario when calling external code because external code might have vulnerabilities that you are not aware of and cannot prevent or fix.

Providing Host Evidence for an Assembly

Evidence is the information about the assembly that the runtime gathers. Evidence provided by the host is called host evidence.

In an application domain, you gain complete control over the host evidence once you start the assemblies. Evidence determines the code groups to which the assembly belongs, and the code groups determine the privileges of the assembly. The common forms of evidence comprise the folder or Web site the assembly is running from along with the digital signatures. You can control the permissions assigned to the assembly by assigning the evidence to an assembly. You can provide evidence for an assembly with the help of two steps. You have to first create a `System.Security.Policy.Evidence` object and then pass it as a parameter to the application domain's overloaded `ExecuteAssembly` method.

When you create an `Evidence` object with the constructor, it requires two object arrays. To this constructor, you must provide one array that represents host evidence and a second array that provides assembly evidence. Alternately, either of the arrays can be null, and unless you have specifically created an assembly evidence object, you will probably have to assign only the host evidence array. You might find it strange that the `Evidence` object takes unspecified object arrays instead of strongly typed `Evidence` objects. However, the evidence can be anything such as a string, an integer, or a custom class. So, in case you are using the evidence types embedded into the .NET Framework, you have to add them to an object array.

The simplest way to control the permissions assigned to an assembly in an application domain is for you to pass the zone evidence by using a `System.Security.Policy.Zone` object and the `System.Security.SecurityZone` enumeration.

Here is a bit of code that demonstrates the use of the `Evidence` constructor. This constructor takes two object arrays by building a `Zone` object, adding it to an object array named `hostEvid`, and then using the object array to create an `Evidence` object named `internetEvid`. At the end, the `Evidence` object is passed to the `ExecuteAssembly` method of application domain along with the assembly filename.

The following code sample, which requires the `System.Security` and the `System.Security.Policy` namespaces, demonstrates this process:

```
object[] hostEvid = {new Zone(SecurityZone.Internet)};
Evidence internetEvid = new Evidence(hostEvid, null);
AppDomain newDomain =
AppDomain.CreateDomain("New_Application_Domain");
newDomain.ExecuteAssembly("TheAssembly.exe", internetEvid);
```

The result of executing this code is that the specified assembly runs in an isolated application domain with only the permission set granted to the Internet_Zone code group. When the application domain starts the assembly, the runtime analyzes the evidence provided. The evidence matches the Internet zone and therefore the runtime assigns it to the Internet_Zone code group. This group, in turn, assigns the Internet permission set, which is extremely restrictive by default.

Configuring Application Domain Properties

The `AppDomainSetup` class is used to provide the CLR with configuration information for a new application domain.

One of the most important properties when creating your own application domain is `ApplicationBase`. The `AppDomainSetup` related properties are used to configure a particular application domain mainly by the runtime hosts. However, any modifications done to the properties of an `AppDomainSetup` instance do not affect any existing `AppDomain`. These updates take effect only on the creation of a new `AppDomain` by calling the `CreateDomain` method with the `AppDomainSetup` instance as a parameter.

Table 6-3 shows the most useful AppDomainSetup properties.

Table 6-3

Properties of the AppDomainSetup class

Property	Description
ActivationArguments	Gets or sets data about the activation of an application domain.
ApplicationBase	Gets or sets the name of the root directory that contains the application. By default, this folder contains the assembly that is loaded from disk or the parent that created the AppDomain by a running assembly. When the runtime needs to complete a type request, it searches for the assembly that contains the type in the directory specified by the ApplicationBase property.
ApplicationName	Gets or sets the name of the application.
ApplicationTrust	Gets or sets an object containing security and trust information.
ConfigurationFile	Gets or sets the name of the configuration file for an application domain. It uses the same format as *Machine.config*, but specifies settings that apply only to the application domain. Typically, the file is named *<Assembly>.config*. For example, if you have an assembly named *MyFirstApp.exe*, the configuration file would be named *MyFirstApp.config*.
DisallowApplication-BaseProbing	Specifies if the application base path and the private binary path are probed when searching for assemblies to load.
DisallowBindingRedirects	Gets or sets a value indicating whether an application domain allows assembly-binding redirection.
DisallowCodeDownload	Gets or sets a value indicating whether Hypertext Transfer Protocol (HTTP) download of assemblies is allowed for an application domain. The default value is set as false. To ensure that services do not download any partially trusted code, you must set this property to true.
DisallowPublisherPolicy	Gets or sets a value indicating whether the publisher policy section of the configuration file is applied to an application domain.
DynamicBase	Gets or sets the base directory where the directory for dynamically generated files is located.
LicenseFile	Gets or sets the location of the license file associated with the domain.
LoaderOptimization	Specifies the optimization policy used to load an executable.
PrivateBinPath	Gets or sets the list of directories under the application base directory that is probed for private assemblies.

To apply these properties to an application domain, create and configure an AppDomainSetup object and pass it (along with an Evidence object) to the AppDomain.CreateDomain method. The following code sample demonstrates this process:

```
// Construct and initialize settings for a second AppDomain.
AppDomainSetup objADS = new AppDomainSetup();
objADS.ApplicationBase = "file://" +
System.Environment.CurrentDirectory;
objADS.DisallowBindingRedirects = false;
```

```
objADS.DisallowCodeDownload = true;
objADS.ConfigurationFile =
AppDomain.CurrentDomain.SetupInformation.ConfigurationFile;
// Create the second AppDomain
AppDomain objAD = AppDomain.CreateDomain("New Domain", null, objADS);
```

CERTIFICATION READY?
Create a unit of isolation for Common Language Runtime in a .NET Framework application by using application domains.
USD 2.3

To examine the properties for the current application domain, use the `AppDomain.CurrentDomain.SetupInformation` object, as the following code sample demonstrates:

AppDomainSetup objADS = `AppDomain.CurrentDomain.SetupInformation;`

```
Console.WriteLine(objADS.ApplicationBase);
Console.WriteLine(objADS.ApplicationName);
Console.WriteLine(objADS.DisallowCodeDownload);
Console.WriteLine(ads.DisallowBindingRedirects);
```

Creating and Consuming Windows Services

THE BOTTOM LINE

Imagine that you need to create an application to perform the inventory calculation for all transactions happening for the day. In addition, you want the application to run automatically in the background on the server start up without any interaction from the user and to update the inventory table in your database with the inventory details. Windows services are an ideal option to meet your need in this case. By using Windows services, you can create constantly running applications that can start automatically when the system boots.

Defining Windows Service

You can write a Windows service to create constantly running applications in the background to meet different functional requirements.

A ***Windows service*** is a process running in the background in its own session, without a user interface. Whenever you start the computer, the Windows service can start running automatically, even before you log on to the system. The ultimate use of Windows services is to enable the developers to create executable applications, which run continuously without any user interaction. Let us look at a few examples. You can consider some of the Windows built-in services, which include Print Spooling, Event Log mechanism, Server (shares folders on the network), Workstation (connects to shared folders), and World Wide Web Publishing (serves Web pages).

You can create a Windows service easily using the Microsoft Visual Studio. In addition, you can also take advantage of the classes provided by the .NET Framework to define and control your Windows service.

FUNCTIONING OF SERVICE APPLICATIONS

You should know the various requirements to follow during the creation and installation of Windows service applications:

- Create an installation component and install the service application before it starts functioning. The installation component helps to install and register the service. The component also creates an entry for the service in the ***Service Control Manager***.
- Attach a debugger to the service's process only after installing and starting your service to debug the service application.
- Log error messages in the Windows event log rather than in the user interface. Also, remember that dialog boxes raised from within a Windows service application are not seen and might cause your program to stop responding because the Windows Service station is not interactive. Windows services run in a separate Windows station, which is a secure object that contains objects like a clipboard, a set of global atoms, and a group of desktop objects. The Windows station is separate from the user's interactive station.

TAKE NOTE*

If you use the Windows service Visual Studio project template, it includes the `Run` method automatically.

TAKE NOTE* Because the Windows service does not run in an interactive station, you cannot see any dialog boxes raised from within a Windows service application.

- Decide which user account will run the Windows services because these services can run immediately after booting the system. Windows services run in their own security context and can start running even before the user logs in to the system.

TAKE NOTE* A service running under the system account has more permissions and rights than those running under a user account.

WARNING If a service has more privileges than required, it could be prone to damages by hackers. Therefore, you should run your service with the fewest privileges possible to minimize potential damage.

Creating a Windows Service

You can create a Windows service using the Visual Studio that can take care of controlling the behavior of your service.

Using the Visual Studio project template Windows service, you can create and build a service project. The Windows service template automatically takes care of inheriting and using the necessary classes required for creating a service, lessening the burden on your part.

CREATE A SERVICE PROJECT

You should perform the steps listed next when building and using a service:

1. Use the Windows service template and create a new service project as shown in Figure 6-3.

TAKE NOTE* The template automatically creates a class inheriting from the service base class `ServiceBase`. In addition, the template also takes care of writing the essential codes to perform basic service functionalities, such as starting a service.

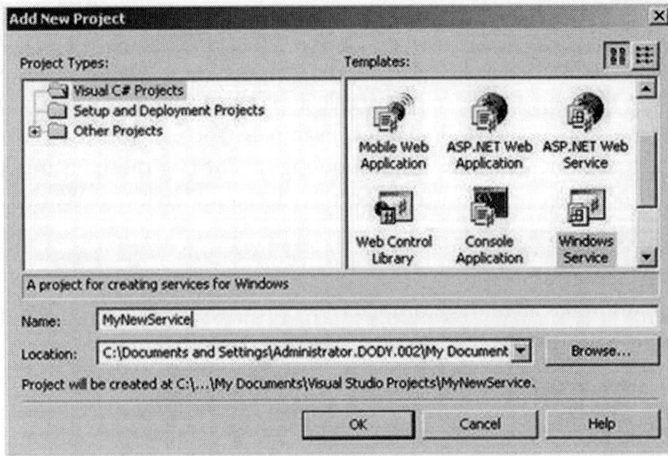

Figure 6-3
The add new project dialog box

2. Configure the created service by writing necessary code for the `OnStart` and `OnStop` methods, and override any other required methods according to your need.
3. Add the required installers for the created service.

TAKE NOTE* In Visual Studio, open the design view for your service. Right click the designer, and click the Add Installer link. By default, the template creates a class containing installers to install the service and any other services associated with your project.

4. Build the project.
5. Create a setup project to install the service.

6. Start the service, using the Services snap-in. You can access the Services snap-in by typing Services.msc at the command prompt.

TAKE NOTE*

In step 5, you create a ***Setup Project*** to install your Windows service. To do this, add a new project to your solution and select the Setup Project template available under the Setup and Deployment Projects type.

Configuring the Service

You must configure the created service to ensure the proper functioning of the service.

CONFIGURE SERVICE

Once you have created the service, you should configure the service application as listed next:

1. In the properties window of your designer, modify the value of the `ServiceBase.ServiceName` property.

TAKE NOTE*

Every service must have a unique name. Therefore, you must always change the default value of the `ServiceBase.ServiceName` property. The `ServiceName` setting enables the operating system and the code to identify the service. For example, you can start a service from the command line by executing Net `Start <ServiceName>`.

2. Add the required code to the `OnStart` method to set up the necessary monitoring that your service may require. To write code for a simple polling, use the `System.Timers.Timer` component. Set parameters on the component and set the `Enabled` property to true.

   The timer then raises the appropriate events periodically at the specified time when the monitoring process takes place.

TAKE NOTE*

The `OnStart` method actually does not perform the monitoring. It returns to the operating system once the service starts. Therefore, it must not loop forever.

TAKE NOTE*

When overriding the `OnShutdown` method, set the `ServiceBase.CanShutdown` to true.

3. Add code to the `OnStop` method to perform any necessary actions to stop your service.
4. Optionally, you can override the `OnPause` and `OnContinue` methods. The `OnPause` method executes when a user pauses your service from the Services snap-in, which rarely happens. The `OnContinue` method executes when a service resumes from a `pause` state.
5. Optionally, you can override the `OnShutdown` method. The `OnShutdown` method executes on shutting down the computer.
6. Optionally, you can override the `OnPowerEvent` method. The `OnPowerEvent` method executes when computer power status has changed and when the computer goes to the suspended mode, which is a common scenario in mobile computers.

TAKE NOTE*

When overriding the `OnPowerEvent` method, set the `ServiceBase.CanHandlePowerEvent` to true.

Creating Install Project for Service

TAKE NOTE*

You explicitly need not write code to include the installer classes discussed previously because the Visual Studio automatically includes them for you.

You have to install your service before starting or debugging it.

Unlike other applications, you cannot just run a service executable file. You must install your service for it to run. Therefore, you cannot debug or run your service directly from the Visual Studio development environment.

The .NET Framework provides two classes you can use to install your service, which include:

- **ServiceInstaller.** Defines the service description, display name, service name, and start type.
- **ServiceProcessInstaller.** Defines the service account settings.

CREATE SERVICE INSTALLER

You should follow the steps listed next to create a service installer using Visual Studio:

1. In Visual Studio, open the design view for your service. Right click the designer and select the *Add Installer* option. Visual Studio creates a `ProjectInstaller` component.
2. Set the `StartType` property of the `ProjectInstaller ServiceInstaller` component to any one of the following values:
   - `Automatic`. In this option, the Windows service starts automatically on booting the system, even before users log in.
   - `Manual`. This is the default value. By setting this value, the Windows service starts manually by user interaction.
   - `Disable`. In this option, the Windows service does not start automatically. Nor can the user start the service without changing the start-up type.
3. Set the `Description` and `DisplayName` property of the `ServiceInstaller` component.
4. Set the `ServicesDependedOn` property with a list of service names, which should run for your service to function. For example, if your service connects to a shared folder, you will need the Workstation service with the service name `LanmanWorkstation`.

TAKE NOTE*

To know the service name, you have to open the Services snap-in (available in the Computer Management console) and double click the service to view its properties and its name found in the *Service Name* attribute.

5. Define the security context for your service by setting the `Account` property of the `ProjectInstaller ServiceProcessInstaller` component to any one of the following values:
   - `LocalService`. In this option, the service runs in the context of an account, which is a nonprivileged user on the local computer, and provides anonymous credentials to remote servers.
   - `NetworkService`. In this option, the service authenticates another computer on the network. This service authentication is not required for anonymous connections such as Web server connections.
   - `LocalSystem`. In this option, the service runs with unlimited privileges and provides the computer's credentials to other remote servers.
   - `User`. This option causes the system to prompt for a valid username and password during service installation, unless you specify values for the `Username` and `Password` properties of the `ServiceProcessInstaller` object. This is the default option.

TAKE NOTE*

To minimize security risks, you can set the `Account` property to `LocalService`. Alternatively, if you set the `Account` property to `LocalSystem`, it increases the security risks by exploiting any vulnerability in your application and takes complete control of the user's computer.

6. Define the service project's start-up object by right clicking the project in the Solution Explorer and then selecting the **Properties** option.
7. In the Project Designer window, on the Application tab, select the required service project from the Startup Object list.
8. Build your project.

At this point, you can either manually install the service using the `InstallUtil` tool or create a Setup Project to provide a wizard-based installation interface and a Windows Installer (MSI) package.

TAKE NOTE*

You can find `InstallUtil.exe` in the *%windir%\Microsoft .NET\Framework\ v2.0.50727* folder.

INSTALLING A SERVICE MANUALLY

To install a service manually, run the `InstallUtil.exe` from the command line by specifying the service name as shown:

```
InstallUtil<yourservice.exe>
```

To uninstall a service manually, run the `InstallUtil.exe` by specifying an option to uninstall, as shown:

```
InstallUtil /u<yourservice.exe>
```

CREATING A SETUP PROJECT FOR SERVICE INSTALLATION

You can use Visual Studio to add a Setup Project that can install the Windows service.

 **CREATE SETUP**

To build a Setup Project for service installation, you should perform the following steps:

1. In the current solution, you should add a Setup Project.
2. To add the output from your service project to your Setup Project, in the Solution Explorer, right click your Setup Project, select Add, and then select Project Output.
3. In the Add Project Output Group dialog box, select the required service project from the project list, then select Primary Output, and then click OK.
4. To add a custom action for installing the service executable file, in the Solution Explorer, right click your Setup Project, select View, and then select Custom Actions.
5. In the Custom Actions editor, right click Custom Actions, and select the Add Custom Action option.
6. In the Select Item In Project dialog box, double click on the Application Folder. Select Add Output, and then select Primary Output. Now, click OK to add the primary output from your service project.
7. Click OK once again to add the primary output to all four nodes of the Custom Actions that include Install, Commit, Rollback, and Uninstall.
8. In the Solution Explorer, right click your Setup Project, and then click Build.

TAKE NOTE*

You can uninstall a service using any of the standard methods: manually, using the Control Panel or automatically using the Windows Installer (MSI) tools.

The service-setup build folder contains a Setup.exe file for the interactive installation of the service and an MSI file for the automatic deployment of the service.

Managing and Controlling Service

You can start a service after installing it, according to the start-up type settings mentioned while defining a service.

The service automatically starts after booting the system, if the service start-up type is set to `Automatic`. But, if the start-up type is set to `Manual`, then you can control the service using the Services snap-in from the command line, from a Windows application, or even from your ASP .NET Web application.

USING SERVICES SNAP-IN

Services snap-in allows you to manage services that are located on local or on remote computers.

 **START A SERVICE USING SERVICES SNAP-IN**

You have to perform the following steps to start the service using the Services snap-in:

1. First, login as an administrator or with any other user account that has the privileges to manage the service. Then select Start, right click Computer, and then select Manage.

TAKE NOTE*

You can also find the Services snap-in in the Windows server 2008 Server Manager, which is a Microsoft Management Console Snap-in.

2. Respond to any UAC prompts that appear (UAC prompts are User Account Control prompts which may appear due to actions that make changes to system-wide settings or to files in %SystemRoot% or %ProgramFiles%).
3. Expand Services and Applications, and then select Services.
4. In the right pane, right click the required service, and then click Start, as shown in Figure 6-4.

Figure 6-4

The Service properties dialog box

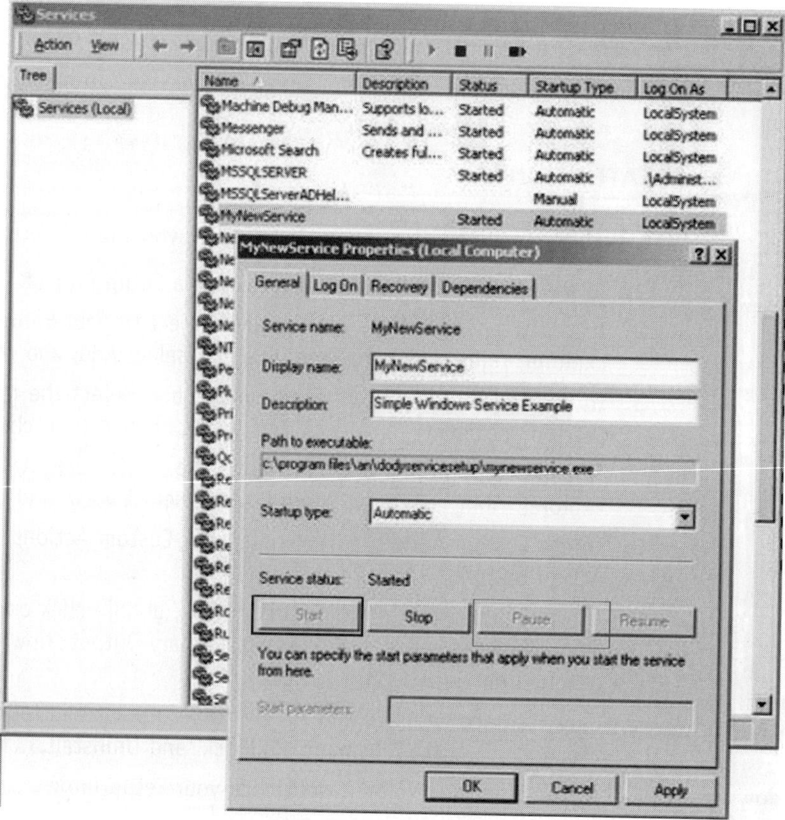

TAKE NOTE*

To control a service from the command line, issue the following command at the command prompt: `Net Start <ServiceName>` or `Net Stop <ServiceName>`

USING WEB APPLICATION

You can also create an ASP.NET Web application to control a service. To control a service from your ASP.NET Web application, you have to use the `System.SystemProcess.ServiceController` class. Using the `ServiceController` class, you can connect to a service running on the local or a remote computer and perform all the administrative tasks on the service. In addition, you can also send custom commands to the services, which is not possible through the Services snap-in.

The following code sample illustrates how to connect to a service using the `ServiceController` class:

```
// Connect to the Server service
ServiceController srvc = new ServiceController("Server");
// Stop the service
srvc.Stop();
// Wait two seconds before starting the service
Thread.Sleep(1000);
// Start the service
srvc.Start();
```

The code then stops and resumes the service after few seconds.

TAKE NOTE*

This code sample requires `System.ServiceProcess` namespace and `System.Threading` namespace. You must add the `System.ServiceProcess` namespace manually in the Visual Studio.

CERTIFICATION READY?
Implement, install, and control a service.
USD 2.1

UNINSTALLING SERVICE

You can uninstall a service by:

- Clicking the Add/Remove Programs in the Control Panel, locating the required service, and selecting Uninstall, or
- Right clicking the program icon for the*.msi* file and selecting Uninstall.

SKILL SUMMARY

This lesson provided a clear understanding on creating and unloading application domains. An application domain is the best way to isolate applications in the .NET Framework. Presence of one or more application domains within a single process minimizes the system overheads. An application domain with a process has its specific configuration and is assigned with distinct security access levels. You can manipulate application domains by using the methods and properties of the `AppDomain` class. You can call the static `App.Domain.Unload` method to perform unloading of the application domain, which involves downloading both the domain and the assemblies within it. It is recommended to limit the rights of an application domain. For example, you can apply the principle of Defense-in-Depth to secure the application when it accesses external code. You can use the `AppDomainSetup` class to provide the CLR with configuration information for a new application domain.

You can use Windows services when there is a need to create applications that need to be running continuously without any user interactions. Windows service provides a mechanism to perform those kinds of tasks that need to run on their own without any user. It is essential to understand the process of creating, configuring, installing, managing, and controlling the service. We have various types of Windows service applications like print spooler, event logger, server, and workstation components.

For the certification examination:

- Understand the benefits of using application domains and processes of its creation along with its unloading.
- Know how to set up application domains by providing limited permissions to minimize the risk of security vulnerability.
- Know how to create, configure, install, manage, and control a service.

■ Knowledge Assessment

Matching

Match the following descriptions to the appropriate terms.

a. `ExecuteAssembly`
b. `DynamicDirectory`
c. `ExecuteAssemblyByName`
d. `CurrentDomain`
e. `SetupInformation`

_______ 1. Method that determines the assembly that runs your application domain.
_______ 2. Property that specifies application domain configuration for a particular instance.
_______ 3. Property that specifies the directory that the assembly resolver searches for dynamically created assemblies.
_______ 4. Method that runs the specified assembly.
_______ 5. Method that runs the assembly contained in the specific file.

True / False

Circle T if the statement is true or F if the statement is false.

T | F 1. You can use Web services to communicate between different application domains.

T | F 2. The flipside of working with application domains is the processwide unrestricted access.

T | F 3. You can directly access the code of external assemblies and application domains.

T | F 4. The Defense-in-Depth principle provides a single level of protection for the application domain.

T | F 5. Restricting permissions to application domain greatly reduces the risk of malicious action caused by the assembly.

Fill in the Blank

Complete the following sentences by writing the correct word or words in the blanks provided.

1. The ____________ property of the `AppDomainSetup` class gets or sets the base directory where the directory for dynamically generated files is located.
2. The ____________ property of the `AppDomainSetup` class specifies the optimization policy used to load an executable.
3. The ____________ class helps control the service from an ASP.NET Web application.
4. The ____________ property of the `ServiceProcessInstaller` component enables you to set the security context for your service application.
5. The ____________ method of the `AppDomain` class runs the code in another application domain.

Multiple Choice

Circle the letter or letters that correspond to the best answer or answers.

1. Which of the following tools can be used to configure application domains? (Choose all that apply.)
   a. Common Language Runtime
   b. Dynamic-link libraries
   c. Internet Information Services manager
   d. .NET Framework configuration
2. Which one of the following properties of the `AppDomain` class represents an integer that uniquely identifies the application domain within a process?
   a. `Int`
   b. `Id`
   c. `Num`
   d. `Di`
3. Which one of the following properties of the `AppDomainSetup` class gets or sets the name of the root directory that contains the application?
   a. `ApplicationTrust`
   b. `ApplicationName`
   c. `ApplicationBase`
   d. `DisallowApplicationBaseProbing`
4. Select the class that is used to create a service installer.
   a. `AddInstaller`
   b. `ServiceProcessInstaller`
   c. `ProcessServiceInstaller`
   d. `ServiceBaseInstaller`

5. Select the statements that are true about Windows services. (Choose all that apply)
   a. Runs in the background without affecting other logged in users.
   b. Can be paused and restarted.
   c. Starts automatically on booting the system.
   d. Can be debugged, and a Windows service application can be started from the MS Visual Studio like other applications.

Review Questions

1. To host your Web applications, you require a Web server such as IIS. Similarly, to run an ASP.NET application, you require the ASP.NET worker process to run in the background. In this case, the IIS and the worker process act as runtime hosts. What are runtime hosts and is it possible to create your own runtime hosts?
2. Windows services are programs that do not have any user interface. Instead, these programs write the output to the logs. Can you use an EXE to start a Windows service?

■ Case Scenarios

Scenario 6-1: Creating Application Domains

Your Web site hosts your online booking system for movies. The Web site is available to the users 24 × 7, so you cannot shut it down to run any background jobs. Your Web site records current bookings from users in a memory table and you want to create an assembly that accesses this data. Create a .NET program that creates an application domain, loads the assembly into the created domain, and also unloads the assembly from the domain you have loaded it to.

Scenario 6-2: Creating Windows Services

Consider that you record all the current bookings into a temporary table in your local database and transfer all the records to your centralized corporate database after every 100 bookings. To monitor the number of records in the temporary table and start the background transfer job, you want to create a Windows service. Create a service that checks the database once every minute to see if the number of bookings has reached 100.

✳ Workplace Ready

Sharing of Data by Application Domains

Many operating systems allow processes to run only one application. Each application thus has its own process space in which it is executed. Application domains are lightweight processes because they require fewer resources than normal processes.

In XYZ Chemicals Inc., a real-time .NET application monitors the temperature of a cooling system. A second real-time .NET application depends on this data to automatically initiate its thermostat control process. These two applications run in the .NET CLR in two different application domains simultaneously. For these applications to work seamlessly, their application domains must share data between them. Considering the fact that these applications have their own address space, how do you think you can make them share the data?

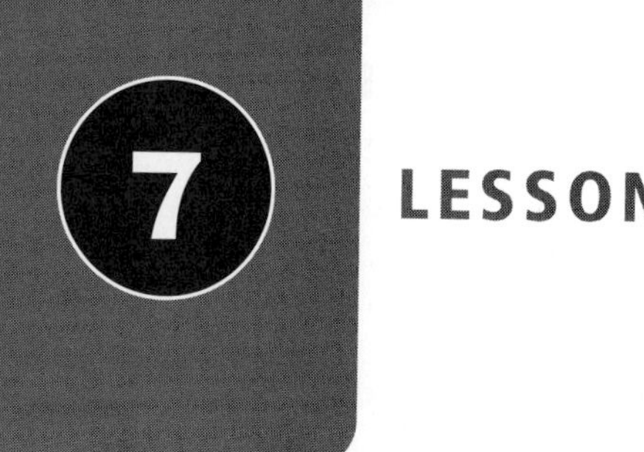

Using Threading and Reflection

OBJECTIVE DOMAIN MATRIX

Technology Skill	Objective Domain	Objective Domain Number
Create and invoke multiple threads.	Develop multi-threaded .NET Framework applications.	2.2
Handle multiple threads.	Develop multi-threaded .NET Framework applications.	2.2
Understand reflection.	Implement reflection functionality in a .NET Framework application.	6.3
Understand reflection.	Create metadata, Microsoft Intermediate Language (MSIL), and a PE file by using the System.Reflection.Emit namespace.	6.3
Work with reflection.	Implement reflection functionality in a .NET Framework application.	6.3
Work with reflection.	Create metadata, MSIL, and a PE file by using the System.Reflection.Emit namespace.	6.3

KEY TERMS

assembly
baking
dynamic assemblies
metadata
Microsoft Intermediate Language (MSIL)
modules
Multi-Threaded Apartment (MTA)
multi-threading
reflection
Single-Threaded Apartment (STA)
thread
thread-safe
type browsers

The configuration of your computer hardware, specifically the processor, determines how fast your system is compared to others. However, developers must write robust programs in a specific manner to take advantage of the processor's speed. Additionally, if an application is designed to allow multi-threading, then that application can efficiently increase the utilization of a single processor because ***multi-threading*** is a technique that allows simultaneous execution of multiple tasks within a single process. Keeping this in mind, the .NET Framework supports the multi-threading concept and allows its developers to write multi-threaded code.

Creating and Invoking Multiple Threads

THE BOTTOM LINE

Processors use threads to execute series of instructions. Therefore, a ***thread*** is a unit of execution within a process. Based on the instructions within the program, the OS creates and manages threads.

Consider threads as paths of execution. The thread carries the step-by-step instructions, while the process provides the isolation. Therefore, a single-threaded application contains just one thread of execution. However, when you need to run multiple tasks, having all tasks on a single thread causes problems. Multiple tasks may include printing a document, downloading a file, and generating a report. If the thread running these tasks required user input, you would have to wait until the method was completed. To handle this problem, you can define a thread for each task. You can simultaneously initiate multiple threads within a single process. This technique is known as multi-threading.

Understanding Thread Basics

Multi-threading, if used properly, improves the performance of your application. On the contrary, if not handled properly, multi-threading can affect the performance of the application too. Therefore, you must understand the basics of threads thoroughly to utilize multi-threading effectively.

To execute an executable, you type the executable name at the command prompt of an OS or double click the executable file. The OS then creates a process to run the executable. After this, the OS loads the executable to the memory space allocated for the process and searches for an entry point inside the executable to begin the execution. Once the OS identifies an entry point, it initiates a thread for the process. The thread then takes over and executes the code at the entry point of the executable. The thread follows the instructions in the executable from that point. This thread created at the entry point is called the main thread of the process. Depending on the code in the executable, the OS may create more threads for the process as needed.

Multi-threading improves the responsiveness and efficiency of your programs. For example, a computer having multiple processors or multiple cores within a single processor can execute multiple threads simultaneously. It is also possible for a single processor to process code from each thread, sequentially switching between the threads. However, switching between threads or processes takes up a lot of time and stresses the memory cache. To optimize the processor's potential, you can use background threads. The .NET Framework allows you to run a thread in the background, while your program continues processing; however, in some circumstances you may incur processor overheads. One such example is when a program and the background thread perform computations. In this case, they do not require any other resource because they alternately wait for the processor time. Therefore, in such cases, multi-threading is a trade-off over processor speed.

In situations where multiple threads try to access a resource at the same time, or when you may want to control the thread, such as to start, pause, resume, or abort background threads, multi-threading can become a complex process.

Threading Classes in .NET

.NET supports multi-threaded operations mainly in two ways—starting your own threads using the `ThreadStart` delegate or using the `ThreadPool` class.

Typically, you create a thread manually using the `ThreadStart` delegate for a voluminous task. However, you can use the `ThreadPool` class when the task is short.

WORKING WITH THREADS

The Thread class is in the System.Threading namespace. The Thread class provides methods and properties that you can use to create and control threads. You can set a sequence to run the threads. You can also find the status of the currently active threads.

Table 7-1 lists several of the methods available in the Thread class.

Table 7-1

Methods of the Thread class

METHOD	DESCRIPTION
Start	Sets the schedule for execution of the thread.
Abort	Throws a ThreadAbortException that signifies that the thread is being terminated.
GetDomain	Specifies the domain in which the current thread is running.
GetData	Retrieves specific information from portions of the current thread.
GetType	Specifies the type of the current instance of the thread.
Join	Blocks all threads until the current thread is terminated.
SetData	Defines the data in a specific portion of the current thread.
Sleep	Blocks the current thread for a specific amount of time, typically a few milliseconds.
ResetAbort	Cancels an abort request for a current thread.

Table 7-2 lists several of the properties provided by the Thread class.

Table 7-2

Properties of the Thread class

PROPERTY	DESCRIPTION
Name	Specifies a name for the thread.
Priority	Prioritizes thread scheduling.
CurrentThread	Returns the currently active thread.
IsAlive	Returns the status of the current thread.
IsBackground	Specifies whether a thread is a background thread.
IsThreadPoolThread	Specifies whether a thread is part of the managed thread pool.

EXPLORING THE THREADSTATE ENUMERATION

You can use the ThreadState enumeration to specify the execution states of a thread, such as Started, Unstarted, or Aborted. Threads are initially in an Unstarted state. However, the unmanaged external threads entering the managed .NET environment will be already in the Running state. You can set an Unstarted thread to a state of running, using the Start method. Some threads that have been discarded are in the Aborted state.

TAKE NOTE*

A single thread can be in multiple states at the same time. For example, a thread can be in Running and Background states at the same time. However, a thread cannot be in both the Aborted and Unstarted state at the same time. The Aborted state denotes that the thread is entering the Stopped state. The Unstarted started state represents a thread that is yet to be started, and the Thread.Start method has not been invoked on the thread.

Table 7-3 lists the members of the ThreadState enumeration.

Table 7-3
Members of the ThreadState enumeration

MEMBER	DESCRIPTION
Running	The thread is up and not blocked, and there is no pending ThreadAbortException.
StopRequested	The thread is being requested to stop. Note that this member is for internal use only.
SuspendRequested	The thread is being requested to suspend.
Background	The thread is running in the background
Unstarted	The Thread.Start method has not been called on the thread.
Stopped	The thread has been stopped.
WaitSleepJoin	The thread is blocked.
Suspended	The thread is suspended.
AbortRequested	The Thread.Abort method has been invoked on the thread, however the thread has not yet received the ThreadAbortException, which will attempt to terminate it.
Aborted	The thread is now dead; however, its state has not yet been changed to Stopped.

Figure 7-1 depicts the states that a single thread can be in when you call the various methods on that thread. The dotted boundary lines indicate temporary thread states that occur when the thread waits for its processing turn.

Figure 7-1
ThreadStates state diagram

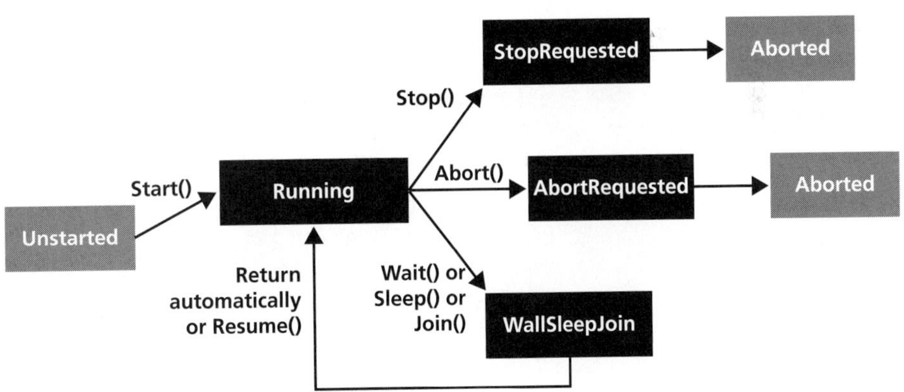

EXPLORING THREADS WITHIN A THREAD POOL

In general, threads in a ThreadPool class are not huge processes. They have a short lifespan.

ThreadPool class enables you to create a pool of threads to post work items and perform asynchronous I/O operations. Work items are a set of background tasks, which does not require you to wait for its completion. Instead, you can continue using your application. It is easy to manage threads in a thread pool. To manipulate threads within a thread pool, you can use several methods provided in the ThreadPool class, as listed in Table 7-4.

Table 7-4

Methods of the ThreadPool class

Method	Description
GetAvailableThreads	Determines the number of available threads, including the currently active thread.
GetMaxThreads	Determines the maximum number of active threads in a thread pool. Any further requests are queued until the thread pool threads become available.
GetMinThreads	Determines the number of idle threads.
QueueUserWorkItem	Queues a thread for execution.
SetMaxThreads	Determines how many requests the thread pool can manage. If the request limit is reached, the requests are queued until the thread pool thread is available.
SetMinThreads	Specifies the number of idle threads the thread pool can maintain.

Creating and Using Threads

.NET Framework provides several methods to manipulate threads. You can use the ThreadStart object to create a thread.

The following code displays a simple multi-threading program. This program creates two different threads that count numbers at a different speed:

```
using System;
using System.Threading;
public class SampleThread
{
   static void Main()
   {
      // Create a thread and start it
       ThreadStart myjob = new ThreadStart(SeparateThread);
      Thread thread1 = new Thread(myjob);
      thread1.Start();

      // Count 0 to 2 once in two seconds
      for (int i = 0; i < 3; i++)
   {
      Console.WriteLine ("First thread: {0}", i);
      // Sleep for 2000ms
      Thread.Sleep(2000);
   }
}

static void SeparateThread()
{
   // Count 0 to 4 once a second
   for (int i = 0; i < 5; i++)
   {
      Console.WriteLine ("Separate thread: {0}", i);
      // Sleep for 1000ms
      Thread.Sleep(1000);
   }
  }
}
```

In this code, the `Sleep` method sets a different time period for the main and the other thread. No other thread can be running when a thread is ready to resume after a sleep spell. This affects the output. Therefore, the results of the execution are different each time.

This code uses the `ThreadStart` class to create and start a thread. Alternatively, you can use the `ThreadPool` class to create and start a thread. In the first method, you create the thread manually, and in the second method, you create a thread and queue it for execution. Therefore, for a long-running task, you must use the manual thread creation process, and when you have many small tasks, you can use the `ThreadPool` object to create thread.

TAKE NOTE*

The threads provided by the `ThreadPool` class are worker threads that run in the background. Therefore, their `IsBackground` property is true. In addition, the thread provided by the `ThreadPool` class will not keep your application running after all foreground threads have exited.

MANAGING THREADS IN A THREAD POOL

You can use the methods and properties in the `ThreadPool` class to schedule a thread that runs in the background. The following code shows how a console application uses the `QueueUserWorkItem` method in the `System.Threading.ThreadPool` class. The console application requests a thread in the thread pool to execute the `PerformProc` method, through the `QueueUserWorkItem` method. The `QueueUserWorkItem` method in turn queues the `PerformProc` method for execution. Whenever a thread in the thread pool is available, the `PerformProc` method executes:

```
static void Main(string[] args)
{
    // Use a pool to queue the task
    ThreadPool.QueueUserWorkItem(PerformProc);
    Console.WriteLine("Main thread works and then sleeps.");
    Thread.Sleep(2000);
}
// Procedure to perform the task
static void PerformProc(Object stateInfo)
{
    Console.WriteLine("Task inside the pool.");
}
```

PASSING PARAMETERS TO THREADS

Another way of scheduling a background method is to pass an object to the method that you want to run in the background. To achieve this, you can use the overloaded `ThreadPool.QueueUserWorkItem` method that accepts a parameter.

The following code shows how to pass an object to a thread:

```
static void Main(string[] args)
{
    string thrdstate = "Thread State!";
    ThreadPool.QueueUserWorkItem(PerformProc, thrdstate);
    Console.WriteLine ("Main thread works and then sleeps.");
    Thread.Sleep(2000);
}
static void PerformProc(Object stateInfo)
{
    string thrdstate = (string)stateInfo;
    Console.WriteLine("Task inside the pool: " + thrdstate);
}
```

CREATING MULTIPLE THREADS

When you want to create multiple threads, you can make multiple calls to the `PerformProc` method as shown:

```
ThreadPool.QueueUserWorkItem(PerformProc,"First Thread");
ThreadPool.QueueUserWorkItem(PerformProc,"Second Thread");
ThreadPool.QueueUserWorkItem(PerformProc,"Third Thread");
ThreadPool.QueueUserWorkItem(PerformProc,"Fourth Thread");
```

TAKE NOTE* A thread pool maintains a queue of threads. The `ThreadPool.QueueUserWorkItem` allocates work to the first available thread so that the specific thread starts working. This means that the work is dequeued by threads in FIFO order. However, due to the sleep method, the result of the execution of the above code may vary at different times. Refer to the section on Creating and Using Threads in this lesson.

TAKE NOTE* The thread pool can typically hold 250 threads at a time for each available processor. If you plan to have more than 250 background threads running simultaneously, you can modify this default value by using the `ThreadPool.SetMaxThreads` method.

CHECKING THE NUMBER OF AVAILABLE THREADS

At times, you may want to know the number of available threads, including the currently active thread. You can determine the number of available threads by using the `ThreadPool.GetAvailableThreads` method.

The following code uses the `GetAvailableThreads` method to evaluate the number of worker threads that can be started:

```
int threadJobs;
int portThreads;
ThreadPool.GetAvailableThreads(out threadJobs, out portThreads);
Console.WriteLine("The number of available threads: " + threadJobs);
Console.WriteLine("The number of available completion port threads: "
+ portThreads);
```

TAKE NOTE* The `PortThreads` parameter in the example returns the number of asynchronous I/O threads that can be initiated.

DIFFERENTIATING BACKGROUND AND FOREGROUND THREADS

The significant difference between a thread running in the foreground from that running in a background is that the background thread cannot stop a process from terminating. However, when all the foreground threads for a process have been terminated, the CLR ends the process. All background threads too are terminated, irrespective of whether the thread is completely executed or not.

CERTIFICATION READY? Develop multi-threaded .NET Framework applications. USD 2.2

The following code syntax shows a background thread:

```
Thread bgThread = new Thread(new ThreadStart(SampleThread.
SeparateThread));
bgThread.Name = "BGThread";
bgThread.IsBackground = true;
bgThread.Start();
```

Handling Multiple Threads

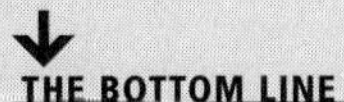

In the current scenario, it is essential to use more than one thread to increase user responsiveness and to process the data required to perform the job simultaneously. On a computer with a single processor, multiple threads can produce this result by availing the short time durations that occur in between user events to process the data in the background. For example, a user can edit a spreadsheet, and at the same time, another thread recalculates other parts of the spreadsheet within the same application.

Threading and Application Design

Consider a multi-threaded application running on a single processor. If you run the same multi-threaded application on a computer with more than one processor, then the application can increase user satisfaction significantly even without any modifications to the code. This is possible only if you use multiple threads in your application.

You can use multiple threads for a single application domain to perform the following tasks:

- Communicate over a network to a Web server and to a database.
- Perform operations that need more time.
- Differentiate tasks of varying priority. For example, a high-priority thread manages time-critical tasks while the low-priority thread performs other tasks.
- Allow the user interface to be responsive when background tasks are being performed during their allocated time.

You can use the `ThreadPool` class to easily handle multiple threads for comparatively shorter tasks that do not have a specific execution schedule and that will not block other threads. Since the `ThreadPool` class queues threads for execution, the `ThreadPool` class cannot handle threads with specific execution schedules. In this case, you must create your own thread. In addition, you can create your own threads, if you need to:

- Set a priority for a task.
- Place threads in a ***Single-Threaded Apartment (STA)***; Objects reside in apartments that can contain one or more threads. STA is a threading model in which each thread lives in its own apartment and all the objects created on that thread live in that apartment.
- Use the `ThreadPool` class to place threads in a multi-threaded apartment; In the ***Multi-Threaded Apartment (MTA)*** model, all the threads created in a process reside in a single apartment.
- Associate a stable identity with the thread. For example, you should use a dedicated thread to abandon that thread, suspend it, or locate it by name.
- Run background threads that interact with the user interface.

TAKE NOTE*

The .NET Framework provides a `BackgroundWorker` component that communicates through events with cross-thread marshaling to the user-interface thread.

You can also create your own threads if you have a task that might run for longer time and may block other tasks.

Managing Threads

When creating applications with multiple threads, you need to create and manage these threads efficiently. This gains control over the thread and, thus, improves its performance.

You can use the `Thread.Create` method to create a thread for effective control. If you use the `ThreadPool.QueueUserWorkItem` method to create a thread, then you need not explicitly start or stop the thread. The thread automatically ends when the method execution stops.

You can perform various operations on a thread by using a `Thread object.` Table 7-5 displays the methods of the `Thread` class, and code samples indicating the corresponding list of operations, which you can perform using the methods.

Table 7-5

Methods of the `Thread` object and their operational features

METHOD	CODE SAMPLE

`Start`	• You can use the class name with the method name to start a thread using a static method, as shown:
	`Thread sampThread = new Thread(new ThreadStart(SampleThread.SeparateThread));`
	`sampThread.Start();`
	• You can use the instance variable instead of the class name, `SampleThread,` to start a thread using an instance method.
	`SampleThread mythread = new SampleThread();`
	`Thread sampThread = new Thread(mythread.SeparateThread);`
	`sampThread.Start();`

`Join`	• You can use the following code to wait for the foreground thread to terminate: `sampThread.Join();` • You can use the `Join` method to ensure the termination of a thread. The caller blocks the thread indefinitely if it does not terminate. • If the thread terminates before calling the `Join` method, this method returns immediately. • This method also changes the state of the calling thread to include the `WaitSleepJoin` state. • You cannot invoke this method on a thread that is in the `Unstarted` state.
`Sleep`	• You can use the following code to block the thread for the specified time: `sampThread.Sleep(Int32 Time);` • Time is the number of milliseconds for which the thread is blocked. • You can specify zero (0) or Infinite to indicate that this thread should be suspended to allow the execution of other waiting threads or to block the thread indefinitely respectively.
`Abort`	• You can use the following code to abort the thread: `sampThread.Abort();` • You must catch the `ThreadAbortException` for your code to respond to the termination of the thread. To finish, you can use the Finally statement to close all the resources.

X REF

You can refer to the section "Working with Threads" under the topic "Threading Classes in .NET" in the lesson "Creating and Invoking Multiple Threads" to learn more about the methods of the `Thread` class.

Exploring Exceptions in Managed Threads

Generally, the Common Language Runtime (CLR) in the .NET Framework allows most of the code to continue working in case of unhandled exceptions in threads. In most cases, unhandled exceptions may result in the termination the application.

The CLR provides certain defensive techniques to manage some of the unhandled exceptions that control the flow of a program. These include:

- A `ThreadAbortException`, thrown in a thread, on calling the `Abort` method.
- An `AppDomainUnloadedException`, thrown in a thread on unloading the application domain in which the thread is executing.
- An internal exception thrown to terminate the thread.

TAKE NOTE*

The runtime can throw an unhandled exception before any managed code tries to install an exception handler. If the managed code cannot handle such an exception, the exception proceeds normally.

Following are the consequences that you may have to deal with if you did not handle the previously mentioned exceptions:

- If any of these exceptions are unhandled in threads that are created by the CLR, then, the exception terminates the thread, but the CLR does not allow the exception to proceed further.
- If these exceptions are unhandled in the main thread, or in threads that entered the runtime from unmanaged code, they continue normally and terminate the application.

EXPOSING THREADING PROBLEMS DURING DEVELOPMENT

Many programming problems cannot be detected when threads stop without terminating the applications. You may face these problems especially with services and other applications that run beyond the stipulated time.

Thread failure results in a gradual degradation of the program state. For example, an application may perform poorly or may hang. Permitting unhandled exceptions in threads to proceed naturally, until the operating system terminates the program, reveals such problems during development and testing. Error reports on program terminations support debugging.

Synchronizing Data for Multi-Threading

When you use multi-threading, you must synchronize the use of shared resources to create a defect-free application.

It is essential to synchronize the calls made by multiple threads with the properties and methods of an object. If this synchronization is not done properly, then, one thread can interrupt the task of another thread and this leaves the object in an invalid state. You can refer to a class whose members are protected from such interruptions as ***thread-safe***.

Table 7-6 displays the various strategies followed by the Common Language Infrastructure to synchronize access to instance and static members of a class.

Table 7-6

Synchronization strategies of the Common Language Infrastructure

STRATEGY	DESCRIPTION
Synchronizing code regions only	Use the `Monitor` class or compiler support for this class to synchronize only the code block that requires it, thus, improving performance.
Synchronizing manually	Use the synchronization objects provided by the .NET Framework class library, such as `Monitor` or `Mutex` object to perform manual synchronization.
Synchronizing contexts automatically	Use the `SynchronizationAttribute` to enable simple, automatic synchronization for `ContextBoundObject` objects.
Synchronizing using the `Synchronized` property	Use the `Synchronized` property provided by certain classes, such as `HashTable` and `Queue` to return a thread-safe wrapper for an instance of the class.

EXPLORING SYNCHRONIZATION OF THREADS

Consider a scenario where two or more threads need to access a shared resource at the same time. Under such a condition, the system needs a synchronization mechanism to ensure that only one thread at a time uses the resource. Mutex is a synchronization primitive that grants exclusive access to only one thread to use the shared resource. If a thread acquires a Mutex, the second thread that wants to acquire that Mutex remains suspended until the first thread releases the Mutex.

The following code samples explain the various operations of the Mutex.

You can use the following code to create a Mutex:

```
// Create a new Mutex that is not associated with any thread.
private static Mutex sampleMtx = new Mutex();
```

You can use the WaitOne method to request ownership of a Mutex. The thread that owns a Mutex can request the same Mutex in repeated calls to the WaitOne method without blocking its execution, as shown in the following code:

> **TAKE NOTE***
> Starting from version 2.0 of the .NET Framework, an AbandonedMutexException is thrown in the next thread that acquires the abandoned Mutex. The earlier versions did not include any such exceptions.

```
// Code to request ownership to a mutex.
sampleMtx.WaitOne();
```

To release ownership of the Mutex, the thread must call the ReleaseMutex method for the same number of times as the thread called the WaitOne method to request ownership of the Mutex. The Mutex class enforces thread identity to release the Mutex only by the thread that acquired it:

```
// Release the Mutex.
sampleMtx.ReleaseMutex();
```

If a thread terminates while owning a Mutex, the Mutex is said to be abandoned. The state of the Mutex is set to signaled and the next thread in the queue gets its ownership.

ANALYZING THE TYPES OF MUTEXES

There are two types of mutexes:

- Unnamed or local mutex
- Named system mutex

Table 7-7 displays the features of these two types of mutexes.

Table 7-7

Features of the Mutex types

TYPE	FEATURES
Local or unnamed mutex	• Exists only within your process. • Any thread in your process that has a reference to the Mutex object, representing the mutex, can use it. • Each unnamed Mutex object represents a separate local mutex.
Named system mutex	• Seen throughout the operating system. • Synchronizes the activities of processes. • You can create a Mutex object that represents a named system mutex by using a constructor that accepts a name. • The operating system object can either be created at the same time or can exist before the creation of the Mutex object. • You can create multiple Mutex objects that represent the same named system. You can use the OpenExisting method to open an existing named system mutex.

MONITORING THE THREADS

The Monitor class controls access to objects by granting a lock for an object to a single thread. An object lock enables you to restrict access to a code block, usually referred to as a critical section. No other thread, except the thread that owns the lock for an object, can acquire its lock. You can also use the Monitor class to ensure that no other thread is allowed to access a section of the application code that the lock owner is executing. However, another thread can execute the code using a different locked object.

Following are the features of the Monitor class:

- The class associates with an object on demand.
- The class is unbound. This implies that you can call it directly from any context.
- You cannot create an instance of the Monitor class.

SYNCHRONIZING DATA USING MONITORS

Monitor objects are able to synchronize access to a region of the code by accepting and releasing a lock on a specific object by using methods, such as Monitor.Enter, Monitor.TryEnter, and Monitor.Exit. After placing a lock on a code region, you can use the following methods:

- The Monitor.Wait method releases the lock if it is held and waits to be notified. On notifying, it returns and obtains the lock again.
- The Monitor.Pulse and the Monitor.PulseAll methods signal for the next thread in the wait queue to proceed.

TAKE NOTE*

The C# lock statement uses the Monitor.Enter and the Monitor.Exit methods to accept the lock and release it respectively. The advantage of using the language statements is that the Try statement includes all the contents in the lock or SyncLock block. In addition, the Try statement has a Finally block to assure the release of the lock.

Every synchronized object includes the following information:

- A reference to the thread that currently holds the lock.
- A reference to a ready queue, which contains the threads that are ready to obtain the lock.
- A reference to a waiting queue, which contains the threads that are waiting for notification of a change in the state of the locked object.

SYNCHRONIZING VALUE TYPES

The Monitor locks reference type objects but does not reference value types. When you pass a value type to Enter and Exit, it boxes separately for each call. Each call creates a separate object and, therefore, Enter never blocks. The code it is allegedly protecting does not actually synchronize. Moreover, the object passed to Exit differs from the object that is passed to Enter, so Monitor throws SynchronizationLockException and displays the message, "Object synchronization method was called from an unsynchronized block of code."

```
private int s;
// The next line of code creates a generic object containing the
value of s each time the code is executed, so that Enter never
blocks.
Monitor.Enter(s);
try
{
   // Code that the monitor protects.
}
```

```
finally
{
    // You must use Finally to ensure that you exit the Monitor.
    // The following line of code creates another object containing
    // the value of s, and throws SynchronizationLockException
    // because the two objects do not match.
    Monitor.Exit(s);
}
```

Understanding Managed Thread States

WARNING You must use ThreadState only in a few debugging scenarios. You should not use ThreadState in your code to synchronize the activities of threads.

At any given time, a thread can be in multiple states. The thread can transform from its current state to a new state based on the action performed on it.

The ThreadState property of a thread provides a bit mask that specifies its current state. A thread is always in either of the possible states in the ThreadState enumeration.

When you create a managed thread, it is in the Unstarted state. The thread remains in the same state until the operating system moves it into the Started state. You can call Start so that the operating system to know that the thread can be started. This does not affect the state of the thread.

TAKE NOTE* If a thread leaves the Unstarted state as an outcome of calling Start, it can never return to its original (Unstarted) state. In addition, a thread can never leave the Stopped state.

Unmanaged threads that enter the managed environment are already in the Started state. In the Started state, the thread can perform various actions to change its current state into a new state. Table 7-8 lists these actions and the resultant states.

Table 7-8

Actions of the thread to change the current state

MEMBER INVOLVED	ACTION	RESULTANT STATE
The specific thread	Responds to the Thread.Start request and begins running	Running
	Calls Thread.Sleep	WaitSleepJoin
	Calls Monitor.Wait on another object	WaitSleepJoin
	Calls Thread.Join on another thread	WaitSleepJoin
	Responds to a Thread.Suspend request	Suspended
	Responds to a Thread.Abort request	Aborted
Another thread	Calls Thread.Start	No change
	Calls Thread.Suspend	SuspendRequested
	Calls Thread.Resume	Running
	Calls Thread.Abort	AbortRequested

Generally, threads are in more than one state at the same time. For example, if you call the Monitor.Wait method to block a thread and another thread calls the Abort method on that same thread, then this thread will be in both the WaitSleepJoin and the AbortRequested states simultaneously. In such a case, the thread receives the ThreadAbortException immediately after it returns from the call to Wait or gets interrupted.

The `Running` state has zero (0) value and therefore you cannot perform a bit test to determine this state. In this code, `state` indicates one of the `ThreadState` enumeration values that specify the state of the current thread:

CERTIFICATION READY?
Develop multi-threaded .NET Framework applications.
USD 2.2

```
// To find if the thread is in Running state
if ((state & (Unstarted | Stopped)) = 0)
```

MORE INFORMATION
You can refer to the "Threading Tutorial" from the MSDN library for further reading and more examples on threading.

Understanding Reflection

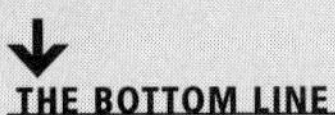

Users expect applications to have extended capabilities. If multi-threading is one technique to improve an application's performance, then ***reflection*** is another that you can use for dynamic type identification. Reflection allows you to obtain information about loaded assemblies and to create assemblies dynamically. Imagine that you are creating an application that must be capable of using third-party tools and assemblies at runtime and it must also be capable of retrieving class information at runtime. Reflection allows you to expose and retrieve class information for this purpose.

.NET offers the `System.Reflection` namespace to support reflection. The methods and properties within the `System.Reflection` namespace help you retrieve information about the assemblies. You can also use the methods to retrieve the ***modules***, members, and parameters within the ***assembly***. You can also access ***metadata*** information of the assembly.

Introducing Reflection

Reflection offers classes to handle assemblies, modules, and related types.

The primary task of the CLR loader is to manage application domains. During compilation, the CLR loads each assembly for the corresponding application domain. It also defines the memory layout of the type hierarchy within each assembly, such as members within types, types within modules, and modules within assemblies.

The process of reflection involves using objects to encapsulate assemblies, modules, and types. At runtime, you can use reflection to create an instance of a type and bind it to an existing object. You can also retrieve the type of an existing object and use the type's methods and properties. Table 7-9 lists the use of some of the reflection classes.

Table 7-9
Uses of reflection classes

Class	Uses
`Assembly`	Defines and loads assemblies and modules stored in the manifest files of the assemblies. It retrieves a type and creates an instance of the type.
`Module`	Learn about the assembly and associated classes for the specific module. Retrieves the global and non-global methods defined on the module.
`ConstructorInfo`	Learn about constructors, such as name, parameters, and access modifier constructors. It uses the `GetConstructor` or `GetConstructors` method of a type to invoke a specific constructor.

Table 7-9 (continued)

CLASS	USES
`MethodInfo`	Learn about the name, return type, parameters, and access modifiers, such as public or private. It also retrieves implementation details of a method, whether abstract or virtual. It uses the `GetMethod` or `GetMethods` method of a `Type` to invoke a method.
`FieldInfo`	Learn about a field, such as name and access modifiers, such as private or public. It determines if the field is a static field. It can also be used to get and set values for a field.
`EventInfo`	Learn about an event, such as the event name, event-handler datatype, custom attributes, declaring type, and the reflected type of an event. It also contains information to add or remove event handlers.
`PropertyInfo`	Learn about a property, such as property name, datatype, declaring type, and reflected type. It also determines whether the property is read-only or writable. It can be used to get and set values for a property.
`ParameterInfo`	Learn about a parameter, such as name and datatype. It also determines if the parameter is assigned as an input or an output. It also determines the placeholder of a parameter in a method syntax.

To manage assemblies, you can use the classes provided in the `System.Reflection.Emit` namespace. These classes can be used to build types at runtime.

Reflection is used to create ***type browsers***. The type browsers help select types and view detailed information about the type you chose. Some programming languages, such as Jscript, use reflections to construct symbol tables.

The `System.Runtime.Serialization` namespace uses reflection to access data and identify the fields. Reflection works indirectly with the classes within the `System.Runtime.Remoting` namespace through the process of serialization.

Understanding Assemblies

Assemblies form the basic infrastructure of .NET Framework applications, allowing the runtime to understand the contents of an application such as its types and resources. Additionally, an assembly makes the deployment of applications easier and enables the runtime to solve versioning problems, which may arise through component-based applications.

During runtime, the CLR looks up the assemblies to execute the code in the correct manner. The general contents of an assembly include:

- **Assembly information.** Includes a manifest file—a metadata—that provides information such as assembly name, strong name, version, and culture information.
- **Type information.** Includes information about the type, such as classes, methods, properties, and constructors associated with the assembly. This also includes parameter information.
- **Code.** Includes the actual code in ***Microsoft Intermediate Language (MSIL)***. During runtime, the CLR converts MSIL into machine code.
- **Resource information.** Includes objects, such as strings, files, and images used in the code.

You can bundle all these contents in a single-file assembly or in a multi-file assembly. If you use a multi-file approach, then you can bundle the assembly manifest, frequently accessed type information, and code in the main assembly file. Alternatively, you can bundle infrequently used types in a separate file called modules, so that it can be downloaded only when necessary. Additionally, you can even move the resources information to a different file that is accessible when required. Figures 7-2 and 7-3 display the contents of a single and multiple file assembly, respectively.

Figure 7-3 represents a multi-file assembly. The assembly manifest that describes the relationship between elements in the assembly, the type metadata, code, and resources are placed in the main assembly file. Additionally, the less frequently used type metadata is placed as a separate module and a large resource file that can be downloaded as needed is placed in its source file. Note that the .NET Framework downloads a file only when a reference is made for accessing it. Therefore, by keeping the rarely accessed code in separate files, you can optimize the code download.

Figure 7-2

Single file assembly

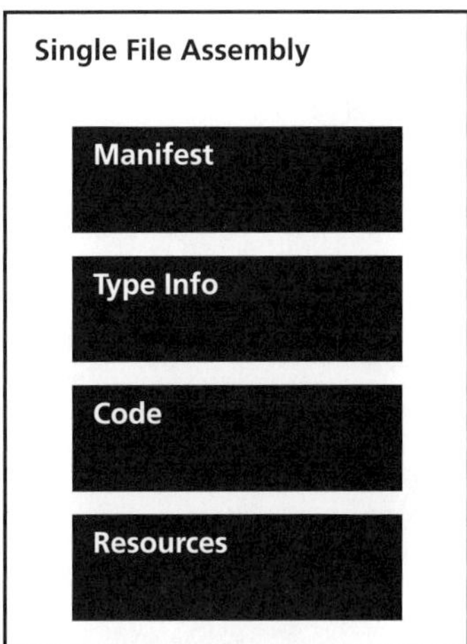

Figure 7-3

Multi-file assembly

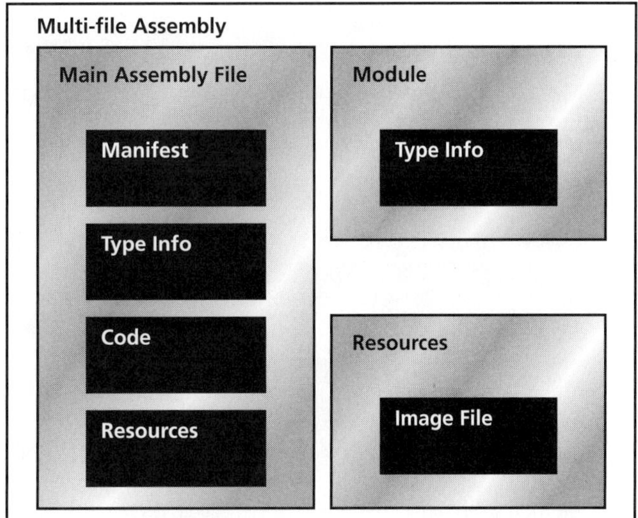

TAKE NOTE*

The assembly manifest links the files that make up a multiple file assembly. Additionally, the CLR manages these files as a single unit.

Introducing Assembly Class

The `Assembly` class represents an assembly.

You can use the `Assembly` class to load assemblies and explore the metadata or types available within assemblies. Additionally, the `Assembly` class also enables you to create objects of the types present in the assembly. The methods and properties within the `Assembly` class can be used to manage assemblies in an application domain. Table 7-10 lists several of the methods of the `Assembly` class.

Table 7-10

Methods of the `Assembly` class

METHOD	TYPE	DESCRIPTION
`CreateInstance`	Method overload	Locates a specific type from an assembly. After it locates the type, it uses the system activator to create an instance of the specific type.
`GetAssembly`	Method	Determines the associated assembly to which a current class belongs.
`GetCallingAssembly`	Method	Determines the associated assembly to which the currently executing method belongs.
`GetCustomAttributes`	Method overload	Retrieves custom attributes for a specific assembly.
`GetEntryAssembly`	Method	Determines the executable process within the application domain.
`GetExecutingAssembly`	Method	Determines the associated assembly that contains the currently executable code.
`GetExportedTypes`	Method	Determines the public types defined in the assembly.
`GetFile`	Method	Determines the `FileStream` for the specified file.
`GetFiles`	Method overload	Determines the files in the file table of an assembly manifest.
`GetLoadedModules`	Method overload	Determines the loaded modules that are part of a specific assembly.
`GetModule`	Method	Retrieves the specified module in an assembly.
`GetModules`	Method overload	Retrieves all the modules that are part of a specific assembly.
`GetName`	Method overload	Retrieves an `AssemblyName`.
`GetReferencedAssemblies`	Method	Retrieves the `AssemblyName` objects for all the assemblies referenced by an assembly.
`GetSateliteAssembly`	Method overload	Retrieves the satellite assembly.
`GetType`	Method overload	Retrieves the `Type` object that represents a specified type.
`GetTypes`	Method	Retrieves the types defined in a specific assembly.
`IsDefined`	Method	Determines if a specified attribute has been applied to the assembly.
`Load`	Method overload	Loads an assembly.
`LoadFile`	Method overload	Loads the contents of an assembly file.
`LoadFrom`	Method overload	Loads an assembly.
`LoadModule`	Method overload	Loads the module associated with the assembly.
`LoadWithPartialName`	Method overload	Retrieves an assembly from the application directory or from the global assembly cache by using a partial name.
`MemberwiseClone`	Method	Creates a shallow copy of the current object.
`ReflectionOnlyLoad`	Method overload	Loads an assembly in a reflection-only context. You can review the assembly content but cannot execute it.
`ReflectionOnlyLoadFrom`	Method	Loads an assembly into the reflection-only context, provided the path is known.

Table 7-11 lists several of the properties of the `Assembly` class.

Table 7-11
Properties of the `Assembly` class

PROPERTY	DESCRIPTION
`CodeBase`	Retrieves the location of the assembly as specified, such as the `AssemblyName` object.
`EntryPoint`	Retrieves the entry point of a specific assembly.
`EscapedCodeBase`	Retrieves the URL. It also includes escape characters that represents codebase.
`Evidence`	Retrieves the evidence for an assembly.
`FullName`	Retrieves the display name of an assembly.
`GlobalAssemblyCache`	Retrieves information about whether or not the assembly was loaded from the global assembly cache.
`Location`	Retrieves the path or UNC location of the loaded file that contains the manifest.
`ReflectionOnly`	Retrieves a Boolean value indicating whether this assembly was loaded into the reflection-only context. *Note:* In this context, the assembly can only be examined but cannot be executed.

Introducing Module Class

A module is a portable executable file, generally a .dll or an application.exe file that contains one or more classes or interfaces.

A single module can contain several namespaces and multiple modules may provide information about a single namespace. One or more modules combined and deployed as unit constitute an assembly.

Table 7-12 lists the methods of the `Module` class.

Table 7-12
Methods of the `Module` class

METHOD	TYPE	DESCRIPTION
`GetCustomAttributes`	Method overload	Used to return custom attributes.
`GetFields`	Method overload	Returns the global fields defined in the module.
`GetField`	Method overload	Returns a specified field.
`GetMethod`	Method overload	Returns a method having the specified criteria.
`GetMethods`	Method overload	Returns the global methods defined in the module.
`GetPEKind`	Method	Retrieves a pair of values indicating the nature of the code in a module and the platform targeted by the module.
`GetType`	Method overload	Returns a specified type.
`GetTypes`	Method	Returns all the types defined within a module.
`IsDefined`	Method	Determines if the specified attribute `Type` is defined within a module.
`IsResource`	Method	Retrieves a value that specifies whether or not the object is a resource.

Table 7-13 lists the properties of the Module class.

Table 7-13

Properties of the Module class

PROPERTY	DESCRIPTION
Assembly	Retrieves the appropriate assembly for an instance of a specific module.
FullyQualifiedName	Retrieves a string representing the fully qualified name. It also returns a path to this module.
Name	Retrieves a string value containing only the name of the module without the path.
ScopeName	Retrieves a string value that is the name of the module.

Introducing Type Class

The Type class represents type declarations.

Type declarations include class types, interface types, array types, value types, enumeration types, type parameters, generic type definitions, and open or closed constructed generic types.

Table 7-14 lists the methods of the Type class.

Table 7-14

Methods of the Type class

METHOD	TYPE	DESCRIPTION
GetConstructors	Method overload	Retrieves the constructors of the current Type.
GetDefaultMembers	Method	Looks up the members associated with the current Type whose DefaultMemberAttribute is set.
GetInterface	Method overload	Retrieves a specific interface implemented or inherited by the current Type.
GetInterfaces	Method overload	When overridden in a derived class, gets all the interfaces implemented or inherited by the current Type.
GetMember	Method overload	Retrieves the specified members of the current Type.
GetMembers	Method overload	Retrieves the member elements, such as properties, methods, fields, and events of the current Type.
GetMethod	Method overload	Retrieves the specified members of the current Type.
GetMethods	Method overload	Retrieves the methods of the current Type.
GetNestedType	Method overload	Retrieves the specific type nested within the current Type.
GetNestedTypes	Method overload	Retrieves the types nested within the current Type.
GetProperties	Method overload	Retrieves the properties of the current Type.
GetProperty	Method overload	Gets a specific property of the current Type.
GetType	Method overload	Retrieves the Type object that represents a specified type.
GetTypeArray	Method	Retrieves the types of the objects in a specified array.
GetTypeCode	Method	Retrieves the underlying type code of the specified Type.
IsDefined	Method	When overridden in a derived class, indicates whether one or more instance of attribute Type is applied to this member. This method is inherited from MemberInfo.

Table 7-15 lists the properties of the Type Class.

Table 7-15

Properties of the Type class

PROPERTY	DESCRIPTION
Assembly	Retrieves the associated assembly that contains the type declaration. In case of generic types, this property returns the assembly that contains the generic types.
AssemblyQualifiedName	Retrieves the associated assembly qualified name of a specific **Type**. It includes the name of the assembly from which the type was loaded.
Attributes	Returns the attributes associated with a specific type.
BaseTypes	Returns the parent type from which the current **Type** inherits.
FullName	Returns the fully qualified name of a specific type. It includes the namespace of the type.
GUID	Retrieves the associated GUID for a type.
IsArray	Determines if the type is an array.
IsClass	Determines if the type is a class.
IsEnum	Determines if the type is an enumeration.
IsGenericType	Determines if the type is a generic type.
IsInterface	Determines if the type is an interface.
IsNested	Determines if the type definition is nested within another type's definition.
IsNestedAssembly	Determines if the type is nested and is available to members of its own assembly.
IsNestedPulic	Determines if the type is declared as public and if it is nested.
IsNotPublic	Determines if the type is not declared as public.
IsPointer	Determines if the type is a pointer type.
IsPrimitive	Determines if the type is a primitive type.
IsPublic	Determines if the type is declared as public.
IsSealed	Determines if the type is sealed.
IsSerializable	Determines if the type is serializable.
IsValueType	Determines if the type is a value type.
IsVisible	Determines if the type is available to code outside its own assembly.
Module	Returns the *.dll* module where the current type is defined.
Name	Is inherited from the **MemberInfo** class and returns the name of the current member.
Namespace	Returns the namespace of the type.

CERTIFICATION READY?
Implement reflection functionality in a .NET Framework application, and create metadata, Microsoft Intermediate Language (MSIL), and a PE file by using the System.Reflection.Emit namespace.
USD 6.3

Working with Reflection

THE BOTTOM LINE

Reflection capabilities in .NET applications involve generating and working with ***dynamic assemblies*** that you can create during runtime. Each assembly's type hierarchy includes assemblies that contain modules, modules that have types, and types that in turn may contain various members. For this purpose, the .NET Framework offers the `System.Reflection.Emit` namespace that provides classes and methods to manage dynamic assemblies. You are most likely dealing with reflection capabilities if you are designing a search engine or a compiler tool. You can use reflection to create dynamic assemblies when you are creating a search engine or a compiler of your own.

A dynamic assembly runs directly from memory. You can store these dynamic assemblies in a disk once they have finished executing. Figure 7-4 depicts the contents of a dynamic assembly. The dynamic assembly is made up of a dynamic module that contains the definition of the dynamic type, You can add members for the dynamic type within the module.

Figure 7-4

Dynamic assembly

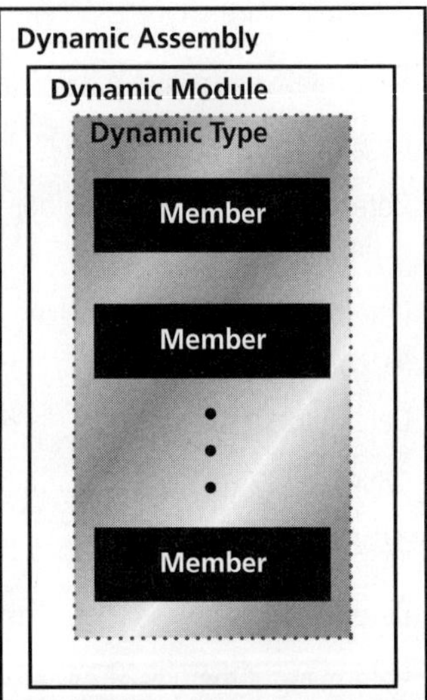

MORE INFORMATION

To know more about the real-time scenarios in which you can use dynamic assemblies, refer to the "Reflection Emit Application Scenarios" from the MSDN library.

Introducing the Emit Namespace

Many .NET compilers implement the `System.Reflection.Emit` namespace to generate the metadata.

You can implement the `System.Reflection.Emit` namespace and the classes within it in script engines and compilers. Compilers can exploit a set of managed types within the `System.Reflection.Emit` namespace through which the compilers can emit metadata and MSIL. The namespace allows you to generate a portable executable (PE) file that you can store on your disk. This process is known as reflection emit.

Table 7-16 displays several classes defined within the `System.Reflection.Emit` namespace.

Table 7-16

Classes of the `System.Reflection.Emit` namespace

CLASS	USE
`AssemblyBuilder`	Builds a dynamic assembly.
`ModuleBuilder`	Builds a dynamic module.
`TypeBuilder`	Builds a dynamic type.
`FieldBuilder`	Builds a field for the dynamic type.
`ConstructorBuilder`	Builds a constructor for a dynamic type.
`MethodBuilder`	Builds a method for a dynamic type.
`ILGenerator`	Emits the MSIL opcodes into the method or the constructor of a dynamic type.
`OpCodes`	Returns a class containing MSIL opcodes.

The `System.Reflection.Emit` namespace also includes a `struct` called `Label`. It is used to define a label for MSIL branching.

Introducing a Case Scenario

TAKE NOTE*

This topic introduces a small code assembly that you will learn to generate dynamically in the next few topics.

You can create a dynamic assembly and save it to a disk for later use. These assemblies can be used in different applications, depending on your requirements.

To create a simple code library assembly, you can use the classes within the `System.Reflection.Emit` namespace. Consider a simple class that extracts names from a text file and displays a random name. The code for this `RandomName` class would be as shown:

```
namespace RandomName
{
  public class RandomName
  {
    private System.Collections.ArrayList m_Names = new System.
Collections.ArrayList();
    private Random m_Random = new Random();

    public RandomName(string filename)
    {
      // Open a text reader from the filename
      System.IO.TextReader tr = System.IO.File.OpenText(filename);
      string name;

      // Add each line as a name in the array list
      while ((name = tr.ReadLine()) != null)
      m_Names.Add(name);

      // Close the text reader
      tr.Close();
  }
  public string GetRandomName()
  {
    int count = m_Names.Count;
```

```
            // If there are no names, return an empty string
            if (count = 0)
            return "";
            // Otherwise, return a random name from the list
            return (string) m_Names[ m_Random.Next(count) ];
        }
    }
}
```

The RandomName class loads all the names from a given text file at runtime. The GetRandomName method retrieves a name at random. You can generate this class dynamically at runtime instead of compiling it in a code library.

GENERATE A CLASS DYNAMICALLY

You need to follow these steps in order to generate the RandomName class discussed in the previous example:

1. Create a dynamic assembly to hold the dynamic modules.
2. Create a dynamic module to hold the dynamically created types, which in this case is the RandomName class.
3. Create a dynamic type to define the RandomName class at runtime.
4. Define the required fields for the RandomName class.
5. Define the constructor for the RandomName class.
6. Define the required method for the RandomName class.
7. Bake the RandomName class or in other words create the RandomName class. Then save the dynamic assembly to disk.

These steps are shown in the following sections.

Creating a Dynamic Assembly

To create dynamic assemblies, you need to use the System.Reflection and System.Reflection.Emit namespaces.

To create a dynamic assembly, you need to invoke the AppDomain.DefineDynamicAssembly method. For example, the following code creates an assembly called myAssembly and saves it to the disk:

```
// Create a weak assembly name
AssemblyName myassembly = new AssemblyName();
// Version the assembly as 1.0.0.0
myassembly.Version = new Version(1, 0, 0, 0);
// Set the assembly name
myassembly.Name = "RandomName";
// Define a dynamic assembly
AssemblyBuilder abuilder = System.AppDomain.CurrentDomain.DefineDynami-
cAssembly(myassembly, AssemblyBuilderAccess.Save);
```

myassembly uses the Save access to save the assembly to a disk. You can also use other accesses, such as Run, to compile and run the assembly without saving it. Alternatively, you can use both the Run and Save accesses to run and save the assembly, respectively.

Creating a Dynamic Module

After you have created a dynamic assembly, you need to define a module within it.

To create a dynamic module you need to invoke the AssemblyBuilder.DefineDynamicModule method. This method creates a single-module assembly called the RandomName (same as the

TAKE NOTE*

By default, all assemblies are saved as dynamic-link libraries. You can create an executable by invoking the `AssemblyBuilder.SetEntryPoint` method. This method generates a console or Windows application assembly.

assembly name, `RandomName`). The following code syntax creates a dynamic module assembly called `RandomName.dll`:

```
// Define a dynamic module

ModuleBuilder mbuilder =
abuilder.DefineDynamicModule("RandomName",
"RandomName.dll");
```

Creating Dynamic Types

You can define and create a type at runtime. These types are known as dynamic types. As per the type hierarchy layout, you now need to create a dynamic type within the dynamic module.

To create a dynamic type such as the `RandomName` type within the dynamic module, use the following code:

```
// Create the public RandomName type (namespace is RandomName)

TypeBuilder tbuilder =
mbuilder.DefineType("RandomName.RandomName",
TypeAttributes.Class | TypeAttributes.Public);
```

This `Type` attribute defines the access modifiers, if public or private. It also specifies if the `Type` is a class or an interface. It also specifies if the `Type` is defined as sealed or abstract. The `TypeBuilder` object in the code syntax is used to construct the `RandomName` class.

Defining Fields for a Dynamic Type

Moving ahead in the type hierarchy of dynamic assemblies, the next step is to define fields within a dynamic type.

To create private fields `m_Names` and `m_Random` within the `RandomName` class, use the following code syntax:

```
// Define two fields (both private)

FieldBuilder m_Names = tbuilder.DefineField("m_Names",
typeof(System.Collections.ArrayList), FieldAttributes.Private);

FieldBuilder m_Random = tbuilder.DefineField("m_Random",
typeof(System.Random), FieldAttributes.Private);
```

You can use the `TypeBuilder.DefineField` method to enter the name, type, and the attributes of the fields.

Defining the Constructor for a Dynamic Type

When the fields are defined for a dynamic type, you need to define the constructor.

DEFINE A CONSTRUCTOR

To define a constructor within the `RandomName` class, follow these steps:

1. Define a public constructor that accepts a single string argument using the `TypeBuilder.DefineConstructor()` method. When a `ConstructorBuilder` is located, you can use `ConstructorBuilder.GetILGenerator()` to emit the MSIL opcodes directly into the constructors. The following code shows how to create a new public constructor:

```
// Create a new constructor (public with one string argument)

ConstructorBuilder cbuilder = tbuilder.DefineConstructor
(MethodAttributes.Public, CallingConventions.Standard, new Type[]
{ typeof(String) });
```

2. Define two local variables, tr and name, of type TextReader and String respectively. Note that you are not emitting debug symbols and therefore, the local variables are unnamed. Use the following code syntax to retrieve the constructor's ILGenerator():

```
// Get the constructor's IL generator
ILGenerator ilg = cbuilder.GetILGenerator();
// Declare the "tr" local
ilg.DeclareLocal(typeof(System.IO.TextReader));
// Declare the "name" local
ilg.DeclareLocal(typeof(System.String));
```

TAKE NOTE*

To emit debug symbols, you can invoke a different method overload of the AssemblyBuilder.DefineDynamicModule() method. You can then use the LocalBuilder.SetLocalSymInfo() method on the LocalBuilder object returned by the TypeBuilder.DeclareLocal() method.

3. Now, call the base constructor. Before invoking the constructor, ensure that you specify the OpCodes.Ldarg_0 argument. This argument is loaded on to the evaluation stack before the base constructor is invoked. Because the constructor is an object method, you need to use the this keyword to reference this object. The following code passes the object reference to the RandomName constructor by using the this keyword and the string argument:

```
// Load "this"
ilg.Emit(OpCodes.Ldarg_0);
// Call the base constructor (no args)
ilg.Emit(OpCodes.Call, typeof(Object).GetConstructor(new
Type[0]));
```

4. Instantiate a new ArrayList object by calling the default constructor and saving it in the field m_Names. The following code syntax instantiates two new random objects by invoking the default constructor and stores them in the m_Names and m_Random fields, respectively:

```
// Load "this"
ilg.Emit(OpCodes.Ldarg_0);
// Create new ArrayList obj
ilg.Emit(OpCodes.Newobj,
   typeof(System.Collections.ArrayList).GetConstructor(new
   Type[0]));
// Store in field "m_Names"
ilg.Emit(OpCodes.Stfld, m_Names);

// Load "this"
ilg.Emit(OpCodes.Ldarg_0);
// Create new Random obj
ilg.Emit(OpCodes.Newobj,
   typeof(System.Random).GetConstructor(new Type[0]));
// Store in field "m_Random"
ilg.Emit(OpCodes.Stfld, m_Random);

// Load constructor argument "filename"
ilg.Emit(OpCodes.Ldarg_1);
// Call File.OpenText(string)
ilg.Emit(OpCodes.Call,
    typeof(System.IO.File).GetMethod("OpenText"));
// Store the result in the "tr" local
ilg.Emit(OpCodes.Stloc_0);
```

5. Define two labels that will construct the `while` loop. The following code syntax defines two labels, `loop` and `exit`, to mark the beginning and end of a while loop:

```
// Define the loop and exit labels for the
// "while" construct
Label loop = ilg.DefineLabel();
Label exit = ilg.DefineLabel();
```

6. Mark the `loop` label. This indicates the `ILGenerator` to associate the next instruction with the label. The instruction that follows is the conditional part of the while loop. The following code syntax uses the `tr.ReadLine()` method and stores the output in the local name. If the name returns a null value, the `ILGenerator` exits the loop:

```
// Mark the loop label
ilg.MarkLabel(loop);
// Load local "tr"
ilg.Emit(OpCodes.Ldloc_0);
// Call tr.ReadLine() (virtual)
ilg.Emit(OpCodes.Callvirt,
    typeof(System.IO.TextReader).GetMethod("ReadLine"));
// Store the result in the local "name"
ilg.Emit(OpCodes.Stloc_1);
// Load the local "name"
ilg.Emit(OpCodes.Ldloc_1);
// Branch to the exit label if "name" is null
ilg.Emit(OpCodes.Brfalse_S, exit);
```

7. Invoke the m_Names.Add() method, if the name is not null to add the name to the name list. Sometimes, when you invoke the Add method, it returns an integer value specifying the index number of the new item. If you are not using this information, you can exit the evaluation stack or continue to run the loop. The following code invokes the m_Names.Add() method in the loop:

```
// Load "this"
ilg.Emit(OpCodes.Ldarg_0);
// Load "m_Names" field
ilg.Emit(OpCodes.Ldfld, m_Names);
// Load local "name"
ilg.Emit(OpCodes.Ldloc_1);
// Call m_Names.Add(object) (virtual)
ilg.Emit(OpCodes.Callvirt,
   typeof(System.Collections.ArrayList).GetMethod("Add"));
// Pop the result of m_Names.Add(object) (unused)
ilg.Emit(OpCodes.Pop);
// Unconditional branch to the loop label
ilg.Emit(OpCodes.Br_S, loop);
// Mark the exit label
ilg.MarkLabel(exit);
// Load local "tr"
ilg.Emit(OpCodes.Ldloc_0);
// Call tr.Close() (virtual)
ilg.Emit(OpCodes.Callvirt,
   typeof(System.IO.TextReader). GetMethod("Close"));
// Emit return opcode
ilg.Emit(OpCodes.Ret);
```

Defining the Method of a Dynamic Type

After creating a constructor, you can define a method for a dynamic type.

DEFINE A METHOD

To build the GetRandomName() method, you can use the ModuleBuilder.DefineMethod() and MethodBuilder.GetILGenerator() methods as shown in the following steps:

1. Define a new public method called GetRandomName. Use the MethodBuilder.GetILGenerator method to retrieve information about ILGenerator.

```
// Define the GetRandomName method
MethodBuilder mtbuilder =
   tbuilder.DefineMethod("GetRandomName",
   MethodAttributes.Public, CallingConventions.Standard,
   typeof(System.String), new Type[0]);
```

2. Define a local variable of type int, called count. Also, define a label called cont within which you will place the loop statements.

```
// Get the IL generator for the method
ilg = mtbuilder.GetILGenerator();
// Declare the "count" local
ilg.DeclareLocal(typeof(int));
// Define the cont label
Label cont = ilg.DefineLabel();
```

3. Load the m_Names fields to the evaluation stack and invoke the ArrayList.get_Count method. Invoking the get_Count method retrieves the corresponding property in C#, which is m_Names.Count.

```
// Load "this"
ilg.Emit(OpCodes.Ldarg_0);
// Load field "m_Names"
ilg.Emit(OpCodes.Ldfld, m_Names);
// Call m_Names.get_Count() (virtual)
ilg.Emit(OpCodes.Callvirt,
   typeof(System.Collections.ArrayList).GetMethod("get_Count"));
// Store in local "count"
ilg.Emit(OpCodes.Stloc_0);
```

4. Add an if statement by loading the local variable count to the evaluation stack and performing a brtrue.s instruction that specifies the steps to follow if the condition is true. When the value returned is a non-zero, the instructions within the label marked cont are executed. If both the conditions are not followed, an empty string is loaded to the evaluation stack.

```
// Load local "count"
ilg.Emit(OpCodes.Ldloc_0);
// Branch if count is not 0
ilg.Emit(OpCodes.Brtrue_S, cont);
// Load the string ""
ilg.Emit(OpCodes.Ldstr, "");
// Return
ilg.Emit(OpCodes.Ret);
```

5. If the local variable returns a non-zero value, mark the cont label where if construct ends. Now load the fields m_Names and m_Random to the evaluation stack. Invoke the m_Random.Next() method. The value that the Next() method returns is passed as a parameter to the m_Names.get_Item method. The get_Item method acts as an indexer. The value returned by the get_Item method is cast to string. Emit the opcodes.

```
// Mark the cont label
ilg.MarkLabel(cont);
// Load "this"
ilg.Emit(OpCodes.Ldarg_0);
// Load field "m_Names"
ilg.Emit(OpCodes.Ldfld, m_Names);
// Load "this"
ilg.Emit(OpCodes.Ldarg_0);
// Load field "m_Random"
ilg.Emit(OpCodes.Ldfld, m_Random);
// Load local "count"
ilg.Emit(OpCodes.Ldloc_0);
// Call m_Random.Next(int) (virtual)
ilg.Emit(OpCodes.Callvirt,
   typeof(System.Random).GetMethod("Next", new Type[] {
typeof(int) }));
// Call m_Names.get_Item(int) (virtual)
ilg.Emit(OpCodes.Callvirt,
   typeof(System.Collections.ArrayList).GetMethod("get_Item"));
// Cast the result to string
ilg.Emit(OpCodes.Castclass, typeof(System.String));
// Return
ilg.Emit(OpCodes.Ret);
```

Baking Dynamic Types and Saving Dynamic Assemblies

After you have created all the elements of the type hierarchy, you need to bake and save the dynamic assembly to disk. The process of ***baking*** marks the completion of the entire type hierarchy.

You need to bake the dynamic assembly before you save it to a disk; otherwise you get a System.NotSupportedException, indicating that the process of creating the RandomName type is not completed. You can use the TypeBuilder.CreateType() to carry out the process of baking. The following code syntax shows how to bake the RandomName type:

```
// "Bake" the RandomName type
tbuilder.CreateType();
```

After the baking is done, you can save the dynamic assembly to a disk using the AssemblyBuilder.Save() method, as shown in the following code:

```
// Save the assembly to the file specified
abuilder.Save("RandomName.dll");
```

You can now compile and run the new assembly. Notice that a new RandomName.dll is created within the same directory. To see the contents of this assembly and verify that the assembly code generated is accurate, you can use the MSIL Disassembler (ildasm.exe) on this file.

Using the Generated Assembly

After a dynamic assembly is generated and stored to a disk, you can reuse this assembly within any application.

USE A DYNAMIC ASSEMBLY

To use a dynamic assembly in an external application, follow these steps:

1. Create a new console application project.
2. Add a reference to the `RandomName.dll` by selecting Add Reference from the Project Menu.
3. Click Browse and select the generated `RandomName.dll` from the location on the disk.
4. Add the following code in the `Main` method of the console application:

```
RandomName.RandomName rdname = new
    RandomName.RandomName("names.txt");
Console.WriteLine("Random Name: " + rdname.GetRandomName());
```

CERTIFICATION READY?
Implement reflection functionality in a.NET Framework application, and create metadata, Microsoft Intermediate Language (MSIL), and a PE file by using the `System.Reflection.Emit` namespace.
USD 6.3

Once you compile it, it prints a random name from the names specified in the names.txt file. If the specified file is not found in the same directory as that of the console application, a `FileNotFound` exception is thrown.

SKILL SUMMARY

This lesson explained the process of creating and managing threads and handling reflection. As a programmer, you have understood the various multi-threading operations in an application built on .NET Framework. A thread represents a unit of execution. You can use multi-threading to increase the responsiveness and efficiency of your programs. It is essential to manage multiple threads in an application competently to have complete control over the functioning of these threads and improve the overall performance of the application. Synchronization of the calls made by multiple threads prevents interruption of tasks performed by individual threads.

Reflection involves the use of objects to encapsulate assemblies, modules, and types. You have understood how the assembly stores information in single or in multiple files. It is important to understand the properties and methods provided by the `Assembly`, `Module`, and `Type` classes. You have also understood the creation of a dynamic assembly, dynamic module, and a dynamic type within the dynamic module. You must first define a field, then a constructor, and finally a method for the dynamic type. Last, you need to bake the dynamic assembly before saving it to disk.

For the certification examination:

- Know how create and invoke multiple threads.
- Understand the ways to manage multiple threads in an application.
- Know how to implement the reflection process in an application.
- Understand the ways to manage dynamic assemblies using reflection.

Knowledge Assessment

Matching

Match the following descriptions to the appropriate terms.

a. `IsDefined`
b. `CodeBase`
c. `Name`
d. `GetProperty`
e. `ScopeName`

_______ 1. Property of the `Assembly` class that gets the location of the assembly as specified originally.

_______ 2. Method of the `Type` class that gets a specific property of the current type.

_______ 3. Property of the `Module` class that gets a string representing the name of the module.

_______ 4. Method of the `Assembly` class that indicates if a specified attribute is applied to the assembly.

_______ 5. Property of the `Module` class that gets a string representing the name of the module with the path removed.

True / False

Circle T if the statement is true or F if the statement is false.

T | F 1. You can use the `SynchronizationAttribute` for automatic synchronization of `ContextBoundObject` objects.

T | F 2. You can perform the bit test to determine if the thread is in the `Running` state.

T | F 3. The process provides the isolation for the application domain and the thread carries out the instructions.

T | F 4. The `ThreadState` enumeration specifies the execution states of a thread.

T | F 5. Threads created in CLR are initially in the `Aborted` state.

Fill in the Blank

Complete the following sentences by writing the correct word or words in the blanks provided.

1. You can use the _________ class to handle multiple threads for shorter tasks that will not block other threads.
2. You must use the _________ method to create a thread to gain effective control over the thread.
3. The ________ property of the `Module` class returns a string value for the name of the module.
4. The ________ method of the `Module` class loads an assembly into the reflection-only context.
5. You can create dynamic assemblies using the ___________ namespace.

Multiple Choice

Circle the letter or letters that correspond to the best answer or answers.

1. What is the new state of a thread when another thread calls the `Thread.Start` method on it?
   a. No change
   b. `Running`
   c. `Suspended`
   d. `Aborted`
2. Which one of the following methods can you use to request ownership of a `Mutex`?
   a. `WaitOne`
   b. `OpenExisting`
   c. `Wait`
   d. None of the above
3. In what state would the external threads be when they are implemented by the CLR?
   a. `Unstarted`
   b. `Running`
   c. `Aborted`
   d. `Suspended`

4. Which of the following methods of the `ThreadPool` class takes a method object as parameter and initiates it as a background thread?
   a. `QueueUserWorkItem`
   b. `GetAvailableThreads`
   c. `SetMaxThreads`
   d. `GetMaxThreads`

5. Which of the following options is not a method of the `Assembly` class?
   a. `GetCallingAssembly`
   b. `GetLoadedModules`
   c. `GetExportedTypes`
   d. `GetCustomAttributes`

Review Questions

1. Consider that your organization has multiple applications that access the HR Information (HRInfo) application to obtain employee data. As all the applications are live, they can simultaneously try to access the HRInfo application. However, your team decides to restrict a single application to access the HRInfo application at a given instance of time. What object would you use to allow single access to the HRInfo application?
2. Your application has a specific requirement to load an assembly into the memory for analysis. However, the assembly must not be executed. Is it possible to achieve this?

■ Case Scenarios

Scenario 7-1: Creating Threads

In the online movie booking Web application, you want to provide the list of upcoming movies to the Web site visitor through the "Get Latest Movies" link. The Web site obtains the list of movies by querying a third-party database, which may take some time depending on the availability of the database. Therefore, you want to make this a background job and allow the user to browse the site in the meantime. Create a .NET routine that creates a thread and initiates the background job to query the database.

Scenario 7-2: Using Reflection

You want your vendors to extend your movie application to create applications for their Web sites. Therefore, you plan to build the reflection facility in your online movie booking Web site application. As a part of this functionality, create a routine to get all the methods defined by all the modules in the currently loaded assembly.

✳ Workplace Ready

Passing Information to Threads

Threads can run in the background or in the foreground of processes. Most often, when you create a background thread, you may want to pass some information to the thread. If you use the `ThreadStart` delegate to start a thread, this delegate does not take any parameters.

XYZ Gaming, Inc. develops a game that displays multiple balls at random for the player to shoot at. Assume that there are certain rules to control the color of the ball that appears next. These balls keep moving on the screen until the player shoots them. You must create separate threads for each ball that appears at random and must pass on the color of the ball to the thread that creates the ball. You cannot pass parameters to the `ThreadStart` object. In this case, how can you pass information to the threads?

Monitoring Application Performance

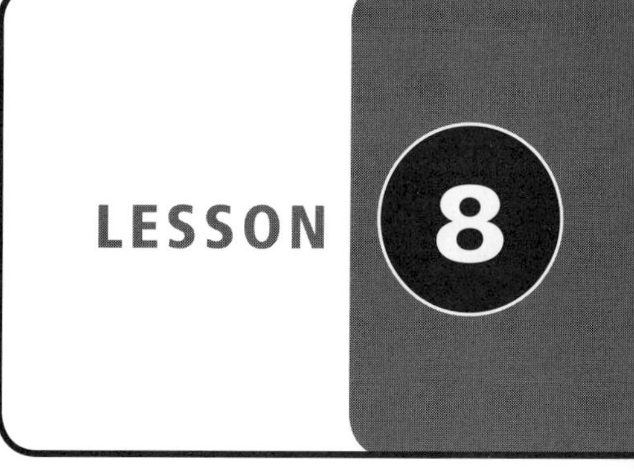

OBJECTIVE DOMAIN MATRIX

Technology Skill	Objective Domain	Objective Domain Number
Maintain event logs.	Manage an event log by using System.Diagnostics namespace.	3.3
Monitor performance of .NET applications.	Manage system processes and monitor the performance of a .NET Framework application by using the diagnostics functionality of the .NET Framework.	3.4
Troubleshoot .NET applications.	Debug and trace a .NET Framework application by using the System.Diagnostics namespace.	3.5
Handle management events.	Embed management information and events into a .NET Framework application.	3.6

KEY TERMS

debugging
debugging attributes
event source
listeners
management events
performance
tracing
Windows event logs
Windows Management Instrumentation (WMI)

As a developer, you should provide robust applications that will withstand complex scenarios, which may occur in the production environment. Robust applications offer better user experience. To provide better user experience, you can make your application log necessary events such as low memory or failure to access a disk to enable system administrators or customer support personnel to track and prevent the error from reoccurring.

You can build dynamic applications by monitoring the ***performance*** of your application throughout the development life cycle. Performance monitoring avoids technical complications that may arise at a later stage. You can also use the various techniques provided by the .NET Framework to manage and troubleshoot your applications.

■ Maintaining Event Logs

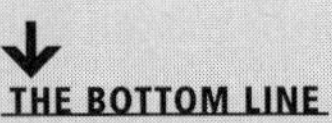

THE BOTTOM LINE

During development or sometimes after implementation, you may find that the application fails abruptly, which could be caused by a number of things. For example, the performance of your application may degrade suddenly due to low memory. At times, your application may not be able to continue because it has been disconnected from the host process or an inability to access a file. In all these cases, it is easy for system administrators to recover the applications if they know the reasons for such failures. Microsoft Windows event logging provides several features that you can use to analyze such failures.

An event is an action that notifies you about hardware or software conditions, which may require the attention of a system administrator. Whenever such events occur, you can design the application in such a way that it makes an entry to an event log. Windows event logging provides a standard user interface and a programming interface through .NET Framework classes for viewing and analyzing event log entries.

Exploring Windows Event Logs

Monitoring the application becomes very easy if you can classify event logs according to the source of events. Microsoft Windows event logging provides you with various event logs for this purpose.

In general, any computer running the latest version of Windows provides three main event logs including several other rarely used event logs, which may vary depending on the Windows version. Table 8-1 lists the default ***Windows event logs***.

Table 8-1

Windows event logs

Event Log	Description
System log	Tracks events that occur on system components such as a device driver.
Security log	Tracks security changes and other violations.
Application log	Tracks events that occur on a registered application.

Apart from these standard event logs, other programs such as Active Directory can create their own default logs. Moreover, you can also create your own custom logs using the classes available in the `System.Diagnostics` namespace.

CLASSIFYING EVENT LOG ENTRIES

When you log an entry in an event log, you can specify the type of that entry. Entries can be categorized into five types:

> **TAKE NOTE***
> It is not appropriate to make an informative entry for a desktop application each time it starts.

- **Error.** When a significant problem that needs immediate user attention arises, you can log an entry into the event log and specify an error type. For example, when your application could not access a service that is up and running, it can log the entry as an error.
- **Warning.** When a problem that does not require immediate attention but may cause issues in the future arises, you can log an entry as a warning. You can generally classify an event as a warning if your application can recover without any disaster such as loss of data or functionality.
- **Information.** When an application successfully completes an important operation, you can log an entry as information. For example, your database server can log an entry once the application has successfully started.

TAKE NOTE*

Both success audit and failure audit events are security events.

- **Success Audit.** You can log an entry as a success audit when access to specified objects such as files, folders, or printers is audited and is successful.
- **Failure Audit.** You can log an entry as a failure audit when access to specified objects such as files, folders, or printers is audited and is a failure.

You can use the Event Viewer, which is the standard user interface to view and manage event logs in the Windows system. Figure 8-1 shows the Event Viewer interface that lists the entries in the Application event log.

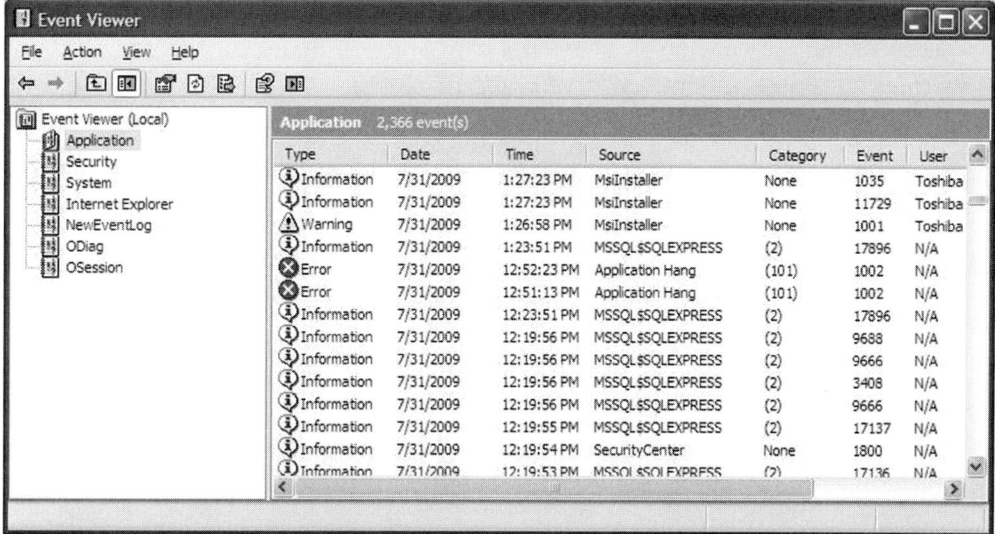

Figure 8-1

Event Viewer

Introducing EventLog Class

At times, in addition to logging error events, it may be necessary for your application to interact with event logs to log information like users logging on or the beginning of a file transfer. During such times, you can use the `EventLog` class provided in the .NET Framework to connect to event logs.

.NET Framework's `System.Diagnostics` namespace provides the `EventLog` class to access and customize Windows event logs.

USING EVENTLOG CLASS

You can use the `System.Diagnostics.EventLog` class to perform the following actions:

- Read and write entries from and to event logs, respectively.
- Create or delete event sources.
- Create or delete logs.
- Respond to log entries.

TAKE NOTE*

You can use the Server Explorer to view a list of event logs for the server to which you have access.

In other words, the `EventLog` class enables you to connect and perform read-write operations into existing event logs that are available on local and remote computers. Moreover, using the `EventLog` class, you can also write your own custom event logs.

Figure 8-2 shows the Server Explorer user interface that lists the available event logs for a given server.

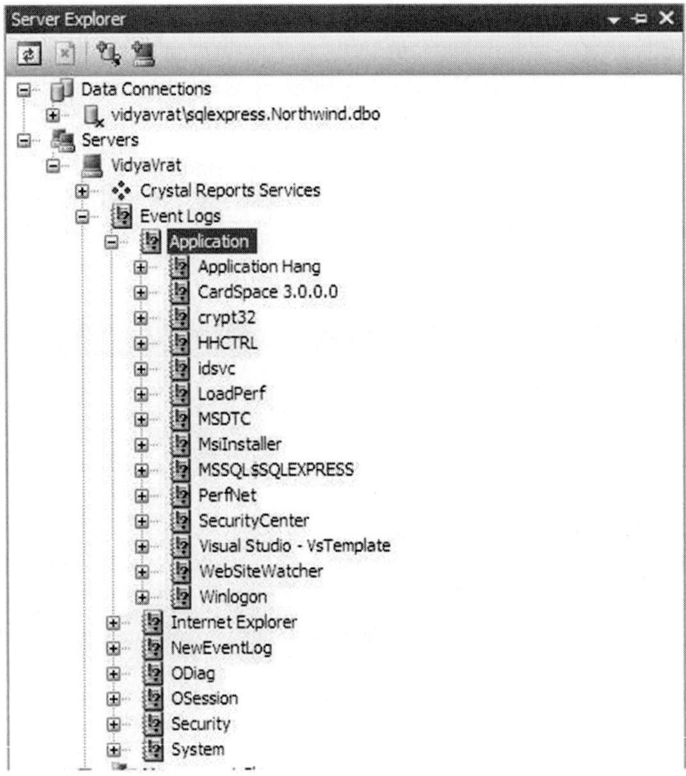

Figure 8-2

Server Explorer

DEFINING SOURCE

Every event in the event log associates itself with a particular source. A source helps in registering your application with the specified event log. Therefore, before writing an event to an event log, you must specify the source of the event. You can specify the ***event source*** by using the `Source` property of the `EventLog` class.

TAKE NOTE*

The value of the `Source` property can be any random string; however, the value should be unique from other sources in your computer. In addition, you need to specify a source for writing a log entry only, not for reading a log entry.

WARNING Because the event source must be unique, the system throws an exception even when you try creating a duplicate source. In addition, attempting to write to an event log before the operating system has refreshed its event sources results in a write operation failure.

If there is no event source available, you must create an event source when installing your application. While doing so, the operating system has time to refresh its list of event sources and necessary configuration.

TAKE NOTE*

You must have administrative rights in the system to create a new source.

You can configure a new event source using the `CreateEventSource` method of the `EventLog` class. If you want your application to write entries to an event log using resource identifiers, instead of specifying string values, you should register the event source with local resources. That is, instead of writing the message directly to the event log, your event source can use the localized resource files that contain message strings based on the culture settings. The Event Viewer uses the resource identifier that indexes the values in the localized resource files to locate and display the corresponding message string from the resource file. You can use the `EventLogInstaller` and `EventSourceCreationData` of the `System.Diagnostics` namespace to configure your event source with resource files.

MORE INFORMATION

To know more about the event source, you can refer to the `EventLog` class section in the MSDN Library. Additionally, for more information about configuring an event source with local resources using the `EvenLogInstaller` and `EventSourceCreationData` classes, refer to the corresponding sections in the MSDN library.

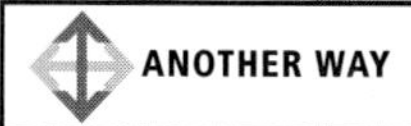

You can also configure a new event source using the `System.Diagnostics.EventLogInstaller` class.

TAKE NOTE*

You can use the source to write entries to only one log at any point in time. Alternatively, an event log can have multiple sources associated with it. Additionally, you must configure a source either to write localized entries using a localized resource file or to write message strings directly. Otherwise, you should register two separate sources for your application to use resource identifiers and direct string values.

EXPLORING EVENTLOG MEMBERS

Tables 8-2 and 8-3 discuss the important properties and methods of the `EventLog` component.

Table 8-2

Important properties of the `EventLog` component

Property	Description
`Entries`	Retrieves the event log contents.
`Log`	Specifies the name of the log to perform read-write operations.
`MachineName`	Specifies the name of the computer on which events have to be logged.
`Source`	Specifies the source of the event to be registered.
`OverflowAction`	Retrieves the configured behavior to store new entries when the event log overflows.

Table 8-3

Important methods of the `EventLog` component

Method	Description
`CreateEventSource`	Overloaded static member that makes an application a valid event source to write event on a specific log.
`DeleteEventSource`	Overloaded static method that removes a registered event source from the event log.
`GetEventLogs`	Overloaded static method that creates an array of all the available event logs on the system.
`RegisterDisplayName`	Enables you to register and specify a localized name for the event log to display it in the Event Viewer.
`ModifyOverflowPolicy`	Enables you to change the configured behavior to write new entries when an event log overflows.
`WriteEntry`	Overloaded method that writes an entry in the event log.
`WriteEvent`	Overloaded method that writes a localized event entry in the event log.
`SourceExists`	Overloaded static method that determines whether the specified event source is registered on the local computer.
`LogNameFromSourceName`	Static method that retrieves the log name to which the specified source is registered.

Creating and Configuring EventLog Instances

For your application to interact with an event log, you need to first create and configure EventLog instances based on your requirements.

CREATING EVENTLOG INSTANCES

Imagine that you are creating a Windows Forms application to interact with an event log. You can create an instance of the EventLog component by any one of the following:

- Drag an instance of the EventLog component from the Components tab of the Toolbox to your form or designer.
- Locate the required log in the server explorer and add it to your designer to create the EventLog instance to point to an existing log.
- Create the EventLog instance programmatically as specified in the following code sample:

```
System.Diagnostics.EventLog MyEventLog = new
System.Diagnostics.EventLog();
```

CONFIGURING EVENTLOG INSTANCES

After you have created an instance of the EventLog component, you need to configure its properties, depending on how you are going to use it. The various requirements and the corresponding EventLog properties that need to be set include:

- If you are required to write entries to a log, you have to do one of the following:
  - Register a source using the CreateEventSource method, if the source already exists and set the Source property to the registered source.
  - Set the MachineName, Log, and Source properties for the component if you are using a new source string.

  The following code sample shows how to configure an EventLog instance with the machine name, log name, and source. The code uses one of the EventLog constructors with the log name, machine name, and source as parameters to the constructor. The EventLog constructor in turn sets the Log, MachineName, and Source properties with the values in the corresponding parameters. Note that the following code sample requires System.Diagnostics namespace:

```
EventLog SampleEventLog = new EventLog("Application", "server1",
"myApp");
SampleEventLog.WriteEntry("Sample Log Entry");
```

- If you are required to read or monitor the entries in a log, set the MachineName and Log properties to specify the corresponding log.
- If it is necessary for your component to receive notification of the EntryWritten event, then set the EnableRaisingEvents property to true. Note that the EntryWritten event occurs when your application makes an entry to an event log in the local computer.

TAKE NOTE*

If MachineName property is not set, the system considers local computer by default.

XREF

For an example of how to register a source using the CreateEventSource method, you can refer to the "Writing Event Log Entry" subsection in the next topic.

Writing to an Event Log

You may want to write to an event log to understand the exact cause of the problem that may occur during the execution of any application.

Once you decide to write to a log, you need to specify the message that is to be written to the log. The message should contain all information related to the problem so that the user can interpret the cause of the problem or error accurately. In addition, the various parameters that you can specify while writing to a log include:

- Entry type
- Event ID
- Event category
- Required binary data to append to the entry

TAKE NOTE*

You can use the EventLogEntryType enumeration in the System.Diagnostics namespace to specify the type of your log entry.

WRITE TO A LOG BY REGISTERING TO A SOURCE

You must perform the following steps to write to a log when you want to register a source explicitly:

1. Register a source with the required log.
2. Create an EventLog instance.
3. Set the Source property of the EventLog component to the name of the registered source.
4. Invoke the WriteEntry method.

TAKE NOTE* When you explicitly register a source, you need not specify the Log property for the component because the name of the log is automatically determined on connecting to the registered source.

WRITE TO A LOG BY SPECIFYING A NEW SOURCE

You must perform the following steps to write to a log when you want to specify a new source string:

1. Create an EventLog instance.
2. Set the Source, MachineName, and Log properties of the EventLog component.
3. Invoke the WriteEntry method. In this case, the WriteEntry method would automatically determine if the source is registered or not. If the source does not exist, it would register the source by itself.

TAKE NOTE* To successfully write to a log, you must register the source with the required log, your application must have write permission to the log it writes, and the message length must not exceed 16K.

WRITING AN EVENT LOG ENTRY

The following sample code shows how to write a simple message to an event log. The code writes to the Application log. The sample code requires System.Diagnostics namespace:

```
if (!EventLog.SourceExists("SampleSource"))
{
   EventLog.CreateEventSource("SampleSource","Application");
}
EventLog MyEventLog = new EventLog();
MyEventLog.Source = "SampleSource";
MyEventLog.WriteEntry("Sample event log entry");
```

TAKE NOTE* You can also use a custom log to record log entries pertaining to your application. However, you may prefer to use the Application log instead of creating a custom because:

- You must create and configure this custom log before attempting to write entries into it.
- You cannot write to a custom log immediately after creating it because the operating system requires time to refresh its registered event sources and their corresponding configuration.
- You have to write your own cleanup and event handling mechanisms for custom logs. However, the Application log has its default configuration.

WRITING A LOCALIZED EVENT LOG ENTRY

If you have to write a localized log entry, you need to specify the event properties with resource identifiers. This is because the Event Viewer uses the resource identifiers to display the corresponding strings from the local resource files for the source. In addition, you must register the source with the required resource file before writing an event using resource identifiers.

The following sample code shows how to write a localized entry to an event log. The sample code requires the `System.Diagnostics` namespace:

```
if (!EventLog.SourceExists("SampleSource"))
{
EventLog.CreateEventSource("SampleSource","MyLog");
}
EventLog MyEventLog = new EventLog();
MyEventLog.Source = "SampleSource";
MyEventLog.WriteEvent(new EventInstance(1, 0), new string[]
{"Sample message"});
```

TAKE NOTE*

You must use the `WriteEvent` method to write a localized event entry to a log as shown in the previous example code. Additionally, use the `EventInstance` class of the `System.Diagnostics` namespace to specify the resource identifier for writing localized entries. Most important, event logging consumes more disk space, CPU time, and other resources; therefore, you should write only necessary and important information to the log.

Reading from an Event Log

You may want to read from an event log to know the actual cause of the problem and to avoid any future complications to your system.

READ FROM AN EVENT LOG

You can read entries from an event log by following these steps:

1. Create an `EventLog` object.
2. Specify the `Log` and `MachineName` properties of the `EventLog` object.
3. Use the `Entries` collection to view the event log entries.

The following example code shows how to read entries from an event log. The code sample requires `System.Diagnostics` namespace:

CERTIFICATION READY?
Manage an event log by using System.Diagnostics namespace.
USD 3.3

```
EventLogEntry MyLogEntries;
EventLog MyEventLog = new EventLog("MyLog","MySystem");
if (MyEventLog.Entries.Count > 0)
{
  foreach (MyLogEntries in MyEventLog.Entries)
    Console.WrieLine(MyLogEntries.Message);
}
else
{
  Console.WriteLine("No entries found in the log.");
}
```

Monitoring Performance of .Net Applications

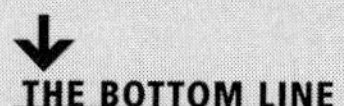

THE BOTTOM LINE

With the help of the Process component, you can monitor process and thread performance. This component allows you to view the currently executing processes and their loaded assemblies, memory usage, and threads. Additionally, the System.Diagnostics namespace enables you to monitor and update performance-related information in performance counters from within your application.

Monitoring Process and Thread Performance

The Process component provides various properties that allow you to perform management-related tasks, such as monitoring process and thread performance.

The Process component allows you to perform most of the Windows process management tasks with ease and speed. It is possible to use this component with processes on local as well as remote computers. On a local computer, you can start and stop a process and query it for specific information. The information may include the names of the modules it has loaded, the start time, and the thread sets. On a remote computer, you cannot start or stop a process, but you can query existing processes to get information.

You must add an instance of the Process component to the class in order to work with the processes in your classes. This allows the class to access the processes on the servers and also to start and stop new processes. In addition, it is possible for other components in your application to call the Process component if they need it to start a new process or manipulate an existing process. When monitoring system performance, it is advisable to use the PerformanceCounter and EventLog components.

VIEWING CURRENTLY EXECUTING PROCESSES

Sometimes, you may need to view all the processes that are executing at a given time. For example, imagine that you want to create an application that facilitates stopping processes that are currently running. In order to achieve this, you must trace all running processes. You could then display the process names in a list box and allow the users to select specific processes when they need to take action on them.

VIEW THE RUNNING PROCESSES

Perform the following steps to view the running processes:

1. Create an array of the type Process.
2. Fill the array with the return value from the GetProcesses method.
3. Iterate through the array using the indexed value to obtain the process name of each process in the array.
4. Write the obtained process name to a console.

The following code snippet shows how to call the GetProcesses method of a Process component to return the process array and write the process name to a console. Note that this code helps you view a list of the processes on the local computer:

```
Process[] currProcesses = Process.GetProcesses();
foreach (Process myProcess in currProcesses)
{
    Console.WriteLine(myProcess.ProcessName);
}
```

Alternatively, to get a list of processes running on a remote computer, you can use one of the overloads of the GetProcesses method. For example, the following code sample gets a list of the processes running on a remote computer named "RemoteComputer." Note that once you get the current list of processes, you can iterate through the array in the same way you did in the earlier code:

```
Process[] currProcesses = Process.GetProcesses("RemoteComputer");
```

VIEWING LIBRARIES LOADED FOR A PARTICULAR PROCESS

To access the loaded libraries of a process, you can use the `Modules` property of the `Process` component. This property returns a collection of the type `ProcessModuleCollection`. This collection includes all the loaded libraries of the target process. You can then traverse through the collection to view all the individual libraries.

INVESTIGATE LIBRARY USAGE

Perform the following steps to investigate the library usage for a process:

1. If the required process was not initiated by a `Process` component, then you must bind that process with a new instance of a `Process` component.
2. To store the module collection, declare an object type `ProcessModuleCollection`.
3. Allocate the modules property to the `ProcessModuleCollection` variable to populate the `ProcessModuleCollection` object with the modules from the target module.
4. Iterate through the `ProcessModuleCollection` object to view and manage individual libraries.

The following code snippet demonstrates how to return all the loaded libraries for Notepad text editor. Note that the following code sample will throw an exception if Notepad is not running on the local computer:

```
Process[] myapps;
ProcessModuleCollection modules;
myapps = Process.GetProcessesByName("notepad");
modules = myapps[0].Modules;
foreach (ProcessModule myModule in modules)
{
Console.WriteLine(myModule.ModuleName);
}
```

VIEWING MEMORY USAGE OF A PROCESS

You can view the memory statistics for a process. The `Process` component provides six properties for this purpose. You can access these properties at runtime to view the memory usage of a process. Each property offers different statistics for memory allocation.

Table 8-4 lists the memory usage properties.

Table 8-4

Memory usage properties of `Process` component

PROPERTY	DESCRIPTION
`PrivateMemorySize64`	Returns the number of bytes the concerned process has allocated, which cannot be shared with other processes.
`PeakVirtualMemorySize64`	Returns the maximum amount of memory the concerned process has allocated, which can be written to the virtual paging file.
`PagedSystemMemorySize`	Returns the amount of memory the system has allocated on behalf of the concerned process that can be written to the virtual memory paging file.
`PagedMemorySize`	Returns the amount of memory the concerned process has allocated that can be written to the virtual memory paging file.
`NonpagedSystemMemorySize`	Returns the amount of memory the system has allocated on behalf of the concerned process that cannot be written to the virtual memory paging file.

INVESTIGATE MEMORY USAGE

Perform the following steps to investigate the memory usage for a process:

1. Bind a process component instance to the process under consideration.
2. Call the `Refresh` method to refresh the property cache, if needed.
3. Reference the appropriate memory usage property and read it.

The following code snippet demonstrates using the `Process` component to read the `PrivateMemorySize64` property for Notepad and assign the returned property value to a variable. The value is then displayed in a console. Note that the code will throw an exception if Notepad is not running on the local computer:

```
long var1;
Process[] var2;
var2 = Process.GetProcessesByName("Notepad");
var1 = var2[0].PrivateMemorySize64;
Console.WriteLine("Memory used: {0}.", var1);
```

MONITORING THREAD USAGE

The `Threads` property of the `Process` component allows you to view the process threads. This property returns a collection type of `ProcessThreadCollection`. The return value contains a collection of `ProcessThread` objects that represent the operating system threads currently being executed in the process. You can traverse through the collection to view all the individual thread properties. *Note:* The primary thread is not necessarily the thread at index 0 of the collection.

INVESTIGATE THREAD USAGE

Perform the following steps to investigate the thread usage for a process:

1. Associate a `Process` component to the process under consideration if the process was not initiated by a `Process` component.
2. Assign the `Threads` property value of the process to an empty `ProcessThread` type collection.
3. Iterate through the array index to check the properties for a single thread.

The following code snippet shows reading the `Threads` property of the Microsoft Word application and assigning the value to an empty array. The `BasePriority` value of the first thread in the process thread array is then read and displayed:

```
ProcessThreadCollection mythreads;
Process[] var1;
var1 = Process.GetProcessesByName("Winword");
mythreads = var1[0].Threads;
Console.WriteLine(mythreads[0].BasePriority.ToString());
```

Monitoring Performance Using Counters

You can use the `PerformanceCounter` component to read the existing, predefined counters and to publish the performance data to custom counters.

Counters help in gathering performance data. All the counter names are stored in the registry. These counters are related to a specific area of system functionality. Some examples of counters include a processor's busy time, memory usage, and the number of bytes received over a network connection.

CREATING PERFORMANCE COUNTERS IN A CATEGORY

You can uniquely identify each counter by its name and its location. The counter information consists of four elements: computer, category, category instance, and counter name.

Counter information must include the category for which the counter measures data. The computer categories include physical components, such as processors, disks, and memory, and the system categories are processes and threads. Fundamentally, each category is associated with a functional element within the computer. Each category has a set of standard counters assigned to it. You can view these counter objects in the Performance object drop-down list of the Add Counters dialog box within System Monitor. Figure 8-3 shows the *Add Counters* dialog box that lists the *Memory* category and the corresponding counters from that category. You must include these counters in the counter path. The performance data is grouped by the category associated with the counters.

Figure 8-3

Add Counters dialog box

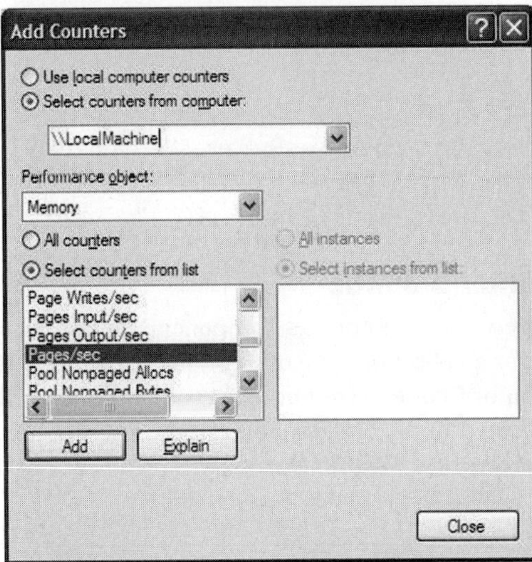

Sometimes several copies of the same category may exist. These copies are referred to as category instances. Every instance has its own set of standard counters allocated. Thus, counter information must include an instance specification if the category of that counter can have more than one instance.

You can use the `NextValue` method of the `PerformanceCounter` class to obtain the current reading of the counter.

The performance counter categories installed in the .NET Framework 2.0 and above use separate shared memory. Each performance counter category has its own memory. Performance counters are not supported in Windows 98 or Windows Millennium Edition (Me).

READ FROM PERFORMANCE COUNTER

To read from a performance counter, perform the following steps:

1. Create an instance of the `PerformanceCounter` class.
2. Set the `CategoryName`, `CounterName` properties.
3. Call the `NextValue` method to take a performance counter reading.

PUBLISH PERFORMANCE COUNTER DATA

To publish performance counter data, perform the following steps:

1. Create one or more custom counters using the `PerformanceCounterCategory.Create` method.
2. Create an instance of the `PerformanceCounter` class.
3. Set the `CategoryName`, `CounterName` properties.
4. Call the `IncrementBy`, `Increment`, or `Decrement` methods, or set the `RawValue` property to change the value of your custom counter.

The following code sample publishes performance counter data. The code registers a custom performance counter category on the local computer by calling the `PerformanceCounterCategory.Create` method. *Note:* The third parameter of the `Create` method in the code indicates that the custom category created can have multiple instances.

```
PerformanceCounterCategory.Create("CategoryName", "CategoryDescription",
PerformanceCounterCategoryType.MultiInstance, "CounterName","CounterDe
scription");
// Create an instance of PerformanceCounter by setting the
CategoryName and CounterName properties through the PerformanceCounter
constructor
PerformanceCounter pc = new PerformanceCounter("CategoryName",
"CounterName", false);
// Set the performance counter value by defining the RawValue property
pc.RawValue = 8;
// Call the Decrement, Increment, and IncrementBy methods to adjust
the counter value relative to the current value
pc.Decrement();
pc.Increment();
pc.IncrementBy(2);
```

Table 8-5 lists important members of the `PerformanceCounter` class.

Table 8-5

Important members of the `PerformanceCounter` class

Member	Description
`NextSample`	Obtains a counter sample and returns the raw or uncalculated value for it.
`NextValue`	Obtains a counter sample and returns the calculated value for it.
`CloseSharedResources`	Frees the performance counter library shared state allocated by the counters.
`BeginInit`	Begins the initialization of the `PerformanceCounter` instance.
`EndInit`	Ends the initialization of the `PerformanceCounter` instance.
`CanRaiseEvents`	Specifies a value indicating whether the component can raise events.
`CategoryName`	Specifies the name of the performance counter category for the current performance counter.
`CounterName`	Specifies the name of the performance counter associated with the `PerformanceCounter` instance.
`CounterType`	Retrieves the counter type of the related performance counter.
`InstanceLifeTime`	Specifies the lifetime of a process.

UNDERSTANDING VARIOUS PERFORMANCE COUNTER CATEGORIES

The `PerformanceCounterCategory` class offers various methods for interacting with counters and categories on the computer. You can define custom categories with the help of the `Create` method, remove categories from the computer using the `Delete` method, view the list of categories using the `GetCategories` method, and retrieve all the counter and instance data associated with a single category by using the `ReadCategory` method.

You should use performance counters to publish the performance data of an application. The categories include physical components like processors, disks, and memory, and system objects like processes and threads. You can also group system counters that are related to the same performance object into a category that indicates their common focus. While creating an instance of the `PerformanceCounter` class, you must first specify the category with which the component will interact and then choose a counter from that category.

Let us consider a Windows counter category example in the Memory category. System counters within this category trace memory data like the number of bytes available and the number of bytes cached. If you need to work with the bytes cached in your application, you must first create an instance of the `PerformanceCounter` component. You must then connect it to the Memory category and then pick the appropriate counter from that category.

The most frequently used categories are Cache, Memory, Objects, PhysicalDisk, Process, Processor, Server, System, and Thread categories. Let us look at a code snippet that illustrates how to create a category and delete a specific category if it exists. *Note*: In the following code snippet, you need to provide values for the parameters. Also, note that before deleting any category you must determine if that specific category exists:

```
PerformanceCounterCategory mypercat = PerformanceCounterCategory.
Create(categoryName, categoryHelp, counterName, counterHelp);
bool exists = PerformanceCounterCategory.Exists(categoryName);
PerformanceCounterCategory.Delete(categoryName);
```

Table 8-6 lists the important members of the `PerformanceCounterCategory` class.

Table 8-6

Important members of `PerformanceCounter-Category` class

MEMBER	DESCRIPTION
`CounterExists`	This overloaded method determines whether a specified counter is registered to a particular category.
`Create`	This overloaded method registers with the system, a custom performance counter category in addition to one or more counters.
`GetCategories`	This overloaded method retrieves a list of the performance counter categories that are registered on a computer.
`GetCounters`	This overloaded method retrieves a list of the counters in the performance counter category.
`ReadCategory`	Reads all the counter and performance object instance data that are associated with the performance counter category.
`CategoryName`	Specifies the name of the performance object that defines the category.
`CategoryType`	Retrieves the performance counter category type.

Debugging with Stack Information

Application ***debugging*** is the process of locating and fixing errors in your application. To enhance the debugging process, the .NET Framework provides you with classes that supply detailed error information.

To debug an error using minimum effort, you need to have detailed information about the error such as the file name, method name, error line number, and the error column number. The `StackTrace` and `StackFrame` classes of the .NET Framework provide the detailed error information that you need.

A stack frame represents a function call on the call stack for the current thread. A stack trace is an ordered collection of one or more stack frames.

The information provided through StackTrace is most informative with debug build configurations.

By default, debug builds include debug symbols; however, release builds do not include these symbols. The debug symbols include information such as file, method name, line number, and column information used in constructing StackFrame and StackTrace objects. Because of code transformations that occurred during optimization, the StackTrace class may not report as many method calls as expected.

Table 8-7 lists the important members of the StackFrame class.

Table 8-7

Members of the StackFrame class

MEMBER	DESCRIPTION
GetFileName	This method gets the file name that contains the executing code.
GetMethod	This method gets the method in which the frame is executing.
GetFileLineNumber	This method gets the line number of the code in the currently executing file.
GetFileColumnNumber	This method gets the column number of the code in the currently executing file.

Table 8-8 lists the important members of the StackTrace class.

Table 8-8

Members of the StackTrace class

MEMBER	DESCRIPTION
GetFrame	This method gets the specified stack frame.
GetFrames	This method returns a copy of all stack frames in the current stack trace.
FrameCount	This property gets the number of frames in the stack trace.

TAKE NOTE*

You can place the code that provides the stack frame information as shown in the previous code sample in the exception-handling block (catch block).

CERTIFICATION READY?
Manage system processes and monitor the performance of a .NET Framework application by using the diagnostics functionality of the .NET Framework.
USD 3.4

Let us look at a code snippet that shows how to create a simple StackTrace class and traverse through its frames to obtain debugging and diagnostic information. The following snippet captures the filename, line number, and column information:

```
StackTrace myst = new StackTrace(true);
string stackIndent = "";
for(int i =0; i< myst.FrameCount; i++)
{
   StackFrame mysf = myst.GetFrame(i);
   Console.WriteLine(stackIndent + " Method: {0}", mysf.GetMethod() );
   Console.WriteLine(stackIndent + " File: {0}", mysf.GetFileName());
   Console.WriteLine(stackIndent + " Line Number: {0}",
mysf.GetFileLineNumber());
   stackIndent += " ";
}
```

■ Troubleshooting .NET Applications

THE BOTTOM LINE

On several occasions, you may find that your Web applications that were up and running may have suddenly hung and crashed. To avoid this scenario, you might want to verify the functionality of your Web applications by checking the flow of their execution in production and development environments. You can use the debugging and ***tracing*** techniques to verify the application's functionality. Tracing is the process in which you record diagnostic information about the application. Debugging Web applications used to be difficult. Now, with the `System.Diagnostics` namespace in the .NET Framework, debugging your Web applications has become a lot easier.

You can use the classes provided by the `System.Diagnostics` namespace to debug and trace the execution of your Web applications.

Understanding Debugging in .NET

As a developer, you probably prefer debugging tools that allow you to create robust debugging code without affecting your application's performance or its size. By using the classes provided by `System.Diagnostics` namespace, you can develop robust debugging code without affecting the performance and size of your application.

Debugging is the process of finding and fixing errors in an application. The .NET Framework provides `System.Diagnostics.Debug` and `System.Diagnostics.Debugger` classes. By using these classes, you can debug and verify the output of your code for specific values, through assertions. Assertion is the process of showing small messages to the user at various points in code. These messages help users determine the exact point at which the code stopped functioning properly. In addition, debugger classes also enable your application to communicate with a debugger.

USING DEBUG CLASS

The `Debug` class provides various methods and properties to help you in debugging your code. You can use the `Debug` class to run the "debug only" code that will not run when you build your application for release.

There are various write methods provided by the `Debug` class. For example, if you want to reduce the number of lines of code to be written, you can use the `WriteIf` and `WriteLineIf` methods, over other Write methods because the `WriteIf` and `WriteLineIf` methods not only write the output but also check for a Boolean condition before writing.

In addition, to provide failure assertions when your code does not produce the expected output value, you can use the `Debug.Assert` method to display an assert dialog box. If you want to display the debug output immediately, you can use the `Debug.AutoFlush` property by setting its value to true.

Tables 8-9 and 8-10 display the important properties and methods of the `Debug` class.

Table 8-9

Important properties of the `Debug` class

PROPERTY	DESCRIPTION
`AutoFlush`	Specifies a Boolean value indicating whether the output of the debug should be written immediately after every write.
`IndentLevel`	Specifies the indent level of the debug output messages.
`IndentSize`	Specifies the number of spaces in an indent.
`Listeners`	Retrieves the listeners collection that is monitoring the debug output.

Table 8-10

Important methods of the Debug class

METHOD	DESCRIPTION
`Assert`	Overloaded static method that displays a message box to show the call stack, based on a condition.
`Fail`	Overloaded static method that throws an error message.
`Flush`	Flushes the output buffer to write to the `Listeners` collection.
`Indent`	Increases the current `IndentLevel`.
`Unindent`	Decreases the current `IndentLevel`.
`Write, WriteLine`	Static overloaded method that writes debug information to the trace listeners.
`WriteIf, WriteLineIf`	Static overloaded method that writes debug information to the trace listeners depending on a condition.

TAKE NOTE*

The listeners help to produce formatted debug message output. When you build your application using the release build, you cannot see the debug messages.

The following code sample uses the `Debug` class to spot the beginning and end of an application. The code writes the debugging output to a text file named *DebugOutput.txt*. Note that in order to write the debug output to a text file, the code adds an instance of the `TextWriterTraceListener` class to the `Listeners` collection. The `TextWriterTraceListener` object in turns redirects the debug output to the specified file:

```
Stream DebugFile = File.Create("DebugOutput.txt");
Debug.Listeners.Add(new TextWriterTraceListener(DebugFile));
Debug.AutoFlush = true;
Debug.WriteLine("Application Starts");
// Your code logic goes here
Debug.WriteLine("Application Ends");
```

You can refer to the topic “Understanding Tracing in .NET” in this lesson to learn about displaying messages with a release build. Additionally, to know more about listeners, you can refer to the “Adding Listeners” section in this lesson.

USING DEBUGGER CLASS

You can use the `Debugger` class to communicate with a debugger, through code, thus enabling communication with a debugger at runtime. Note that you can use the Visual Studio debugger to debug your applications only during the design time. However, you can use the `Debugger` class to enable your application to be debugged even after it is deployed to the live environment.

The `Debugger` class allows you to log messages, set up breakpoints, and check for an attached debugger.

You can use the `IsAttached` property of the `Debugger` class to determine if a debugger object is attached. Table 8-11 discusses the important methods of the `Debugger` class.

Table 8-11

Important methods of the Debugger class

METHOD	DESCRIPTION
`Break`	Indicates a breakpoint to the attached debugger.
`IsLogging`	Checks if logging is enabled by the attached debugger.
`Launch`	Launches and attaches a debugger if it is not already attached.
`Log`	Logs a message for the attached debugger.

Setting Application Behavior Using Debug Attributes

Imagine that you might want to change the display of a particular type or variable in the current debug window. There also may be times when you would like to hide or skip certain parts of code from debugging, which you think may affect the debugging process. .NET Framework provides you with various ***debugging attributes*** to enrich your debugging experience.

The `System.Diagnostics` namespace provides various debugging attributes, each of which you can use to support and enhance debugging. The list of debugging attributes includes:

- `DebuggerBrowsableAttribute`
- `DebuggerDisplayAttribute`
- `DebuggerHiddenAttribute`
- `DebuggerNonUserCodeAttribute`
- `DebuggerStepperBoundaryAttribute`
- `DebuggerStepThroughAttribute`
- `DebuggerTypeProxyAttribute`
- `DebuggerVisualizerAttribute`

SETTING PROPERTY/FIELD DISPLAY BEHAVIOR

You can use the `DebuggerBrowsableAttribute` class to set the display behavior of a property or field in the debugger window. Table 8-12 lists the display states that you can specify for your property or field in the `DebuggerBrowsableAttribute` constructor through the `DebuggerBrowsableState` enumeration.

Table 8-12

Display state values of the `DebuggerBrowsableState` enumeration

DISPLAY STATE	DESCRIPTION
`Never`	Never displays the specified field or property.
`Collapsed`	Displays the specified field or property in the collapsed state. This is the default display behavior.
`RootHidden`	Hides the specified member; however, displays its element objects if the member is an array or collection.

The following code sample shows how to use the `DebuggerBrowsableAttribute` to hide the property languages, which is an `ArrayList` collection, and display only its elements:

```
[DebuggerBrowsable(DebuggerBrowsableState.RootHidden)]
public static ArrayList languages = new ArrayList();
```

SETTING THE TYPE RENDERING

You can use the `DebuggerDisplayAttribute` class to set the type rendering in the debugger window. You can apply this attribute to classes, structures, delegates, enumerations, fields, properties, and assemblies.

While declaring the `DebuggerDisplayAttribute`, you can specify the required properties or fields to display and even call the methods of your class to provide the result.

The following code sample shows how to use the `DebuggerDisplayAttribute` to specify the rendering of the Employee class in the debugger window:

```
[DebuggerDisplay("{id} Designation={empdesig}")]
public class Employee
{
    private int id;
    private string empdesig;
}
```

SETTING DISPLAY PROXY FOR TYPE

You can use the DebuggerTypeProxyAttribute class to display a proxy for your type. That is, using the DebuggerTypeProxyAttribute, you can change the display of your type by substituting it with a proxy. The debugger, then, instantiates the proxy, and the proxy in turn renders your class.

You can use the DebuggerTypeProxyAttribute when debugging complex classes with numerous member variables. Some of these variables may not even be required to be included in the debugging process. The proxy class helps you display only the essential variables in the debugger window.

The proxy class must have one public constructor that should accept an argument of the type it displays. The following sample code shows you how to use the DebuggerTypeProxyAttribute to display a custom view of the employee type in the debugger window through a proxy class:

```
[DebuggerTypeProxy(typeof(EmployeeProxy))]
class Employee
{
   private string empId;
   private string empDesig;
   internal class EmployeeProxy
   {
      private Employee _employee;
      public string empIdproxy;
      public string empDesigproxy;
      public EmployeeProxy(Employee emp)
      {
          _employee = emp;
      }
   }
}
```

TAKE NOTE* Generally, you can define the proxy class for the type as a nested internal class as shown in the sample code. Internal classes have full access to all the private members of the containing type. Additionally the debugger window shows only the public members of the proxy class and not its private or protected members.

STEPPING THROUGH A TYPE

You can use the DebuggerStepThroughAttribute class to make the debugger skip a type during the "Step into" debug process. However, DebuggerStepThroughAttribute allows setting a breakpoint for a method in the type to which you have attached it.

You can use the DebuggerStepThroughAttribute for classes, structures, constructors, and methods. The following sample code shows how to make the debugger skip the methods in the static class Sample using the DebuggerStepThroughAttribute:

```
[DebuggerStepThrough()]
public static class Sample
{
   // Your class variables and methods goes here
}
```

STEPPING THROUGH DESIGNER CODE

You can use the DebuggerNonUserCodeAttribute to make the debugger step through the designer-created code during the "Step into" debug process. This helps avoid complications during the debugging process by only allowing the debugger to step into the user-created code.

However, unlike the DebuggerStepThroughAttribute, the DebuggerNonUserCode-Attribute will not allow you to set a breakpoint in the method for which you have declared this attribute. You can apply the DebuggerNonUserCodeAttribute to classes, structures, methods, constructors, and properties.

The following code sample uses the DebuggerNonUserCodeAttribute to step through the designer created dispose method:

```
[DebuggerNonUserCode()]
protected override dispose(bool disposing)
{
   If (disposing && components != null )
      components.Dispose();
   SampleBase.Dispose(disposing);
}
```

HIDING CODE FROM DEBUGGER

You can use the DebuggerHiddenAttribute to hide a method from the debugger to avoid the debugger stepping into the method. Additionally, this attribute does not allow setting breakpoints in the methods for which you have declared this attribute.

The following code sample specifies the DebuggerHiddenAttribute for the DisplayName method to hide it from the debugger:

```
[DebuggerHidden()]
public DisplayName(string name)
{
   Console.Write(name);
}
```

SKIPPING THE STEP THROUGH TO RUNNING CODE

You can use the DebuggerStepperBoundaryAttribute when you debug your code in a multi-threaded environment. When applying DebuggerNonUserCodeAttribute to your code, the debugger skips the designer-created code and steps into the next user-created code. However, during context switches on a thread, the next user-created code that executes may not correspond to the previous running code of the debugging process. The DebuggerStep perBoundaryAttribute helps you eliminate this experience during debugging by allowing you to skip the step through of the debugging process to the running code.

For example, you can use the DebuggerStepperBoundaryAttribute when you want to step through a code module in Thread 1 and at the same time run the same code module in Thread 2. You can also use the DebuggerStepperBoundaryAttribute along with the Debu ggerNonUserCodeAttribute as shown next in the code that follows. The Debugger Non-UserCodeAttribute in the following code snippet instructs the debugger to step through the class during the "Step into" debug process. However, when the debugger encounters the DebuggerStepperBoundaryAttribute, the debugger skips that step-into process:

```
[DebuggerNonUserCode]
class Sample
{
   public void firstMethod()
   {
      nextMethod();
   }
   [DebuggerStepperBoundary]
   public void nextMethod()
   {
      //your code can come here
   }

}
```

IDENTIFYING VISUALIZERS

Visualizers are components of the Visual Studio debugger user interface that create an interface such as a dialog box to display variables or objects in a suitable way depending on their data types. For example, a bitmap visualizer interprets and displays graphics represented by a bitmap structure.

You can write your own visualizers to extend the existing functionality of the Visual Studio debugger user interface. You can package the collection of classes you write to extend a visualizer in a separate assembly know as the visualizer type.

You can use the `DebuggerVisualizerAttribute` to identify the assembly level visualizers during the debugging process. This attribute provides information about the visualizer type and its name displayed in the UI.

Apart from assemblies, you can also apply this attribute to classes and structures. This attribute has several overloaded constructors. Fundamentally, the `DebuggerVisualizerAttribute` constructor takes two arguments—one that specifies the visualizer type or visualizer type name and the other that specifies the type or type name of the object source of the visualizer.

The code creates a visualizer user interface by inheriting from `DialogDebuggerVisualizer` class, which is responsible for displaying the user interface. In order to use the class, the `SampleVisualizer` overrides the `Show` method of the `DialogDebuggerVisualizer` class. The overridden `Show` method in the code displays the view of the received object, which in this case is string data:

```
[assembly:DebuggerVisualizer(typeof(SampleVisualizer),
typeof(VisualizerObjectSource),Target = typeof(System.String))]
public class SampleVisualizer: DialogDebuggerVisualizer
{
   protected void Show(IDialogVisualizerService windowService,
   IVisualizerObjectProvider objectProvider)
   {
   object dataToDisplay = (object)objectProvider.GetObject();
   Button MyButton = new Button();
   MyButton.Text = dataToDisplay.ToString();
   windowService.ShowDialog(MyButton);
   }
}
```

MORE INFORMATION

To know more about how to use this given assembly code, refer to "Writing a Visualizer in C# Walkthrough" from the MSDN section. This discusses the various ways in which you can utilize the visualizer type in .NET applications.

Understanding Tracing in .NET

Monitoring and tracing the execution of your code running in the production environment can help you determine the exact cause of a problem such as a hang or crash of your application. `System.Diagnostics` namespace provides classes that help you monitor the output of the execution of your code, even in release builds.

Recall that tracing is the process in which you record diagnostic information about the application. The `System.Diagnostics` namespace provides the `Trace` class, which you can use both during debug and release builds.

USING TRACE CLASS

The `Trace` class provides the same methods and properties as the `Debug` class to help you trace the execution of your code. However, unlike the `Debug` class, Trace class methods have the `ConditionalAttribute` attribute with the value of `TRACE` applied to them. This indicates to the compiler that it should ignore the methods with this attribute if "TRACE" is not defined as a conditional compilation symbol. You can define the conditional compilation symbol using the compiler command-line switches such as `/define:TRACE` or by adding directives in the source code such as `#define TRACE`. However, by default, Visual Studio .NET compiles Release builds with the TRACE conditional compilation constant defined.

You can also use BooleanSwitch and TraceSwitch classes to provide a dynamic control of the traced output. The BooleanSwitch class provides an on-off switch to control output. The TraceSwitch class also provides a multilevel switch to control traced output. By using these classes in combination with the Trace class, you can emit messages according to their importance.

TAKE NOTE*

You can use the Level property of the TraceSwitch class to emit messages according to their importance by defining the initial level of your trace switch in your application's configuration file. The TraceLevel enumeration defines the values that you can set to the level. When you change the Level property through your code, the corresponding TraceError, TraceWarning, TraceInfo, and TraceVerbose read-only properties of the TraceSwitch class are updated because each value of the TraceLevel enumeration corresponds to one of these properties.

The following code sample emits a warning and informational message in the trace output according to the switch value set in the Level property of the TraceSwitch class:

```
static TraceSwitch SampleTraceSwitch = new TraceSwitch("MyTraceSwitch",
"Tracing My Application");
static public void TraceSwitchOutput()
{
    //Emitting warning tracing
    if(SampleTraceSwitch.TraceWarning)
    {
        Trace.Write("Sample warning message");
    }
    //Emitting informational tracing
    if(SampleTraceSwitch.TraceInfo)
    {
        Trace.WriteLine("Sample message");
    }
}
```

TAKE NOTE*

You can use the configuration file to configure the properties of the TraceSwitch class to control tracing and debugging output without recompiling your code.

ADDING LISTENERS

You can also add ***listeners*** to the Trace class, similar to adding listeners to the Debug class, to customize the tracing output. Trace listeners are objects that can receive trace output and divert it to an output device or location such as a monitor or file.

TAKE NOTE*

If you add a listener to either the Debug or Trace class, the same listener automatically gets added to the other class. For example, if you add a listener to the Debug class, the same listener gets added to the Trace class.

By default, when you run the application directly from Visual Studio, the trace uses the DefaultTraceListener listener and displays the output in the output window of the Visual Studio environment. However, if you want to send the trace output to other sources such as the console or a file, you can add any one of the several listeners provided by the System.Diagnostics namespace to the Trace class.

Table 8-13 lists the various listeners and their purpose.

Table 8-13
Listeners

LISTENER	PURPOSE
ConsoleTraceListener	Sends the tracing or debugging output to the console or to the standard error stream.
DelimitedListTraceListener	Sends the tracing or debugging output to a delimited text file.
EventLogTraceListener	Sends the tracing or debugging output to an event log.
XmlWriterTraceListener	Sends the tracing or debugging information as an XML encoded data to a text file or stream.
TextWriterTraceListener	Sends the tracing or debugging output to a text file or a stream, such as the FileStream.
EventSchemaTraceListener	Sends the tracing or debugging output to an XML-compliant log file.

TAKE NOTE*
TraceListener is the abstract base class for all the listeners.

ASSOCIATING TRACING WITH SOURCE

To find the actual source of the trace messages, you can use the TraceSource class of the System.Diagnostics namespace. The TraceSource class provides properties and methods to trace the execution of your code and associate the trace messages with the actual source.

You can associate a specific trace source with the trace messages arriving from a particular code component. This helps you streamline and divert all the trace messages of that component to a particular destination. The TraceSource class uses the trace listeners to identify and catch the tracing data. In addition, you can easily control the trace output from the TraceSource through settings in the configuration file. You can use the configuration file to identify where to send the trace output and to specify the level of tracing.

The following code sample shows how to create a trace source for an application. The code sample traces error events using the TraceSource object and writes the trace messages in default trace listener:

```
using System;
using System.Diagnostics;
public class UsingTraceSource
{
   private static TraceSource SampleSource = new TraceSource("MyApp");
   static void Main(string[] args)
   {
      SampleSource.TraceEvent(TraceEventType.Error, 1, "Message
      representing the error");
      SampleSource.Close();
      return;
   }
}
```

To make this code write to a text file, you can edit the configuration file of your application as shown next. The setting configures a TextWriterTraceListener listener for the trace source. Note that the trace source is identified by the name of the associated application. In addition, note that the setting removes the default trace listener for this source. The trace switch for the listener is configured as TraceWarning:

```
<configuration>
  <system.diagnostics>
    <sources>
      <source name="MyApp">
        <listeners>
          <add name="textListener"
type="System.Diagnostics.TextWriterTraceListener"
initializeData="TraceOutput.log" />
          </add>
          <remove name="Default"/>
        </listeners>
      </source>
      </sources>
      <switches>
        <add name="newSwitch" value="TraceWarning" />
      </switches>
      </system.diagnostics>
    </configuration>
```

CERTIFICATION READY?
Debug and trace a .NET Framework application by using the System. Diagnostics namespace.
USD 3.5

TAKE NOTE*

The configuration file for the `TraceSource` exists in the same folder as your application executable file. In addition, the configuration file has the same name as your application with the .config extension. For example, if your executable application name is *MyApp.exe*, then the configuration file for the corresponding `TraceSource` has the name MyApp.exe.config.

GROUPING CORRELATED TRACES

You can tag traces that come from different logical operations with an operation-unique identity. This tagging helps you identify and segregate the traces based on logical operations. You can use the `CorrelationManager` class of the `System.Diagnostics` namespace to store an operation-unique identity in a thread-bound context. The `CorrelationManager` then automatically tags every trace event of the thread with that stored identity.

Handling Management Events

The .NET Framework provides an event infrastructure, such as the Windows Management Instrumentation (WMI) that allows management of events. Along with the ***Windows Management Instrumentation*** (***WMI***) infrastructure, the .NET Framework also provides the `System.Management` namespace that contains classes and methods to provide access to management events about the system, devices, and applications tied to the WMI infrastructure.

Members of the `System.Management` namespace and the WMI programmable code can be used together to manage events and event handling processes. In WMI, every event, publication of an event, or subscription to an event, is a WMI object. You can use these WMI objects just as you use any other WMI class or instance.

MORE INFORMATION

The WMI infrastructure helps you manage data and operations on Windows-based operating systems. To learn more about the Windows Management Instrumentation (WMI) infrastructure, refer to the "Windows Management Instrumentation" section in the MSDN library.

Accessing Management Information in .NET

To handle management information, WMI infrastructure uses the classes and methods provided in the `System.Management` namespace.

The `System.Management` namespace provides classes and methods to control management information and ***management events***, specifically for system devices and applications managed by the WMI infrastructure. For example, your application can query required management information such as the amount of free disk space through the classes derived from `ManagementObjectSearcher` and `ManagementQuery`. You can also use the `ManagementEventWatcher` class to subscribe to numerous management events, such as backing up the system configurations at a specified time of the day, every day.

Table 8-14 lists some of the frequently used classes within the `System.Management` namespace.

Table 8-14

Classes of the `System.Management` namespace

CLASS	DESCRIPTION
`CompletedEventArgs`	Contains data for a completed event.
`ConnectionOptions`	Defines the configuration for a WMI connection.
`DeleteOptions`	Provides options for deleting a management object.
`EnumerationOptions`	Contains a base class for all query and enumeration-related objects.
`EventArrivedEventArgs`	Contains data for the `EventArrived` event. The properties of this class specify how the event was triggered and if it was a new event.
`EventQuery`	Specifies arguments for a WMI event query.
`EventWatcherOptions`	Defines options for monitoring management events.
`InvokeMethodOptions`	Defines options for invoking management methods.
`ManagementBaseObject`	Is a base class for management objects. It also contains the basic elements of a management object.
`ManagementEventArgs`	Is a virtual base class that holds information for a management event.
`ManagementEventWatcher`	Is used to subscribe to temporary event notifications.
`ManagementException`	Contains information about management exceptions.
`ManagementObject`	Is an instance of a WMI object.
`ManagementObjectCollection`	Contains several WMI management objects.
`ManagementObjectSearcher`	Searches a collection of management objects based on an event query.
`ManagementQuery`	Is an abstract base class for all management query objects.

TAKE NOTE*

In addition to the classes within the `System.Management` namespace, there are various delegates and enumeration options that you can use for event queries.

Retrieving Collections of Management Objects

Devices such as adapters or file systems that are managed by the operating system are referred to as management objects in Windows-based operating systems. You can use the `ManagementObjectSearcher` class of the `System.Management` namespace to retrieve collections of management objects such as network adapters or all disk drives on a system.

The ManagementObjectSearcher class can be used to acquire a collection of management objects, based on a specific query. This is one of the most frequently used classes of the System.Management namespace. You can use the ManagementObjectSearcher class to determine key management information about a specific device, disk, or process. You can use an instance of this class and pass it to a WMI query.

You can use the properties and methods of this class along with other options, such as the ManagementScope and EnumerationOptions, to process complex management events. When used in conjunction with the ManagementScope class of the System.Management namespace, the ManagementObjectSearcher class retrieves WMI namespaces that can run your queries.

The ManagementObjectSearcher class contains members, such as constructors, methods, events, and properties that you can use in your queries. These members retrieve a collection of management objects.

Table 8-15 lists the frequently used members of the ManagementObjectSearcher class.

Table 8-15

Members of ManagementObjectSearcher class

Member	Description
ManagementObjectSearcher	This is a constructor overload. It initializes an instance of the ManagementObjectSearcher class. You can use the options within this constructor to invoke a management information query.
CreateObjRef	This method creates an object proxy, which contains all relevant information to communicate with remote objects.
Get	This method executes a query within a specified scope. It retrieves a collection of management objects from the ManagementObjectCollection that corresponds to the query.
GetType	This method returns the type of the current instance.
ToString	This method retrieves the name of the object.
CanRaiseEvents	This is a property of the ManagementObjectSearcher class. This property returns a value determining if the object or component can raise an event.
Events	This property lists the available event handlers associated with the object.
Options	This property allows you to specify the options for searching an object.
Query	This property allows you to specify or retrieve the query for the ManagementObjectSearcher class.
Scope	This property allows you to define a scope within which the query will search for objects.
Disposed	This is an event of the ManagementObjectSearcher class. This event is raised when the object or component is discarded using the Dispose method.

The following code sample retrieves a collection of objects for the specified class, in this case the Win32_NetworkConnection, through which you can view the active network connections in your Windows-based environment. It uses a foreach statement through the retrieved collection and displays the active NetworkConnection objects:

```
using System;
using System.Management;
```

```
public class SearchNetworkAdapterObjects
{
   public static int Main(string[] args)
   {
     ManagementObjectSearcher ms = new ManagementObjectSearcher
("Select * from Win32_NetworkConnection");
       foreach (ManagementObject NetworkConnection in ms.Get())
       {
         Console.WriteLine(NetworkConnection.ToString());
       }
    }
   }
```

Querying Management Information

WMI allows you to query for management information, based on a set of criteria.

In distributed application systems, the query is run on the system for which you seek the required management information. This procedure allows you to process the query request without exposing the management information to everyone on the network. Only the processed output is sent across the network to the intended recipient.

The WMI infrastructure offers the following classes within the `System.Management` namespace to query management information:

- `ManagementQuery`
- `EventQuery`
- `ObjectQuery`

USING MANAGEMENTQUERY CLASS

All management query objects are implemented from the abstract base class provided in the `ManagementQuery` class. The following code shows the usage of the `ManagementQuery` class in a C# environment:

```
public abstract class ManagementQuery: ICloneable
```

The `ManagementQuery` class includes methods and properties to carry out a query in order to retrieve management information of a system. Table 8-16 lists some of the methods of the `ManagementQuery` class.

Table 8-16

Members of the `ManagementQuery` Class

Member	Description
`ParseQuery`	This method is used to distinctly parse the query string, such as the class name property and the condition property, and then assign the respective values.
`QueryLanguage`	This property specifies or retrieves a query language that will be used in the query string.
`QueryString`	This property defines the format of the query string as text.

USING EVENTQUERY CLASS

The `EventQuery` class is used when querying WMI events. The `EventQuery` object or any instance of it is included in the `ManagementEventWatcher` class. The `ManagementEventWatcher` class is used to subscribe to specific WMI events. The following code represents the C# syntax for the `EventQuery` class:

```
public class EventQuery: ManagementQuery
```

You can manipulate the EventQuery object type using the EventQuery members such as the constructors, methods, and properties.

Table 8-17 lists some of the members of the EventQuery class.

Table 8-17

Members of the EventQuery class

MEMBER	DESCRIPTION
EventQuery	This constructor is overloaded to initialize a new instance of the EventQuery class.
ParseQuery	This method is used to distinctly parse the query string, such as the class name property and the condition property, and then assign the respective values.
QueryLanguage	This property is inherited from ManagementQuery. It specifies or retrieves the query language for a query string.
QueryString	This property is inherited from ManagementQuery and defines the query to use the text format.

You can use the EventQuery object and its members to determine how a client or recipient receives notification when an instance of Win32_Process is created. The following code sample creates a WMI event query in text format using the EventQuery object. The code creates a query that retrieves the running instances of the Win32_Process class (for example, an instance of Notepad). The query string uses the InstanceCreationEvent class and specifies a Where condition by setting the TargetInstance property of the InstanceCreationEvent to Win32_Process:

```
EventQuery equery = new EventQuery();

equery.QueryString="SELECT * FROM" + "InstanceCreationEvent" +
“WHERE TargetInstance isa \"Win32_Process\"");
```

USING OBJECTQUERY CLASS

ObjectQuery is a type of management query that retrieves classes and instances. The following code shows the representation of the ObjectQuery class in a C# program:

```
public class ObjectQuery: ManagementQuery
```

Like ManagementQuery and EventQuery, ObjectQuery has constructors, methods, and properties to manage management query objects.

Table 8-18 lists some of the members of the ObjectQuery class.

Table 8-18

Members of the ObjectQuery class

MEMBER	TYPE	DESCRIPTION
ObjectQuery	Constructor overload	Provides options for initializing a new instance of the ObjectQuery class.
ParseQuery	Method	Used to distinctly parse the query string, such as the class name property and the condition property, and then assign the respective values.
QueryLanguage	Property	Allows you to specify the query language that your query string will use, including the format of the query string.
QueryString	Property	Defines the format of the query in a text format.

Handling Event Subscriptions and Consumptions

An important aspect of running applications in distributed systems is the ability to determine why events are raised. The enterprise applications are huge applications; they handle and manage a huge volume of data and resources, so it is very important to track such events.

The most common way to keep track of events is to use centralized logs that can be frequently monitored to analyze them. The WMI infrastructure has a system to manage such events. It allows events to be published, filtered, subscribed to, and logged in using a specific combination of criteria for each application. In WMI infrastructure, every event, publication, and subscription is a WMI object.

TRACKING MANAGEMENT EVENTS

The WMI event-handling capabilities can be easily configured using standard code that is supported by WMI. Similarly, you can use classes and instances in the same way you would for any WMI class. You can subscribe to a WMI event and define it to be triggered for a specific condition. In such cases, you define permanent event consumers. These WMI events are raised when the defined condition is met. For example, a permanent event consumer that handles the daily backup operations can be set to run every night at a certain hour. You can also configure additional conditions like restricting or allowing the number of times the backup operations run.

SUBSCRIBING TO MANAGEMENT EVENTS

The `System.Management` namespace allows you to subscribe to management events. These WMI events notify the recipient when a specific event is raised within the OS, devices, or applications in the managed environment. You can subscribe to the event that is most relevant to you by specifying it in an event query, and you can also specify the criteria for the subscribed events within your query. The `ManagementEventWatcher` class can be used to subscribe to event notification based on specified criteria.

The `ManagementEventWatcher` class members, such as the constructor, methods, and properties, can be utilized to handle subscription requests and set the criteria. The following code shows the C# representation of the `ManagementEventWatcher` class:

```
public class ManagementEventWatcher: Component
```

Table 8-19 lists some of the constructors of the `ManagementEventWatcher` class.

Table 8-19

Members of the `ManagementEventWatcher` class

Member	Type	Description
`ManagementEventWatcher`	Constructor	Is overloaded to initialize a new instance of the `ManagementEventWatcher` class based on the WMI event query.
`Start`	Method	Used to subscribe to events and set the criteria. It delivers them asynchronously using the `EventArrived` event.
`Stop`	Method	Used to discard synchronous and asynchronous subscription to events.
`WaitForNextEvent`	Method	Waits for the next event that meets the criteria specified in the query to arrive then returns it to the recipient.
`CanRaiseEvents`	Property	Specifies whether a component can raise an event.
`Events`	Property	Retrieves a list of event handlers associated with the component.
`Options`	Property	Specifies or retrieves options to watch for events.
`Query`	Property	Specifies the criteria for events.
`Scope`	Property	Defines the scope where the events have to be monitored.

After you subscribe to a WMI event, consumption of the events can be carried out synchronously and asynchronously. The following code displays the method of subscribing to WMI intrinsic events and consumes them synchronously. The code sample creates a WMI event query to get an instance of the generated `Win32_PrintJob` by supplying `InstanceCreationEvent` as the event class. The event query in the code then creates a `ManagementEventWatcher` object to subscribe to events that matches the query. The code sample then receives the event synchronously by calling the `WaitForNextEvent` method. Note that the code sample requires a print job to be generated for it to receive the notification:

CERTIFICATION READY?
Embed management information and events into a .NET Framework application.
USD 3.6

```
using System;
using System.Management;
public class NotifyWin32PrintProcesses
{
  public static void Main(string[] args)
  {
    // Create a WMI event query to get an instance of the generated
Win32_PrintJob by supplying InstanceCreationEvent as the event class
WqlEventQuery query = new WqlEventQuery("InstanceCreationEvent",
"TargetInstance isa""Win32_PrintJob""");
    // Create a ManagementEventWatcher object to subscribe to events
that match the query
    ManagementEventWatcher mw = new ManagementEventWatcher();
    // Call the WaitForNextEvent method of the ManagementEventWatcher
class to receive the event synchronously
    ManagementBaseObject mBaseObj = mw.WaitForNextEvent();
    // Display the name of the print job
    Console.WriteLine("Name of the Print Job Created: " +
((ManagementBaseObject)mBaseObj["TargetInstance"])["Name"]);
  }
    // Stop the ManagementEventWatcher
    mw.Stop();
}
```

SKILL SUMMARY

This lesson explained how to monitor application performance by maintaining event logs, using performance counters, using debugging techniques, and embedding management information into your .NET applications.

You have learned how to use the various programming interfaces of the .NET Framework to view and analyze event log entries. In addition, you also learned how to use the `EventLog` component to perform read-write operations to an event log. As a developer, you have understood how to monitor the process and thread performance by using performance counters.

Additionally, you have learned to troubleshoot your .NET applications using the various debugging and tracing techniques provided in the .NET Framework. You have also learned how to apply various debugging attributes to your code to enhance and support your debugging experience.

You also learned about the .NET Framework's Windows Management Instrumentation infrastructure and the `System.Management` namespace to manage events and event handlers. You have understood how to configure the WMI to track management events using standard WMI programming syntax. Additionally, you know how to subscribe to WMI events using the `ManagementEventWatcher` component. You have also learned the various `Query` classes to query management information on a system.

For the certification examination:

- Know how to maintain event logs using the `System.Diagnostics` namespace.
- Understand the process of monitoring the performance of .NET applications using the diagnostics functionality.
- Know how to troubleshoot your .NET applications using debug and trace functionalities of the .NET Framework.
- Know how to create .NET applications with management information and events.

■ Knowledge Assessment

Matching

Match the following descriptions to the appropriate terms.

a. `PagedSystemMemorySize`
b. `EventQuery`
c. Event source
d. `CorrelationManager`
e. `ManagementEventWatcher`

_______ 1. Queries WMI events.
_______ 2. Returns the amount of memory the system has allocated on behalf of the concerned process that can be written to the virtual memory paging file.
_______ 3. Tags every trace event of the operation-unique identity in a thread-bound context.
_______ 4. Registers applications with the event log.
_______ 5. Subscribes to event notification based on specified criteria.

True / False

Circle T if the statement is true or F if the statement is false.

T | F 1. You must specify a source for reading from an event log.
T | F 2. You can configure a source for writing both localized entries and direct strings.
T | F 3. You can associate tracing messages of a particular component with a specified `Trace` object.
T | F 4. The counter information must include an instance specification if a category can have more than one instance.
T | F 5. `EventQuery` can be used to query the `System.Management` namespace.

Fill in the Blank

Complete the following sentences by writing the correct word or words in the blanks provided.

1. You can create and delete logs using ________ component.
2. You can use the ______________ enumeration to specify the log entry type.
3. You can use __________ class to query WMI events.
4. __________ and ____________ classes help you output trace and debug information based on importance.
5. The ______________ component helps reading existing predefined counters and publishing performance data to custom counters.

Multiple Choice

Circle the letter that corresponds to the best answer.

1. Which of the following classes in the `System.Diagnostics` namespace should you use to write to an event log using resource identifiers?
   a. `EventInstance`
   b. `EventLogInstaller`
   c. `EventSourceCreationData`
   d. `EventLog`
2. Which of the following listener classes should you use to output the debug information to an XML compliant log file?
   a. `TraceListener`
   b. `XmlWriterTraceListener`
   c. `EventSchemaTraceListener`
   d. `EventLogTraceListener`
3. Which of the following debugging attributes should you use to step through the designer generated code?
   a. `DebuggerNonUserCodeAttribute`
   b. `DebuggerUserCodeAttribute`
   c. `DebuggerStepThroughAttribute`
   d. `DebuggerStepperBoundaryAttribute`
4. Which of the following properties should you use for accessing the loaded libraries of a process?
   a. `Modules`
   b. `Module`
   c. `ProcessThread`
   d. `Threads`
5. Which of the following features should you use to get a collection of management objects?
   a. `ManagementObjectSearcher`
   b. `ManagementObjectCollection`
   c. `ManagementBaseObject`
   d. `ManagementQuery`

Review Questions

1. Consider that you want to locate a running instance of Windows Word. Is it possible for you to locate the instance using the `Process` object?
2. How can you find if a specified category contains the instance of a specified counter on all the machines in your network?

■ Case Scenarios

Scenario 8-1: Querying Log Information

You want to include the event logging functionality in your online movie booking application. As a first step, write a program to query all the logs that are available in a remote computer, say your Web server.

Scenario 8-2: Monitoring Instances

Consider that your online movie application allows the use of a specific tool, say ABC.exe. The users can open many instances of this tool. However, if multiple users open this tool, then site performance may be impacted. Therefore, as a first step, write an administrative routine that can display the number of instances of this tool.

✳ Workplace Ready

Choosing the Appropriate Tracing Approach

.NET offers various classes to help you write trace messages to various mediums such as console or text files. You must choose the correct tracing classes per your requirements. XYZ Integrated, Inc. develops a data-critical application. Their programmers want to include tracing support to be able to debug the application at a later stage. Their team decides that trace messages must appear in the console and should be written to a text file. Suggest the best approach for the programmers to take.

LESSON 9 Securing Applications, Users, and Data in .NET

OBJECTIVE DOMAIN MATRIX

Technology Skill	Objective Domain	Objective Domain Number
Explore CAS.	Implement code access security to improve the security of a .NET Framework application.	5.1
Explore CAS.	Control code privileges by using the System.Security.Policy classes.	5.6
Explore CAS.	Modify the code access security policy at the computer, user, and enterprise level by using the code access security policy tool.	5.8
Protect assemblies with declarative security.	Implement code access security to improve the security of a .NET Framework application.	5.1
Protect assemblies with declarative security.	Control permissions for resources by using the System.Security.Permission classes.	5.5
Protect methods with imperative and declarative security.	Implement code access security to improve the security of a .NET Framework application.	5.1
Protect methods with imperative and declarative security.	Control permissions for resources by using the System.Security.Permission classes.	5.5
Authenticate users.	Implement a custom authentication scheme by using the System.Security.Authentication classes.	5.3
Authenticate users.	Control permissions for resources by using the System.Security.Permission classes.	5.5
Authenticate users.	Access and modify identity information by using the System.Security.Principal classes.	5.7
Authorize users.	Implement a custom authentication scheme by using the System.Security.Authentication classes.	5.3
Authorize users.	Control permissions for resources by using the System.Security.Permission classes.	5.5
Authorize users.	Access and modify identity information by using the System.Security.Principal classes.	5.7
Work with access control lists.	Implement access control by using the System.Security.AccessControl classes.	5.2
Explore data encryption.	Encrypt, decrypt, and hash data by using the System.Security.Cryptography classes.	5.4

KEY TERMS

access control entries (ACE)
asymmetric encryption
authentication
authorization
ciphertext
code access security (CAS)
code access security policy tool (Caspol.exe)
code groups
declarative security
discretionary access control list (DACL)
evidence
imperative security
role-based security (RBS)
security demand
security override
symmetric encryption
system access control list (SACL)

When you create an application, you must consider the security of the application from different aspects. You must secure your application resources, and at the same time, protect your application from hacker attacks.

The .NET Framework offers security from two perspectives: code and role. ***Code access security (CAS)*** enables you to secure your application code through declarations made by the code. ***Role-based security (RBS)*** enables you to secure your application resources by using roles to authenticate and authorize users. Authenticating users is the process of identifying users based on their roles, and authorizing users is the process of verifying the user rights to access your application resources. In addition, you can use CAS and RBS to authenticate and authorize resources that can access your application.

.NET also permits you to manage the Windows access control lists to control access to resources. Last but not least, you can secure data during transmission by using the cryptographic services offered by the .NET Framework.

Exploring CAS

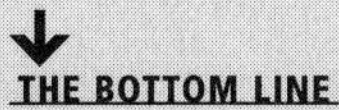

The .NET Common Language Runtime (CLR) provides code access security (CAS) to check the identity of your code. You can use CAS to restrict the resources that your code can access. For example, you can prevent a Web application from transferring data through the Internet or accessing the hard disk.

Introducing CAS

Every code that runs on a computer or server has access to the protected resources and operations on that computer or server. Code access security is a security mechanism that helps you limit these access permissions for your code.

The .NET Framework provides a security mechanism known as code access security (CAS) that enables you to identify and assign permission to applications. You can use CAS to restrict the resources that your code can access to prevent any security vulnerability. You can use the CAS mechanism in the following scenarios:

- When you want your code to access only specified types of resources such as specific files or directories to ensure security.
- When you want to prevent any malicious code from accessing your code or accessing resources through your code.
- When you want to provide an identity for your code that the runtime can recognize; the runtime uses this identity to decide what kind of access your code can have for accessing secured resources.

The CAS model enables system administrators to set security policy for your applications. That is, an administrator can decide what type of permissions to set for your application to restrict it from accessing specific resources or from performing privileged actions. The CLR enforces this security policy at runtime.

UNDERSTANDING ELEMENTS OF CAS

The CAS model is comprised of different elements that together create rules, which the common language security system applies to your application. Table 9-1 lists the various elements of CAS.

Table 9-1

CAS elements

ELEMENT	DESCRIPTION
Application domain host	Each .NET Framework application runs in an application domain. An application is executed under the control of a host that creates the application domain and loads assemblies into the application domain.
Permission sets	Permission determines the type of access a code can have. For example, the FileIOPermission determines whether the code can access a specific file or directory. Permission sets are a collection of permissions. For example, the Internet permission set includes the minimum set of permissions required to protect your code from the risks presented by malicious assemblies. Administrators can specify permission sets for a code group. These permission sets are called named permission sets because they have a name, description, and at least a single permission. Administrators use named permission sets to establish or enhance the security policies for code groups. You can link more than one code group with the same named permission set.
Code groups	You can create a logical grouping of code with a specified membership condition. Any code or assembly that meets the membership condition becomes part of that code group. For example, the members of the Internet_Zone code group include all the code running from the Internet. When you apply permission sets for a code group, the permission sets apply to all the assemblies contained within that code group. An administrator can set the security policy for managing code groups.
Policy levels	These policy levels are enterprise, machine, user, and application domain. Each level has its own hierarchy of code groups and permission sets.
Evidence	The CLR utilizes evidence to identify an assembly and to determine the code group of an assembly. The runtime can gather two types of evidences from the assembly—host evidence and assembly evidence. Host evidence provides details about the source from which the assembly originates, for example, the site from which the assembly was downloaded. Assembly evidence is the custom evidence provided by the assembly developer.

MORE INFORMATION

To learn more about how the CLR uses these types of evidence to make decisions about the security policy, refer to the Evidence section from the MSDN library.

UNDERSTANDING THE FUNCTIONS OF CAS

The CAS model provides the following functionality:

- **Enables the configuration of security policy.** As explained earlier, CAS allows administrators to configure security policy for your applications. Administrators can associate a permission set with a code group, which then applies to all the members of that code group.

- **Enables defining and granting permissions.** CAS enables you to define permissions for your code to access a secured resource or to perform privileged operations. Additionally, CAS grants permissions to the loaded assembly by checking its evidence and applying the appropriate security policy configured by the administrator.
- **Enables code to demand permissions and digital signatures.** CAS enables your code to demand a permission to ensure that the code and its caller have the required permissions to access the secured resources. Additionally, your code can also demand that its caller contain a required digital signature.
- **Enables the CLR to throw security exceptions.** At runtime, CAS allows the CLR to determine whether the code can have access to secured resources or perform the required action by performing a stack walk. During this stack walk, the CLR compares permissions granted to each caller with the required demand permission. If any of the callers do not possess the demanded permission, then the CLR throws a security exception and prevents the code from accessing the secured resources.

Figure 9-1 depicts a working CAS model. When an application is installed, the .NET server hosts the assembly and gathers evidence from it. The system administrator configures the security policy for the installed assembly. Imagine that a client calls this application assembly and the CLR loads the assembly into memory. The runtime identifies the assembly using evidence and grants permission to the assembly as configured in the security policy. Whenever the code in the assembly accesses a secured resource, it demands a specified permission from the runtime, and the runtime performs a stack walk to ensure that the corresponding caller possess the demanded permission. If the caller does not possess the demanded permission, the runtime throws a security exception. Otherwise, the runtime allows the code to access the secured resource.

Figure 9-1

Working of CAS

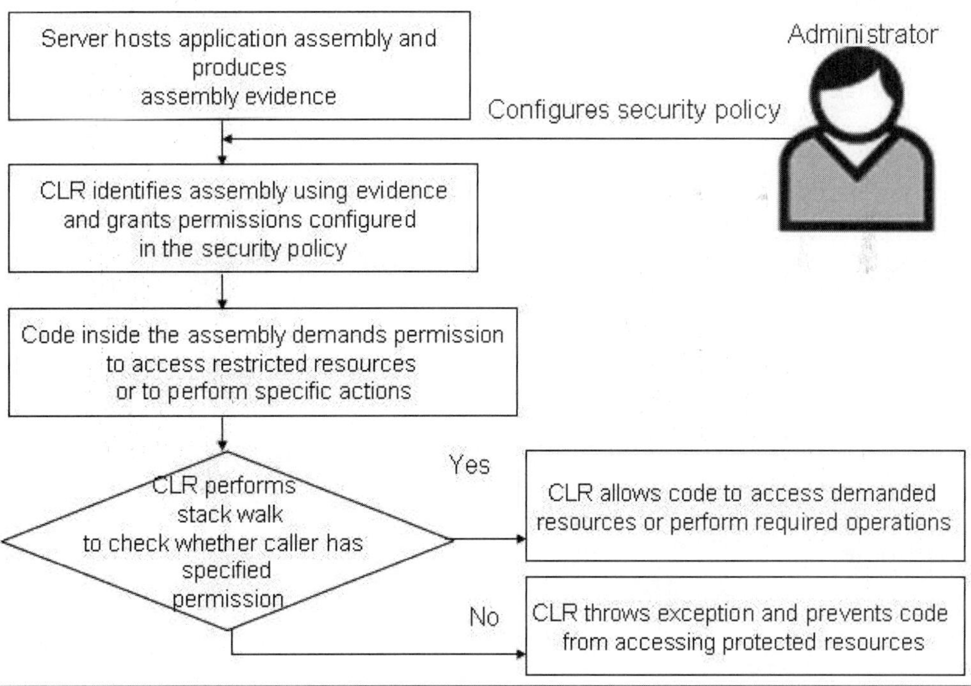

MORE INFORMATION

To learn more about CAS refer to the "Code Access Security" section from the MSDN library. Stack walk is the process in which the runtime checks all the callers of a particular code higher in the stack for a specific permission. To understand stack walk and permission grants refer to the "Introduction to Code Access Security" section from the MSDN Library.

Exploring Security and Policy Classes

The System.Security namespace provides the underlying structure of the CLR security system. Additionally, the System.Security.Policy namespace provides classes that create the rules, which the security policy system then applies.

EXPLORING THE SECURITY NAMESPACE

The System.Security namespace includes the following base classes for defining and granting permissions to code. For example, the CodeAccessPermission class defines the base class that you can use to create a custom permission.

Table 9-2 lists the classes in the System.Security namespace.

Table 9-2

Classes in the System.Security namespace

CLASS	DESCRIPTION
AllowPartiallyTrustedCallersAttribute	Facilitates strong-named assemblies to be called by partially trusted code.
CodeAccessPermission	Defines the underlying structure of all code access permissions.
HostProtectionException	Depicts the exception that is thrown when a denied host resource is detected.
HostSecurityManager	Allows the control and customization of security behavior for application domains.
NamedPermissionSet	Defines a permission set having a name and description associated with it.
PermissionSet	Represents a collection that holds different types of permissions.
SecureString	Depicts a text that should be kept confidential. The text is encrypted for privacy when being used, and deleted from computer memory when no longer needed.
SecurityContext	Encapsulates and propagates all security-related data for execution contexts transferred across threads.
SecurityCriticalAttribute	Specifies that a code or an assembly performs security-critical operations.
SecurityState	Provides a base class for requesting the security status of an action from the AppDomainManager object.
SecurityTransparentAttribute	Specifies that an assembly cannot cause an elevation of privilege.
SecurityTreatAsSafeAttribute	Identifies the nonpublic SecurityCriticalAttribute members that are accessible by transparent code within the assembly.
SuppressUnmanagedCodeSecurityAttribute	Permits managed code to call into unmanaged code without a stack walk.
UnverifiableCodeAttribute	Tags the modules that contain unverifiable code.
VerificationException	Depicts the exception thrown when the security policy requires code to be type safe and when the verification process is unable to verify that the code is type safe.
XmlSyntaxException	Depicts the exception thrown when there is a syntax error in XML parsing.

MORE INFORMATION

These classes form the base of the .NET security system. All the other classes and namespaces discussed in this lesson are built on the classes in this namespace. To know more about each of these classes, refer to the corresponding section in the MSDN library.

EXPLORING THE SECURITY POLICY NAMESPACE

The `System.Security.Policy` namespace contains classes to define and use membership conditions, code groups, and evidence. Evidence classes and membership conditions help in creating policy statements and determining the granted permission set. Code groups encapsulate a rule placed hierarchically in a policy level.

Table 9-3 lists the important classes available in the `System.Security.Policy` namespace.

Table 9-3

Important classes in the `System.Security.Policy` namespace

Class	Description
`AllMembershipCondition`	Represents a membership condition matching all code.
`CodeConnectAccess`	Specifies the granted network resource access of the code.
`CodeGroup`	Represents the abstract base class for all the code groups.
`FileCodeGroup`	Enables granting permission to code assemblies. This permission matches the membership condition to manage files placed in the code assemblies.
`Evidence`	Provides an input to security policy decisions by defining the required set of information.
`PermissionRequestEvidence`	Defines evidence representing permission requests.
`PolicyLevel`	Represents the runtime security-policy level.
`PolicyStatement`	Represents the policy statement of a code group object that describes the permissions and other information that applies to the code with particular evidence.

Modifying Security Policy Using CASPOL

Your code can have custom permissions other than those defined in the default security policy, but you must update the default security policy to include your custom permissions.

The default security policy includes only the built-in permission sets. To use your own custom permissions for your code, you should add the custom permissions to the default security policy.

ADD CUSTOM PERMISSIONS TO SECURITY POLICY

Perform the following steps to include your custom permissions to the default security policy:

1. Create a new named permission set, which includes your custom permission.
2. Generate an .xml file through code that contains the XML representation of the newly created named permission set.
3. Add the newly created named permission set to the default security policy by using the ***code access security policy*** **tool (Caspol.exe).**

TAKE NOTE*

Caspol.exe allows you to add the .xml file containing custom permissions to the security policy on the computer in which the code executes. In addition, Caspol.exe allows you to modify machines, users, and enterprise-level CAS policies. You can execute Caspol.exe from the Visual Studio command prompt. The navigation path for this command prompt is Start→All Programs→Microsoft Visual Studio→Visual Studio Tools→Visual Studio Command Prompt. Note that you can also use the .NET Framework configuration tool (Mscorcfg.exe) to update the default security policy with your custom permissions.

MORE INFORMATION

Caspol.exe provides various options to configure security policies. To learn more about these options, you can refer to the "Code Access Security Policy Tool" section in the MSDN library.

The following command line shows how to supply the .xml file, which in this case is "custompermissionset.xml" to Caspol.exe. The –`addpset` option adds the custom permissions contained in the specified .xml file to the security policy. The –`machine` option indicates that this permission set applies to the machine level security policy.

```
caspol -machine -addpset custompermissionset.xml
```

Once you have added your custom permissions to the default security policy, you have to update the security policy about the assembly containing the custom permissions and the code to which it has to grant the permission.

UPDATE THE SECURITY POLICY

To update the default security policy, you must:

1. Add the assembly to the list of trusted assemblies.
2. Inform the security policy about the code that should be granted your custom permission.

ADDING THE ASSEMBLY TO THE TRUSTED ASSEMBLIES LIST

You can gain the full trust for your assembly by adding it to the list of trusted assemblies. After you add your assembly to the trusted assemblies list using Caspol.exe, you must also add assemblies that your permission class references. You can use the following command to add an assembly to the trusted assemblies list:

TAKE NOTE*

Caspol.exe will not add an assembly to the full-trust list if the assembly does not have a strong name.

```
caspol -addfulltrust custompermissionset.dll
```

You can view the list of fully trusted assemblies using the following command:

```
caspol -listfulltrust
```

CONFIGURING POLICY TO GRANT YOUR CUSTOM PERMISSION

You must associate your new permission set with the appropriate code groups. This association enables the security policy to grant the custom permission to the specific code. You can achieve this by modifying an existing code group or by adding a new code group that identifies the set of code that should be granted your custom permission. The following Caspol.exe command is used to make `custompermissionset` the permission set granted to code that meets the membership condition of the `LocalIntranet` code group:

```
caspol -user -chggroup 1.2. custompermissionset
```

The label 1.2 represents the `LocalIntranet` code group. You can display all the code groups and their associated labels using the following command:

```
caspol -list
```

You can view the list of permission sets using the following command:

```
caspol -listpset
```

EXPLORING CASPOL

The code access security policy tool helps users and administrators update security policies at any level—machine, user, or enterprise. The following are examples of policy updates at different levels:

- **Example 1.** Imagine that a permission set containing a custom permission is added to machine policy. This custom permission is implemented in *NewPerm.exe,* which references classes in *NewMem.exe*. You must add both these assemblies to the trusted assemblies list. You can use the following command to add the *NewPerm.exe* assembly to the full trust list for the machine policy:

  ```
  caspol -machine -addfulltrust NewPerm.exe
  ```

  The following command adds the NewMem.exe assembly to the full-trust list for the machine policy:

  ```
  caspol -machine -addfulltrust NewMem.exe
  ```

CERTIFICATION READY?
Implement CAS to improve the security of a .NET Framework application.
USD 5.1

- **Example 2.** You can use the following command to add the *MyPerm* permission set to the user policy:

  ```
  caspol -user -addpset MyPerm.xml MyPerm
  ```

CERTIFICATION READY?
Control code privileges by using the `System.Security.Policy` classes.
USD 5.6

- **Example 3.** You can use the following command to change the permission set with name *MyPerm* to the permission set contained in *mynewpset.xml:*

  ```
  caspol -chgpset MyPerm mynewpset.xml
  ```

- **Example 4.** You can use the following command to recover the most recently saved machine policy:

  ```
  caspol -machine -recover
  ```

CERTIFICATION READY?
Modify the code access security policy at the computer, user, and enterprise level by using the code access security policy tool.
USD 5.8

- **Example 5.** You can use the following command to remove the code group labeled 1.2. This command also removes any child code groups associated with this code group:

  ```
  caspol -remgroup 1.2.
  ```

- **Example 6.** You can use the following command to remove *MyPermset* from the user policy level:

  ```
  caspol -rempset MyPermset
  ```

■ Protecting Assemblies with Imperative and Declarative Security

THE BOTTOM LINE

Because your class libraries may access system resources and unmanaged codes frequently, when programming errors occur in your application, your application is exposed to security vulnerabilities. Therefore, you must secure your class libraries to avoid malicious attacks through any vulnerability in your code. The .NET Framework allows you to provide security for your applications at the assembly level. You can provide assembly level security by using attributes to declare the security information metadata above the assembly code. This is called ***declarative security***. By doing so, you can ensure that administrators who deploy your application are aware that your application only requires minimum permissions to run. You can use the various security permission attributes available in the .NET Framework to declare the permissions required for your code.

Understanding Security Permissions

You can set security permissions to protect your code or application from malicious attacks.

With the help of security permissions settings, the CLR ensures that the code performs only the restricted operations that it is supposed to perform. Thus, security permissions provide a way for the runtime to implement restrictions on managed code.

The three kinds of permissions that you can set for your application include code access permissions for providing access to protected resources, identity permissions for providing access to particular identity, and role-based security permissions for providing access to users based on roles.

Following are the main purposes of using security permissions:

- Your assembly code can demand that its calling codes have defined permissions. For example, by demanding a specified permission for your code, you can ensure that your code is only executed by codes that have the specified permission. You can also use demands to recognize the identity of the code caller.
- Your code can verify that it contains all the essential permissions for it to run.
- Your code uses permissions to deny access to callers and protect resources. For example, your code can deny file access to a particular location, thus preventing the valuable resources from an untrusted code.
- You can use the various built-in permission classes provided by the runtime and implement your own custom permission classes.

ANALYZING SECURITY ELEMENTS

The important elements that you should consider when imposing security for your class libraries include:

- **Security demand.** You can apply demands at the class and method levels to demand that the callers of your code have the specified permissions. The security demand initiates a stack walk. During the stack walk, the runtime examines all the callers of your code on the stack to make sure they have the specified permission to access your code. The three types of security demands that you can place in your code include demands, link demands, and inheritance demands.
- **Security override.** You can apply overrides at the class and method levels to overrule some of the runtime security decisions. Unlike the security demand, the security override stops stack walks. Additionally, it also limits the access of callers who already contain certain granted permissions. The three types of security overrides that you can place in your code include assert, deny, and permit only.

Table 9-4 discusses the types of security demands and security overrides.

Table 9-4

Types of demands and overrides

SECURITY ACTION	DESCRIPTION	SECURITY ACTION TIME
Demand	When you use **Demand** in your code, any application that includes your code will execute only if all the callers have the permissions specified in the demand. Note that you should use demands only to secure custom resources with custom permissions. This is because the majority of the built-in classes in the .NET Framework already contain demands. Therefore, when you impose demands on these classes, it will cause a redundant stack walk, which could affect the efficiency of your code.	Runtime

Table 9-4 (continued)

SECURITY ACTION	DESCRIPTION	SECURITY ACTION TIME
`LinkDemand`	When you use `LinkDemand` in your code, the CLR performs only one check. It checks that the immediate calling assembly has the permission specified by your code. If the calling assembly of your code does not have sufficient permission to link to your code, the runtime throws an exception and does not perform linking. Linking takes place when you bind your code to a type reference.	Just-in-time
`Inheritance Demand`	When you use `InheritanceDemand` at the class level, only the code with the specified permission can inherit that class. When you place the inheritance demands at the method level, only the methods with the specified permissions can override your method.	Load time
`Assert`	You can call `Assert` on permission classes and on the `PermissionSet` class. By placing asserts on your code, you can inform the runtime security system that it should not check the callers of your code for the specified asserted permission, instead, it should check your code for the specified permission.	Runtime
`Deny`	By placing a `Deny` permission on your code, you can prevent access to specified resources. That is, you can deny permission for a specified resource even though the callers of your code possess the permission to access that resource. For example, if you do not want the caller of your code to access a specified file or directory, you can place deny file permissions on your code.	Runtime
`PermitOnly`	You can use `PermitOnly` when you want only the specified resources to be accessed through your code. For example, if you want the caller of your code to access only a specified file or directory, you can place permit only file permissions on your code.	Runtime

TAKE NOTE*

You should use overrides with extreme care. To improve code performance during its interaction with the runtime security system, you can use a combination of demands and overrides. For example, if method A needs to perform multiple operations, and if for every one of those operations, your code places a demand permission to the runtime, then the runtime performs stack walk for each of those operations to determine whether your code and the callers of your code possess the specified demand permission. This increases the performance overhead of your application. To reduce the overhead caused by security demands, you can use demands and overrides together. That is, the code inside method A can place a demand and an assert for permission X. When you place an assert after a demand, the runtime performs stack walk only once. Asserts make the runtime check only your code for the specified asserted permission, and they stop subsequent checks on all the callers of your code.

X REF

Refer to Table 9-6 in the "Protecting Methods with Imperative and Declarative Security" section for a list of permission classes that you can use in the imperative syntax.

Exploring the Security Types

You can place the security demands and security overrides for your code either declaratively through attributes or imperatively through code at runtime.

USING IMPERATIVE SECURITY

When using ***imperative security***, you can use the instances of the permission classes to make security calls. You can use imperative security to specify a permission or permission set for your code.

TAKE NOTE*

To create a group of permissions, you can use the PermissionSet and NamedPermissionSet classes.

When using the imperative syntax to specify a single permission, you should initialize the state data of the corresponding permission object before making security calls using that object. For example, if you use the FileDialogPermission object, you can use its constructor to specify the type of access to use to retrieve files or folders through a File dialog box.

The following code sample uses imperative syntax to demand that the AccessthroughFileDialog method and its callers have the FileDialogPermission to open the files through File dialog box:

```
public class SampleClass
{
    public SampleClass()
    {
        //Constructor
    }
    public void AccessthroughFileDialog()
    {
        //Using imperative syntax to demand FileDialogPermission
        FileDialogPermission fdialogperm = new
FileDialogPermission(FileDialogPermissionAccess.Open);
        fdialogperm.Demand();
        //Rest of the method implementation goes here
    }
}
```

Note that if the call to the Demand method of the FileDialogPermission object fails, the remaining part of the code is not executed.

TAKE NOTE*

You can use imperative security to perform demands and overrides only; you cannot use it to perform security requests. You can use imperative syntax when the information required to initialize the permission state is available only during runtime.

USING DECLARATIVE SECURITY

With the declarative security type, you can use attributes to embed security information in the metadata of your code. You can apply attributes to assembly, class, or class members to specify the required request type, demand, or override.

Similar to imperative security, you should initialize the state data of the permission object while using the declarative security calls.

TAKE NOTE*

All built-in permissions contain an attribute to which you can pass a SecurityAction enumeration to specify the required security type. Additionally, you can also specify values for the parameters that are specific to individual permissions.

The following code uses the declarative syntax to request permission. Because the code places the declarative call before the Method1 method of the SampleClass, the permission applies only to this method. The code passes a SecurityAction.Assert enumeration value to the FileDialogPermissionAttribute and specifies that callers of this method do not need to possess FileDialogPermission to open the files through the File dialog box. This is because SecurityAction.Assert informs the runtime not to check callers for the FileDialogPermission:

```
public class SampleClass
{
    public SampleClass()
    {
```

```
        // Unsecured constructor
    }
    [FileDialogPermissionAttribute(SecurityAction.Assert, Open = true)]
    public void Method1()
    {
        // Method 1 implementation goes here
    }
    public void Method2()
    {
        // Method 2 implementation goes here
    }
}
```

TAKE NOTE*

System administrators use the *Permission View Tool* to examine assemblies and to set up security policy. If you do not explicitly request the required permissions for your application, the Permission View Tool will not show the necessary information about these permissions for your applications, which makes administration of your application difficult.

Requesting Permissions at Assembly Level

You can use requests in your applications to inform the runtime security system about permissions that your application may or may not need.

You can request permissions for your code using declarative syntax. During the creation of the assembly, the compiler places the requested permissions in the assembly manifest. Then, the runtime determines the required permissions to grant to the assembly at load time.

Your code should always request permissions to ensure that:

- The code runs correctly on execution.
- The code is granted only the required permissions.

By requesting permissions, you can let your administrator know about the minimum permissions required for your applications. This lets your system administrator adjust the security policy accordingly.

Table 9-5 lists the different types of permission requests and their description.

Table 9-5

Types of permission requests

Request	Description
Requesting minimum permissions	Use the `RequestMinimum` flag to request the minimum permissions that your code must have for it to run.
Requesting optional permissions	Use the `RequestOptional` flag to specify the optional permissions that your code can have. However, your code can run properly even without these optional permissions.
Requesting permission refusal	Use the `RequestRefuse` flag to specify the permissions that you never wanted your code to get, even if the security policy allows those permissions to be granted for your code.
Requesting built-in named permission sets	Use the built-in named permission sets such as `Nothing`, `Execution`, `FullTrust`, `Internet`, `LocalIntranet`, and `SkipVerification`, instead of requesting individual permissions.
Requesting XML-encoded permissions	Use XML representations of custom permission sets to request permission.

USING REQUESTMINIMUM FLAG

By using the `RequestMinimum` flag, you can inform the runtime that it should not allow your code to run without the required set of specified permissions.

The following example illustrates how the runtime works when you set the RequestMinimum flag for your assembly. Imagine that you have set the FileIOPermission to your assembly through the RequestMinimum flag, as shown in the following code:

```
[assembly: FileIOPermission(SecurityAction.RequestMinimum,
Unrestricted = true)]
namespace Sample
{
  class Test
  {
    static void Main(string[] args)
    {
      try
      {
        DirectoryInfo myDir = new
DirectoryInfo(@"c:\myDir");
        if (myDir.Exists)
          Console.WriteLine("The folder already exists");
        else
          myDir.Create();
      }
      catch(SecurityException e)
      {
        Console.WriteLine("Directory creation cannot be permitted" +
e.ToString());
      }
    }
  }
}
```

When you execute this application from a local intranet zone whose default permission set does not include FileIOPermission, your assembly will fail to load, and an exception will be thrown. This is because the code requests FileIOPermission as a minimum requirement through the RequestMinimum flag. Therefore, when loading your assembly, the CLR understands that your assembly needs the FileIOPermission for proper execution. However, the local Intranet permission set would not grant the FileIOPermission to your assembly. In this case, you get a FileLoadException.

TAKE NOTE*

When you run the earlier console application from your personal computer, it is granted full trust and therefore it loads and executes successfully. However, if you run the same application in a partial-trust zone such as a local intranet zone, which does not include FileIOPermission in its permission set, the application will fail to load because it requires FileIOPermission at a minimum for it to run successfully.

USING REQUESTOPTIONAL FLAG

You can use the RequestOptional flag to inform the runtime that it can allow your code to run even without the specified set of permissions. Consider the following code sample. The code sets the FileIOPermission as an optional permission for an assembly by specifying the RequestOptional flag:

```
[assembly: FileIOPermission(SecurityAction.RequestOptional,
Unrestricted = true)]
namespace Sample
{
   // The class code goes here
}
```

In this case, when the runtime examines the assembly, it understands that it can allow the assembly to run, even if the assembly is not granted the `FileIOPermission`. However, when the assembly loads, the runtime throws a `FileIOPermission` exception if that permission is not granted for your assembly.

TAKE NOTE*

When using `RequestOptional` permissions, you should place your code inside a try catch block. This enables your code to handle any exceptions that might be thrown if it is not granted the specified optional permissions. Additionally, when you specify `RequiredOptional` permissions, the runtime takes the union of the `RequiredMinimum` and `RequiredOptional` permissions for your assembly and does not let any other permission be granted for your assembly.

USING REQUESTREFUSE FLAG

At times, you may be concerned that your code could be used to access certain system resources illicitly. In this case, you can inform the runtime that it should not grant your code the specified set of permissions by using the `RequestRefuse` flag.

CERTIFICATION READY?
Implement CAS to improve the security of a .NET Framework application.
USD 5.1

For example, imagine that your application must read data from a file but should not edit the data. In this case, you can refuse any file-write permissions for your application. By refusing the write permissions, you can protect the file data from your code in case of an error or malicious attack.

The following code sample refuses the `FileIOPermission` for an assembly by specifying the `RequestRefuse` flag:

CERTIFICATION READY?
Control permissions for resources by using the `System.Security.Permission` classes.
USD 5.5

```
[assembly: FileIOPermission(SecurityAction.RequestRefuse, Unrestricted =
true)]
namespace Sample
{
    // The class code goes here
}
```

■ Protecting Methods with Imperative and Declarative Security

THE BOTTOM LINE

You must protect classes or methods in your assembly from calling codes to ensure that unauthorized operations or access to system resources does not happen through your code. You can use the `System.Security.Permissions` namespace provided in the .NET Framework to implement security permissions either imperatively or declaratively for your classes or methods.

Understanding the Permissions Namespace

You can use the various permission classes and attributes available in the `System.Security.Permissions` namespace to restrict malicious access to resources through your code.

Table 9-6 lists the important classes available in the System.Security.Permissions namespace.

Table 9-6

Important classes of System.Security.Permissions namespace

CLASS	PURPOSE
EnvironmentPermission	Controls access to system and user environment variables.
FileDialogPermission	Controls access to files and folders through a File dialog box.
FileIOPermission	Controls access to files and folders.
IsolatedStorageFilePermission	Specifies the allowed usage of a private virtual file system.
ReflectionPermission	Controls access to nonpublic types and members through the System.Reflection APIs and to certain features of the System.Reflection.Emit APIs.
ZoneIdentityPermission	Defines identity permissions for the zone from which the code originates.

Table 9-7 lists the important attributes available in the System.Security.Permissions namespace.

Table 9-7

Important attributes of System.Security.Permissions namespace

ATTRIBUTE	PURPOSE
EnvironmentPermissionAttribute	Allows security actions for EnvironmentPermission to be applied to code declaratively.
FileDialogPermissionAttribute	Allows security actions for FileDialogPermission to be applied to code declaratively.
IsolatedStorageFilePermissionAttribute	Allows security actions for IsolatedStorageFilePermission to be applied to code declaratively.
ReflectionPermissionAttribute	Controls access to nonpublic types and members through the System.Reflection APIs and controls certain features of the System.Reflection.Emit APIs.
ZoneIdentityPermissionAttribute	Allows security actions for ZoneIdentityPermission to be applied to code declaratively.
FileIOPermissionAttribute	Allows security actions for FileIOPermission to be applied to code declaratively.

Using Declarative Security to Protect Classes and Methods

You can apply demands and overrides declaratively on classes, methods, and even nested classes.

When you place a declarative security check at the class level, the check applies to all the members of the class. When you place a declarative security check at the member level, the check applies to only that particular member. In addition, any declarative security check placed at the member level overrides the permission specified at the class level.

TAKE NOTE*

You can place demands and overrides declaratively using attributes to specify necessary security information. Additionally, declarative security is evaluated during compile time. That is, when you compile the corresponding class or methods on which you place declarative security, the security information for that class or method is placed in the metadata section of the assembly.

USING DEMANDS

You can use security demands declaratively by using the corresponding permission attributes. The following code sample uses the `FileIOPermissionAttribute` demand for the `AccessFile` method to specify that the method and all the callers of the method must possess the `FileIOPermission` to read the files in the directory, C:\MyFiles. Note that the first line of the code uses the escape sequence \\ to indicate to the CLR that it should read it as C:\MyFile:

```
[FileIOPermissionAttribute(SecurityAction.Demand, Read =
"C:\\MyFiles")]
public void AccessFile()
{
   // Method implementation goes here
}
```

USING LINK DEMANDS

When you place a link demand on an entire class, it does not protect any static constructor if present. However, the link demand protects the other members of the class. In addition, the link demand makes the runtime check only the immediate calling assembly of your code for the specified permission. Therefore, unlike `Demand`, `LinkDemand` does not allow the runtime to perform a full stack walk. When a security check fails or the immediate calling assembly does not possess the specified permission, the link demand causes the runtime to throw a security exception.

The following code sample uses `LinkDemand` to specify that the method and the immediate caller of the method, `AccessFile`, must have the `FileIOPermission` to read the files in the directory C:\MyFiles:

```
[FileIOPermissionAttribute(SecurityAction.LinkDemand, Read =
"C:\\MyFiles")]
public void AccessFile()
{
   // Method implementation goes here
}
```

USING INHERITANCE DEMANDS

You can use inheritance demands at the class level to specify that the classes that inherit this class must have the specified permission. Or you can apply an inheritance demand on a specific method in class A to indicate that all the classes that derive from class A must have the specified permission to override that method.

The following code sample places the `InheritanceDemand` on `SampleClass` to specify that any class that inherits from `SampleClass` must have the `FileIOPermission` to read all the files in the "C:\MyFiles" directory:

```
[FileIOPermissionAttribute(SecurityAction.InheritanceDemand, Read =
"C:\\MyFiles")]
   public class SampleClass
   {
   public SampleClass()
   {
       // Constructor
```

```
    }
    public void ReadingCustomResource()
    {
        // Reads a custom resource
    }
}
```

The following code sample places the `InheritanceDemand` on a method residing in a class. The code uses a `FileIOPermissionAttribute` to provide read access to the files in the directory, C:\MyFiles, as an inheritance demand on the method named `myMethod`. This means that all classes that derive from `myClass` can override `myMethod` only if they have the `FileIOPermission` with read access to the specified directory:

```
public class MyClass
{
    public MyClass()
    {
        // Class constructor
    }
[FileIOPermissionAttribute(SecurityAction.InheritanceDemand,
Read = "C:\\MyFiles")]
    public myMethod()
    {
        // Method implementation goes here
    }
}
```

USING ASSERT

In some situations, you may want to enable your code to perform actions that it has permission to do irrespective of whether its callers have permission to perform that action. In such cases, you can use the `Assert` action.

The following sample code uses the `Assert` method to override security checks. The code places an assert on `FileIOPermission` to specify that your code may access the file, sample.txt, with this permission. The runtime security system does not check the callers of your code for the `FileIOPermission` to access the file:

```
[FileIOPermission(SecurityAction.Assert, All = @"C:\Sample.txt")]
public void SampleWriteMethod()
{
StreamWriter swriter = new StreamWriter(@"C:\Sample.txt");
swriter. Write("Sample Message");
swriter. Close();
}
```

TAKE NOTE*

Do not use asserts in situations where you suspect that other code can use your code to access a resource that you have protected using permissions. Alternatively, you could use assertions on your code to assert permissions that are not necessary for the caller of your code to possess. For example, consider that your assembly code accesses a specified resource such as a file from an isolated storage, which is a private virtual file system. The code that uses your library may not possess `IsolatedStorageFilePermission` because it does not know what your code performs internally. In this case, if you think it is not necessary for the callers of your code to have `IsolatedStorageFilePermission` to access the isolated storage, you can assert `IsolatedStorageFilePermission` for your code.

USING DENY

You can use the Deny action to deny a caller's access to a resource even if the caller has access permission to that resource. The following code sample uses the Deny method to override security checks. The code places Deny on SampleClass to specify that the security system must deny the ReflectionPermission for the right to view private members through reflection. That is, using this declarative denial, the method in the code cannot read private members of a type through reflection:

```
[ReflectionPermissionAttribute(SecurityAction.Deny, TypeInformation =
true)]
public class SampleClass
{
   public SampleClass()
   {
   }
   public void UsePublicMembers()
   {
      // Use public members through reflection
   }
}
```

USING PERMIT ONLY

You can use the PermitOnly action to override security checks similar to the Deny security action. However, instead of specifying the permissions that must be denied access to specific resources, you specify the permission that must only be permitted to access the resource. The following code sample uses the PermitOnly security action. The code specifies that callers of the ReadRegistry method cannot access all protected resources. However, they can access the interface resources. Thus, you grant only the user interface permission and deny all other permissions:

```
[UIPermissionAttribute(SecurityAction.PermitOnly, Unrestricted=true)]
public void ReadRegistry()
{
   // Use UI resource
}
```

Using Imperative Security to Protect Classes and Methods

You can use imperative security to check only on the methods of your class, not on the class itself.

You can apply demands and overrides imperatively by creating the required security permission objects programmatically. When demands and overrides are applied imperatively, they are only evaluated at runtime.

Additionally, when you place security demands imperatively inside your methods, the runtime performs a security check for the specified permission when executing your method. If the security check fails, the system throws a SecurityException, disallowing the execution of the rest of the code in the method. To avoid this, you should handle the exception using a try catch block.

TAKE NOTE*

You cannot apply link demand and inheritance demand imperatively because the link demand occurs when your code links to a type reference. Therefore the security check occurs when your assembly is compiled (compile time) and not during its execution (runtime). Similarly, the security check for an inheritance demand occurs when your assembly is loaded (load time) and not during its execution.

USING DEMANDS

When you call the `Demand` method for a specific permission in your code, you instruct the runtime that the code and all the callers of the code must have that permission.

CREATE DEMAND IMPERATIVELY

You can use the following steps to place a demand at the method level:

1. Create an instance of the required permission class.
2. Call the `Demand` method of the instance.

The following code sample places a `RegistryPermission` demand on all callers of the `ReadingRegistryVariables` method to control the access of registry variables. The following code sample instantiates an instance of the `RegistryPermission` class by specifying read access to specific registry variables:

```
public void ReadingRegistryVariables()
{
   RegistryPermission regperm = new
RegistryPermission(RegistryPermissionAccess.Read, "HKEY_LOCAL_MACHINE\\
RESOURCEMAP\\System Resources\\Physical Memory");
   try
   {
      // Perform RegistryPermission demand by calling the
RegistryPermission.Demand() method
      regperm.Demand();
      // If demand fails, a security exception is thrown and the rest
of the code in this method does not execute.
      // Code to read registry variables goes here.
      }
      catch(SecurityException e)
      {
         Console.WriteLine(e.ToString());
      }
}
```

TAKE NOTE*

If you want to assert multiple permissions for your code, you should use a `PermissionSet` object. Otherwise, the system throws a `SecurityException`.

X REF

To learn more about the `PermissionSet` class, refer to Table 9-2 under the "Exploring the Security and Policy Classes" topic.

USING ASSERT

You can assert permission for your code when you want to bypass the security checks for all the callers of your code. This in turn avoids multiple stack walks performed by the runtime because `Assert` makes the runtime check only your code for the specified permission and not the callers. The runtime only performs a stack walk once for the current stack frame. You can use assert when you have full trust on all the subsequent assemblies that can call your code.

CREATE ASSERT IMPERATIVELY

You can use the following steps to place an assert at the method level:

1. Create an instance of the required permission class.
2. Call the `Assert` method of the instance.

The following sample code asserts `EnvironmentPermission` to specify that the `AccessEnvironmentVariable` method must have a read access to the environment variable NUMBER_OF_PROCESSORS. However, the security system does not check the callers of your code for the `EnvironmentPermission`:

```
public void AccessEnvironmentVariable()
{
   // Create an instance of EnvironmentPermission specifying the
access to read "NUMBER_OF_PROCESSORS" environment variable
```

```
    EnvironmentPermission envperm = new
EnvironmentPermission(EnvironmentPermissionAccess.Read, "NUMBER_OF_
PROCESSORS");
    // Assert the created environment permission object
    envperm. Assert();
    // Read the environment variable
    string NoOfProcessors = Environment.GetEnvironmentVariable("NUMBER_
OF_PROCESSORS");
    // Display the value of the environment variable
    Console. WriteLine("Number of processors: " + NoOfProcessors);
}
```

USING DENY

You can use the Deny method to deny security permissions for your callers even if they have that permission.

CREATE DENY IMPERATIVELY

You can use the following steps to place Deny at the method level:

1. Create an instance of the required permission class.
2. Call the Deny method of that instance.

The following code sample uses the Deny method on the RegistryPermission to prevent callers of the method from accessing registry variables. The code creates an instance of the RegistryPermission class by specifying fully restricted access to the registry variables. It then denies the permission to all callers of the ReadData method even if they posses permission to access the registry values:

```
public void ReadData()
{
    // Create RegistryPermission object with fully restricted access
by specifying the PermissionState.None enumeration in the constructor
    RegistryPermission regperm = new RegistryPermission(PermissionState.
None);
    // Place deny on the RegistryPermission object
    regperm. Deny();
    // Rest of the method code goes here
}
```

USING PERMITONLY

You can use the PermitOnly method to permit the callers of your code to access only the specified resources.

CREATE PERMITONLY IMPERATIVELY

CERTIFICATION READY?
Implement CAS to improve the security of a .NET Framework application.
USD 5.1

CERTIFICATION READY?
Control permissions for resources by using the System.Security.Permission classes.
USD 5.5

You can use the following steps to place PermitOnly at the method level:

1. Create an instance of the required permission class.
2. Call the PermitOnly method of the instance.

The following code sample uses the PermitOnly method to specify to the runtime that all callers of the SampleRead method can access only the specified registry variables, even if they possess the permission to read all the registry variables:

```
public void SampleRead()
{
    // Create a registry permission object by specifying the read
access to the given registry variable
```

```
    RegistryPermission regperm = new
RegistryPermission(RegistryPermissionAccess.Read, "HKEY_LOCAL_MACHINE\\
RESOURCEMAP\\System Resources\\Physical Memory");
    // Permit access to only the specified registry variables
    regperm. PermitOnly();
}
```

Authenticating Users

THE BOTTOM LINE

In a network, multiple users may request access to resources simultaneously. Applications employ two complementary and related mechanisms to determine who can access information resources over the network. These mechanisms are ***authentication*** and ***authorization***.

Understanding Authentication

User authentication is a process of determining the identity of the requesting entity.

Authentication is the process of obtaining credentials from a user and using those credentials, typically user ID and password, to verify that user's identity.

DETAIL THE USER AUTHENTICATION PROCESS

The typical steps for user authentication process are:

1. The user accesses the application.
2. The application calls the authentication module.
3. The application's authentication module prompts for user credentials to check the authenticity of the user.
4. The user provides credentials.
5. The application verifies the user credentials and provides access only if the user has provided the appropriate credentials. For unauthenticated users, the application restricts the access.
6. The authenticated user starts interacting with the application.

Figure 9-2 depicts this user authentication process.

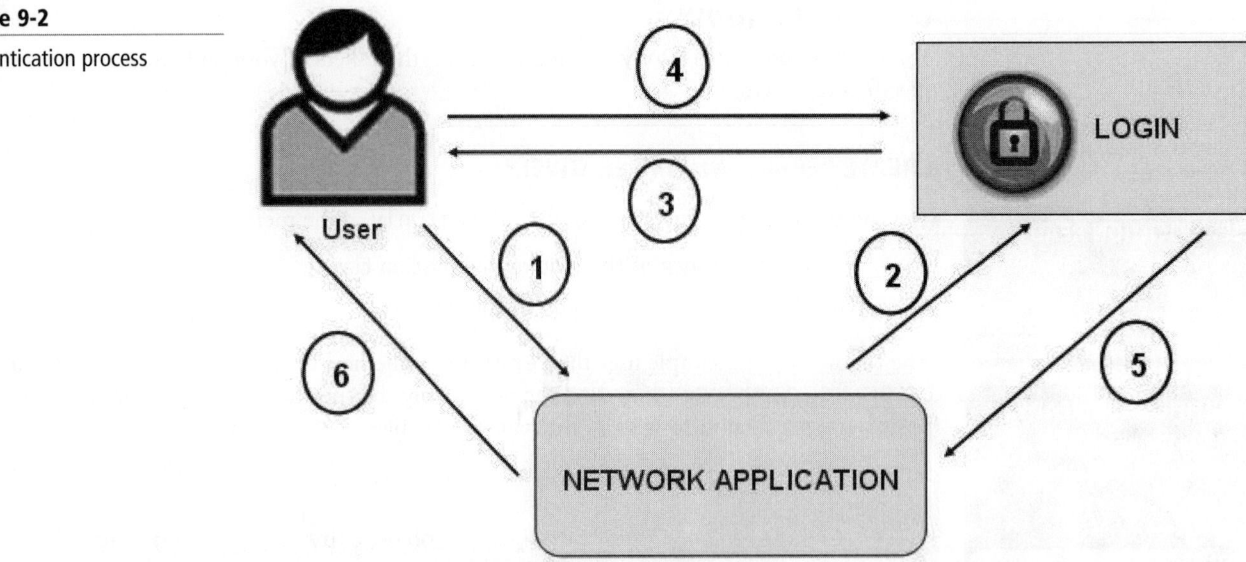

Figure 9-2

Authentication process

Managed code can determine the identity of a principal using the `Principal` object, which holds a reference to an `Identity` object. The `Identity` and `Principal` objects are similar to user and group accounts. In .NET Framework, `Identity` objects represent users, and roles represent memberships and security contexts. The .NET `Principal` object encapsulates both an identity object and a role.

Applications built in .NET Framework grant rights to the principal based on its identity. The `Identity` object encapsulates information about the user or entity being validated and contains a name and an authentication type.

The .NET Framework defines a `GenericIdentity` object, which you can use in custom logon scenarios. The Framework also provides a `WindowsIdentity` object that can be used if the application needs to rely on Windows authentication. You can even define your own custom identity class for custom user information. All the `Identity` classes implement the `IIdentity` interface.

The `Principal` object specifies the security context under which the code is executed. The .NET Framework offers a `GenericPrincipal` object and a `WindowsPrincipal` object. You can also define your own custom principal classes. All the `Principal` classes implement the `IPrincipal` interface.

If the runtime is unable to trace the `Principal` object belonging to the creator of the thread, it follows the default policy for `Principal` and `Identity` object creation. By default, the runtime uses `Principal` and `Identity` objects that represent unauthenticated users. However, these objects are not generated until the code attempts to access them.

The trusted code that creates an application domain can set the application domain policy. This policy in turn controls construction of the default `Principal` and `Identity` objects. The application domain-specific policy is applicable for all execution threads in that application domain. A trusted host inherently has the capability to set this policy. However, the managed code that sets this policy must have the `System.Security.Permissions.SecurityPermission` to control the domain policy.

The following example uses the `GenericIdentity` class in conjunction with the `GenericPrincipal` class to build a custom authentication scheme.

USE THE GENERICIDENTITY AND GENERICPRINCIPAL CLASSES

You must perform the following steps to authenticate using the `GenericIdentity` and the `GenericPrincipal` classes:

1. Create an instance of the `GenericIdentity` object and initialize it with the required identity name:

   ```
   GenericIdentity CustomIdentity = new GenericIdentity("CustomUser");
   ```

2. Create an instance of the `GenericPrincipal` class and initialize it with the `GenericIdentity` object created in Step 1 and a string array. The string array must represent the roles that you want to associate with this principal. The following example specifies a string array to represent the administrator role:

   ```
   String[] MyRole = {"Administrator", "Admin"};
   GenericPrincipal CustomPrincipal = new
   GenericPrincipal(CustomIdentity, MyRole);
   ```

3. Attach the principal to the current thread. You must perform this step only if your application scenario requires repeated validation of the principal object:

   ```
   Thread. CurrentPrincipal = CustomPrincipal;
   ```

Exploring Classes Related to Authentication

The .NET Framework offers three different sets of authentication classes for Windows-based authentication, non-Windows-based authentication, and custom authentication.

The `System.Security.Principal` namespace defines a principal object depicting the security context under which the code is executed. Table 9-8 lists the base classes of the `System.Security.Principal` namespace.

Table 9-8

Classes of the `System.Security.Principal` namespace

Class	Description
`GenericIdentity`	Depicts a generic user.
`GenericPrincipal`	Depicts a generic principal.
`IdentityNotMappedException`	Depicts an exception if an identity of a principal could not be mapped to a known identity.
`IdentityReference`	Depicts an identity.
`IdentityReferenceCollection`	Represents a collection of `IdentityReference` objects.
`NTAccount`	Represents a user or a group account.
`SecurityIdentifier`	Represents a security identifier (SID).
`WindowsIdentity`	Represents a Windows user.
`WindowsImpersonationContext`	Represents the Windows user before an impersonation operation.
`WindowsPrincipal`	Permits the code to check the Windows group membership of a Windows user.

The `WindowsIdentity` and the `WindowsPrincipal` classes represent a Windows user. Table 9-9 lists the methods of the `WindowsIdentity` class.

Table 9-9

Methods of the `WindowsIdentity` class

Method	Description
`GetAnonymous`	Returns an object that depicts an anonymous user.
`GetCurrent`	Returns an object that depicts the current Windows user.
`Impersonate`	Permits the code to impersonate a different Windows user.

Table 9-10 lists the properties of the `WindowsIdentity` class.

Table 9-10

Properties of the `WindowsIdentity` class

Property	Description
`AuthenticationType`	Returns the type of authentication used to identify the user.
`Groups`	Returns the groups to which the current Windows user belongs.
`ImpersonationLevel`	Returns the impersonation level for the user.
`IsAnonymous`	Specifies if the user account is identified as an anonymous account by the system.
`IsAuthenticated`	Specifies whether the user has been authenticated by Windows.
`IsGuest`	Specifies if the user account is identified as a Guest account by the system.
`IsSystem`	Specifies if the system identifies the user account as a System account.
`Name`	Gets the Windows logon name for the user.

Table 9-11 lists the methods of the `WindowsPrincipal` class.

Table 9-11

Methods of the `Windows Principal` class

METHOD	DESCRIPTION
`IsInRole`	Determines if the current principal belongs to the specified Windows user group.

Table 9-12 lists the properties of the `WindowsPrincipal` class.

Table 9-12

Properties of the `Windows Principal` class

PROPERTY	DESCRIPTION
`Identity`	Returns the identity of the current principal.

The generic and the Windows security classes implement the `IPrincipal` and the `IIdentity` interfaces. The `IPrincipal` interface defines the basic functionality of a principal object; the `IIdentity` interface defines the basic functionality of an identity object. Therefore, if you want to create your own custom authentication classes then, you must implement the `IPrincipal` and `IIdentity` interfaces.

EXAMINING USER AUTHENTICATION

You can use the `WindowsIdentity` class to determine the identity of users and their authentication type. This class allows you to determine whether you can authorize the currently logged on users to execute privileged actions.

The following code sample uses the `WindowsIdentity` class to determine the identity of a currently logged on user:

```
// Retrieve the Windows identity of the currently logged on user
WindowsIdentity userIdentity = WindowsIdentity.GetCurrent();
// Retrieve user's Windows logon name
string userName = userIdentity.Name;
Console. WriteLine("User's logon name" + username);
// Check if user is authenticated
if (userIdentity.IsAuthenticated)
{
   // Retrieve the type of user authentication
   string authenticationType = userIdentity.AuthenticationType;
   Console. WriteLine("User authentication type" + authenticationType);
}
// Determine the type of account the user belongs to
if(userIdentity.IsAnonymous)
Console. WriteLine("User belongs to Anonymous account");
if(userIdentity.IsGuest)
Console. WriteLine("User belongs to Guest account");
if(userIdentity.IsSystem)
Console. WriteLine("User belongs to system account");
```

Exploring the Authentication Namespace

The `Authentication` namespace provides various enumerations to describe the security of a connection.

The `Authentication` namespace provides the following two classes:

- `AuthenticationException`
- `InvalidCredentialException`

The AuthenticationException class is the exception that occurs when authentication fails for an authentication stream. When you get this exception, you can retry authentication with a different set of user credentials. If the authentication fails even with alternate user credentials, then the runtime throws the InvalidCredentialException, which represents the exception you get when authentication fails for an authentication stream and cannot be retried. The methods and properties for both the authentication exception classes are similar.

Table 9-13 lists the methods of the AuthenticationException class.

Table 9-13

Methods of the AuthenticationException class

Method	Description
GetBaseException	Returns the exception that is the root cause of one or more subsequent exceptions.
GetObjectData	Sets the SerializationInfo with information about the exception.
GetType	Returns the runtime type of the current instance.

Table 9-14 lists the properties of the AuthenticationException class.

Table 9-14

Properties of the AuthenticationException class

Property	Description
Data	Returns a collection of key-value pairs that provide additional user-defined information about the exception.
InnerException	Returns the Exception instance that caused the current exception.
Source	Gets or sets the name of the application or the object that caused the error.
Message	Returns a message that describes the current exception.
StackTrace	Returns a string representation of the frames on the call stack at the time the current exception occurred.
TargetSite	Returns the method that raised the current exception.

In addition to the exception classes, the Authentication namespace provides various enumerations that you can use to set the properties of the SslStream class. Table 9-15 lists the enumerations provided by the Authentication namespace.

Table 9-15

Enumerations in the Authentication namespace

Enumeration	Description
CipherAlgorithmType	Provides valid cipher algorithms for the SslStream.CipherAlgorithm property.
ExchangeAlgorithmType	Provides possible algorithms for creating a public key shared by both the client and the server. In addition, it also provides values for the SslStream.KeyExchangeAlgorithm property.
HashAlgorithmType	Specifies the algorithm for generating message-authenticating codes (MAC) and provides values for the SslStream.HashAlgorithm property.
SslProtocols	Specifies the various versions of SslProtocols.

MORE INFORMATION
You can refer to the corresponding sections of the MSDN library to learn more about the members of the various enumerations we've discussed.

MORE INFORMATION
You can refer to the MSDN library to learn how to use the `SslStream` class to perform client-server communication.

CERTIFICATION READY?
Implement a custom authentication scheme by using the `System.Security.Authentication` classes.
USD 5.3

CERTIFICATION READY?
Control permissions for resources by using the `System.Security.Permission` classes.
USD 5.5

CERTIFICATION READY?
Access and modify identity information by using the `System.Security.Principal` classes.
USD 5.7

The following code snippet shows a `TcpClient` that uses the `SslStream` object to communicate with a server through the Secure Socket Layer (SSL) security protocol. The code displays the security algorithm associated with the `SslStream` object. The code also throws an `AuthenticationException` if the server authentication fails and closes the connection:

```
// Create a TCP/IP client socket for the specified client and port
TcpClient client = new TcpClient("clientmachine", 440);
// Create the SslStream using the client's network stream
SslStream stream = new SslStream(client.GetStream());
try
{
   // Authenticate using the default authentication; Note that the
name of the server, which in this case is "servermachine", must match
the name on the server's certificate
   stream. AuthenticateAsClient("servermachine");
   // Display the properties specifying the security algorithm value
associated with the SslStream object
   Console. WriteLine("Cipher Algorithm" + stream.CipherAlgorithm);
   Console. WriteLine("Hash Algorithm" + stream.HashAlgorithm);
   Console. WriteLine("Key exchange algorithm" + stream.
KeyExchangeAlgorithm);
   Console. WriteLine("Protocol", stream.SslProtocol);
}
catch(AuthenticationException e)
{
   // Authentication fails
Console. WriteLine(e.Message);
   // Close the connection
   client. Close();
}
```

Authorizing Users

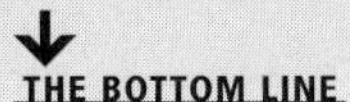

THE BOTTOM LINE

Authentication and authorization are connected processes that must be completed successfully if a user wants to access a particular part of the application.

Whenever a user logs on to an application, the authentication process happens first followed by the authorization of the user. While authentication verifies user credentials, the authorization process determines resources such as services, printers, servers, and network devices that the authenticated user is permitted to access. Certain applications do not restrict or validate an authenticated user. However, even such applications authorize the user as an anonymous user.

You can use authorization to verify whether a user has access to a specific part of an application. For example, imagine that only users with the role of manager can generate and print an MIS report and other users can only view a generated report. When a user clicks on the link to generate the MIS report in your application, your code must check that the role of the user is Manager. If the user is a Manager, then your application must allow the user to generate the report. If the user is not a Manager, then your application must prevent the user from generating a report.

Understanding Authorization

User authorization is a process that allows users access to permitted resources only.

Authorization is a process that ensures that the principal object is allowed to perform the requested action. This process uses information about the principal's identity to determine which resources that principal can access.

DETAIL THE USER AUTHORIZATION PROCESS

The typical steps for the user authorization process are:

1. An authenticated user tries to access one of the options in the application.
2. The application verifies whether the authenticated user has permission to access that part of the application.
3. If the user has access permissions, then the application allows the user to access that part of the application.
4. If the user does not have the required access permissions, then the application throws a security exception.

Figure 9-3 depicts the user authorization process.

Figure 9-3

Authorization process

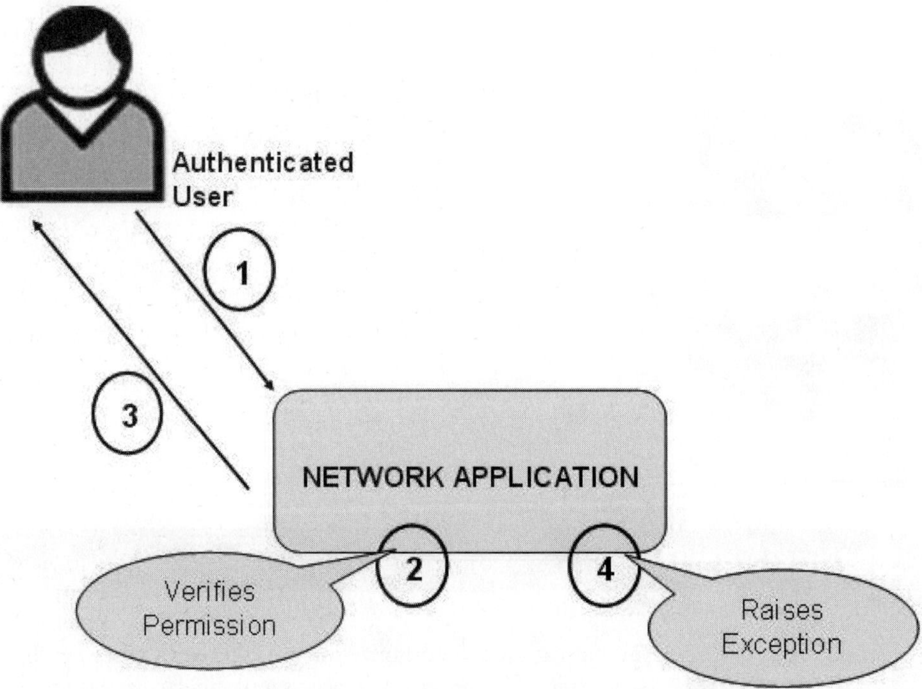

Authentication and authorization processes help you implement role-based security. Financial as well as business applications make use of roles when implementing security policy. For example, an application may restrict access to specific pages in a Web site, depending on the role of the user posting the request.

In addition, role-based security proves helpful in a scenario where an application demands multiple approvals before completing an action. One example of an application could be a purchasing system. Here, any employee can generate a purchase request; however, only a manager can convert it into a purchase order after verifying the details of the request.

Role-based security in .NET Framework supports authorization by collecting information about the principal. This information is built from an associated identity that is available to the current thread. Role-based security in .NET Framework supports an identity based on a Windows account as well as a custom identity not linked to a Windows account.

Applications made in .NET Framework can make authorization decisions based on the principal's identity, role membership, or both. A role is a named set of principals such as a purchase officer or a manager. Alternatively, a principal can be a member of one or more roles. For example, a user can perform the role of a warehouse supervisor and a warehouse manager. As a result, role membership can be used to determine whether a principal is authorized to perform a requested action.

The `PrincipalPermission` object enables the CLR to perform authorization. The `PrincipalPermission` class represents the role that the principal must match and is compatible with both declarative and imperative security checks.

Exploring Classes Related to Authorization

The `System.Security.Permissions` namespace defines classes that control access to operations and resources based on security policy.

The `System.Security.Permissions` namespace consists of various base classes. The `PrincipalPermission` class allows various checks against the active principal using the language constructs defined for both declarative and imperative security actions.

Table 9-16 lists the methods of the `PrincipalPermission` class.

Table 9-16

Methods of the `PrincipalPermission` class

METHOD	DESCRIPTION
`Copy`	Creates and returns an identical copy of the current permission.
`Demand`	Specifies whether the current principal matches the principal specified by the current permission at runtime.
`Intersect`	Creates and returns a permission that is the intersection of the current permission and the specified permission.
`IsSubsetOf`	Specifies whether the current permission is a subset of the specified permission.
`IsUnrestricted`	Specifies whether the current permission is unrestricted.
`ToXml`	Creates an XML encoding of the permission along with its current state.

The `PrincipalPermissionAttribute` class allows you to apply security actions to the code by using declarative security.

Table 9-17 lists the methods of the `PrincipalPermissionAttribute` class.

Table 9-17

Methods of the `PrincipalPermissionAttribute` class

METHOD	DESCRIPTION
`CreatePermission`	Creates and returns a new PrincipalPermission.
`IsDefaultAttribute`	Indicates if the value of this instance is the default value for the derived class.

Table 9-18 lists the properties of the `PrincipalPermissionAttribute` class.

Table 9-18

Properties of the `PrincipalPermissionAttribute` class

PROPERTY	DESCRIPTION
`Action`	Gets or sets a security action.
`Name`	Gets or sets the name of the identity associated with the current principal.
`Role`	Gets or sets membership in a specified security role.

Granting Permissions through Roles

The role-based security (RBS) model supports a permission object, `PrincipalPermission`, similar to the permission objects provided in the CAS model.

The `PrincipalPermission` object depicts the identity and role that a particular principal object must possess to execute.

Consider an example to implement the `PrincipalPermission` class imperatively. The following code snippet creates a new instance of the `PrincipalPermission` class and initializes it with the name and role that the users must have to access your code:

```
String myidentity = "Smith";
String myrole = "Manager";
PrincipalPermission myprincipalPerm = new
PrincipalPermission(myidentity, myrole);
```

For success during the runtime security check, the specified identity and role must match. When you create the `PrincipalPermission` object with a null identity string, it indicates that the identity of the principal can be anything. Similarly, when you pass a null role string to the `PrincipalPermission` object, it indicates that the principal can be a member of any role or no roles at all.

You can implement a similar permission declaratively by using the `PrincipalPermission-Attribute` class. The following code snippet declaratively initializes the identity:

```
PrincipalPermissionAttribute(SecurityAction.Demand, Name = "Smith",
Role = "Manager")]
```

The following code snippet uses the `PrincipalPermissionAttribute` class to declaratively specify that a principal can have any name, but must have the "Manager" role:

```
[PrincipalPermissionAttribute(SecurityAction.Demand, Role =
"Manager")]
```

Performing Role-Based Security Checks

For the imperative or declarative security check to occur, you must make a security demand for an appropriately constructed `PrincipalPermission` object.

Once you have defined the `Identity` and `Principal` objects, you perform security checks against them by:

- Using imperative security checks
- Using declarative security checks
- Accessing the `Principal` object directly

The managed code can use imperative or declarative security checks to determine whether a particular principal object:

- Is a member of a known role
- Has a known identity
- Represents a known identity acting in a role

USING IMPERATIVE SECURITY CHECKS

To execute an imperative security check, use the `Demand` method of the `Principal Permission` object to determine whether the current principal object represents the specified identity, role, or both.

Consider an example to ensure that a `GenericPrincipal` object matches the `Principal Permission` object. An imperative check is advisable in a situation where many methods or other assemblies in the application domain must make role-based determinations.

The following code snippet creates a `GenericIdentity` and a `GenericPrincipal` object to create a valid administrator:

```
GenericIdentity CustomIdentity = new GenericIdentity("User1");
String[] Str1 = {"Administrator"};
GenericPrincipal CustomPrincipal = new GenericPrincipal
(CustomIdentity, Str1);
Thread. CurrentPrincipal = CustomPrincipal;
```

The following code snippet creates a `PrincipalPermission` object and demands the permission to check if the current user is same as the generic identity created in the previous code snippet:

```
PrincipalPermission CustomPermission = new PrincipalPermission
("User1", "Administrator");
CustomPermission. Demand();
```

PERFORMING DECLARATIVE SECURITY CHECKS

When performing declarative security checks, you can place the demands at the class level and on individual methods, properties, or events. Consider that you have a declarative demand set at both the class and member level. In this case, the declarative demand on the member overrides the demand at the class level.

CERTIFICATION READY?
Implement a custom authentication scheme by using the `System.Security.Authentication` classes.
USD 5.3

The following code example illustrates declarative security. The `PrincipalPermission Attribute` defines the principal that the current thread must have to invoke the method:

```
[PrincipalPermissionAttribute(SecurityAction.Demand, Name = "User1",
Role = "User")]
```

ACCESSING A PRINCIPAL OBJECT DIRECTLY

Using imperative and declarative demands to invoke role-based security checks is the primary mechanism for checking and enforcing the identity and role membership. However, you may want to access the `Principal` object and its associated `Identity` object directly to perform the authorization tasks without creating permission objects. Consider a case where you do not want to make use of declarative or imperative demands because you do not want an exception to be the default behavior for validation failure. To achieve this, you can use the static `CurrentPrincipal` property on the `System.Threading.Thread` class to invoke the `Principal` object and call its methods.

CERTIFICATION READY?
Control permissions for resources by using the `System.Security.Permission` classes.
USD 5.5

Once you obtain the `Principal` object, you can use a conditional statement to control access to your code based on the principal name, as in:

CERTIFICATION READY?
Access and modify identity information by using the `System.Security.Principal` classes.
USD 5.7

```
WindowsPrincipal CustomPrincipal = (WindowsPrincipal)Thread.
CurrentPrincipal;
if (CustomPrincipal.Identity.Name == "Smith")
{
    // Provide access to specific functionality
}
```

Working with Access Control Lists

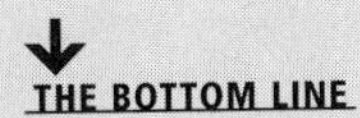

Your Web application may need to create files or folders in a computer file system. In such scenarios, you should assign a set of permissions to the respective object to be accessed by your application. By attaching a list of permissions to an object, you can make sure that your application can access the object only if it has the corresponding permissions. This enables you to protect the object and the important data from hackers who may attack the data through your application.

Using access control list (ACL), you can protect your data or object by defining a list of permissions for an object. ACL enables you to specify whom or what can access your object and the type of operation that you would like to allow on the object. You can use the classes provided in the `System.Security.AccessControl` namespace of the .NET Framework to create these lists for your objects.

Understanding ACL

You can use the managed ACL API provided in the .NET Framework to protect several types of resources. The ACL API helps you manage the ACLs programmatically.

Microsoft Windows NT and the later versions of Windows use the following objects to protect resources such as files and folders:

- ***Discretionary access control list (DACL)***: An access control list controlled by the owner of an object. This list specifies the access that specific users or groups can have to the object.
- ***System access control list (SACL)***: An access control list that controls the generation of audit messages for attempts to access a securable object.
- ***Access control entries (ACE)***: An entry in an access control list. An ACE contains a set of access rights and a security identifier (SID) that identifies a trustee for whom the rights are allowed, denied, or audited.

By using the classes in the `System.Security.AccessControl` namespace, you can easily access these Windows ACLs programmatically.

USING ACCESS CONTROL LISTS

DACLs possess many ACEs that associate an account or groups of accounts with a set of permissions for accessing an object. Thus, using DACLs and ACEs, you can set the required permissions for user accounts to access protected resources. For example, to disallow all the user accounts to access a file, you can create an ACE and apply it to the DACL of that file.

SACLs enable you to control audit messages associated with a resource. Audit messages specify the security related events that are logged in the security event log. For example, SACL allows you to ensure that all the successful attempts to write to a file are logged in the event log. Similar to DACLs, you can also create ACEs for SACLs to define the audit rules for the resource. However, unlike access ACEs, audit ACEs do not examine the accounts for a set of permissions. For example, to log all the successful attempts to open a particular file, you can create an audit ACE and apply it to the SACL.

Exploring Access Control Classes

You can use the classes in the `System.Security.AccessControl` namespace to control access and audit security related actions on protected resources.

Table 9-19 lists the primary classes of the `System.Security.AccessControl` namespace, which allows you to create and modify ACLs easily with respect to key technological areas.

Table 9-19

Primary classes of `System.Security.AccessControl` namespace

CLASS	PURPOSE
`AuthorizationRule`	Determines access to protected resources.
`AccessRule`	Represents user identity, an access mask, and an access control type (allow or deny) for accessing resources.
`AuditRule`	Represents user identity and an access mask for auditing resources.

Table 9-19 (continued)

Class	Purpose
`CryptoKeyAuditRule`	Contains an audit rule for a cryptographic key.
`CryptoAccessRule`	Contains an access rule for a cryptographic key.
`FileSystemAccessRule`	Represents an abstract access control entry, which defines the access rule for a file or directory.
`FileSystemAuditRule`	Represents an abstract access control entry, which defines the audit rule for a file or directory.
`DirectorySecurity`	Contains the access control and audit rule for a directory.
`FileSecurity`	Contains access and audit rules for a file or directory.
`RegistryAccessRule`	Represents the set of access permissions allowed or denied for a user or group to access a registry key.
`RegistryAuditRule`	Represents the set of access permissions to be audited for a user or group to access a registry key.
`MutexAccessRule`	Represents the set of access permissions allowed or denied for a user or group to access a named mutex.
`MutexAuditRule`	Represents the set of access permissions to be audited for a user or group to access a named mutex.
`SemaphoreAccessRule`	Represents the set of access permissions allowed or denied for a user or group to access a named semaphore.
`SemaphoreAuditRule`	Represents the set of access permissions to be audited for a user or group to access a named semaphore.

Configuring ACL

You can configure the access control and audit settings for an existing file or folder using the appropriate access control methods.

You can use the classes in the `System.Security.AccessControl` namespace to create and modify ACLs. You can then associate these ACLs with the required resources.

SPECIFYING ACCESS CONTROL AND AUDIT FOR NEW OBJECTS

If you want your application to create a new file or folder, you can use the following procedure to specify the ACL for that new file or folder using the .NET Framework's ACL classes.

SPECIFY ACL

To specify ACL when creating a new file or folder, your application should:

1. Create one or more instances of `FileSystemAccessRule` or `FileSystemAuditRule` to represent the specified rules.
2. Add the instances created to a new `FileSecurity` or `DirectorySecurity` instance.
3. Create a new file or folder by passing the `FileSecurity` or `DirectorySecurity` instance to the corresponding method or constructor.

The following code sample creates a new file system access rule and sets this rule to a new file using a `FileSecurity` object. The code uses the `FileSystemAccessRule` constructor to create a file system access rule that takes the following parameters:

- The name of the user account that the access rule will be applied to
- The type of rights to access the file
- The type of access rule that specifies whether to allow or deny the access rule

```
// Create an instance of FileSystemAccessRule for the specified user
account "user1" with full control access rights to access the created
file
FileSystemAccessRule accessRule = new FileSystemAccessRule("user1",
FileSystemRights.FullControl, AccessControlType.Allow);
// Create an instance of FileSecurity object
FileSecurity fsecurity = new FileSecurity();
// Add the created FileSystemAccessRule object to the FileSecurity
instance
fsecurity. AddAccessRule(accessRule);
// Create the new file by passing the FileSecurity object to the
Create method
File. Create(@"C:\myfile.txt", 12, FileOptions.None, fsecurity);
```

TAKE NOTE*

You can pass the file or directory security instance by using any of the overloaded file or directory creation methods or constructors. As shown in the previous code sample, the `File.Create` method accepts a file security parameter, which your application can use to set ACLs when creating the file.

SPECIFYING ACCESS CONTROL AND AUDIT FOR EXISTING OBJECTS

The ACL classes in the .NET Framework allow you to perform modifications to an access or audit rule for an existing file or folder. Consider that you want to access ACLs programmatically to modify access or audit specifications for an existing file or folder.

MODIFY ACL

To modify ACL for an existing file or folder, your application should:

1. Retrieve the `FileSecurity` or `DirectorySecurity` instance from an existing file or folder through the `GetAccessControl` method.
2. Create one or more instances of `FileSystemAccessRule` or `FileSystemAuditRule` to represent the specified rules.
3. Add the access or audit instances created to the `FileSecurity` or `DirectorySecurity` instance retrieved.
4. Preserve the retrieved `FileSecurity` or `DirectorySecurity` instance through the `SetAccessControl` method.

ADDING AN ENTRY

You can use the `AddAccessRule` method of the `FileSecurity` object to add an ACL entry for a file and a valid user or group account. You can then use the `SetAccessControl` method of the `File` class to apply the access rule to the specified file for the specified user or group account.

The following code sample uses the `SetAccessControl` method to add an ACL entry for the specified file and account. The `AddEntry` method in the following code sample accepts the following four arguments:

- File name on which the ACL entry has to be made
- User account for which the access right or permission has to be set
- Permission indicating the access rights on the file such as reading or opening the file
- Access type indicating whether to allow or deny the permission

```
public static void AddEntry(string fname, string userAccount,
FileSystemRights permission, AccessControlType accessType)
{
   // Retrieve a FileSecurity object for the current security
settings
FileSecurity fSecurity = File.GetAccessControl(fname);
   // Add the new access rule to the file security
fSecurity. AddAccessRule(new FileSystemAccessRule(userAccount,permission,
accessType));
   // Set the added access settings to the file
   File. SetAccessControl(fname, fSecurity);
}
```

REMOVING AN ENTRY

You can use the RemoveAccessRule method of the FileSecurity object to remove an ACL entry for a file and a valid user or group account. You can then apply the new rule to the file using the SetAccessControl method of the File class.

The RemoveEntry method accepts the following four arguments:

- File name on which the ACL entry has to be removed
- User account for which the access right or permission has to be removed
- Permission indicating the access rights on the file
- Access type indicating the type of access control in the given file for the account

The following code sample uses the RemoveEntry method to remove an ACL entry for a specified file and a specified account:

```
public static void RemoveEntry(string fname, string userAccount,
FileSystemRights permission, AccessControlType accessType)

{
   // Get a FileSecurity object representing the current security
settings for the given file
   FileSecurity fSecurity = File.GetAccessControl(fname);
   // Remove the FileSystemAccessRule from the security settings for
the specified account
   fSecurity. RemoveAccessRule(new FileSystemAccessRule(userAccount,
permission,accessType));
   // Set the modified access settings
   File.SetAccessControl(fname, fSecurity);
}
```

CERTIFICATION READY?
Implement access control by using the System.Security.AccessControl classes.
USD 5.2

Exploring Data Encryption

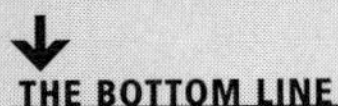

THE BOTTOM LINE

There is lack of security when you use public services such as the Internet for communication. Unauthorized elements can read or modify the data communicated over the Internet. You can use the science of information security, referred to as cryptography, to secure the means of communication. Cryptography focuses mainly on data integrity and authentication.

Understanding Cryptography Basics

Various cryptography techniques are available to protect applications from exposing confidential data. A developer trying to develop a cryptographic algorithm and technique must be highly proficient in handling mathematical problems. However, cryptography classes provided by .NET wrap up all complex cryptographic algorithms, so that the developers can use them to encrypt and decrypt information without understanding the implementation of the underlying algorithms.

TAKE NOTE*

A key is a randomly generated set of numbers or characters to facilitate encryption and decryption of information.

Cryptography is the art of scrambling characters to secure information. This helps in restricting the data access to specific users, because only the users who know the technique that was used to scramble the characters can rearrange them to read the information correctly.

Features of cryptography include:

- Encrypting the data to change the appearance of the plaintext. Encrypting plaintext leads to unreadable volume of data, referred to as ***ciphertext***. This helps maintain the secrecy of information from all restricted persons, including those who can see the encrypted data.
- Decrypting involves the process of transforming the ciphertext back to its original plaintext.
- Setting the key that represents the string of bits to encrypt and decrypt the information.

EXPLORING THE TYPES OF CRYPTOGRAPHY

Two types of cryptography are symmetric and asymmetric encryptions.

Symmetric encryption is commonly referred to as secret key encryption. It is also known as conventional or single key encryption and has been in practice before the advent of public key encryption. The symmetric encryption type requires that all communicating parties share a common key. Encrypting and decrypting the information is based on this single key. In this encryption type, the security of the information depends on the secrecy level of the single secret key.

Asymmetric encryption is commonly referred to as the public key encryption. In this encryption type, each sender encrypts the data using a public key that is known to everybody, and the recipients decrypt the received encrypted data with a private key that is known only to them. That is, though both the communicating parties know the public key, only the individual who possesses the private key has information about the key. Encrypting and decrypting the information is based on the public-private key pair. This means that for encryption or decryption, you must have at least one public key and one private key. This key pair is mathematically related to each other such that the decryption of the data can occur only with the private key that corresponds to the public key that encrypts the data.

Exploring Cryptography in .NET

The .NET Framework consists of cryptographic objects that support common algorithms and perform operations, such as hashing, encrypting, and generating digital signatures. You can use these features to sign and encrypt a document.

Developers use cryptographic objects for specific purposes. Table 9-20 lists the cryptographic services provided by the .NET Framework.

Table 9-20

Cryptographic services in .NET Framework

SERVICE	DESCRIPTION
Secret key encryption algorithms	• Uses a single secret key • Operates on varying lengths of buffers • Functions faster when compared to public key encryption algorithms • Performs cryptographic transformations on large streams of data

Table 9-20 (continued)

SERVICE	DESCRIPTION

	• Involves the following .NET classes:
	  ○ `AesManaged`
	  ○ `DESCryptoServiceProvider`
	  ○ `HMACSHA1`
	  ○ `RC2CryptoServiceProvider`
	  ○ `RijndaelManaged`
	  ○ `TripleDESCryptoServiceProvider`
	• Examples include Data Encryption Standard (DES), TripleDES, and Rivest Cipher (RC2)

Public key encryption algorithms	• Uses a private key that is not disclosed to others and a public key that can be shared with others
	• Operates on a fixed length of buffers
	• Possesses a larger key space in comparison with the secret key algorithms
	• Transfers small amounts of data
	• Involves the following .NET classes:
	  ○ `DSACryptoServiceProvider`
	  ○ `RSACryptoServiceProvider`
	  ○ `ECDiffieHellman` (base class)
	  ○ `ECDiffieHellmanCng`
	  ○ `ECDiffieHellmanCngPublicKey` (base class)
	  ○ `ECDiffieHellmanKeyDerivationFunction` (base class)
	  ○ `ECDsaCng`
	• Examples include Rivest, Shamir, and Adleman (RSA); Digital Signature Algorithm (DSA); and Diffie-Hellman

Digital signatures	• Uses the public key algorithms
	• Authenticates the identity of a sender with a valid public key
	• Protects the data integrity
	• Involves the following .NET classes:
	  ○ `DSACryptoServiceProvider`
	  ○ `RSACryptoServiceProvider`
	  ○ `ECDsa` (base class)
	  ○ `ECDsaCng`

Hash values	• Involves smaller binary values of fixed length known as hash values that represent numerical pieces of data
	• Converts binary values of an arbitrary length using hash values
	• Ensures message integrity and authenticates the sender
	• Involves the following .NET classes:
	  ○ `HMACSHA1`
	  ○ `MACTripleDES`
	  ○ `MD5CryptoServiceProvider`
	  ○ `RIPEMD160`

Table 9-20 (continued)

Service	Description
	◦ SHA1Managed ◦ SHA256Managed ◦ SHA384Managed ◦ SHA512Managed
Random number generation	• Forms the basis for several cryptographic operations • Generates cryptographic keys that make prediction of the output impossible • Involves the `RNGCryptoServiceProvider` class
ClickOnce manifests	• Involves the following cryptography classes to receive and verify information about manifest signatures for applications based on ClickOnce technology: ◦ The `ManifestSignatureInformation` class obtains information about a manifest signature and applying its `VerifySignature` method overloads. ◦ The `ManifestKinds` enumeration specifies the manifests to verify. The result of the verification is one of the `SignatureVerificationResult` enumeration values. ◦ The `ManifestSignatureInformation Collection` class collects the read-only `ManifestSignatureInformation` objects of the verified signatures.
Suite B support	• Consists of the following Suite B set of cryptographic algorithm, published by the National Security Agency (NSA): ◦ Advanced Encryption Standard (AES) algorithm with key sizes of 128, 192, and 256 bits for encryption ◦ Secure Hash Algorithms SHA-1, SHA-256, SHA-384, and SHA-512 for hashing ◦ Elliptic Curve Digital Signature Algorithm (ECDSA), using curves of 256-bit, 384-bit, and 521-bit prime moduli for signing ◦ Elliptic Curve Diffie-Hellman (ECDH) algorithm, using curves of 256-bit, 384-bit, and 521-bit prime moduli for the key exchange and secret agreement
Cryptography next generation (CNG) classes	• Provides a managed wrapper around the native CNG functions • Includes "Cng" in their names • Consists of the CngKey container class that forms the abstract class to store and use CNG keys • Uses CngKey class for additional operations, including opening, creating, deleting, and exporting keys • Involves the following .NET classes: ◦ CngProvider ◦ CngAlgorithm ◦ CngProperty

Exploring the Cryptography Classes

TAKE NOTE*

Table 9-21 lists only some of the classes in the `System.Security.Cryptography` namespace.

The .NET Framework provides various classes to perform cryptographic tasks. You must combine classes effectively to create a successful cryptographic solution.

The `System.Security.Cryptography` namespace provides various classes to secure encoding and decoding of data and to perform cryptographic operations, such as hashing, random number generation, and message authentication. Table 9-21 lists these classes along with their description.

Table 9-21

Classes in the `System.Security.Cryptography` namespace

Class	Type	Description
`AsymmetricAlgorithm`	Abstract base class	Inherits all the implementations of asymmetric algorithms.
`AsymmetricKeyExchangeDeformatter`	Base class	Derives all the asymmetric key exchange deformatters.
`AsymmetricKeyExchangeFormatter`	Base class	Derives all the asymmetric key exchange formatters.
`AsymmetricSignatureDeformatter`	Abstract base class	Derives all the implementations of asymmetric signature deformatters.
`AsymmetricSignature Formatter`	Base class	Derives all the implementations of asymmetric signature formatters.
`CngAlgorithm`	Class	Encapsulates the name of an encryption algorithm.
`CngAlgorithmGroup`	Class	Encapsulates the name of an encryption algorithm group.
`CryptoAPITransform`	Non-inherited class	Transforms the data cryptographically.
`CryptoConfig`	Class	Accesses the cryptography configuration information.
`CryptographicException`	Class	Represents the exception that is thrown when an error occurs during a cryptographic operation.
`CryptographicUnexpectedOperationException`	Class	Represents the exception that is thrown when an unexpected error occurs during a cryptographic operation.
`CryptoStream`	Class	Defines a stream that links data streams to cryptographic transformations.
`DeriveBytes`	Abstract base class	Inherits all the classes that derive byte sequences of a specified length.
`DSA`	Abstract base class	Inherits all the implementations of the Digital Signature Algorithm (DSA).
`DSACryptoServiceProvider`	Non-inherited class	Defines a wrapper object to access the Cryptographic Service Provider (CSP) implementation of the DSA algorithm.
`DSASignatureDeformatter`	Class	Verifies a DSA PKCS#1 v1.5 signature.
`DSASignatureFormatter`	Class	Creates a DSA signature.

Table 9-21 (continued)

Class	Type	Description
DES	Base class	Derives all the Data Encryption Standard (DES) implementations.
DESCryptoServiceProvider	Non-inherited class	Defines a wrapper object to access the CSP version of the DES algorithm.
HashAlgorithm	Base class	Derives all the implementations of cryptographic hash algorithms.
HMAC	Abstract base class	Derives all the implementations of Hash-based Message Authentication Code (HMAC).
HMACMD5	Class	Uses the MD5 hash function to compute a HMAC.
HMACSHA1	Class	Uses the SHA1 hash function to compute a HMAC.
RandomNumberGenerator	Abstract base class	Derives all the implementations of cryptographic random number generators.
Rijndael	Base class	Inherits all the implementations of the Rijndael symmetric encryption algorithm.
RijndaelManaged	Non-inherited class	Accesses the managed version of the Rijndael algorithm.
RijndaelManagedTransform	Non-inherited class	Performs a cryptographic transformation of data using the Rijndael algorithm.
SHA1	Class	Computes the SHA1 hash for the input data.
SHA1Cng	Class	Provides a cryptography next generation (CNG) implementation of the Secure Hash Algorithm (SHA).
SHA1CryptoServiceProvider	Non-inherited class	Uses the implementation provided by the CSP to compute the SHA1 hash value for the input data.
SHA1Managed	Class	Uses the managed library to compute the SHA1 hash for the input data.
SignatureDescription	Class	Provides information about the properties of a digital signature.
StrongNameSignatureInformation	Class	Contains the strong name signature information for a manifest.
SymmetricAlgorithm	Abstract base class	Inherits all the implementations of symmetric algorithms.

Generating and Verifying a Digital Signature for a File

Digital signature is an identity proof that you can include with the encrypted data to protect it from undetected changes.

Digital signature cryptographic technique depends on hashing the data and encrypting the hash value with your private key. You can also verify the authenticity of this signature by using the data and the public key that corresponds to the private key used for signing the data. You can use the DSA algorithm to generate a digital signature for a file.

GENERATE A DIGITAL SIGNATURE

You can perform the following steps to generate a digital signature using the DSA algorithm:

1. Create the DSA object:

```
DSACryptoServiceProvider mysigner = new
DSACryptoServiceProvider();
```

2. Declare a stream to extract the data to be signed from the file:

```
FileStream myfile = new FileStream("C:\\mydata.bin",
FileMode.Open, FileAccess.Read);
```

3. Store the data to be signed in a byte array:

```
BinaryReader myreader = new BinaryReader(myfile);
byte[] mydata = myreader.ReadBytes((int)myfile.Length);
```

4. Call the `SignData` method to store the signature:

```
byte[] mysignature = mysigner.SignData(mydata);
```

5. Export the public key:

```
string pKey = mysigner.ToXmlString(false);
```

6. Display the signature:

```
Console.WriteLine("Signature of the file: " + Convert.
ToBase64String(mysignature));
```

7. Release the resources:

```
myreader.Close();
myfile. Close();
```

VERIFY A DIGITAL SIGNATURE

You can perform the following steps to verify a digital signature created using the DSA algorithm.

1. Create the DSA object:

```
DSACryptoServiceProvider myverifier = new
   DSACryptoServiceProvider();
```

2. Import the digital signature and the public key:

```
myverifier.FromXmlString(pKey);
```

3. Create a `FileStream` object to store the data to be verified:

```
FileStream myfile = new FileStream("C:\\mydata.bin",
   FileMode.Open, FileAccess.Read);
```

4. Store the data to be verified in a byte array:

```
BinaryReader myreader = new BinaryReader(myfile);
byte[] mydata = myreader.ReadBytes((int)myfile.Length);
```

TAKE NOTE*

Note that pKey used in Step 2 of this step list is the same public key that you used to create the signature. Therefore add the code in this step list to the code in the previous step list to create and verify a digital signature.

5. Call the VerifyData method to verify the signature and display appropriate messages:

```
if (myverifier.VerifyData(mydata, mysignature))
   Console. WriteLine("Verified Signature");
else
   Console. WriteLine("Unable to verify signature");
```

6. Release the resources:

```
myreader.Close();
   myfile. Close();
```

Using Hash to Verify Data Integrity

You can use the hash algorithms provided in the .NET Framework to protect data integrity.

Hash algorithms provide a hash value that is unique to a specific file or piece of data. A hash algorithm helps you ensure that hackers have not modified the specified file or data. For example, to ensure the data integrity of a file, you create and store the hash of the file. Your application can in turn verify the integrity of the file by calculating its hash value and comparing it with the stored hash value of that file. If the two hash values match, then the file has not been modified by any attackers.

CREATE A HASH VALUE USING SHA1 HASH ALGORITHM

MORE INFORMATION

Apart from the classes discussed already, to learn how to implement the other cryptography classes listed in Table 9-21, refer to the corresponding sections in the MSDN Library.

You can compute the hash value for your data using the SHA1 algorithm provided through the SHA1CryptoServiceProvider class in .NET. As explained earlier, the SHA1 algorithm is a hash algorithm that lets you create a hash value for your data. The size of the hash value generated using the SHA1 algorithm is 160 bits. You can perform the following steps to compute a hash value using SHA1 algorithm:

1. Create the SHA1CryptoServiceProvider object:

```
SHA1 Sha = new SHA1CryptoServiceProvider();
```

2. Create a FileStream object for the file that contains the data to be hashed:

```
FileStream fs = File.Open("C:\\data.bin", FileMode.Open,
   FileAccess.Read);
```

CERTIFICATION READY?

Encrypt, decrypt, and hash data by using the System.Security.Cryptography classes.

USD 5.4

3. Call the ComputeHash method of the SHA1CryptoServiceProvider object to compute the hash code for the specified file bypassing the newly created FileStream object and storing the resultant hash code of the file in a byte array:

```
byte[] hashCode = Sha.ComputeHash(fs);
```

SKILL SUMMARY

This lesson introduced you to various techniques for securing your applications, checking users' identities, and protecting your data. You can use Code Access Security (CAS) to provide security by monitoring the code. The System.Security and the System.Security.Policy namespaces consist of various classes to work with security features. You can update the security policy using Code Access Security Policy Tool (CASPOL). The System.Security.Permission namespace provides various permission classes and attributes to restrict malicious access to resources through your code.

You can authenticate a user by checking that user's identity with help of login credentials, such as user ID and password. The System.Security.Principal namespace consists of various classes associated with the authentication process. The Authentication namespace consists of the AuthenticationException and the InvalidCredentialException classes. Authorization is the process of determining whether an authenticated user has permission to access resources such as services, printers, servers, and network devices. The `System.Security.Permission` namespace consists of various classes associated with the authorization process. You can perform imperative or declarative security checks after defining the `Identity` and `Principal` objects. You can also access the `Principal` object and its associated `Identity` object directly to perform the authorization tasks without creating permission objects.

The `System.Security.AccessControl` namespace provides various classes for creating Access Control Lists (ACLs) for your objects. You can use ACLs to protect your data or object by defining a list of permissions for an object.

You can use cryptography to communicate securely using either symmetric or asymmetric encryptions. The `System.Security.Cryptography` namespace provides various classes to secure encoding and decoding of data and perform operations, such as hashing, random number generation, and message authentication.

For the certification examination:

- Know how to implement CAS to improve the security of a .NET Framework application.
- Know how to secure applications at the assembly level.
- Know how to implement security permissions imperatively or declaratively for your classes or methods.
- Learn to authenticate users to grant access.
- Learn to provide authorization to resources for authenticated users.
- Understand the use of ACL to protect the data or object.
- Understand the role of cryptography in securing the data.

■ Knowledge Assessment

Matching

Match the following descriptions to the appropriate terms.

a. `HostProtectionException`
b. `HostSecurityManager`
c. `SecurityTransparentAttribute`
d. `SecurityTreatAsSafeAttribute`
e. `SecurityContext`

_______ 1. This class allows the control and customization of security behavior for application domains.

_______ 2. This class depicts the exception that occurs when a denied host resource is detected.

_______ 3. This class identifies the nonpublic `SecurityCriticalAttribute` members that are accessible by transparent code within the assembly.

_______ 4. This class specifies that an assembly cannot cause an elevation of privilege.

_______ 5. This class encapsulates and propagates all security-related data for execution contexts transferred across threads.

True / False

Circle T if the statement is true or F if the statement is false.

T | F 1. Data Encryption Standard (DES) is an example of secret key encryption algorithm.

T | F 2. Public key encryption algorithms operate on varying lengths of buffer.

T | F 3. You cannot define your own identity class.

T | F 4. While performing declarative security checks, the demands can be placed at the class level as well as on individual methods, properties, or events.

T | F 5. ACE associates an account or group of accounts with a set of permissions for accessing an object.

Fill in the Blank

Complete the following sentences by writing the correct word or words in the blanks provided.

1. ________ and ________ encryptions are the two types of cryptography.
2. The ______ class of the `System.Security` namespace represents a collection that contains different types of permissions.
3. The random number generation service involves the _________ class.
4. ________ and _________ are the two types of security that you can use to interact with the runtime security system.
5. The __________ security override allows you to inform the runtime to stop checking for callers' permissions.

Multiple Choice

Circle the letter or letters that correspond to the best answer or answers.

1. What is the full form of DSA?
   a. Digital Signature Algorithm
   b. Double Signature Algorithm
   c. Digital Signing Algorithm
   d. Digital Signature Access
2. Which class provides a cryptography next generation (CNG) implementation of the Secure Hash Algorithm (SHA)?
   a. `SHA1`
   b. `SHA1Cng`
   c. `SHA1CryptoServiceProvider`
   d. `SHA1CryptographyNextGeneration`
3. Which of the following flags can you use to specify the least number of required permissions for your assembly?
   a. `RequestOptional`
   b. `RequestMinimum`
   c. `RequestRefuse`
   d. `RequestRequired`
4. Which of the following security demands can you use to specify the permissions that a method that overrides your method should have?
   a. `InheritanceDemand`
   b. `Demand`
   c. `PermitOnly`
   d. `LinkDemand`

5. Which of the following security actions should you use to specify that all the callers of your code should access only a particular resource?
   a. PermitOnly
   b. Deny
   c. Assert
   d. Demand

Review Questions

1. Imagine that your user account has `FullTrust` access to a file. You execute an assembly from a code group that grants Read permission to the code group. Which actions do you think you can perform on the file and why?
2. Imagine that your method must throw an exception if the caller does not possess a specific permission. Which security action should you use to throw an exception in this scenario?

■ Case Scenarios

Scenario 9-1: Using CASPOL

You have implemented CAS in your movie application and created an assembly that defines a permission set named `ClientPermissionSet`. You want to assign this permission set to all the users under the `LocalIntranet` code group. How can you achieve this?

Scenario 9-2: Using Windows Authentication

Consider that your online movie application must authenticate users based on their Windows user account. Write code to check whether the current user is a valid Windows user.

✳ Workplace Ready

Using Role-Based Authorization

.NET Framework offers a wide range of security classes to implement security through code-based and role-based approaches. You can use role-based security to authenticate and authorize users to access specific parts of your application.

XYZ Bank is building an object-oriented application to computerize its activities. The Bank wants to implement a custom authentication scheme based on a defined set of roles. As a solution architect of the bank, suggest the classes that you will use and the approach that you will take to implement this authentication scheme.

LESSON

Extending Capabilities of .NET Applications

OBJECTIVE DOMAIN MATRIX

TECHNOLOGY SKILL	OBJECTIVE DOMAIN	OBJECTIVE DOMAIN NUMBER
Create and send email messages.	Send electronic mail to a Simple Mail Transfer Protocol (SMTP) server for delivery from a .NET Framework application.	6.4
Enable globalization in applications.	Format data based on culture information.	7.1
Create regular expressions.	Enhance the text handling capabilities of a .NET Framework application, and search, modify, and control text in a .NET Framework application by using regular expressions.	7.3
Encode and decode text.	Enhance the text handling capabilities of a .NET Framework application, and search, modify, and control text in a .NET Framework application by using regular expressions.	7.3

KEY TERMS

culture-specific values
decoding
encoding
globalization
invariant culture
mutable
neutral culture
regular expressions
Simple Mail Transfer Protocol (SMTP)
specific culture

When you develop an application, you may have to address specific requirements such as sending email to users or enabling the application to be world ready. In some scenarios, you may have to extract legacy data from text files or documents and covert the data to a specific format per your business requirements. Each of the functionalities mentioned here are special requirements that extend the capabilities of your application. .NET Framework offers separate namespaces that provide classes to address these requirements.

Creating and Sending Email Messages

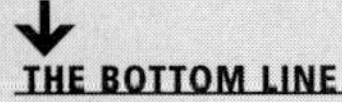

Based on your business requirements, you may have to send logon information to users from your Windows or Web applications. You may also want to enable your applications to send error messages to the application administrators. To build these capabilities into your applications, you need specific classes that enable you to create and send email messages. The .NET Framework provides a namespace that allows you to create and send email messages from your .NET applications.

Exploring the Mail Namespace

You can create and send emails from your Windows and Web applications by using the `System.NET.Mail` namespace available in the .NET Framework.

The `System.NET.Mail` namespace provides classes that help you create and send electronic messages to a ***Simple Mail Transfer Protocol (SMTP)*** server for delivery.

Table 10-1 discusses the important classes of the `System.NET.Mail` namespace.

Table 10-1

Important classes of the `System.Net.Mail` namespace

Class	Description
`Attachment`	Allows you to add an attachment to an email message.
`MailAddress`	Represents the email address of a sender or a recipient.
`MailAddressCollection`	Allows you to create a list of addresses associated with an email.
`MailMessage`	Allows you to create an email message that you can send through `SmtpClient` class.
`SmtpClient`	Enables an application to send email by using SMTP.
`SmtpPermission`	Allows you to control access to SMTP servers imperatively. This is a permission.
`SmtpPermission Attribute`	Allows you to control access to SMTP servers declaratively.

Table 10-2 lists the important methods of the `SmtpClient` class, which allow you to send email messages to the designated SMTP server.

Table 10-2

Important methods of the `SmtpClient` class

Method	Description
`Send`	Sends an email message to an SMTP server for delivery and blocks the calling thread during the message transmission.
`SendAsync`	Sends an email message without blocking the calling thread.
`SendAsyncCancel`	Enables you to cancel an asynchronous operation that sends an email message.
`OnSendCompleted`	Raises the `SendCompleted` event. You can handle this event to perform an action after the email message is sent.

Table 10-3 lists the important properties of the `SmtpClient` class.

Table 10-3

Important properties of the `SmtpClient` class

PROPERTY	DESCRIPTION
`Credentials`	Specifies the credentials used to authenticate the sender.
`DeliveryMethod`	Specifies the way to handle the outgoing email messages.
`EnableSsl`	Specifies if the SMTP uses a secure socket layer for encrypting the connection.
`Host`	Specifies the IP address or name of the host used for SMTP transactions.
`Port`	Specifies the port used for SMTP transactions.
`ServicePoint`	Retrieves the network connection for transmitting email messages.
`TargetName`	Specifies the name of the service provider used for authentication when using extended protection.

Creating Email Messages

The .NET Framework offers separate classes to compose different parts of an email such as the recipient, subject, message body, and attachments.

You can construct email messages by using the following three classes of the `System.NET.Mail` namespace:

- `MailMessage`
- `MailAddress`
- `Attachment`

INTRODUCING THE MAILMESSAGE CLASS

You can use the various properties of the `MailMessage` class to specify different parts of an email message such as the sender, recipients, and contents of the email. Table 10-4 lists the important properties of the `MailMessage` class.

Table 10-4

Important properties of the `MailMessage` class

PROPERTY	DESCRIPTION
`Attachments`	Retrieves the attachment collection that stores data attached to the current email message.
`AlternateViews`	Specifies copies of an email message in several formats.
`BCC`	Retrieves the address collection, which holds the blind carbon copy (BCC) recipients for the current email message.
`Body`	Specifies the body of the email message.
`BodyEncoding`	Specifies the encoding for the message body.
`CC`	Retrieves the address collection, which holds the carbon copy (CC) recipients for the current email message.
`From`	Specifies the from address for the current email message.
`Priority`	Specifies the priority of the current email message.

Table 10-4 (continued)

PROPERTY	DESCRIPTION
`ReplyTo`	Specifies the address that can receive the replies for the current email message.
`Sender`	Specifies the sender's address for the current email message.
`Subject`	Specifies the subject line for the current email message.
`SubjectEncoding`	Specifies the encoding that encodes the subject content for the current email message.
`To`	Specifies the address collection that holds the recipients for the current email message.
`IsBodyHtml`	Specifies a value indicating whether the mail message body is in HTML format.

INTRODUCING THE MAILADDRESS AND ATTACHMENT CLASSES

The `MailAddress` class enables the `SmtpClient` and `MailMessage` classes to store address information for an email message. You can use the properties of the `MailAddress` class to retrieve different portions of an email address for an email message, which include host, user, and an optional display name.

Table 10-5 lists the important properties of the `MailAddress` class.

Table 10-5

Important properties of the `MailAddress` class

PROPERTY	DESCRIPTION
`Address`	Retrieves the email address of the current instance.
`DisplayName`	Retrieves the display name collected from the address information.
`Host`	Retrieves the host portion of the address.
`User`	Retrieves the user information from the address.

In addition to sending messages through an email, you can also send additional files as attachments with the contents of the email. The `MailMessage` class uses the `Attachment` class to add attachments to email messages. You can use the `MailMessage.Attachments` collection to add an attachment to your email message. Your attachment could be a string, stream, or file name.

To specify the content in an attachment, you can use any of the constructors of the `Attachment` class. Table 10-6 lists the important properties of the `Attachment` class.

Table 10-6

Important properties of the `Attachment` class

PROPERTY	DESCRIPTION
`ContentDisposition`	Retrieves the MIME content disposition for the current attachment.
`Name`	Specifies the name of the MIME content type associated with the current attachment.
`NameEncoding`	Specifies the encoding used to encode the current attachment.

CONSTRUCTING AN EMAIL

You can create a simple email message by attaching a content string as an inline attachment with the message. The `CreateInlineAttachment` method in the following code sample receives an argument type of `string` that contains the text to be attached to the email message:

```
public static void CreateInlineAttachment(string attachmentText)
{
   // Creates a message using the MailMessage class
   MailMessage inlineAttachmentMessage = new MailMessage("mymail@me
.com","yourmail@you.com","Text Attachment","This email contains an
inline text attachment");
   // Attaches the text message to the email message
   Attachment stringAttachment = new Attachment(attachmentText);
   ContentType ctype = stringAttachment.ContentType;
   ctype.MediaType = MediaTypeNames.Text.Plain;
   inlineAttachmentMessage.Attachments.Add(stringAttachment);
}
```

The `CreateInlineAttachment` method uses the following objects:

- An overloaded constructor of the `MailMessage` class to create an email message. This constructor accepts the following parameters: sender address, recipient address, subject, and a message body string.
- An instance of the `Attachment` class (`stringAttachment`) to create an inline attachment from the `attachmentText` parameter of the `CreateInlineAttachment` method.
- An instance of the `ContentType` class (ctype) to set the content type of the attachment as plain text.
- The `Add` method of the `Attachments` collection of the `MailMessage` class to add the `stringAttachment` object to the email.

You can also send email messages that have HTML formatted body content. The following code sample uses the `IsBodyHtml` property of the `MailMessage` class to indicate that the mail message body is in HTML format:

```
MailMessage nwmessage = new MailMessage();
nwmessage.From = new MailAddress("mymail@me.com", "Me");
nwmessage.To.Add(new MailAddress("yourmail@you.com", "You"));
nwmessage.Subject = "Create HTML Mail";
// Specify an HTML message body
nwmessage.Body = "<html><body><h1>My Message To You</h1><br>Sending
you an <b>HTML message</b>.</body></html>";
nwmessage.IsBodyHtml = true;
```

This code uses an instance of the `MailMessage` class to create a message and add sender, recipient, subject, and message body details to that message.

Sending Email Messages

You can send email messages using the methods available in the `SmtpClient` class.

You can use any of the overloads of the `Send` or `SendAsync` methods of the `SmtpClient` class to send an email from your Windows or Web application.

ANALYZING THE REQUIREMENTS FOR SENDING MESSAGES

Before sending an email using the send methods, you should consider the following requirements:

- You can set the `Host` and `Port` settings through either the configuration file settings or using the `SmtpClient(String,Int32)` constructor.
- You must supply the necessary credentials to the mail server, if required. You can specify the credentials through the `UseDefaultCredentials` or `Credentials` properties.

Additionally, to avoid any uncaught exceptions you must always use the send methods inside a try catch block. The various exceptions that may occur while sending a mail message to the SMTP server include:

- **ArgumentNullException.** This occurs when From, To, or message is a null reference.
- **ArgumentOutOfRangeException.** This occurs when there are no recipients in To, Cc, and Bcc.
- **InvalidOperationException.** This occurs in one or more of the following conditions:
  - When the current SmtpClient has still some pending asynchronous messages to be sent.
  - When the Host is a null reference or an empty string.
  - When the Port is zero.
- **ObjectDisposedException.** This occurs when you try to access a disposed object.
- **SmtpException.** This occurs when the server connection or server authentication fails or when the operation has timed out.
- **SmtpFailedRecipientException.** This occurs when a Send or SendAsync operation cannot be completed for the specified recipients.

TAKE NOTE*

In case of an Smtp Exception, you can check the StatusCode property to find the reason for the operation failure.

SENDING THE MESSAGE SYNCHRONOUSLY

You can send messages to the SMTP server either synchronously or asynchronously. The SendInlineAttachment method in the following code sample uses the Send method to send the specified mail message synchronously by blocking the thread. The method receives the mail message through an argument type of MailMessage, which it then sends to the SMTP server:

```
public static void SendInlineAttachment(string mailServer,
MailMessage message)
{
    // Sends the message by including the default network credentials
    SmtpClient sclient = new SmtpClient(mailServer);
    sclient. Credentials = CredentialCache.DefaultNetworkCredentials;
    try
    {
        sclient. Send(message);
    }
    catch (Exception ex)
    {
        Console. WriteLine(ex.ToString());
    }
}
```

TAKE NOTE*

You can use the Timeout property of the SmtpClient class to specify a time-out value to make sure that the Send method returns after the specified amount of time.

The SendInlineAttachment method does the following:

- Receives two parameters—mail server name and mail message.
- Uses an instance of the SmtpClient class to send an email message.
- Uses the default network credentials to send the email.
- Catches an exception when sending the message and displays the error message.

SENDING THE MESSAGE ASYNCHRONOUSLY

You can use the SendAsync method to send the specified mail message asynchronously, without blocking the thread. The SendInlineAttachment method in the following code sample receives the mail message through a MailMessage argument type, which it then sends to the SMTP server:

```
public static void SendInlineAttachment(string mailServer,
MailMessage message)
{
```

```
    // Sends the message by including the default network credentials
    SmtpClient sclient = new SmtpClient(mailServer);
    sclient.Credentials = CredentialCache.DefaultNetworkCredentials;
    // Adds an event handler to handle the completion of the operation
and notify the user
    sclient.SendCompleted += new SendCompletedEventHandler
(SendCompletedHandler);
    try
    {
        string userState = "Sample message";
        // The userState can be any object, for example a string
constant that allows the callback method to identify this send operation
        sclient.SendAsync(message, userState);
        message.Dispose();
    }
    catch (Exception ex)
    {
        Console.WriteLine(ex.ToString());
    }
}
```

This code:

- Receives two parameters—mail server name and mail message.
- Uses an instance of the `SmtpClient` class to send an email message.
- Uses the default network credentials to send the email.
- Adds an event handler to the `SendCompleted` event of the `SmtpClient` class to receive notification when the email has been sent or if the operation has been cancelled.
- Catches an exception when sending the message and displays the error message.

The following sample code shows the event handler for the `SendCompleted` event:

```
private static void SendCompletedHandler(object sender,
AsyncCompletedEventArgs e)
{
    if (e.Cancelled)
    {
        Console.WriteLine("Send operation canceled");
    }
    if (e.Error != null)
    {
        Console.WriteLine(e.Error.ToString());
    }
    else
    {
        Console.WriteLine("Message sent successfully.");
    }
}
```

CERTIFICATION READY?
Send electronic mail to a Simple Mail Transfer Protocol (SMTP) server for delivery from a .NET Framework application.
USD 6.4

Enabling Globalization in Applications

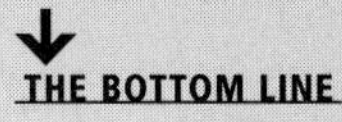

While designing and developing your Windows or Web applications, it is a good practice to keep in mind the various users of your application. By this, you can build a single application that can be used globally. To enable globalization, .NET Framework provides you with services that you can use to easily develop and distribute your application to the global audience.

Understanding .NET Globalization

Using the classes provided in the .NET Framework, you can create applications that can adapt to various cultures worldwide.

The method of designing and developing a software product to suit multiple cultures is called ***globalization***. Globalization adds support for input, display, and output of a defined set of language scripts that are related to a particular geographic locality.

Each geographic area has a specific culture that follows different conventions for displaying date, time, numbers, currency, and other information. The .NET Framework provides classes that facilitate the modification of ***culture-specific values*** in your application.

INTRODUCING GLOBALIZATION NAMESPACE

You can use the classes in the `System.Globalization` namespace for writing applications that target a global audience. These classes define culture-specific information such as language, calendars, date and time, currency, and numbers. Table 10-7 discusses the important classes of the `System.Globalization` namespace.

Table 10-7

Important classes of `System.Globalization` namespace

CLASS	DESCRIPTION
`Calendar`	Represents the yearly calendar showing weeks and months.
`CompareInfo`	Implements methods for comparing culture-sensitive string data.
`CultureInfo`	Provides information about a specific culture such as the culture name, writing system, calendar used, date format, and sort strings.
`DateTimeFormatInfo`	Defines the formatting of DateTime values based on the culture.
`DaylightTime`	Defines the period of daylight savings time.
`NumberFormatInfo`	Defines the formatting of numeric values based on the culture.
`RegionInfo`	Provides information about the country or region.
`StringInfo`	Provides advanced globalization functionalities by enabling you to split a string into text elements and iterate through the text elements.
`TextInfo`	Provides advanced globalization functionalities by defining the text properties that relate to a specific writing system.

Formatting Culture and Region Information

You can use the `CultureInfo` and `RegionInfo` classes to provide culture-specific and region-specific formatting in your application, respectively.

PROVIDING CULTURE-SPECIFIC FORMATTING

You can render culture-specific information in your application by using the `CultureInfo` class. This class enables you to access culture-specific objects that contain information about culture-specific operations. For example, using the `CultureInfo` class, you can access `DateTimeFormatInfo` and `NumberFormatInfo` classes that provide formatting of dates and numbers based on the culture.

The `CultureInfo` class provides a unique culture-specific identifier, which is a standard international numeric abbreviation. This culture identifier contains essential elements that uniquely identify the installed cultures. You can either use the predefined culture identifiers or define your own custom identifiers for your application.

Consider the following when creating your own custom cultures for your application:

- Your custom cultures can contain values exceeding the standard Microsoft-shipped cultures range.
- You must keep in mind the user's choice of culture values that your application must support.
- Custom cultures always override default values. Therefore, because country names or date formats may keep changing, the culture data cannot be stable. For this reason, you should use the invariant culture or a specific format for date-time formatting when your application serializes such unstable culture data.

You can generally group cultures as:

- ***Invariant culture.*** You can specify an invariant culture by name using an empty string or using its identifier. An invariant culture is associated only with the English language and is culture-insensitive.
- ***Neutral culture.*** A neutral culture associates itself with a language and not with a country or region. For example, to specify the neutral French culture, you can use the neutral name fr.
- ***Specific culture.*** A specific culture associates itself with both language and country or region. For example, to specify the specific French culture of France, you can use the specific name fr-FR.

TAKE NOTE* The defined cultures depict the hierarchy as invariant → neutral → specific. The `CultureInfo.Parent` property enables you to determine the parent associated with a culture type. Therefore, when defining custom cultures, you should take care to define the `Parent` property in order to conform to this hierarchical pattern.

All culture values, including predefined cultures but not the invariant culture, are dynamic. This is because the country or region can change the predefined specific cultures. You should always obtain culture data at runtime in your application. Table 10-8 lists the important properties of the `CultureInfo` class.

Table 10-8

Important properties of the `CultureInfo` class

PROPERTY	DESCRIPTION
`CompareInfo`	Retrieves the `CompareInfo` object that defines the string comparison for the culture.
`CultureTypes`	Retrieves the culture type of the current `CultureInfo` object.
`CurrentCulture`	Retrieves the `CultureInfo` object that represents the culture used by the current thread.
`DateTimeFormat`	Specifies the `DateTimeFormatInfo` object that defines the date-time format of the culture.
`InvariantCulture`	Retrieves the `CultureInfo` object that is invariant.
`IsNeutralCulture`	Determines whether the current `CultureInfo` object represents a neutral culture.
`Name`	Retrieves the culture name.
`NumberFormat`	Specifies the `NumberFormatInfo` object that defines the number format of the culture.
`Parent`	Gets the `CultureInfo` object that represents the parent culture of the current `CultureInfo` object.
`TextInfo`	Retrieves the `TextInfo` object that defines the writing system of the culture.

Table 10-9 lists the important methods of the `CultureInfo` class.

Table 10-9

Important methods of the `CultureInfo` class

METHOD	DESCRIPTION
`CreateSpecificCulture`	Creates a `CultureInfo` object that represents the specific culture associated with the specified name.
`GetCultureInfo`	Retrieves a cached, read-only culture object.
`GetCultures`	Retrieves the list of supported cultures for a specified `CultureTypes` parameter.
`GetFormat`	Retrieves an object defining the formatting of the specified type.
`ReadOnly`	Returns a read-only wrapper around the specified `CultureInfo` object.
`ToString`	Returns a string containing the name of the current `CultureInfo` object.

Table 10-10 lists the `CultureTypes` enumeration of the `System.Globalization` namespace, which defines the types of culture lists that you can retrieve using the `CultureInfo.GetCultures` method.

Table 10-10

Values of the `CultureTypes` enumeration

NAME	DESCRIPTION
`NeutralCultures`	Language specific cultures, including the invariant culture
`SpecificCultures`	Country or region specific cultures
`InstalledWin32Cultures`	Cultures installed in the Windows operating system
`AllCultures`	Cultures supported by the .NET Framework, including neutral, specific, and custom cultures, and cultures installed in the Windows operating system
`UserCustomCulture`	User-created custom cultures
`ReplacementCultures`	User-created custom culture that replaces cultures shipped with the .NET Framework
`WindowsOnlyCultures`	Cultures installed only in the Windows operating system
`FrameworkCultures`	Cultures shipped with the .NET Framework that is neutral and specific

PROVIDING REGION-SPECIFIC FORMATTING

You can use the `RegionInfo` class to obtain country or region specific information. Unlike the `CultureInfo` class, the `RegionInfo` class does not depend on the language or culture of the user. You can specify the `RegionInfo` name by using the two-letter code defined in ISO 3166 for country or region. For example, CN represents China and DE represents Germany. Note that the `RegionInfo` name is not case sensitive.

Although you can use just a country or region name, such as US for a `RegionInfo` object, it is always best to use culture names with a `RegionInfo` object. For example, you can use en-US for English (United States) with a `RegionInfo` object. This is because certain `RegionInfo` properties such as `DisplayName` require both the language and the country or region names. Also, your application can lose important data if it creates a new `RegionInfo` object using only the neutral culture name 'en' for a specific culture such as en-US.

Table 10-11 discusses the important members of the RegionInfo class.

Table 10-11

Important members of the RegionInfo class

MEMBER	TYPE	DESCRIPTION
ToString	Method	Returns a string containing the name of the current RegionInfo object.
CurrencyEnglishName	Property	Retrieves the name of the currency used in the country or region in English.
CurrencySymbol	Property	Retrieves the currency symbol of the country or region.
CurrentRegion	Property	Retrieves the RegionInfo object representing the country or region used by the current thread.
DisplayName	Property	Retrieves the full name of the country or region in the language of the localized version of .NET Framework.
IsMetric	Property	Determines whether the country or region uses the metric system for measurements.
Name	Property	Gets the name for the current RegionInfo object.
GeoId	Property	Retrieves a unique identification number for a geographical region, country, city, or location.

Formatting Numbers

In your applications, you can use the NumberFormatInfo class to define how numeric values are formatted based on the culture.

TAKE NOTE*

You cannot create a NumberFormatInfo object for a neutral culture.

You can use the NumberFormatInfo class to provide culture-specific currency information, decimal separators, and other numeric symbols.

CREATING A NUMBERFORMATINFO OBJECT

You must perform different steps to create a number formatting object for specific cultures or invariant cultures.

CREATE A NUMBERFORMATINFO OBJECT FOR A SPECIFIC CULTURE

Perform the following steps to create a NumberFormatInfo object for a specific culture:

1. Create a CultureInfo object for the specific culture.
2. Retrieve the NumberFormatInfo object through the CultureInfo.NumberFormat property.

CREATE A NUMBERFORMATINFO OBJECT FOR A CURRENT CULTURE

Perform the following step to create a NumberFormatInfo object for the culture of the current thread:

1. Use the NumberFormatInfo.CurrentInfo property.

CREATE A NUMBERFORMATINFO OBJECT FOR A INVARIANT CULTURE

Perform the following step to create a NumberFormatInfo object for the invariant culture:

1. Use the NumberFormatInfo.InvariantInfo property for a read-only version or use the NumberFormatInfo constructor for a writeable version.

The following code sample gets a read-only invariant culture `NumberFormatInfo` instance using the `InvariantInfo` property:

```
NumberFormatInfo nfReadOnly = NumberFormatInfo.InvariantInfo;
```

The following code sample gets a writable invariant culture `NumberFormatInfo` instance, using the `NumberFormatInfo` constructor. You can create a writable instance to allow your application to store user-defined formatting:

```
NumberFormatInfo nfWritable = new NumberFormatInfo();
```

TAKE NOTE* When a user chooses to override the current culture settings of Windows or when the `CultureInfo.UseUserOverride` property is set to true, then the system retrieves the `CultureInfo.NumberFormat` from the user settings.

Table 10-12 lists the important properties of the `NumberFormatInfo` class.

Table 10-12

Important properties of the `NumberFormatInfo` class

PROPERTY	DESCRIPTION
`CurrencyDecimalDigits`	Specifies the number of decimal places to use in currency values.
`CurrencyNegativePattern`	Specifies the format pattern for negative currency values.
`CurrencyPositivePattern`	Specifies the format pattern for positive currency values.
`CurrencySymbol`	Specifies the string to use for the currency symbol.
`CurrentInfo`	Retrieves a read-only `NumberFormatInfo` object that formats values based on the current culture.
`InvariantInfo`	Retrieves the default read-only `NumberFormatInfo` object for the invariant culture.
`NumberDecimalDigits`	Specifies the number of decimal places to use in numeric values.
`PercentDecimalDigits`	Specifies the number of decimal places to use in percent values.
`PercentSymbol`	Specifies the string to use for the percent symbol.

The `NumberFormatInfo` class provides various standard formatting patterns stored in its properties; that is, the properties are associated with various standard format specifiers—currency, decimal, scientific, fixed-point, general, number, percent, round-trip, and hexadecimal.

USING CURRENCY FORMAT

You should use C or c to specify the currency format. The `NumberFormatInfo` properties associated with the currency format include `CurrencyDecimalDigits`, `CurrencyDecimalSeparator`, and other currency-related properties. The number that represents a currency amount is converted to a string. The following example includes a double value that represents a currency amount with a currency format specifier for the invariant culture:

```
double CurrencyValue = 54367.987;
Console.WriteLine(CurrencyValue.ToString("C2", CultureInfo.
InvariantCulture));
// Displays the output as 54,367.99
```

Note that in this code, the precision specifier indicates the required number of decimal places to appear in the formatted output value.

USING DECIMAL FORMAT

You should use D or d to specify the decimal format. This format can only be used for integral types. When you use this format, the system converts a number to a string of decimal digits (0–9). If the number is negative, the system prefixes the number with a minus sign. The following sample code formats an integer value with the decimal format specifier:

```
int decimalValue = 89709;
Console. WriteLine(value.ToString("D7"));
// Displays the output as 0089709
```

Note that in this code, the precision specifier D7 indicates the minimum number of digits that need to appear in the resultant output string.

USING SCIENTIFIC FORMAT

You should use E or e to specify the scientific or exponential format. The system converts the given number to a string in the form "–d.ddd . . . E+ddd" or "–d.ddd . . . e+ddd," in which d indicates a digit (0–9):

> **TAKE NOTE*** The exponent always contains a plus or minus sign with a minimum of three digits.

```
double scientificValue = 99998.6789;
Console.WriteLine(scientificValue.ToString("E4", CultureInfo.
InvariantCulture));
// Displays the output as 9.9999E+004
Console.WriteLine(scientificValue.ToString("e4", CultureInfo.
InvariantCulture));
// Displays the output as 9.9999e+004
```

USING FIXED-POINT FORMAT

You should use F or f to specify the fixed-point format. When you use the fixed-point format, the system converts the number to a string in the form "–ddd.ddd . . ." in which each d indicates a digit (0–9). The following sample code formats an integer value with the fixed-point specifier for the invariant culture:

```
int numberValue = -12345;
Console. WriteLine(numberValue.ToString("F3", CultureInfo.
InvariantCulture));
// Displays the output as -12345.000
```

Note that in this code, the precision specifier indicates the required number of decimal places.

USING GENERAL FORMAT

You should use G or g to specify the general format. When you use the general format, depending on the number and the precision specifier present, the system converts the number to the most compact of either fixed-point or scientific notation. If you omit the precision or assign a value of zero for the precision, the system takes the default precision of the number type. The following code sample formats the floating-point value with the general format specifier for the specific French culture:

```
double dvalue;
dvalue = 56789.6789;
Console. WriteLine(dvalue.ToString("G", CultureInfo.CreateSpecific
Culture("fr-FR")));
// Displays the output as 56789,6789
```

USING NUMBER FORMAT

You should use N or n to specify the number format. When you use the number format, the system converts the number to a string in the form "–d,ddd,ddd.ddd . . .," in which the d indicates a digit (0–9); the, indicates a thousands separator between number groups; the – indicates a negative sign; and the . indicates a decimal point.

The following sample code formats a floating-point value with the number format specifier for the invariant culture:

```
double dvalue = -12667.7689;
Console.WriteLine(dvalue.ToString("N",
CultureInfo.InvariantCulture));
// Displays the output as -12,667.77
```

USING PERCENT FORMAT

You should use P or p to specify the percent format. When you use the percent format, the system converts the number to a string representing a percent and multiplies the number by 100 to present it as a percentage. The system uses the `NumberFormatInfo.PecentNegativePattern` or `NumberFormatInfo.PercentPositivePattern` properties to define the percent. The following code sample formats a floating-point value with the percent format specifier for the invariant culture:

```
double percentValue =.1457013;
Console.WriteLine(percentValue.ToString("P1", CultureInfo.
InvariantCulture));
// Displays the output value as 14.6%
```

USING ROUND-TRIP FORMAT

> **TAKE NOTE***
> When you use the round-trip specifier, the system ignores any precision specifier, if present.

You should use R or r to specify the round-trip format. You can use this format only for the `Single` or `Double` types. When you use the round-trip specifier, the system converts the numeric value to a string and parses the string back into the same numeric value because the string representation contains all the significant digits required for formatting. The following sample code formats a double value with the round-trip format for the specific French culture:

```
double doubleValue;
doubleValue = Math.PI;
Console.WriteLine(doubleValue.ToString("r",
CultureInfo.CreateSpecificCulture("fr-FR")));
// Displays the output as 3,1415926535897931
```

USING HEXADECIMAL FORMAT

> **TAKE NOTE***
> When you use any specifier other than the standard specifiers discussed earlier, the system throws a `FormatException` at runtime.

You should use X or x to specify the hexadecimal format. This format can only be used for integral types. When you use the hexadecimal format, the system converts the number to a string of hexadecimal digits. The following sample code formats an integer value with the hexadecimal format:

```
int hexValue;
hexValue = 0x1267e;
Console.WriteLine(hexValue.ToString("x"));
// Displays the output as 1267e
Console.WriteLine(hexValue.ToString("X"));
// Displays the output as 1267E
```

USING CUSTOM FORMAT

You can also use custom patterns to format numeric values. To use custom patterns, you should make the `NumberFormatInfo` object writable and then save your custom patterns in the properties of the `NumberFormatInfo` object appropriately. Table 10-13 lists some of the custom numeric format specifiers.

Table 10-13

Custom numeric format specifiers

Specifier	Description
`0`	Allows any digit present in the 0 position of the formatted value to be copied to the resultant string. If no digit is present at the 0 position in the formatted value, then no value is copied to the resultant string. This specifier displays leading 0s in the formatted value even if the specifier uses 0 in that position.
`#`	Copies any digit present in the # position of the formatted value to the resultant string. If no digit is present at the # position in the formatted value, then no value is copied to the resultant string. This specifier does not display any leading 0s in the formatted value even if the specifier uses # in that position.
`.`	Represents the location of the decimal separator in the formatted value.
`,`	Represents the thousands separator specifier and a number scaling specifier.
`%`	In the presence of the % symbol in a format string, the system multiplies the number by 100 before formatting it.
`'ABC' or "ABC"`	Characters enclosed within single quotes or double quotes do not affect formatting and are copied as is to the resultant string.
`;`	Enables sections to be separated for positive, negative, and zero numbers in the format string.

The following code sample uses the custom format specifier # in the custom format string to display the numeric data in its place. The rest of the characters appear as is in the resultant string:

```
Double sampleDouble = 7325481395;
String result = sampleDouble.ToString( "(###) ### - ####" );
// Output value of result is "(732) 548 - 1395"
```

EXPLORING PERMITTED NUMERIC STRING STYLE

You can use the `NumberStyles` enumeration of the `System.Globalization` namespace to determine the styles permitted in numeric string arguments in the parse methods of the numeric base-type classes. Table 10-14 lists the members of the `NumberStyles` enumeration.

Table 10-14

Members of the `NumberStyles` enumeration

Member	Description
`None`	Specifies that none of the bit values be allowed.
`AllowLeadingWhite`	Specifies that the parse method should ignore the leading white-space character during parsing.
`AllowTrailingWhite`	Specifies that the parse method should ignore the trailing white-space character during parsing.
`AllowLeadingSign`	Specifies that the numeric string can have a sign at the beginning of the number.
`AllowTrailingSign`	Specifies that the numeric string can have a sign at the end of the number.

Table 10-14 (continued)

MEMBER	DESCRIPTION
`AllowParenthesis`	Specifies that the numeric string can have a single pair of parenthesis enclosing the number.
`AllowDecimalPoint`	Specifies that the numeric string can have a decimal point.
`AllowThousands`	Specifies that the numeric string can contain group separators.
`AllowExponent`	Specifies that the numeric string can be in exponential notation.
`AllowCurrencySymbol`	Specifies that the numeric string has to be parsed as currency if it contains the currency symbol. Otherwise, it is parsed as a number.
`AllowHexSpecifier`	Specifies that the numeric string represents a hexadecimal number.
`Integer`	Indicates that the `AllowLeadingWhite`, `AllowTrailingWhite`, and `AllowLeadingSign` styles be used.
`HexNumber`	Indicates that the `AllowLeadingWhite`, `AllowTrailingWhite`, and `AllowHexSpecifier` styles be used.
`Number`	Indicates that the `AllowLeadingWhite`, `AllowTrailingWhite`, `AllowLeadingSign`, `AllowTrailingSign`, `AllowDecimalPoint`, and `AllowThousands` styles be used.
`Float`	Indicates that the `AllowLeadingWhite`, `AllowTrailingWhite`, `AllowLeadingSign`, `AllowDecimalPoint`, and `AllowExponent` styles be used.
`Currency`	Indicates that all styles, except `AllowExponent` and `AllowHexSpecifier`, be used.
`Any`	Indicates that all styles, except `AllowHexSpecifier`, be used.

Formatting DateTime

You can format date and time values in your application using the `DateTimeFormatInfo` class based on the culture.

The `DateTimeFormatInfo` class provides culture specific date patterns, time patterns, and AM or PM designators.

CREATING DATETIMEFORMATINFO OBJECT

You must perform different steps to create date-time formatting objects for the specific culture and invariant culture.

CREATE A DATETIMEFORMATINFO OBJECT FOR A SPECIFIC CULTURE

You can perform the following steps to create a `DateTimeFormatInfo` object for a specific culture:

1. Create a `CultureInfo` object for the specific culture.
2. Retrieve the `DateTimeFormatInfo` object through the `CultureInfo.DateTimeFormat` property.

The following code sample creates a `DateTimeFormatInfo` object for the Thai culture:

```
DateTimeFormatInfo dtInfo = new CultureInfo("th-TH").DateTimeFormat;
```

CREATE A DATETIMEFORMATINFO OBJECT FOR A CURRENT CULTURE

You can perform the following to create a `DateTimeFormatInfo` object for the culture of the current thread:

1. Use the `DateTimeFormatInfo.CurrentInfo` property.

The following code sample creates a `DateTimeFormatInfo` object for the current culture:

```
DateTimeFormatInfo dtInfo = DateTimeFormatInfo.CurrentInfo;
```

CREATE A DATETIMEFORMATINFO OBJECT FOR AN INVARIANT CULTURE

You can perform the following to create a `DateTimeFormatInfo` object for the invariant culture:

1. Use the `DateTimeFormatInfo.InvariantInfo` property for a read-only version or use the `DateTimeFormatInfo` constructor for a writeable version.

The following code sample creates a read-only `DateTimeFormatInfo` object for the invariant culture:

```
DateTimeFormatInfo dtInfo = DateTimeFormatInfo.InvariantInfo;
```

The following code sample creates a writable `DateTimeFormatInfo` object for the invariant culture to store user-defined formatting values in its properties:

```
DateTimeFormatInfo dtInfo = new DateTimeFormatInfo();
```

TAKE NOTE*

You cannot create a `DateTimeFormatInfo` object for a neutral culture.

When a user chooses to override the current culture settings of Windows or when the `CultureInfo.UseUserOverride` property is set to true, then the system retrieves the `CultureInfo.DateTimeFormat` from the user settings.

Table 10-15 lists the important properties of the `DateTimeFormatInfo` class.

Table 10-15

Important properties of the `DateTimeFormatInfo` class

PROPERTY	DESCRIPTION
`AMDesignator`	Specifies the string designator for ante meridiem (AM) hours.
`PMDesignator`	Specifies the string designator for post meridiem (PM) hours.
`Calendar`	Specifies the calendar to use for the current culture.
`CurrentInfo`	Retrieves a read-only `DateTimeFormatInfo` object for formatting values based on the culture.
`DateSeperator`	Specifies the string that separates the year, month, and day in a date.
`InvariantInfo`	Retrieves a read-only default `DateTimeFormatInfo` object that formats values for the invariant culture.

Table 10-15 (continued)

PROPERTY	DESCRIPTION
`FullDateTimePattern`	Specifies the format pattern for the long date and long time values associated with the "F" format pattern.
`IsReadOnly`	Determines whether the `DateTimeFormatInfo` object is read-only or not.
`TimeSeperator`	Specifies a string that separates the hour, minutes, and seconds in the time.
`LongDatePattern`	Specifies the format pattern for a long date value that is associated with the "D" format pattern.
`LongTimePattern`	Specifies the format pattern for a long time value that is associated with the "T" format pattern.
`ShortDatePattern`	Specifies the format pattern for a short date value that is associated with the "d" format pattern.
`ShortTimePattern`	Specifies the format pattern for a short time value that is associated with the "t" format pattern.
`YearMonthPattern`	Specifies the format pattern for a year and month value that is associated with the "y" and "Y" format patterns.
`MonthNames`	Specifies a one-dimensional array type of `String` that contains the culture-specific full names of the months.
`DayNames`	Specifies a one-dimensional array type of `String` that contains the culture-specific full names of the days of the week.

USING STANDARD PATTERNS

You can format the date and time values using the standard patterns. You must use a single format specifier for a standard date and time format string. Table 10-16 lists the available standard patterns for the `DateTimeFormatInfo` object.

Table 10-16

Standard date and time format specifiers

SPECIFIER	DESCRIPTION
d	Represents a custom date and time format string defined by the current `ShortDatePattern` property.
D	Represents a custom date and time format string defined by the current `LongDatePattern` property.
f	Represents a combination of the long date (D) and short time (t) patterns, separated by a space.
F	Represents a custom date and time format string defined by the current `FullDateTimePattern` property.
g	Represents a combination of the short date (d) and short time (t) patterns, separated by a space.
G	Represents a combination of the short date (d) and long time (T) patterns, separated by a space.
`M, m`	Represents a custom date and time format string defined by the current `MonthDayPattern` property.

Table 10-16 (continued)

SPECIFIER	DESCRIPTION
`O, o`	Represents a custom date and time format string using a pattern that preserves time zone information.
`R, r`	Represents a custom date and time format string defined by the `DateTimeFormatInfo.RFC1123Pattern` property.
`s`	Represents a custom date and time format string defined by the `DateTimeFormatInfo.SortableDateTimePattern` property.
`t`	Represents a custom date and time format string defined by the current `ShortTimePattern` property.
`T`	Represents a custom date and time format string defined by the current `LongTimePattern` property.
`u`	Represents a custom date and time format string defined by the `DateTimeFormatInfo.UniversalSortableDateTimePattern` property.
`U`	Represents a custom date and time format string defined by the current `FullDateTimePattern` property.
`Y, y`	Represents a custom date and time format string defined by the current `YearMonthPattern` property.

The following sample code uses the standard format strings with date and time values:

```
// Create a datetime object and retrieve the current date and time
DateTime sampleDate = DateTime.Now;
// Create a new datetime format specifier object
DateTimeFormatInfo formatSpecifier = new DateTimeFormatInfo();
// Create a specific culture object
CultureInfo specificCul = new CultureInfo("en-US");
// Create a new custom date and time pattern
formatSpecifier.MonthDayPattern = "MM-MMMM, ddd-dddd";
// Use the DateTimeFormat from the culture related to the current
thread
Console.WriteLine(sampleDate.ToString("f"));
// For example, if the SampleDate value is 10/10/2009 9:45:30PM, and
assuming that the current culture is en-US, the format specifier f
produces the output as Saturday, October 10, 2009 9:45 PM.
Console.WriteLine(sampleDate.ToString("M"));
// For example, if the SampleDate value is 10/10/2009 9:45:30PM, and
assuming that the current culture is en-US, the format specifier M
produces the output as October 10
// Use the DateTimeFormat from the specific culture
Console.WriteLine(sampleDate.ToString("m", specificCul));
// For example, if the SampleDate value is 10/10/2009 9:45:30PM, the
format specifier m produces the output as October 10
// Use the settings of the DateTimeFormatInfo object
Console.WriteLine(sampleDate.ToString("m", formatSpecifier));
// For example, if the SampleDate value is 10/10/2009 9:45:30PM, the
format specifier m produces the output as October 10 for the speci-
fied MonthDayPattern
```

USING CUSTOM PATTERNS

Similar to the standard patterns, you can also format the date and time values using the custom patterns. However, unlike the standard patterns, the custom date and time format strings consist of one or more custom numeric format specifiers. When using custom patterns, you need to set the associated properties of a writable `DateTimeFormatInfo` object. Table 10-17 lists some of the custom patterns for the `DateTimeFormatInfo` object.

Table 10-17

Custom date and time format specifiers

SPECIFIER	DESCRIPTION
`d`	Represents the day of the month as a number (1–31) and formats a single-digit day without a leading 0.
`dddd` (you can add any number of additional specifiers)	Represents the full name of the day of the week as specified in the current `DateTimeFormatInfo.DayNames` property.
`F`	Represent the tenths of a second in a date and time value. No value is displayed if the digit is 0.
`H`	Represents the hour as a number (0–23) and formats a single-digit hour without a leading 0.
`K`	Represents the time zone information of a date and time value.
`m`	Represents the minute as a number (0–59) and formats a single-digit minute with a leading 0.
`mm,mm`	Represents the minute as a number (00–59) and formats a single-digit minute with a leading 0.
`M`	Represents the month as a number (1–12) and a single-digit month is formatted without a leading 0.
`s`	Represents a second as a number (0–59).
`t`	Represents the first character of the AM/PM designator defined in the current `DateTimeFormatInfo.AMDesignator` or `DateTimeFormatInfo.PMDesignator` property.
`y`	Represents the year as a one- or two-digit number. If the year has more than two digits (e.g., 2009), then only the two low-order digits (09) appear in the result. In addition, if the first digit of a two-digit year is 0, then the number is formatted without a leading 0.
`:`	Represents the time separator defined in the current `DateTimeFormatInfo.TimeSeparator` property.
`/`	Represents the date separator defined in the current `DateTimeFormatInfo.DateSeparator` property.
`"`	Displays the literal value of any string between two quotation marks.
`'`	Displays the literal value of any string between two apostrophes.

The following sample code uses the custom format string with date and time values:

```
DateTime sampleDate;
sampleDate = new DateTime(2009, 9, 30, 17, 9, 1);
Console.WriteLine(sampleDate.ToString("h:m:s.F t",
CultureInfo.InvariantCulture));
// Displays the output as 5:9:1 P
sampleDate = new DateTime(2009, 9, 30, 19, 27, 15);
Console.WriteLine(sampleDate.ToString("dddd dd MMMM",
CultureInfo.CreateSpecificCulture("en-US")));
// Displays the output as Wednesday 30 September
```

Creating Custom Cultures

When the predefined culture does not provide the formatting required for your application, .NET Framework allows you to create a custom culture.

EXPLORING THE CULTUREANDREGIONINFOBUILDER CLASS

You can use the `CultureAndRegionInfoBuilder` class to create a new culture or override an existing culture. Once you have created a custom culture, you can install it on your computer and allow it to be used by all the applications that run on your computer. In addition, you can use the `CultureInfo` class to create an instance of a registered custom culture.

Table 10-18 lists the important methods of the `CultureAndRegionInfoBuilder` class.

Table 10-18

Important methods of the `CultureAndRegionInfoBuilder` class

METHOD	DESCRIPTION
LoadDataFromCultureInfo	Defines the properties of the current `CultureAndRegionInfoBuilder` object with the corresponding properties of the specified `CultureInfo` object.
LoadDataFromRegionInfo	Defines the properties of the current `CultureAndRegionInfoBuilder` object with the corresponding properties of the specified `RegionInfo` object.
Register	Stores the current `CultureAndRegionInfoBuilder` object as a custom culture on the local computer and makes this custom culture available to applications residing on the local computer.
Save	Writes an XML representation of the current `CultureAndRegionInfoBuilder` object to the specified file.
Unregister	Deletes a custom culture from the local computer.

TAKE NOTE*

When creating new cultures, you can populate the properties of a `CultureAndRegionInfoBuilder` object with existing `CultureInfo` and `RegionInfo` objects by using the `LoadDataFromCultureInfo` and `LoadDataFromRegionInfo` methods.

Table 10-19 lists the important properties of the CultureAndRegionInfoBuilder class.

Table 10-19

Important properties of the CultureAndRegionInfoBuilder class

PROPERTY	DESCRIPTION
AvailableCalendars	Specifies an array of calendars supported by the current CultureAndRegionInfoBuilder object.
CultureName	Retrieves the name of the created culture.
CultureTypes	Retrieves the CultureTypes value, which describes the culture represented by the current CultureAndRegionInfoBuilder object.
NumberFormat	Specifies a NumberFormatInfo object.
Parent	Specifies the CultureInfo object representing the parent culture of the current custom culture.
RegionName	Retrieves the name of the country or region for the current CultureAndRegionInfoBuilder object.
TextInfo	Specifies the TextInfo object that defines the writing system associated with the current custom culture.

USING CULTUREANDREGIONMODIFIERS ENUMERATION

You must pass a CultureAndRegionModifiers enumeration as one of the parameters to the CultureAndRegionInfoBuilder class constructor to define its instance. You can then use this CultureAndRegionInfoBuilder instance to create a custom culture. Table 10-20 lists the values of the CultureAndRegionModifiers enumeration.

Table 10-20

Values of the CultureAndRegionModifiers enumeration

VALUE	DESCRIPTION
None	Indicates a specific, supplementary custom culture that can be entirely new or an extension of an existing .NET Framework culture or Windows locale.
Neutral	Indicates a neutral custom culture for a specific language.
Replacement	Indicates a custom culture that replaces an existing .NET Framework culture or Windows locale.

TAKE NOTE* Your custom culture can contain a combination of a specific culture or a neutral culture. It could also be a combination of a replacement culture or a supplement culture.

CREATING CUSTOM CULTURES

You can use the CultureAndRegionInfoBuilder class to create a custom culture.

CREATE A CUSTOM CULTURE

Perform these steps to define and create custom cultures:

1. Use a CultureAndRegionInfoBuilder object to define and name the custom culture.
2. Modify the properties of the CultureAndRegionInfoBuilder object according to your needs.

3. Register the custom culture using the `Register` method. During this task, the registration process takes care of the following tasks:
   - Creating the .nlp file, which contains the information specified in the `CultureAndRegionInfoBuilder` object.
   - Storing the .nlp file in the %WINDIR%\Globalization system directory and preparing .NET Framework to search for the same directory when there is a request to create a new culture.
4. Specify the name of the custom culture in a `CultureInfo` class constructor.

The following code sample creates a custom culture named `SampleCustomCulture` that extends the existing French culture provided by the .NET Framework. The code passes the `None` value of the `CultureAndRegionModifiers` enumeration to the `CultureAndRegionInfoBuilder` constructor to indicate that the custom culture is a specific supplementary culture:

```
CultureAndRegionInfoBuilder myCulture = new CultureAndRegionInfoBuilder
("SampleCustomCulture", CultureAndRegionModifiers.None);
CultureInfo frenchCulture = new CultureInfo("fr-FR");
// Loads culture information from the existing French culture
myCulture.LoadDataFromCultureInfo(frenchCulture);
// Loads region information from the existing French culture
myCulture.LoadDataFromRegionInfo(frenchCulture);
// Register the SampleCustomCulture
myCulture.Register();
// Create a CultureInfo object for the SampleCustomCulture and display
the culture name
CultureInfo customCulture = new CultureInfo("SampleCustomCulture");
Console.WriteLine("My Custom Culture Name", customCulture.Name);
```

TAKE NOTE*

You can create an entirely new culture or a culture that replaces an existing .NET Framework culture or Windows locale. Only users with the administrative rights on the computer can register a custom culture.

Comparing and Sorting Culture Information

Alphabetical order and conventions for sorting data differ from one culture to another, so it is a good practice for an application to compare and sort data on a per-culture basis. .NET Framework provides a class that performs culture-sensitive comparisons and sorting for this purpose.

You can use the methods of the `CompareInfo` class of the `System.Globalization` namespace to provide culture-sensitive string comparisons.

USING COMPAREINFO METHODS

The `CompareInfo` property of the `CultureInfo` class, which is an instance of the `CompareInfo` class, can be used to define how to compare and sort strings for a specific culture. The `String.Compare` method then uses this information to compare strings.

The following code sample compares the two given strings using the `String.Compare` method based on the French culture. That is, the `String.Compare` method in the sample code uses the casing rules and the alphabetic order of individual characters, specific to the French culture, for comparison. The Compare method returns an integer value as the comparison result based on the relationship between the two compared strings. For example, the comparison value returns the following values:

- A negative value if `firstStr` is less than `secondStr`
- A zero if `firstStr` is equal to `secondStr`

- A positive value if `firstStr` is greater than `secondStr`

```
string firstStr = "Coté";
string secondStr = "côte";
// Set the CurrentCulture to French for France
Thread.CurrentThread.CurrentCulture = new CultureInfo("fr-FR");
// Compare the two strings
int comparisonResult = String.Compare(firstStr, secondStr);
// Display the result of comparison
Console.WriteLine("The result of the comparison of strings for the
French culture is" + comparisonResult);
```

Because certain cultures support multiple sort orders, you can override the default sort order by specifying a predefined alternate sort order identifier.

SPECIFY AN ALTERNATE SORT ORDER

Perform the following steps to specify an alternate sort order:

1. Create a `CultureInfo` object using the alternate sort order identifier.
2. Obtain a `CompareInfo` object by using the `CultureInfo.CompareInfo` property or by using the `CompareInfo.GetCompareInfo` method, specifying the alternate sort order specifier.

X REF

You can refer to the "Comparing and Sorting Data for a Specific Culture" section in the MSDN library to get a list of alternate sort order identifiers.

You can use the overloaded `IndexOf` method of the `CompareInfo` class to search a character or substring within a specified string. The following code sample uses the `IndexOf` method to search for a character in the given string for a specified culture:

```
// Initialize a string and a character
string sampleString = "Æble";
char findCharacter = 'Æ';
// Use the CultureInfo for Danish in Denmark.
CultureInfo danishCulture = new CultureInfo("da-DK");
// Use the IndexOf method to search a character
int searchResult = danishCulture.CompareInfo.IndexOf(sampleString,
findCharacter);
// Display the search result
Console. WriteLine("The result of the search operation is " +
searchResult);
```

TAKE NOTE*

You can use the overloaded `Sort` method of the `Array` class to sort arrays based on the `CurrentCulture` property. You can use the `SortKey` class of the `System.Globalization` namespace to support culture-sensitive sorting.

ANALYZING THE NEED FOR CULTURE-INSENSITIVE STRING OPERATIONS

You already know that you can use culture-sensitive string operations to compare and sort data on a per-culture basis. However, it does not yield appropriate results when you want the results to be culture-independent. In such situations, you must use culture-insensitive string operations in your applications.

You can use culture-insensitive string operations in the following cases:

- When your application uses the result of string operations internally. For example, if your application works with file names, persistence formats, or symbolic information that it does not display to the user.
- When your application uses the result of string operations, irrespective of the culture; for example, if your application uses string comparison methods for comparing a string to find out whether the string is a recognized XML tag.
- When your application uses the result of string operations for a security decision.

Exploring Best Practices in Globalization

You need to follow best practices to develop an effective application for global use.

When developing applications for global audience, you should follow certain guidelines. Table 10-21 lists the recommended practices to be followed in various scenarios when developing a global application.

Table 10-21

Recommended practices in globalization

SCENARIO	RECOMMENDED PRACTICE
Developing an application for global use	Use Unicode standards in your application
Setting culture properties	Use the `CultureInfo` class. For example, you can use the `CultureInfo.CurrentCulture` property for number formatting, date and time formatting, and for any other formatting tasks
Disallowing the override of `CultureInfo` property settings by user-settings	Set the `CultureInfo.useUserOverride` property to false
Displaying text	Use the `System.Drawing` namespace
Sorting and comparing data in an application	Use the culture-sensitive `SortKey` and `CompareInfo` classes
Encoding data	Use encoding classes in the `System.Text` namespace
Ensuring security	Use `UTF8Encoding` class for its error detection feature

CERTIFICATION READY?
Format data based on culture information.
USD 7.1

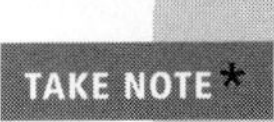

Before releasing your application in the production environment, always test its functionality on international operating system versions with international data. Additionally, use culture-insensitive operations wherever required.

MORE INFORMATION

You can refer to the "Best Practices for Developing World-Ready Applications" section in the MSDN library to know more about the best practices followed in creating world-ready applications.

Creating Regular Expressions

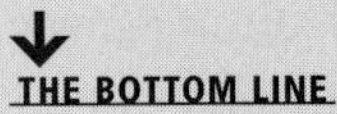

You can use ***regular expressions*** to manipulate text with ease. Regular expressions are powerful tools to build applications such as HTML processors and log file parsers that deal extensively with strings.

Regular expressions offer extensive pattern-matching notations that allow you to parse large amounts of text to find specific character patterns. In addition, regular expressions allow you to extract, edit, replace, and delete text substrings from a text string.

Microsoft .NET Framework regular expressions include features such as right-to-left matching and on-the-fly compilation. Right-to-left matching denotes parsing the string from right to left. On-the-fly compilation facilitates compilation of the regular expressions at the time they are used for parsing, and .NET Framework regular expression classes are included in the base class library.

Manipulating Strings

The `System.Text.StringBuilder` class enables you to build and manipulate strings.

The `StringBuilder` class in the `System.Text` namespace manages and formats `String` objects without creating intermediate instances of a `String` object. Alternatively, if you use a `String` object, you have to write multiple statements to perform successive string operations that produce intermediate string data. In addition, you may require more memory to store the intermediate string data.

You can refer to the section "Encoding and Decoding Text" in this lesson to learn about encoding `System.Text` namespace classes.

You can use the `StringBuilder` class to build strings and work with regular expressions. This class denotes an object similar to a string whose value is a ***mutable*** sequence of characters. The resultant string is said to be mutable because the value of the object can be modified after it has been created. You can perform various modifications on the string including appending, removing, replacing, or inserting characters. In addition, you should use `StringBuilder` object when performance is a major issue in your application because a `StringBuilder` object always maintains a buffer to accommodate the concatenation of new data during concatenation operations and appends new data at the end of the buffer. It allocates memory, only when allocated buffer is very small to accommodate the concatenated data. You can use the `StringBuilder` object especially when concatenating a random number of user input strings.

Most of the methods that modify an instance of the `StringBuilder` class return a reference to that same instance. This feature of the `StringBuilder` class allows you to write a single statement that chains successive operations, one after another.

`StringBuilder` class capacity is the maximum number of characters the instance can store at any given time. This capacity is greater than or equal to the length of the string representation of the instance value. You can also increase or decrease the capacity using the `Capacity` property or `EnsureCapacity` method of the `StringBuilder` class. However, the capacity cannot be less than the value of the `Length` property.

You can concatenate new data to an existing `StringBuilder` object by using the `Concat` and `AppendFormat` methods. The concatenation operation always creates a new object from the existing string and the new data specified. A `StringBuilder` object retains a buffer to hold the concatenated data. You can use a `StringBuilder` object for a concatenation operation if an arbitrary number of strings are to be concatenated.

Table 10-22 lists the `StringBuilder` class methods that are used when working with regular expressions.

Table 10-22

Methods of the `StringBuilder` class

Method	Description
`Append`	Appends the string representation of a specified object to the end of the specified instance.
`AppendFormat`	Appends the string returned by processing a composite format string, which contains none or more format items to the instance.
`AppendLine`	Appends the default line terminator or a copy of a specified string and the default line terminator to the end of the instance.
`EnsureCapacity`	Ensures that the capacity of the instance of `StringBuilder` is at least the specified value.

Table 10-22 (continued)

METHOD	DESCRIPTION
`Insert`	Inserts the string representation of a specified object into a specific instance at a specified character position.
`Remove`	Deletes the specified range of characters from the specified instance.
`Replace`	Replaces all the occurrences of a specified character or string in the specified instance with another specified character or string.
`ToString`	Converts the value of a `StringBuilder` object to a `String` object.

Table 10-23 lists the properties of the `StringBuilder` class that are used when working with regular expressions.

Table 10-23

Properties of the `StringBuilder` class

PROPERTY	DESCRIPTION
`Capacity`	Gets or sets the maximum number of characters that can be contained in the memory allocated by the current instance.
`Chars`	Gets or sets the character at the specified character position in the specified instance.
`Length`	Gets or sets the length of the current `StringBuilder` object.
`MaxCapacity`	Gets the maximum capacity of the specified instance.

The following code sample manipulates a string using the `StringBuilder` class. The code creates a new `sbaddress` object and uses the `AppendLine` method to append two lines of text to it. The code then inserts a , character at the 16th character position of the `sbaddress` object. Note that both the `AppendLine` and `Insert` methods return a reference to the `sbaddress` object and do not create a new intermediate string data:

```
System.Text.StringBuilder sbaddress = new Sytem.Text.
StringBuilder(50);
// Appends first line of string data
sbaddress.appendLine("Lamplighter Park ");
// Appends second line of string data
sbaddress.appendLine("15501 NE 10th ST");
Console.WriteLine(sbaddress.To.String());
// Produces the output as LampLighter Park
15501 NE 10th ST in two lines
// Inserts a comma character at the 16th position
sbaddress.Insert(16,',');
Console.WriteLine(sbaddress.ToString());
// Produces the output as LampLighter Park,
15501 NE 10th ST in two lines
```

MORE INFORMATION

Refer to the "Regular Expression Language Elements" section of the *.NET Framework Developer's Guide* to learn how to create regular expressions.

Building Regular Expressions

The `System.Text.RegularExpressions` namespace provides classes to represent regular expression patterns and to provide information about the specified regular expression. Additionally, the namespace also contains classes that enable you to access the resultant values of pattern matching performed on a given text.

The System.Text.RegularExpressions namespace provides regular expression functionalities that may be used from any platform or language that runs within the Microsoft .NET Framework.

Table 10-24 lists the classes of System.Text.RegularExpressions namespace.

Table 10-24

Classes in the RegularExpressions namespace

CLASS	DESCRIPTION
Capture	Depicts the results of a single subexpression capture and represents the resultant substring of that successful capture.
CaptureCollection	Depicts a sequence of capture substrings that result from the set of captures by a single capturing group.
Regex	Represents a single read-only regular expression.
Group	Denotes the results from a single capturing group where a capturing group can capture none or more strings in a single match.
GroupCollection	Represents a collection of captured groups of strings and returns the set of captured groups that result from a single match.
Match	Represents the results from a single regular expression match.
MatchCollection	Represents the set of successful matches that result from an iterative application of a regular expression pattern to the same input string.

MORE INFORMATION

Table 10-24 lists the very important classes from the System.Text.RegularExpressions namespace. The examples in the following sections use the various classes listed previously to demonstrate the application of these classes. To get details about the members of this class, you must read the corresponding class and member description from the MSDN library.

SPECIFYING REGULAR EXPRESSIONS

You can use the Regex class to specify a regular expression pattern to parse larger text. Additionally, methods of the Regex class enable you to manipulate the given text with the specified regular expression pattern.

By default, the regular expression engine caches the 15 most recently used static regular expressions. You can also increase the default cache size by modifying the value of the CacheSize property.

Tables 10-25 and 10-26 list the important members of the Regex class.

Table 10-25

Methods of Regex class

METHOD	DESCRIPTION
GetGroupNames	Retrieves the array of capturing group names associated with the regular expression.
GetGroupNumbers	Returns an array of capturing group numbers assigned to the group names in an array.
GroupNameFromNumber	Gets the group name associated with the specified group number.
GroupNumberFromName	Gets the group number associated with the specified group name.
IsMatch	Determines if the regular expression finds a match in the input string.
Match	Searches an input string for a substring that matches a regular expression pattern and returns the first occurrence of the substring in the string as a single Match object.
Matches	Searches an input string for a substring that matches all occurrences of a regular expression and returns all the successful matches.

Table 10-26

Properties of Regex class

PROPERTY	DESCRIPTION
CacheSize	Gets or sets the maximum number of entries in the current static cache of compiled regular expressions.
Options	Gets the options supplied to the **Regex** constructor.
RightToLeft	Specifies a Boolean value to denote the search direction of the regular expression; the value is true if the expression searches from right to left and is false if the expression searches from left to right.

TAKE NOTE*

For all the examples given in this section, you must include the System.Text.RegularExpressions namespace.

The CheckValidity method checks the validity of a given phone number and displays an appropriate message. The following code samples check the given strings for a specified regular expression pattern using the Regex class:

```
public static CheckValidity(string phno)
{
   // Define a group of three, three, and four digits, each group
separated by a hyphen to represent a phone number
   Regex phoneRx = new Regex("\d(3)-\d(3)-d(4)");
   // Check the received phno string with the defined regular expres-
sion pattern
   if(phoneRx.IsMatch(phno))
   {
      Console.WriteLine("Valid Phone Number");
   }
   else
   {
      Console.WriteLine("Invalid Phone Number");
   }
}
```

The MatchText method matches the given text with a Regex object, displaying the matches found:

```
public static MatchText(string sampleText)
{
   // Define a regular expression pattern that includes a newline
character, characters in the 3–7 range, and any nonword character
   string myPattern = @"\n[3–7]\W+";
   // Create a Regex object with the defined pattern
   Regex matchRegex = new Regex(myPattern);
   // Find the match of Regex pattern in the given text and store it
in a MatchCollection object
   MatchCollection matchcol = matchRegex.Matches(sampleText);
   // Display the found matches by iterating through the
MatchCollection object
   foreach(Match match in matchcol)
   Console.WriteLine(match.Value);
}
```

Imagine a string that holds the specified address. The following example uses a Group Collection object, which contains a series of Group objects, to capture three groups namely street name, city name, and state name from the given address string. The regular expression pattern in code defines a group of three-word characters with each group separated by a comma and a space. Note that the first `Group` object in a `GroupCollection` object returned by the `Match.Groups` property contains the entire `Match` string:

```
string address = "Capricorn Drive, Hillsborough, NJ";
// Define a regular expression pattern
string pattern = @"(\w+\s\w+),\s(\w+),\s(\w+)";
// Match the given pattern in the specified text and store the found
group of matches in a Match object
Match match = Regex.Match(address, pattern);
// Retrieve the collection of Group objects from the found match in a
GroupCollection object
GroupCollection groups = match.Groups;
// Display the value in each Group object
Console.WriteLine(groups[1].value);
Console.WriteLine(groups[2].value);
Console.WriteLine(groups[3].value);
// The output is
// Capricorn Drive
// Hillsborough
// NJ
```

The following code sample defines a regular expression pattern that matches a string containing a decimal number pattern and replaces a specific character. The code uses the `Regex.Replace` method to replace the decimal point (.) with a comma (,):

```
string pattern = @"\d+(\.?\d+)";
Regex regx = new Regex(pattern);
string txt = "12.345";
txt = regx.Replace(txt, ",");
Console. WriteLine (txt);
// The output is
// 12,345
```

The following code sample takes two parameters—source string and search text. The code retrieves the position of a given search text in a specified source string. The code sample uses the `CaptureCollection` object to achieve this. Note that the usage of `CaptureCollection` object is best appreciated when you use complex regular expressions involving large text:

```
public RetrieveIndex(string sourcetext, string searchtext)
{
   GroupCollection groupcol;
   CaptureCollection capturecol;
   // Returns all the matches found in the given string in a
MatchCollection object
   MatchCollection matchcol = Regex.Matches(sourcetext, searchtext);
   // Retrieve each match object containing the string that matches
the provided pattern by iterating through the MatchCollection object
   foreach (Match match in matchcol)
   {
      // Retrieve the captured groups from the Match object in a
Groupcollection object
      groupcol = match.Groups;
   //Iterate through the captured groups to retrieve an individual
Group object
   foreach (Group group in groupcol)
   {
      // Retrieve the collection of captured characters from the
individual Group object using the Group.Captures property in a
CaptureCollection object
```

CERTIFICATION READY?
Enhance the text handling capabilities of a .NET Framework application, and search, modify, and control text in a .NET Framework application by using regular expressions.
USD 7.3

```
        capturecol = group.Captures;
        // Iterate the CaptureCollection object to retrieve the indi-
vidual capture and display its corresponding position in the given
text through the Capture.Index property
        foreach (Capture capture in capturecol)
        Console.WriteLine("The captured word" + capture + "found at
position" + capture.Index);
        // For example, if the given text is "I have a blue car and
blue shirt," then the output displayed is
        // The captured word blue found at position 9
        // The captured word blue found at position 22
    }
}
```

Encoding and Decoding Text

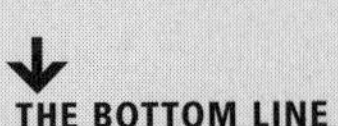

Encoding is the process of placing a sequence of characters, such as letters, numbers, and symbols, in a specialized format in order to transmit or store data. ***Decoding*** is the reverse process of encoding in which you convert the format of the encoded data back to its original sequence of characters. Apart from globalization, data communication, and storage, these processes play an important role in networking. For example, consider an online shopping application that requires credit card information from the users to complete their purchases. To secure the credit card details from hackers during its transmission through the network, you can use the encoding process. This process allows you to protect the users' credit card information.

X REF
Recall that you have learned about the `System.Text` namespace in the "Manipulating Strings" section.

Exploring the Text

The .NET Framework includes a number of specialized classes to perform encoding and decoding of the text.

The `System.Text` namespace consists of classes that enable you to encode and decode character arrays.

Table 10-27 lists the `System.Text` namespace encoding and decoding classes.

Table 10-27

Encoding and decoding classes in the `System.Text` namespace

FUNCTIONALITY	CLASS	DESCRIPTION
Encoding	`Encoding`	Represents a character encoding and is the abstract base class for all the encoding classes.
	`ASCIIEncoding`	Represents an ASCII character encoding of Unicode characters and inherits from the abstract base `Encoding` class.
	`EncodingInfo`	Provides basic information about an encoding.
	`UnicodeEncoding`	Represents a UTF-16 encoding of Unicode characters and inherits from the abstract base `Encoding` class.
	`UTF32Encoding`	Represents a UTF-32 encoding of Unicode characters and inherits from the abstract base `Encoding` class.
	`UTF7Encoding`	Represents a UTF-7 encoding of Unicode characters and inherits from the abstract base `Encoding` class.
	`UTF8Encoding`	Represents a UTF-8 encoding of Unicode characters and inherits from the abstract base `Encoding` class.

Table 10-27 (continued)

FUNCTIONALITY	CLASS	DESCRIPTION
Encoder	`Encoder`	Converts a set of characters into a sequence of bytes.
	`EncoderExceptionFallback`	Throws an `EncoderFallbackException` when an input character cannot be converted to an encoded output byte sequence.
	`EncoderExceptionFallbackBuffer`	Throws an `EncoderFallbackException` when an input character cannot be converted to an encoded output byte sequence.
	`EncoderFallback`	Provides a failure-handling mechanism, referred to as a fallback, when an input character cannot be converted to an encoded output byte sequence.
	`EncoderFallbackBuffer`	Passes a string to an encoding operation that is produced in place of an input character that cannot be encoded.
	`EncoderFallbackException`	Represents an exception that is thrown when an encoder fallback operation fails.
	`EncoderReplacementFallback`	Provides a failure-handling mechanism, referred to as a fallback, when an input character cannot be converted to an encoded output byte sequence. The fallback emits a user-specified replacement string in place of the original input character.
	`EncoderReplacementFallback Buffer`	Represents a substitute input string that is produced when the original input character cannot be encoded.
Decoder	`Decoder`	Converts a sequence of encoded bytes into a set of characters.
	`DecoderExceptionFallback`	Throws a `DecoderFallbackException` when an input character cannot be converted to an encoded output byte sequence.
	`DecoderExceptionFallback`	Throws a `DecoderFallbackException` when an encoded input byte sequence cannot be converted to a decoded output character.
	`DecoderExceptionFallbackBuffer`	Throws a `DecoderFallbackException` when an encoded input byte sequence cannot be converted to a decoded output character.
	`DecoderFallback`	Provides a failure-handling mechanism, referred to as a fallback, when an encoded input byte sequence cannot be converted to an encoded output character.
	`DecoderFallbackBuffer`	Passes a string to a decoding operation that is produced in place of an output character when an input byte sequence cannot be decoded.
	`DecoderFallbackException`	Represents an exception that is thrown when a decoder fallback operation fails.
	`DecoderReplacementFallback`	Provides a failure-handling mechanism, referred to as a fallback, when an input byte sequence cannot be converted to an output character. The fallback emits a user-specified replacement string in place of a decoded input byte sequence.
	`DecoderReplacementFallback Buffer`	Represents a substitute output string that is produced when the original input byte sequence cannot be decoded.

Understanding Encoding of Text

When using encoding in globalized applications that adapt to worldwide cultures, the developers need to have a thorough understanding of the character encoding to work with multilingual and multiscript text data.

TAKE NOTE*

Unicode standard encoding follows a universal character-encoding scheme, which assigns a numeric value, known as code point, to each character used in the scripts of the supported languages. Unicode Transformation Format (UTF) provides a way to encode this code point.

Characters are abstract units that are represented by various character schemes or ***code pages***. Code pages are unique numbers provided to identify those character schemes. For example, Unicode UTF-32 encoding represents characters as sequences of 32-bit integers; Unicode UTF-7 encoding represents the same characters as sequences of 7-bit bytes.

Applications use encoding to map character representations from the native character scheme to other schemes. Correspondingly, applications use decoding to map characters from nonnative schemes to the native scheme. For example, your application can convert a Unicode UTF-16 character scheme to a nonnative scheme such as Unicode UTF-32 encoding. The UTF-16 character scheme that represents characters as sequences of 16-bit integers is the native character stream for the `char` type in .NET Framework. UTF-32 encoding represents characters as sequences of 32-bit integers.

X REF

You can refer to the details of the base classes for these character schemes from the previous topic, "Exploring the Text."

Computers employ several character encodings. The base character schemes for encoding are:

- **ASCII encoding.** This scheme facilitates the conversion of Unicode characters to and from single 7-bit ASCII characters.
- **Multiple encoding.** This scheme facilitates the conversion of characters to and from various specified encodings.
- **UTF-16 Unicode encoding.** This scheme facilitates the conversion to and from UTF-16 encoding that represents characters as sequences of 16-bit integers.
- **UTF-8 Unicode encoding.** This scheme facilitates the conversion of characters to and from UTF-8 encoding that represents characters as sequences of one to four bytes.

ANALYZING THE ENCODING CLASS

You can use the `Encoding` class to convert different encodings to Unicode encoding and vice versa. However, it is always better to use the appropriate derived classes of the `Encoding` class for specific conversions.

TAKE NOTE*

Encoding can operate on Unicode characters but not on arbitrary binary data such as byte arrays. If you need to encode arbitrary binary data into text, you must use a binary-to-text encoding, such as uuencode, that is implemented by methods such as `Convert.ToBase64CharArray`.

Table 10-28 enumerates the important methods of the `Encoding` class.

Table 10-28

Important methods of the `Encoding` class

METHOD	DESCRIPTION
`Convert`	Converts a byte array from one encoding to another.
`GetByteCount`	Override this method in a derived class to calculate the number of bytes produced by encoding a set of characters.
`GetBytes`	Override this method in a derived class to encode a set of characters into a sequence of bytes.
`GetCharCount`	Override this method in a derived class to calculate the number of characters produced by decoding a sequence of bytes.
`GetChars`	Override this method in a derived class to decode a sequence of bytes into a set of characters.

Table 10-28 (continued)

METHOD	DESCRIPTION
`GetDecoder`	Override this method in a derived class to get a decoder that converts an encoded sequence of bytes into a sequence of characters.
`GetEncoder`	Override this method in a derived class to get an encoder that converts an encoded sequence of Unicode characters into an encoded sequence of bytes.
`GetEncoding`	Returns an encoding for the specified code page.
`GetEncodings`	Returns an array containing all encodings.
`GetHashCode`	Returns the hash code for the current instance.
`GetMaxByteCount`	Override this method in a derived class to calculate the maximum number of bytes obtained by encoding the specified number of characters.
`GetMaxCharCount`	Override this method in a derived class to calculate the maximum number of characters produced by decoding the specified number of bytes.
`GetPreamble`	Override this method in a derived class to return a sequence of bytes that specifies the encoding used.
`GetString`	Override this method in a derived class to decode a sequence of bytes into a string.
`IsAlwaysNormalized`	Obtains a value specifying whether the current encoding is always normalized.

Table 10-29 enumerates the properties of the `Encoding` class.

Table 10-29

Important properties of the `Encoding` class

PROPERTY	DESCRIPTION
`ASCII`	Obtains an encoding for the ASCII (7-bit) character set.
`BigEndianUnicode`	Obtains an encoding for the UTF-16 format using the big endian byte order.
`BodyName`	Obtains a name for the current encoding that your email applications can use with mail agent body tags.
`CodePage`	Obtains the code page identifier of the current encoding.
`DecoderFallback`	Obtains or sets the `DecoderFallback` object for the current `Encoding` object.
`Default`	Obtains an encoding for the current ANSI code page of the operating system.
`EncoderFallback`	Obtains or sets the `EncoderFallback` object for the current `Encoding` object.
`EncodingName`	Obtains the human-readable description of the current encoding.
`HeaderName`	Obtains a name for the current encoding that your email applications can use with mail agent header tags.

Table 10-29 (continued)

PROPERTY	DESCRIPTION
IsBrowserDisplay	Obtains a value specifying whether the browser clients can use the current encoding to display content.
IsBrowserSave	Obtains a value specifying whether the browser clients can use the current encoding to save content.
IsMailNewsDisplay	Obtains a value specifying whether the mail and news clients can use the current encoding to display content.
IsMailNewsSave	Obtains a value specifying whether the mail and news clients can use the current encoding to save content.
IsReadOnly	Obtains a value specifying whether the current encoding is read-only.
IsSingleByte	Obtains a value specifying whether the current encoding uses single-byte code points.
Unicode	Gets an encoding for the UTF-16 format using the little endian byte order.
UTF32	Gets an encoding for the UTF-32 format using the little endian byte order.
UTF7	Gets an encoding for the UTF-7 format.
UTF8	Gets an encoding for the UTF-8 format.
WebName	Obtains the name registered with the Internet Assigned Numbers Authority (IANA) for the current encoding.
WindowsCodePage	Obtains the Windows operating system code page that most closely corresponds to the current encoding.

TAKE NOTE*

You can refer to the Encoding class description notes from the MSDN library to view the list of encodings supported by the .NET Framework and their corresponding code pages.

USING ENCODING METHODS IN YOUR APPLICATIONS

The following code sample shows the conversion of a string from one encoding to another using the appropriate methods of the Encoding class:

```
using System;
using System.Text;
public class ConversionClass
{
   public static void Main()
   {
      // Create a Unicode string to encode
      string uniString = "Converting from Unicode to ASCII";
      // Create the encoding objects
      Encoding fromunicode = Encoding.Unicode;
      Encoding toascii = Encoding.ASCII;
      // Convert the Unicode string into a byte[] array
      byte[] uniBytes = fromunicode.GetBytes(uniString);
      // Perform the conversion from Unicode to ASCII encoding; The
Convert overload used in the example takes five parameters: Source
encoding, Destination encoding, byte array to be converted, starting
index for conversion, number of bytes to be converted
      byte[] ascBytes = Encoding.Convert(fromunicode, toascii, uniB-
ytes, 0, uniBytes.Length);
```

```
            // Convert the new ascii byte[] array into an ascii string
            string ascString = toascii.GetString(ascBytes);
            // Display the original and the converted string
            Console.WriteLine("Unicode string: {0}", uniString);
            Console.WriteLine("ASCII string: {0}", ascString);
        }
    }
```

Understanding Encoder

The members of the Encoder class facilitate the conversion of a set of characters into a sequence of bytes.

You must use the GetEncoder method of an Encoding implementation to get an instance the Encoder class.

An Encoder object performs the following functions:

- Maintains state information between successive calls to the GetBytes or Convert methods. This state information enables the Encoder object to encode character sequences between blocks correctly.
- Stores trailing characters at the end of data blocks and uses these trailing characters in the next encoding operation.

EXPLORING THE ENCODER CLASS

Table 10-30 enumerates the important methods of the Encoder class.

Table 10-30

Important methods of the Encoder class

METHOD	TYPE	DESCRIPTION
Convert	Overloaded method	Converts an encoded byte sequence to a string or array of characters.
GetByteCount	Overloaded method	Calculates the number of bytes produced by encoding a set of characters.
GetBytes	Overloaded method	Encodes a set of characters into a sequence of bytes.
Reset	Method	Sets the encoder back to its initial state.

Table 10-31 enumerates the properties of the Encoder class.

Table 10-31

Properties of the Encoder class

PROPERTY	DESCRIPTION
Fallback	Obtains or sets an EncoderFallback object for the current Encoder object.
FallbackBuffer	Obtains the EncoderFallbackBuffer object linked with the current Encoder object.

TAKE NOTE* The GetByteCount method determines the number of resultant bytes in encoding a set of Unicode characters; the GetBytes method performs the actual encoding.

You must understand the following points before reading the next coding example:

- You need an `Encoding` object to specify the encoding used to define the source data. The example uses Unicode encoding.
- You can access the `Encoder` object through the `GetEncoder` method of the Encoding object.
- The `Encoder` object can maintain state between successive calls to the `GetBytes`, `GetByteCount`, and `Convert` methods. Therefore, you must use a Boolean variable to specify the flush status.
- The `GetByteCount` method accepts four parameters: source character array, starting index, number of characters to encode, and flush status.
- The `GetBytes` method accepts six parameters: source character array, starting index, number of characters to encode, destination byte array, index of the encoded byte, and flush status.

The following code sample shows the conversion of an array of Unicode characters into blocks of bytes using a specified encoding. The code displays the converted array of characters in separate lines and uses the `Encoder` object to encode:

```
using System;
using System.Text;
public class EncoderConversion
{
  public static void Main()
  {
    // Create a Unicode character array representing Alpha, Beta,
    and Gamma to encode
    Char[] chars = new Char[]
    {
      '\u03b1', '\u03b2', '\u03b3'
    };
    // Create an Encoding object to set the required encoding
    Encoding encoding = Encoding.Unicode;
    // Create an Encoder object to set the required encoding
    Encoder coder = encoding.GetEncoder();
    // Declare a Boolean to maintain state between calls to the
    GetBytes and GetByteCount methods
    bool bFlushSt = false;
    // Declare a byte array to hold the converted bytes
    Byte[] bchar;
    Console. WriteLine("Characters: ");
    // Encode each character
    for(i=0; i<=2; i++)
    {
      // Set the flush state on last call to Getbytes to true

    if (i==2)
      bFlushSt = true;
    // Initialize the byte array to hold the converted bytes
    bchar = new Byte[coder.GetByteCount(chars, i, 1, bFlushSt)];
    // Call the GetBytes method to convert the current element of
    the character array to a byte array
      coder.GetBytes(chars, i, 1, bchar, 0, bFlushSt);
      // Display the converted character
      foreach (Object obj in bChar)
      {
        Console.Write("[{0}]", obj);
      }
```

```
            Console. WriteLine("\n");
        }
    }
}
```

X REF

You can refer to the details of the Decoder class in the previous topic, "Exploring the Text."

Understanding Decoder

The members of the Decoder class facilitate the conversion of a sequence of encoded bytes into a set of characters.

You must use the GetDecoder method of an Encoding implementation to get an instance of the Decoder class.

A Decoder object performs the following functions:

- Maintains state information between successive calls to GetChars or Convert methods. This state information enables the Decoder object to decode byte sequences between data blocks correctly.
- Stores trailing bytes at the end of data blocks and uses these trailing characters in the next decoding operation.

EXPLORING THE DECODER CLASS

Table 10-32 enumerates the methods of the Decoder class.

Table 10-32

Methods of the Decoder class

METHOD	TYPE	DESCRIPTION
Convert	Overloaded method	Converts an encoded byte sequence to a string or array of characters.
GetCharCount	Overloaded method	Calculates the number of characters produced by decoding a sequence of bytes.
GetChars	Overloaded method	Decodes a sequence of bytes into a set of characters.
Reset	Method	Sets the decoder back to its initial state.

Table 10-33 enumerates the properties of the Decoder class along with its corresponding functions.

Table 10-33

Properties of the Decoder class

PROPERTY	DESCRIPTION
Fallback	Obtains or sets a DecoderFallback object for the current Decoder object.
FallbackBuffer	Obtains the DecoderFallbackBuffer object linked with the current Decoder object.

TAKE NOTE*

The GetCharCount method determines the number of resultant characters in decoding a sequence of bytes and the GetChars method performs the actual decoding.

The following code sample shows the use of a `Decoder` to convert a byte array into a character array. The code encodes a string into a byte array and then converts the byte array into a character array.

You must understand the following points before reading the example:

- You need an `Encoding` object to specify the encoding used to define the source data. The example uses Unicode encoding.
- You can access the `Decoder` object through the `GetDecoder` method of the Encoding object.
- The `GetCharCount` method accepts three parameters: source byte array, starting index, and number of bytes to decode.
- The `GetChars` method accepts five parameters: source byte array, starting index, number of bytes to decode, destination char array, and the index of the decoded char.

```
using System;
using System.Text;
public class DecoderConversion
{
  public static void Main()
  {
    // Create a Unicode string to encode into a byte array
    string uniString = "Alpha";
    // Create the encoding object
    Encoding fromunicode = Encoding.Unicode;
    // Convert the Unicode string into a byte[] array
    byte[] uniBytes = fromunicode.GetBytes(uniString);
    // Create a Decoder object
    Decoder coder = fromunicode.GetDecoder();
    // Decode the byte into character using Decoder
    int charcount = coder.GetCharCount(uniBytes, 0, uniBytes.
Length);
    Char[] chararr = new Char[charcount];
    coder.GetChars(uniBytes, 0, charcount, chararr, 0);
    // Display the character array
    Console.WriteLine("Converted Characters:");
    foreach (Object obj in chararr)
    {
      Console.WriteLine("[{0}]", obj);
    }
  }
}
```

HANDLING EXCEPTIONS DURING ENCODING

Your application may not be able to encode or decode a character because exact character mapping in the target encoding or decoding schemes is not available. You must design your application so that it throws exceptions to handle such failures. You can use the `EncoderFallbackException` or the `DecoderFallbackException` classes to handle such exceptions.

You can use two different mechanisms when handling such exceptions, namely best-fit fallback mechanism and replacement string fallback mechanism. In the best-fit strategy (the default .NET encoding behavior), your application uses a similar character in the target encoding or decoding schemes for mapping. In the replacement strategy, your application can specify a replacement string for the specified character.

TAKE NOTE*

Because there is a high possibility of data loss when using the best-fit strategy, your application should use this strategy sparingly. In addition, you can only use the best-fit fallback strategy for encoding, not for decoding. Therefore, it is recommended that you use either the standard predefined fallback classes or custom fallback classes to handle conversion failures during an encoding or decoding process in your application.

Selecting the Appropriate Encoding Technique

You must carefully analyze the available techniques before you adopt a technique to use to encode and decode.

You can generally use Unicode encodings such as a `UTF8Encoding`, `UnicodeEncoding`, or `UTF32Encoding` over `ASCIIEncoding`. However, you may prefer `UTF8Encoding` because it is faster when compared to other Unicode encodings.

COMPARING UTF8ENCODING WITH ASCIIENCODING

You can use `UTF8Encoding` and `ASCIIEncoding` to encode the content in ASCII. Though these encodings are identical, `UTF8Encoding` is superior to `ASCIIEncoding` in many aspects. Table 10-34 highlights the differences between `UTF8Encoding` and `ASCIIEncoding`.

Table 10-34

Differences between UTF8 Encoding and ASCIIEncoding operations

UTF8ENCODING	ASCIIENCODING
Represents all Unicode character values (0–255).	Supports only the Unicode character values between U+0000 and U+007F because it uses 7-bit representation.
Detects errors and enhances security.	Does not detect errors.
Performs faster than all the encodings, even if the content is totally ASCII.	Performs slower than `UTF8Encoding`.
Suitable for most legacy applications and therefore is a better option than using `ASCIIEncoding`.	Is suitable only for certain legacy applications.

CERTIFICATION READY?
Enhance the text handling capabilities of a .NET Framework application, and search, modify, and control text in a .NET Framework application by using regular expressions.
USD 7.3.

TAKE NOTE*

You should prefer `UTF8Encoding` over `ASCIIEncoding` even in legacy applications. This is because when a non-ASCII character is encoded with `ASCIIEncoding`, every non-ASCII character is encoded into a question mark (?). Therefore, there is a possibility of data loss.

SKILL SUMMARY

This lesson introduced different fields through which you can extend the capabilities of your application. You learned how to construct and send email messages using the classes in the `System.NET.Mail` namespace. You can use the `MailMessage, Attachment,` and `MailAddress` classes to construct the various parts of an email. The `StmpClient` class helps you send an email message that you have constructed using a `MailMessage` object. Mail messages can have inline or external attachments. You can send emails synchronously or asynchronously using the separate send methods provided in the `StmpClient` class.

You can prepare world-ready applications by creating global, culture-sensitive applications. The .NET Framework offers the `System.Globalization` namespace to develop applications for a global audience. You can use the `CultureInfo` class and `RegionInfo` class to provide culture-specific and region-specific formatting in your application. The `NumberFormatInfo` and `DateFormatInfo` classes in the `System.Globalization` namespace help you format numbers and date-time information according to specific cultures. You can modify the cultures installed with your .NET Framework or create custom cultures based on them.

Regular expressions enable you to search and manipulate text in a large string. The `StringBuilder` class in the `System.Text` namespace helps you create large mutable arrays of characters. You can use the `Regex` class from the `System.Text.RegularExpressions` namespace to create regular expressions. You can use classes such as `Match`, `Capture`, `Group`, and their collection classes to find and extract specific text or characters from a large string.

Conversion of data into a specific format by including special characters is termed encoding and the reverse process is termed decoding. .NET offers various classes in the `System.Text` namespace that enable encoding and decoding of arrays that consist of bytes and characters.

For the certification examination:

- Know how to create and send email messages through .NET applications.
- Know how to create world-ready .NET applications with globalization facilities.
- Know how to create and use regular expressions in .NET applications to manipulate text.
- Know how to encode and decode data through .NET applications.

Knowledge Assessment

Matching

Match the following descriptions to the appropriate terms.

a. `EnsureCapacity`
b. `MaxCapacity`
c. `Length`
d. `Capacity`
e. `CacheSize`

_______ **1.** Gets the maximum capacity of the specified instance.

_______ **2.** Maintains the capacity of the instance of the `StringBuilder` object to at least the specified value.

_______ **3.** Gets or sets the maximum number of characters that can be contained in the memory allocated by the current instance.

_______ **4.** Gets or sets the maximum number of entries in the current static cache of compiled regular expressions.

_______ **5.** Gets or sets the size of the current `StringBuilder` object.

True / False

Circle T if the statement is true or F if the statement is false.

T | F 1. The `SendAsync` method sends the email message without blocking the thread.

T | F 2. You can use the `MailAddress` class to add attachments to the message.

T | F 3. You should use a culture-insensitive string operation when your application uses the string operation result for security reasons.

T | F 4. You cannot increase or decrease the capacity of the `StringBuilder` class.

T | F 5. Best fit is a strategy generally used for decoding, and not for encoding.

Fill in the Blank

Complete the following sentences by writing the correct word or words in the blanks provided.

1. You can use the ________________ class to send email messages using SMTP.
2. The _________ property of the `MailMessage` class indicates that the body of the mail message is in HTML format.
3. You can use the _________ enumeration while creating custom cultures.
4. You can concatenate new data to an existing `StringBuilder` object using the _______ and __________ methods.
5. _________ encoding scheme detects errors and enhances security.

Multiple Choice

Circle the letter or letters that correspond to the best answer or answers.

1. Which of the following exceptions occurs when email could not be delivered to all recipients?
   a. `SmtpException`
   b. `SmtpFailedRecipientException`
   c. `ObjectDisposedException`
   d. `InvalidOperationException`
2. Select all the classes that you can use in constructing an email message.
   a. `MailMessage`
   b. `SmtpClient`
   c. `Attachment`
   d. `MailAddress`
3. Which of the following classes can you use to provide culture-sensitive string comparisons?
   a. `CompareInfo`
   b. `String`
   c. `CultureInfo`
   d. `CurrentCulture`
4. Which of the following classes depicts a mutable string of characters?
   a. `StringBuilder`
   b. `String`
   c. `RegEx`
   d. `Encoding`
5. Which property of the `Encoding` class obtains the human-readable description of the current encoding when overridden in a derived class?
   a. `EncodingName`
   b. `BodyName`
   c. `HeaderName`
   d. `Default`

Review Questions

1. You are developing an application that must be deployed in your branch office located in Denmark. Even though you have a specific culture to use, your organization requires a different number formatting. What should you do to create the required application?
2. Consider that you have a file encoded in ASCII. Which decoding types can you use to decode this file and why?

 Case Scenarios

Scenario 10-1: Building an Email Facility

Your clients place their orders through your client application. You need to send emails to users confirming their order along with the generated eticket through the application. Write a program to compose and send an email message with the generated eticket as an attachment from your application using the default credentials.

Scenario 10-2: Validating User Input

Imagine that you must create an application to accept movie reviews from users who booked their tickets through your application. Users can type short reviews of 300 characters and provide a display name of 25 characters along with the review. You must validate the reviews submitted by the user for ' and any special symbols such as @ and #. Write code to achieve this.

✳ Workplace Ready

Extracting Data

You face countless challenges when building applications in the real world. Often, you may have to write code to interface between various applications that your organization already has and the new applications that you intend to build. You may have to extract data from old legacy systems and import it into the new database.

ABC Financial Services, Inc. plans to migrate data from its client report documents to an SQL Server database. They have to repeat this exercise periodically whenever they get a client report, so they plan to write a .NET program to extract data from the reports. You are supposed to extract only the data, leaving the labels and the formatting in the report. As their solution architect, suggest the best approach to achieve this.

Programming .NET Interoperability

LESSON 11

OBJECTIVE DOMAIN MATRIX

TECHNOLOGY SKILL	OBJECTIVE DOMAIN	OBJECTIVE DOMAIN NUMBER
Work with COM components in .NET Framework.	Expose COM components to the .NET Framework and the .NET Framework components to COM.	6.1
Work with .NET types in COM applications.	Expose COM components to the .NET Framework and the .NET Framework components to COM.	6.1
Control marshaling of data.	Call unmanaged DLL functions in a .NET Framework application, and control the marshaling of data in a .NET Framework application.	6.2

KEY TERMS

blittable types
COM callable wrapper (CCW)
data marshaling
interop assembly
interop-specific attributes
non-blittable types
private assemblies
runtime callable wrapper (RCW)
shared assemblies
Type Library Importer tool (Tlbimp.exe)
wrapper classes

Component Object Model (COM) and .NET Framework share many common concepts such as component reusability and language independence. In fact, the software development community perceives that .NET Framework is a natural succession to COM. During development, you may have to access existing COM components from the .NET assemblies and use .NET assemblies in COM components. For this backward and forward compatibility, you can use the `System.Runtime.InteropServices` namespace provided by the .NET Framework.

■ Working with COM Components from .NET Framework

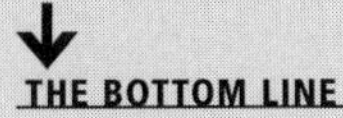

Your .NET applications may have to interact with external applications outside the .NET environment to access functionalities implemented in those external applications. When the required functionalities already exist in COM components, you can access those functionalities and avoid implementing them from scratch. For this purpose, the .NET Framework allows you to access and incorporate COM components in your .NET applications and import the required COM types.

Managing Clients in COM and .NET

Although COM provides features similar to the .NET Framework, it differs from the .NET Framework in some important ways. Therefore, the managed clients of your .NET Framework will not be able to interact with COM objects, directly.

The COM and .NET Framework differ in how they manage their clients. Table 11-1 lists the differences between COM and .NET Framework.

Table 11-1

Differences between COM and .NET Framework

COM	.NET FRAMEWORK
Client applications must manage the lifetime of a COM object.	The .NET Framework runtime manages the lifetime of all its objects.
A COM client interacts through an interface to know about the services of the COM object.	A .NET client uses reflection to know about the functionality of an object.

The .NET Framework execution environment manages the location of .NET objects that reside in the memory, and the execution environment updates all references to these objects whenever it moves these objects in memory to other locations for performance reasons. However, unmanaged clients in the .NET Framework depend on these objects to locate them. These unmanaged clients do not have a proper method to handle objects when the location of an object is not fixed. COM objects contain unmanaged code that, when compared to the .NET managed clients, complicates the interoperability between COM and .NET.

USING WRAPPER CLASSES

To manage the differences between COM components and .NET Framework, the .NET Framework runtime uses ***wrapper classes,*** which enable interaction of the managed .NET clients with the unmanaged COM objects. By using these wrapper classes, the runtime makes it appear to the managed clients that they are interacting with a method inside their environment although they are actually interacting with methods from external environments. The two wrappers provided by the Common Language Runtime (CLR) for COM and .NET interoperability include:

- ***Runtime callable wrapper (RCW).*** When a managed client requires an interaction with the methods of a COM object, the .NET runtime environment creates a runtime callable wrapper to conceal the differences in the reference mechanism of COM and .NET Framework.
- ***COM callable wrapper (CCW).*** When a COM client requires an interaction with the methods of a .NET object, the runtime creates the managed object and a COM callable wrapper as a proxy for the managed object.

EXPOSING COM COMPONENTS TO MANAGED CODE

You can use the existing COM components in managed code as middle-tier business applications or as independent functionalities. To access COM objects, your application should adhere tightly to the programming standards of the Component Object Model.

COM components contain a type library file that includes all the type information about the methods and classes available in the component DLL. For example, the component contains high-level interfaces required by your application to operate with speech engines. To use this COM component in your .NET application, you must import the type library of this component and build an interop application from that library.

ACCESS COM COMPONENTS

Perform the following steps to access COM components from the .NET Framework:

1. Import the type library that contains the required COM type definitions.
2. Define the imported COM types in your .NET assembly.
3. Compile an interop project that refers to the assemblies containing the imported COM types.
4. Install or deploy the interop application.

Importing Type Library as an Assembly

To facilitate the interaction of managed clients of your .NET application with a COM object, you need to first generate metadata of the COM type library in an assembly.

A COM component stores its type definitions in a type library, but .NET components built using CLS-compliant compilers store the type metadata in an assembly. Therefore, you need to import the required COM type library and generate the type metadata in an ***interop assembly***. When you do so, the clients of your .NET applications feel that they are interacting with a method inside the .NET environment. Table 11-2 lists the various methods that you can use to generate the type metadata in an interop assembly.

Table 11-2

Techniques to generate type metadata in an interop assembly

TECHNIQUE	DESCRIPTION
Use Visual Studio	You can add a reference to the required COM type library in Visual Studio. Visual Studio will then automatically generate the interop assembly for you.
Use the ***Type Library Importer tool (Tlbimp.exe)***	You can use Tlbimp.exe, which is a command-line tool that converts all the type definitions contained in a COM type library to metadata within an assembly.
Use the `TypeLibConverter` class	You can use the methods of the `TypeLibConverter` class to convert the type definitions in a type library to metadata, within an assembly.

TAKE NOTE*

Similar to standard wrappers, you can create custom wrappers to define COM types manually. That is, when you cannot access the required type library or if the information given in the type library is not correct, you can create a duplicate type definition of the required COM object in managed source code. To obtain the metadata in an assembly, you can compile this managed source code using a compiler, which targets the runtime. However, creating a custom wrapper involves the use of advanced techniques, which you may not need with the availability of automated tools.

For more information about how to use `TypeLibConverter` class for converting a type library to an assembly, refer to the topic "Exploring Interop Classes" in this lesson. For more information about creating custom wrappers for converting a type library to an assembly, refer to the topic "Customizing Runtime Callable Wrappers" in this lesson.

USING VISUAL STUDIO

When adding a reference to the required COM type library, Visual Studio checks for a primary interop assembly. A primary interop assembly is a unique assembly supplied by the vendor that contains the definitions of types that are available in the COM type library. Only one primary interop assembly can exist for a COM type library; the publisher of the COM type library signs this assembly with a strong name. If a primary interop assembly exists for a COM type library, then Visual Studio uses the existing assembly before creating a new interop assembly.

ADD A TYPE LIBRARY REFERENCE

You can use the following steps to add a type library reference in Visual Studio:

1. Manually install the required COM DLL or EXE file on your computer or use a Windows Installer.
2. In the Visual Studio environment, select Project and then choose References.
3. Click the COM tab and choose the appropriate type library from the Available References list. If the Available References list does not list the required type library, browse for the required type library file.
4. Click OK to add the reference.

USING THE TLBIMP .EXE TOOL

Using the ***Type Library Importer tool (Tlbimp.exe),*** you can convert the type definitions contained in a COM type library to the corresponding definitions in .NET Framework's runtime assembly. The importer tool produces a binary file that contains the type metadata within an interop assembly as the output.

TAKE NOTE*

You can check the output file produced by the Type Library Importer tool using the Ildasm.exe tool. Additionally, using the Tlbimp.exe, you can convert only the entire type definitions contained in a type library to the corresponding type metadata and not a subset of the type.

You can execute the `Tlbimp.exe` tool from the command prompt as shown:

```
tlbimp TypeLibFile [Options]
```

In this command line, `TypeLibFile` indicates the mandatory argument that contains the name of the COM type library file. `Options` indicates the optional parameters. For example, by using the `/keyfile:` or `/keycontainer:` option, you can assign a strong name, which is a globally unique name for the generated assembly. When you execute the Tlbimp.exe tool, it creates a namespace with the same name as the source COM type library.

The following code sample generates the assembly SampleAssembly.dll from the Sample.tlb type library using the Tlbimp.exe tool. The code uses the `/out:` switch to generate an interop assembly with a name other than the name of the COM type library:

```
tlbimp Sample.tlb /out:SampleAssembly.dll
```

TAKE NOTE*

It is always a good practice to give the interop assembly a unique name that is different from the original COM type library. This helps in differentiating the interop assembly from the source COM DLL. Additionally, this also avoids issues that can occur from having duplicate names because COM identifies a type by GUID and allows duplicate definitions of a single type among multiple type libraries. However, .NET identifies each type differently with the full namespace and assembly reference, even if the same type is contained in multiple assemblies. Therefore, the name you assign for an interop assembly must be unique to operate efficiently within the managed environment.

MORE INFORMATION

For more information about creating custom wrappers for converting type library to assembly, refer to the topic "Type Library Importer (Tlbimp.exe)" from the MSDN Library.

Exploring the Interop Classes

You can use the members of the `System.Runtime.InteropServices` namespace in your .NET applications to interoperate with COM services.

The `System.Runtime.InteropServices` namespace provides various attribute classes for controlling marshaling behavior. For example, the `DllImportAttribute` class lets you access unmanaged APIs by defining the platform-invoke methods. In addition, the `MarshalAsAttribute` class lets you specify how marshaling of data happens between managed and unmanaged code.

ANALYZING THE CLASSES OF SYSTEM.RUNTIME.INTEROPSERVICES NAMESPACE

Table 11-3 discusses the important classes of the `System.Runtime.InteropServices` namespace and their purpose.

Table 11-3

Important classes of the `System.Runtime.InteropServices` namespace

CLASS	PURPOSE
`ClassInterfaceAttribute`	When a class is exposed to COM, the `ClassInterfaceAttribute` specifies the type of the generated class interface if an interface is generated.
`CoClassAttribute`	When a coclass is imported from a COM type library, `CoClassAttribute` specifies the class identifier of that coclass.
`ComConversionLossAttribute`	Indicates that information about a class or interface was lost during the import process.
`ComEventInterfaceAttribute`	Identifies the source interface and the generated class during the import of a coclass from a type library. The generated class implements the methods of the event interface.
`ComSourceInterfacesAttribute`	Identifies a list of interface event sources for the attributed class.
`DllImportAttribute`	Specifies the static entry point of an unmanaged dynamic-link library.
`GuidAttribute`	Allows you to specify an explicit `System.Guid` by overriding the automatic generation of GUID
`ImportedFromTypeLibAttribute`	Indicates that the types defined in an interop assembly were defined originally in the source COM type library.
`InterfaceTypeAttribute`	Specifies the type of a managed interface when exposed to COM. For example, you can use `InterfaceTypeAttribute` to indicate if a managed interface is dual, dispatch-only, or an `IUnKnown` interface.

Table 11-3 (continued)

CLASS	PURPOSE
`Marshal`	Provides various methods that you can use when your managed code interacts with an unmanaged code. For example, you can use `Marshal` class methods to allocate unmanaged memory, copy unmanaged memory blocks, convert managed types to unmanaged types, and for several other functionalities that involve interaction with unmanaged code.
`MarshalAsAttribute`	Specifies the marshaling of data between managed and unmanaged code.
`OutAttribute`	Indicates that data should be marshaled from the called method back to the calling method.
`PrimaryInteropAssembly Attribute`	Indicates the primary interop assembly.
`TypeLibConverter`	Exposes services that enable the conversion of a COM type library to an interop assembly and vice versa.

USING THE TYPELIBCONVERTER FOR TYPE LIBRARY CONVERSION

You can use the methods of the `TypeLibConverter` class to convert coclasses and interfaces in a COM type library to metadata within an interop assembly.

When you use the `TypeLibConverter` class to convert type library to metadata programmatically, your code produces the same output as the Tlbimp.exe tool. In addition, you can use the `TypeLibConverter` class to convert an in-memory type library to metadata, which is not possible using the Tlbimp.exe tool.

Table 11-4 lists the important methods of the `TypeLibConverter` class.

Table 11-4

Important methods of the `TypeLibConverter` class

METHOD	TYPE	DESCRIPTION
`ConvertAssemblyTo TypeLib`	Method	Converts an assembly to a COM type library.
`ConvertTypeLibTo Assembly`	Overloaded method	Converts a COM type library to an interop assembly.
`GetPrimaryInterop Assembly`	Method	Retrieves the name and code base of a primary interop assembly for a given type library.

The following code sample uses the `TypeLibConverter` class to convert a COM type library to an interop assembly by using one of the overloads of the `ConvertTypeLibToAssembly` method, which takes the following arguments in this order:

- **typelib.** An `Object` loaded with the original type library
- **assemblyname.** A `String` value containing the file name of the converted COM assembly
- **flags.** A `TypeLibImporterFlags` value mentioning any special settings to indicate that the generated assembly is a primary interop assembly

- **notifysink.** An ITypeLibImporterNotifySink interface implemented by the caller to handle any events and to return the appropriate assembly if reference to another type library is found during conversion
- **publickey.** A byte array containing the public key
- **keypair.** A StrongNameKeyPair containing the public and private cryptographic key pair
- **assemblyNamespace.** A String value containing the namespace name of the generated interop assembly
- **assemblyVersion.** A Version object indicating the version of the generated interop assembly

TAKE NOTE*

Another overload to the ConvertTypeLibToAssembly method takes the following seven parameters:

- A typeLib object of type Object
- A String object containing the name of the assembly
- A TypeLibImporterFlags value indicating any special settings to indicate that the generated assembly is a primary interop assembly
- An object of type ITypeLibImporterNotifySink
- A byte array containing the public key
- A StrongNameKeyPair containing the public and private cryptographic key pair
- A Boolean value indicating link time or runtime stack walk check for UnmangedCode permission

```
TypeLibConverter sampleConverter = new TypeLibConverter();
SampleEventHandler handleConversionEvent = new SampleEventHandler();
AssemblyBuilder myAssembly = sampleConverter.ConvertTypeLibToAssembly
(typeLib,"SampleLib.dll", 0, handleConversionEvent, null, null, null,
null);
myAssembly. Save("SampleLib.dll");
```

Note that the sample code assumes that the object typeLib is already loaded with the required type library successfully. In addition, the code does the following:

- Passes null reference to the publickey and keypair arguments without generating a strong name for the generated assembly.
- Passes the handleConversionEvent object of the sampleEventHandler class that implements the ITypeLibImporterNotifySink to the ConvertTypeLibToAssembly method in order to handle any events that may occur during the conversion process.
- Calls the AssemblyBuilder.Save method to save the generated interop assembly.

TAKE NOTE*

You can assign null reference for the publickey and keypair arguments of the ConvertTypeLibToAssembly method only when the value of the flags does not equal to TypeLibImporterFlags.PrimaryInteropAssembly. In other words, you must specify the publickey or the keypair argument when converting a primary interop assembly. However, specifying both may result in an invalid method signature for the generated assembly.

The following code sample shows the SampleEventHandler class that implements the ITypeLibImporterNotifySink interface:

```
public class SampleEventHandler: ITypeLibImporterNotifySink
{
   public void ReportEvent( ImporterEventKind eventKind, int
eventCode, string eventMsg )
   {
```

```
        // You can handle a warning or error event here depending on
the value of the eventCode parameter
    }
    public Assembly ResolveRef( object typeLib )
    {
        // If a reference to another type library is found during con-
version, you should resolve the reference here and return the appro-
priate assembly
    }
}
```

TAKE NOTE*

You can use the `TypeConverter` class in the `System.ComponentModel` namespace to convert specialized data types into string representation and vice versa. In addition, you can also use the `TypeConverter` class to access standard values and subproperties. For more information about the `TypeConverter` class, refer to the MSDN Library.

Understanding the Conversion Process

All the conversion techniques discussed earlier to convert a COM type library to a .NET assembly follow specific conversion rules to convert the various type information contained within a type library.

The following sections describe the conversion rules specific to the imported type library, modules, types, members, and parameters.

EXPLORING THE CONVERSION OF TYPE LIBRARIES

The conversion process includes different conversion rules for converting the various type information contained within a type library.

When converting a type library, the conversion process keeps all the type definitions of the type library in the imported namespace. For example, in the following sample code, the conversion process imports all the type definitions of the `SampleLib` type library into the `SampleLib` assembly:

```
// Representation of a sample COM type library
library SampleLib
{
    interface SampleInterface {};
    coclass SampleCoClass {};
};
// SampleLib namespace after conversion
namespace SampleLib
{
    interface SampleInterface {};
    class SampleCoClass {};
};
```

EXPLORING THE CONVERSION OF MODULES

When a COM type library contains one or more modules with definitions of constants and methods, only the constants defined inside the modules are imported. The generated assembly contains only the empty implementations of the methods that a direct method calls to the original COM component.

The conversion process imports the constants within the modules as public constant static members of a class, which has the same name as the original module. The following code shows a sample COM library containing a module with constant definitions and the corresponding converted type library in an interop assembly:

```
// Representation of a sample COM type library
library SampleConstants
{
   module Constants
   {
      const short sampleConstant1 = 110;
      const short sampleConstant2 = 220;
   };
};
// Converted types in an interop assembly
public class Constants
{
   public const short sampleConstant1 = 110;
   public const short sampleConstant2 = 220;
}
```

EXPLORING THE CONVERSION OF TYPES

Generally, when the type library contains various types, the conversion process imports all the types with the same name from the source type library.

Table 11-5 lists the conversion process of various types contained within a type library.

Table 11-5

Conversion process of various types

TYPE	CONVERSION PROCESS
Interface	When the type library contains an interface, the importer leaves all `IUnknown` and `IDispatch` methods during conversion and retains the `GuidAttribute` for the interface to maintain the interface identifier assigned in a type library. Additionally, the importer retains `InterfaceTypeAttribute` unless the interface derives from `IDispatch`.
Class	When the type library contains a class, the importer creates a managed class with the same name as the corresponding `coclass` in the type library appended with the word Class. For example, a coclass named Account in the type library becomes AccountClass in the generated assembly. Additionally, the importer adds an interface with the same name as the `coclass`, applying the `CoClassAttribute`.
Structure	When the type library contains a structure, the importer converts the structure as metadata. Note that if a field inside a structure is a reference type, the importer imports the type as an IntPtr, applying the `ComConversionLossAttribute`. The use of `ComConversionLossAttribute` indicates that the data was lost during the import process.
Enumeration	When the type library contains an enumeration, the importer imports it as a managed Enum type.
Typedefs	When the type library contains a type definition, the importer imports only the parameters and fields as the underlying types. For example, the importer imports a parameter of type DRESSSIZE as an integer, since DRESSSIZE is an alias for an integer.

MORE INFORMATION
To know more about the conversion of types and for specific examples refer to the "Imported Type Conversion" section from the MSDN library.

EXPLORING THE CONVERSION OF MEMBERS

Table 11-6 lists the conversion process of members within the type library.

Table 11-6
Conversion process of members

MEMBER	CONVERSION PROCESS
Methods	When a type library contains methods, the importer produces a method signature for the .NET Framework. This method signature is equivalent to the method signature of the source COM object.
Properties	When the interface contained within the type library contains properties, the importer creates the property with one or more accessor methods for that property. These accessor methods help to get or set the property values.
Events	In COM, an event sink implements the interface and an event source, such as a coclass, consumes it. A type library does not contain the connection-point interfaces that connect these event sinks to the appropriate event sources. However, the .NET event model is quite different from this COM connection-point model. Therefore, to interoperate between these different event models, the importer creates various types to enable your .NET managed application to sink events that are used by unmanaged COM classes. These newly created types use the managed .NET event model.

MORE INFORMATION
To know more about the conversion of members and for specific examples refer to the "Imported Member Conversion" section from the MSDN library.

XREF
For more information on parameter marshaling, you can refer to the "Controlling Data Marshaling" topic from this lesson.

EXPLORING THE CONVERSION OF PARAMETERS

The parameters of a method in COM may have an `In`, `Out`, or both `In/Out` attributes to depict the proposed flow of data between objects. Using these attributes, the conversion process determines the marshaling of every parameter between managed and unmanaged code. Marshalling is the technique that defines the rules for converting data from a specific format defined by the source environment (here it is COM) to a specific format understood by the target environment (here it is .NET).

Creating COM Types in Managed Code

TAKE NOTE*
Note that when the clients of a .NET application obtain and release a COM object's reference, the .NET runtime keeps the reference count on the COM object, just like any other COM client would.

Once the COM type library is converted into an assembly within the .NET environment, your .NET application clients can use the types defined in that assembly as any other managed type.

Any managed client that needs to interact with a COM type can create a new instance of that COM type in the same way it would create an instance of the .NET type. Moreover, the managed client can also get the information of the required class through metadata. In addition, the client can check the method syntax either through an object viewer or by using reflection.

To be more precise, the managed clients of your .NET application can obtain and release a reference to a running COM object in the similar way they obtain and release a reference to any other running managed object.

To use the type information contained within the assembly from your .NET client, you must first examine the assembly and resolve the signature of the required methods.

EXAMINING AND INSTANTIATING A COM OBJECT

> **TAKE NOTE***
> Alternatively, you can also view the metadata in a hierarchical tree view by using the Microsoft intermediate language (MSIL) disassembler (Ildasm.exe). The Ildasm.exe is a graphical tool; you can use this tool to get readable descriptions of the metadata.

When you import the COM type library containing a coclass, the metadata for that coclass remains in an interop assembly having the same name as the original COM type library. However, as discussed earlier, you can explicitly give a different name to the interop assembly. For example, let us consider that a type library `AccountLib` contains a coclass named `Account`. During the conversion process, the converter or the importer tool that you use, assigns the same name AccountLib.dll as the type library for the generated assembly. In addition, the importer imports the coclass with the same name `Account` within the generated AccountLib.dll as metadata. Therefore, whenever your .NET clients refer to the `Account` class inside the AccountLib.dll, they should use the fully resolved name of the class as `AccountLib.Account`.

You can determine the COM type information within an assembly using the `System.Type` class provided by the .NET Framework. The `System.Type` class provides the complete type information only if the required COM type has accompanying metadata. If the required COM type does not contain metadata, then you can obtain less type information using the `Type` class.

Once you have learned about the signature of the necessary methods, you can perform early-bound activation on the COM object using minimal code. The following code sample activates a COM object through an interop assembly. The sample code uses the `AccountLib` assembly discussed previously and instantiates the `Account` class contained in the `AccountLib` assembly. Note that this is exactly the same way you access a managed .NET class:

```
using System;
using AccountLib;
public class AccountApp
{
    public static void Main(String[] Args)
    {
        Account act = new Account();
        . . .
    }
}
```

USING MEMBERS OF AN ACTIVE COM OBJECT

Once you have instantiated a COM class through an interop assembly, you can use all the members of that class and catch events raised on the server. Because a COM component exposes its methods through interfaces, you can call the required methods either on the interface or directly on the COM coclass.

The following code sample shows how to call a method on a COM object. The code assumes that the `Account` coclass exposes a `GetAccountDetails` method through its default interface and calls that method on the `Account` coclass:

```
acctDetails = act.GetAccountDetails(act.AcctNo, out AcctBalance);
```

> **TAKE NOTE***
> A managed client can pass parameters to a COM object just as it would pass parameters to a .NET object because the COM interop service takes care of marshaling data types. For example, when a managed client passes the type `System.String` to a method on a COM object, the COM interop service converts the type to `BSTR`.

Just like calling a method on a COM object, you can also use and modify the properties of a COM object through an interop assembly. The following code sample sets a property of a coclass on a COM object through an interop assembly. The sample code assumes that the `Account` coclass exposes an `AccountNumber` property and sets the same:

```
act. AccountNumber = Convert.ToInt16(numberStr);
```

Note that `numberStr` is a C# string type.

Whenever a COM server raises events, a managed client handles the events the same way it handles any other managed events because, during the conversion process of a type library, the converter creates delegates, which you can connect to your event handlers. Additionally, if you are releasing a COM object explicitly, you should call the `Collect` method of the `GC` class twice because the COM objects that raise events require two Garbage Collector (GC) collections before the release. If the COM objects do not raise any events, then you can call the `GC.Collect` method only once to release the COM object explicitly.

MORE INFORMATION

When a COM object throws an exception, the .NET runtime can automatically map the returned failure HRESULT to specific .NET exceptions, which can be caught and handled in the managed code. In addition, the .NET runtime populates the mapped exception with the error information provided in the returned failure HRESULT. To know more about handling COM exceptions in a managed environment, refer to the "Handling COM Interop Exceptions" section from the MSDN library.

Compiling a Project with COM Types

After importing a COM type library within an interop assembly, you must compile the interop project, which contains reference to your interop assembly.

You can compile a COM interop project, which contains references to one or more interop assemblies, as you compile any other managed project. You can use the Visual Studio environment or a command-line compiler to compile a COM interop project.

When compiling an interop project using a command-line compiler, you should use the `/reference` compiler switch to refer to the name of the assembly containing the imported COM type.

Deploying a Project with COM Types

TAKE NOTE*

You must install all COM components associated with an application in the Windows registry. In the previous example, if ClientA.exe and ClientB.exe reside on different computers, you must register the required COM components on each client computer.

After you compile your interop project, you must install or deploy your interop application for the managed clients to use it.

Your interop application should contain the following:

- A .NET client assembly
- Interop assemblies that contain distinct imported COM type libraries
- Registered COM components

An interop assembly may or may not contain strong names. If an assembly is signed by the publisher by supplying the `/keyfile` option in the command-line Tlbimp.exe tool, you can install the assembly into the global assembly cache (GAC). If an assembly does not have a strong name or if it is not signed, you should install the assembly on the client's computer as a private assembly.

CERTIFICATION READY?
Expose COM components to the .NET Framework and the .NET Framework components to COM.
USD 6.1

When installing an assembly for private use, you should install the application.EXE file and the interop assembly in the same directory structure. For example, imagine that ClientA.exe and ClientB.exe use your unsigned interop assembly. ClientA.exe and ClientB.exe have their own directory structures. Therefore, you need to install your interop assembly, say AccountLib.dll, twice in the directories of your client application.

Additionally, when your assembly has a strong name and if multiple applications use it, you must install the assembly in the GAC. Then, all the applications can use that single copy of your interop assembly.

Working with .NET Types in COM Applications

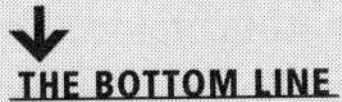

You may have to build .NET applications that your existing COM clients need to consume. In these applications, a managed .NET type must be consumable from the unmanaged COM code. Therefore, you must create these .NET applications with certain considerations such as deciding the correct accessor type and including appropriate custom attributes. This helps you to simplify interoperability between COM and .NET.

Creating a managed .NET type and consuming that type from an unmanaged COM code are two different tasks. The .NET managed code you create must qualify for interoperability.

Understanding Exposure of .NET Types

You must consider the requirements of COM interop at design time if you want to expose types from a .NET assembly to COM applications. This is because an application written for the .NET environment deals with managed code and an application written to be used with .NET and COM must have the ability to deal with managed and unmanaged code. In addition, the conversion of .NET assembly to COM type library follows strict rules that impact the way in which you write code.

You should adhere to guidelines listed in Table 11-7, if you want the managed types such as class, interface, structure, and enumeration to integrate with COM types seamlessly.

Table 11-7

Guidelines to expose managed types

GUIDELINE	DESCRIPTION
Ensure that the managed types are public.	Only public types in an assembly are registered and exported to the type library and therefore only public types are visible to COM.
Ensure that the types have a public default constructor that can be activated from COM.	The managed and public types are visible to COM. However, without a public default constructor, COM clients cannot create the type.
Ensure that you do not have abstract types.	COM does not support abstract types.
Ensure that classes implement interfaces explicitly.	The COM interop facilitates automatic interface generation referred to as class interface. However, it is better to create an explicit interface rather than allowing the interop to generate the interface. This is because the automatically generated class interface does not support further versioning of the interop assembly.
Make all the methods, properties, fields, and events public to make them visible to COM.	Members of public types must also be public because all the public types and members are visible to COM by default. If you want to restrict this visibility of public type or its members, then you must use the `ComVisibleAttribute`

Not all managed types are visible to COM. Certain features of managed types exposed to other managed code, such as parameterized constructors, static methods, and constant fields, are not exposed to COM.

The inheritance hierarchy of a managed type is flattened when the .NET type is exported to COM. For example, when you export a .NET type, the `GetType` method from the `System.Object` base class is also available to the COM client if your .NET assembly references that method.

Your .NET assembly version changes every time you rebuild it. For every new version, a new GUID is created when you register the assembly. Thus, a new GUID is assigned for an assembly even if you rebuild the assembly without making any changes to that assembly. COM operates on GUID and therefore treats every new type library with a new GUID as separate entities. If you want to prevent this, you can use the `GuidAttribute` class to specify a GUID explicitly to the assembly.

Using Attributes for Interoperability

The `System.Runtime.InteropServices` namespace provides ***interop-specific attributes*** to control the outcome of automatic assembly generation by COM interop tools or APIs.

The interop-specific attributes offered by the `System.Runtime.InteropServices` namespace are divided based on their actions. Attribute categories:

- Applied by you at design time
- Applied by COM interop tools and APIs during the conversion process
- Applied either by you or COM interop

You can apply interop-specific attributes to types, methods, properties, parameters, fields, and other members.

Table 11-8 describes the design-time attributes that you can apply to the managed source code. Occasionally, the COM interop tools might also apply these attributes.

Table 11-8

Design-time attributes for COM interoperability

ATTRIBUTE	DESCRIPTION
`ClassInterfaceAttribute`	Allows you to control the type of interface generated for a class.
`CoClassAttribute`	Recognizes the CLSID of the original `coclass` imported from a type library.
`ComUnregisterFunctionAttribute`	Specifies that a method should be called when the assembly is unregistered from COM.
`ComVisibleAttribute`	Renders types invisible to COM for which the attribute value equals false.
`DispIdAttribute`	You can explicitly assign a COM Dispatcher Identifier (DISPID) for a method or field using this attribute. DISPID is a 32-bit signed integer that uniquely identifies a method, property, or field in an interface.
`InAttribute`	Specifies that data should be marshaled in to the caller.
`OutAttribute`	Specifies that the data in a field or parameter must be marshaled from a called object back to its caller.

Table 11-9 describes the conversion-tool attributes that COM interop tools apply during the conversion process. These are not used at the design time.

Table 11-9

Conversion-tool attributes for COM interoperability

ATTRIBUTE	DESCRIPTION
`ComAliasNameAttribute`	Specifies the COM alias for a parameter or field type.
`ComEventInterface Attribute`	Recognizes the source interface and also the class that implements the methods of the event interface.
`ImportedFromTypeLib Attribute`	Indicates that the assembly was originally imported from a COM type library.

Consider an example that uses one of these attributes. The following code snippet demonstrates assigning explicit DISPID to members of a class:

```
using System.Runtime.InteropServices;
public class MyDispID
{
    public MyDispID()
    {
    }
    [DispId(1)]
    public void CustomMethod()
    {
    }
    [DispId(2)]
    public int CustomField;
}
```

Bundling an Assembly for COM

For most of the .NET types, a type library is necessary when consumed by a COM application.

The following guidelines help the COM developers know about the managed types they plan to incorporate in the application:

- For COM, some managed types are invisible, some are visible but not creatable, and some are both visible and creatable. An assembly can have a combination of invisible, visible, not creatable, and creatable types. You should identify the types in an assembly that you intend to expose to COM, especially when those types are a subset of the types exposed to the .NET Framework.
- Managed classes that implement the class interface generated by the COM interop have versioning restrictions. You cannot change the members in a class after you generate an interface for the class using the COM interop service. This is because COM clients may not understand the altered member of the class.
- You must install the unsigned assemblies as private assemblies on the user's machine. However, you can install the strong-named assemblies that are signed by a publisher into the GAC.

You can generate a type library using the following options provided by the .NET Framework:

- Type Library Exporter
- `TypeLibConverter` Class
- Assembly Registration Tool
- .NET Services Installation Tool

MORE INFORMATION
To know how to generate a type library using any of these tools, refer to the corresponding sections in the MSDN library.

In these four cases, only public types defined in the assembly that you supply are incorporated in the generated type library.

Deploying an Assembly for COM

You can either deploy an assembly as a private assembly or a shared assembly for the use of COM clients.

Assemblies can be of two types:

- ***Private assemblies.*** Private assemblies are available only to clients in the same directory structure as that of the assembly.
- ***Shared assemblies.*** Shared assemblies are available to any local COM application. To share an application, you should install the assemblies into the GAC. All the shared assemblies must be strong named. You can use the global assembly cache tool (Gacutil.exe) to add an assembly to the GAC as follows:

```
gacutil /i AccountLib.dll
```

MORE INFORMATION
You must register an assembly before you can use it from a COM client. To learn how to register assemblies in the Windows registry, refer to the "Registering Assemblies with COM" section from the MSDN library.

If a COM component references a type from this shared AccountLib.dll assembly, then the component uses the Microsoft .NET Runtime Execution Engine (Mscoree.dll) to locate the shared assembly.

Consuming a Managed Type from COM

You can use a managed type from COM by following the basic steps outlined in this topic.

CONSUME A MANAGED TYPE

To consume a managed type from COM:

1. **Deploy an application for COM access.** A strong-named assembly can be installed in the GAC and this requires a signature from its publisher. Assemblies that are not strong named must be installed in the application directory of the client.
2. **Register assemblies with COM.** You must register the types in an assembly to consume them in COM. If an installer does not register the assembly, instruct COM developers to use Regasm.exe. For the COM clients to use the .NET class transparently, Regasm.exe adds information about the class to the system registry. Alternatively, you can use the RegistrationServices class to achieve the same functionality.
3. **Reference .NET types from COM.** COM developers can reference types in an assembly using the same tools and techniques that they currently use. If you use the Type Library Exporter tool to convert an assembly into a type library file (.tlb), then you should reference the TLB file with the #import directive to use the .NET object members from an unmanaged C++ client. While referencing a type library from C++, you must specify the `raw_interfaces_only` option. Alternatively, you can import the definitions in the base class library, Mscorlib.tlb.
4. **Call a .NET object.** COM developers can call methods on the .NET object the same way they call methods on any unmanaged type. For example, the COM `CoCreateInstance` API activates .NET objects.

CERTIFICATION READY?
Expose COM components to the .NET Framework and the .NET Framework components to COM.
USD 6.1

■ Controlling Data Marshaling

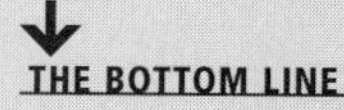

THE BOTTOM LINE

Data marshaling refers to the technique of making the data ready for processing or transporting over a network. It involves gathering the data and transforming it into a standard format before it is transmitted over a network so that the data can move beyond network boundaries. The converted data stream corresponds with the packet structure of the network transfer protocol to facilitate its movement around the network. Sections of data are collected in a message buffer before they are marshaled. After transmission of this data, the receiving computer converts the marshaled data back into an object.

Interop marshaling specifies the rules for passing data in method arguments and returning values between managed and unmanaged memory during method calls. Interop marshaling is a runtime activity performed by the Marshaling service of the CLR.

You can use the platform invoke service or the COM Interop service to control interop marshaling. Platform invoke service enables you to place method calls for unmanaged code inside your managed code. COM Interop service allows you to access managed code from unmanaged code and vice versa.

Understanding Default Marshaling

Marshaling allocates unmanaged memory, copies the unmanaged memory blocks, and converts managed to unmanaged types.

TAKE NOTE*

Marshaling of generic types is not advocated.

MORE INFORMATION

To know more about the default marshaling behavior of the various types, refer to the "Default Marshaling Behavior" section from the MSDN Library.

Interop marshaling follows certain built-in rules. These rules define the way in which data associated with method parameters behave when passing between managed and unmanaged memory. These rules control marshaling activities, such as:

- Control transformation of data types
- Allow or prevent a recipient from changing data received through parameters and return those changes to the sender
- Control circumstances in which the marshaler provides performance optimizations

The interop marshaling services include marshaling arrays, Boolean types, characters, classes, delegates, objects, strings, and value types.

Marshaling Data with Platform Invoke

To call functions exported from an unmanaged library, a .NET Framework application requires a function prototype in managed code that represents the unmanaged function.

When marshaling data, you can use the platform invoke service that helps managed code call unmanaged functions implemented in dynamic-link libraries (DLLs), such as those available in the Win32 API. This service locates and invokes an exported function and marshals its arguments, such as integers, strings, arrays, and structures across the required interoperation boundary.

CONSUME EXPORTED DLL FUNCTIONS

Perform the following steps to consume exported DLL functions from .NET applications:

1. **Identify functions in DLLs.** To identify a DLL function you must specify the following elements:
   a. Function name, for example, `MessageBox`.
   b. Name of the DLL file in which you can locate the implementation; for example, you can find the `MessageBox` function in user32.dll.
2. **Store the unmanaged functions from the DLL.** To group the unmanaged functions, you can:
   a. Use an existing class
   b. Create an individual class for each unmanaged function
   c. Create one class that contains a set of related unmanaged functions

   It is essential to wrap a frequently used DLL function in a managed class to encapsulate platform functionality. This method is not mandatory for all instances. If you are programming in C#, you must declare DLL functions within a class. Within a class, you define a static method for each DLL function that you want to call.
3. **Create prototypes in managed code.** You can use the DllImportAttribute to identify the DLL and the unmanaged function. Mark the method with the static and extern

modifiers. For example, the following code creates a managed prototype for using the MessageBox function from user32.dll:

```
using System.Runtime.InteropServices;
[DllImport("user32.dll")]
public static extern int MessageBox(IntPtr hWnd, String
disptext, String wcaption, uint type);
```

4. **Call a DLL function.** You can call the method on your managed class like you call other managed methods in your application. However, passing structures and implementing callback functions are exceptions.

When passing structures or classes to unmanaged code using the platform invoke service, you must provide additional information to preserve the original layout and alignment.

A callback function is code within a managed application that helps an unmanaged DLL function complete a task. Calls made to a callback function pass indirectly from a managed application to a DLL function and then back to the managed implementation.

ANALYZING THE DLLIMPORTATTRIBUTE CLASS

The `DllImportAttribute` class specifies that the attributed method be exposed by unmanaged DLL as a static entry point. This class is available in the `System.Runtime.InteropServices` namespace.

Following are the features of the `DllImportAttribute`:

- You can apply this attribute to methods.
- This attribute provides the information needed to call a function exported from an unmanaged DLL. You only need to supply the name of the DLL containing the entry point.
- You can apply this attribute directly to C# method definitions.

The following code example demonstrates how to use the `DllImportAttribute` to import the Win32 `MessageBox` function. The code further calls the imported method:

```
using System;
using System.Runtime.InteropServices;
class Example
{
   // Use DllImport to import the Win32 MessageBox function and
specify the character set used by the dll
   [DllImport("user32.dll", CharSet = CharSet.Unicode)]
   // Create a prototype
   public static extern int MessageBox(IntPtr hWnd, String disptext,
String wcaption, uint type);
   static void Main()
   {
      // Call the MessageBox function using platform invoke
      MessageBox(new IntPtr(0), "Calling Windows MessageBox from .NET
code", "Using Platform Invoke", 0);
   }
}
```

MARSHALING STRINGS

You can use the platform invoke service to copy string parameters and to convert them from Unicode (.NET Framework format) to ANSI (unmanaged format), as required. Due to the immutable property of managed strings, platform invoke does not copy them back from unmanaged memory to managed memory when the function returns.

Following are the various marshaling options used by platform invoke when dealing with strings:

- When marshaling strings by value, platform invoke passes strings as `In` parameters.
- When it needs to return string types as results from unmanaged code, platform invoke returns them as strings.
- When passing strings by reference, platform invoke passes strings as `In/Out` parameters using a `StringBuilder` object.
- When you pass string in a structure by value, platform invoke passes strings in a structure that is an `In` parameter.
- When you pass a structure containing character pointers (`char*`) by reference, platform invoke passes strings in a structure that is an `In/Out` parameter. The unmanaged function expects a pointer to a character buffer and the buffer size is a member of the structure.
- When you pass a structure containing character arrays (`char[]`) by reference, platform invoke passes strings in a structure that is an `In/Out` parameter. The unmanaged function expects an embedded character buffer.
- When you pass a class containing character pointers (`char*`) by value, platform invoke passes strings in a class (a class is an `In/Out` parameter). The unmanaged function expects a pointer to a character buffer.
- When you pass a class containing character arrays (`char[]`) by value, platform invoke passes strings in a class (a class is an `In/Out` parameter). The unmanaged function expects an embedded character buffer.
- When you pass an array of strings by value, platform invoke creates an array of strings that is passed by value.
- When you pass an array of structures that contain strings by value, platform invoke creates an array of structures that contain strings and the array is passed by value.

MORE INFORMATION
For a specific example on each of the marshaling options, refer to the "Marshaling Strings" section from the MSDN library.

MORE INFORMATION
For more information about marshaling classes, structures, and unions, refer to the "Marshaling Classes, Structures, and Unions" section from the MSDN library.

MARSHALING CLASSES

In the .NET Framework, classes are classified as reference types that have fields, properties, events, and static and nonstatic methods. When you pass a class by value, platform invoke passes the class with integer members as an `In/Out` parameter.

MORE INFORMATION
For more information about marshaling arrays, refer to the "Marshaling Arrays of Types" section from the MSDN library.

MARSHALING ARRAYS

An array in managed code is a reference type that contains one or more elements of the same type. In spite of being reference types, arrays are passed as `In` parameters to unmanaged functions. This behavior keeps changing, and the managed arrays are passed to managed objects as `In/Out` parameters.

TAKE NOTE*
When you pass arrays of structures containing strings, members of the array can be changed.

Marshaling Data with COM Interop

You can make use of COM interop to utilize COM objects from managed code and to expose managed objects to COM. Marshaling data with the COM interop service mostly provides the correct marshaling behavior.

You can customize interop wrappers by supplying the marshaler with additional type information. This customization includes the following processes:

- **Customization of COM callable wrappers (CCW).** This process describes the way to marshal the data types explicitly using the `MarshalAsAttribute` at design time.
- **Customization of runtime callable wrappers (RCW).** This process describes the way to adjust the marshaling behavior of types in an interop assembly and to define COM types manually.

CUSTOMIZING COM CALLABLE WRAPPERS

Recall that you use CCW to call a managed code from COM clients. You can use the Type Library Exporter (Tlbexp.exe) tool to convert a managed type library to a COM type library. You can export a managed DLL directly without customizing the wrapper. Alternatively, you can customize the CCW to modify marshaling behavior, compile the CCW, and then use the tool to export the DLL.

Customizing a CCW is a simple and direct task. The type you want to expose to a COM client may have nonstandard marshaling requirements. In this case, you must apply the `System.Runtime.InteropServices.MarshalAsAttribute` to a method parameter, class field, or return value to change the marshaling behavior. Figure 11-1 depicts the process of customizing CCW.

Figure 11-1

Customizing data marshaling in DLLs

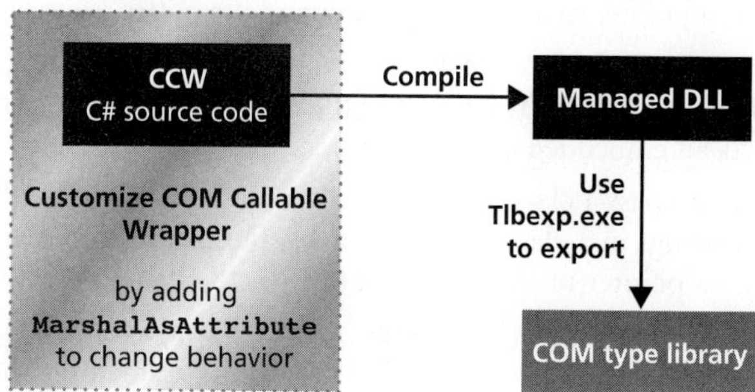

When the COM interop marshals data from managed code to unmanaged code, the interop marshaler recognizes the following representations of the data being passed:

- ***Blittable*** value types have common memory representations in both managed and unmanaged environments. Therefore, these types do not require conversion when passed between managed and unmanaged code and do not require special handling by the interop marshaler. For example, a 16-byte integer is always marshaled to a 16-byte integer. The interop marshaler uses the managed signature to determine the data representation.
- ***Non-blittable*** types have dissimilar memory representations in managed and unmanaged environments and hence require marshaling. For non-blittable types, the interop marshaler recognizes the managed representation from its method signature, but cannot do so for the unmanaged representation. In order to marshal non-blittable types, you can use either of the following techniques:
  - Permit the marshaler to infer the representation from the managed representation.
  - Supply the unmanaged data representation explicitly.

A good example to demonstrate data representations is the conversion of a string to a BSTR type when marshaling takes place from managed to unmanaged code. You can change this default behavior by explicitly applying the `MarshalAsAttribute` to marshal the string to another type, such as LPWSTR.

The following examples show the application of the `MarshalAsAttribute` to a parameter, field, or return value within the source of the type definition:

a. Application of the `MarshalAsAttribute` to a parameter:

```
public void Mymethod([MarshalAs(UnmanagedType.LPWStr)]String
message);
```

b. Application of the `MarshalAsAttribute` to a field within a class:

```
class MsgText
{
    [MarshalAs(UnmanagedType.LPWStr)]
  public String message;
}
```

c. Application of the MarshalAsAttribute to a return value:

```
[return: MarshalAs(UnmanagedType.LPWStr)]
public String GetMyMessage();
```

TAKE NOTE* You can set the System.Runtime.InteropServices.UnmanagedType enumeration to specify the desired format of the unmanaged type.

You can also use the MarshalAsAttribute to specify the required additional information in cases where the interop marshaler requires more information than is provided by the managed and unmanaged data format. For example, to marshal an array, you need additional information such as the element type, rank, size, and bounds of the array.

CUSTOMIZING RUNTIME CALLABLE WRAPPERS

The CLR produces an RCW from the metadata in an interop assembly. In contrast with the other assemblies, the import of type libraries leads to the generation of interop assemblies. The import process generally produces precise interop assemblies; however, sometimes you may need to modify the interop assembly to produce a custom RCW. Some examples follow:

- One or more types in the unmanaged assembly require additional marshaling information.
- A type library contains many specialized types that the marshaler cannot recognize.
- A large COM type library may contain types that are redundant for an application. You can eliminate the need to deploy these types by creating an interop assembly from managed source code.
- You can avoid deploying redundant types by using an RCW source code that contains only the required portion of types from the large source type library.

To customize the RCW by applying additional or different marshaling instructions, you can either edit the interop assembly or create custom wrappers manually. Figure 11-2 depicts the process of editing the assembly and creating custom wrappers.

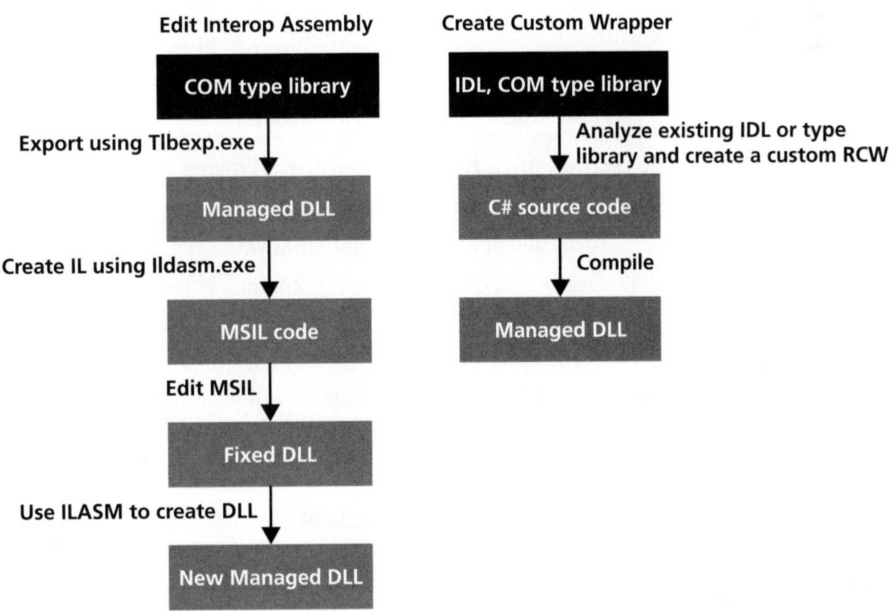

Figure 11-2

Customizing data marshaling in imported type libraries

You can edit the interop assembly to search for problematic syntax and replace it with alternative syntax. This method works better for minor marshaling changes. The Type Library Importer (Tlbimp.exe) converts almost all the COM method signatures into managed signatures. However, many other types require additional information that you can specify by editing the interop assembly.

EDIT THE INTEROP ASSEMBLY

The following steps indicate how to edit an interop assembly and the marshaling changes in Microsoft Intermediate Language (MSIL):

1. Generate the initial interop assembly using Tlbimp.exe; for example, to produce an assembly called AccountLib.dll from AccountLib.tlb, type the following command at the command prompt:

   ```
   tlbimp AccountLib.tlb /out:AccountLib.dll
   ```

2. At the command prompt, type the following command to generate MSIL for the assembly:

   ```
   ildasm AccountLib.dll /out:AccountLib.il
   ```

3. Edit the MSIL as needed.
4. At the command prompt, type the following command to create a new AccountLib.dll defining the proper syntax:

   ```
   ilasm AccountLib.il /dll
   ```

TAKE NOTE* The MSIL assembler (Ildasm.exe) tool generates a portable executable file (.exe) or an assembly (.dll) from Microsoft Intermediate Language (MSIL), which stores MSIL and the required metadata.

TAKE NOTE* Declaring COM types manually is a complicated task that requires a working knowledge of the Type Library Importer (Tlbimp.exe), the default behavior of the interop marshaler, and COM.

You can create a custom wrapper manually based on an existing Interface Definition Language (IDL) file or type library. This method works better when an entire library of specialized types is available or when you require the RCW source code.

CREATE A CUSTOM RCW MANUALLY

The creation of an RCW involves the following steps:

1. Analyze an IDL file or type library file to confirm the classes and interfaces that need to be included in the custom RCW.
2. Create a source file in a CLS-compliant language and declare the types.

TAKE NOTE* When you create a custom RCW, you will manually perform the type conversion activity provided by the Type Library Importer (Tlbimp.exe).

CERTIFICATION READY?
Call unmanaged DLL functions in a .NET Framework application, and control the marshaling of data in a .NET Framework application.
USD 6.2

3. After completing the declarations, compile the file similar to compiling any other managed source code.
4. As with the types imported with Tlbimp.exe, certain types require additional information that you can add directly to your code.

TAKE NOTE* Refer to the section “Edit the Interop Assembly” to perform Step 4.

SKILL SUMMARY

This lesson introduced you to COM and .NET interoperability. COM and .NET Framework show variations in the way they manage their clients. To allow interoperation between COM and .NET, the .NET Framework runtime uses wrapper classes, such as runtime callable wrapper (RCW) and COM callable wrapper (CCW).

To consume a COM component in your .NET application, you must convert the type library into an assembly. You can generate the type metadata in an interop assembly by using Visual Studio, the Type Library Importer tool (Tlbimp.exe), or the `TypeLibConverter` class.

To consume a managed .NET type from an unmanaged COM code, you must confirm that the created .NET managed code is eligible for interoperability. You must convert the .NET assembly to a type library to consume it from a COM client. You can generate a type library by using either the Type Library Exporter or the `TypeLibConverter` class or the Assembly Registration tool or the .NET Services Installation tool.

You can use platform invoke or the COM interop service to control interop marshaling. You can control the marshaling of certain types such as classes using the COM interop service only. You can customize interop wrappers by providing the marshaler with supplementary type information.

For the certification examination:

- Know how to use COM components in .NET applications.
- Know how to use .NET types in COM applications.
- Understand the process of data marshaling with platform invoke and COM interop.

Knowledge Assessment

Matching

Match the following descriptions to the appropriate terms.

a. `DllImportAttribute`
b. `GuidAttribute`
c. `InAttribute`
d. `MarshalAsAttribute`
e. `StructLayoutAttribute`

_______ **1.** Specifies that data should be marshaled in to the caller.

_______ **2.** Maintains the interface identifier assigned in a type library.

_______ **3.** Specifies the marshaling of data between managed and unmanaged code.

_______ **4.** Permits access of unmanaged APIs by defining platform invoke methods.

_______ **5.** Controls the character set used by a marshaled type.

True / False

Circle T if the statement is true or F if the statement is false.

T | F **1.** To customize COM callable wrappers, types must have a public default constructor.

T | F **2.** C-style arrays are one-dimensional typed arrays with a fixed lower bound of 1.

T | F **3.** You cannot assign a different name to your interop assembly that contains the imported type definitions.

T | F **4.** You can compile your interop project either using a command-line compiler or using the Visual Studio environment.

T | F **5.** `OutAttribute` specifies that data should be marshaled in to the caller.

Fill in the Blank

Complete the following sentences by writing the correct word or words in the blanks provided.

1. By default, the interop marshaler passes an array as ________ parameter.
2. Unmanaged arrays are either _______ arrays or ________ arrays with fixed or variable length.
3. You can import a COM type library into your .NET assembly as metadata using ________ command-line tool.
4. The ________ class provides methods to convert coclasses and interfaces of COM type library into metadata within an assembly.
5. The inheritance hierarchy of a managed type is __________ once the type is exported to COM.

Multiple Choice

Circle the letter or letters that correspond to the best answer or answers.

1. Which is the default format of a Boolean parameter in COM calls?
   a. `UnmanagedType.U1`
   b. `UnmanagedType.Bool`
   c. `UnmanagedType.VariantBool`
   d. None of the above
2. Which attribute can you use for platform invoke declarations?
   a. `StructLayoutAttribute`
   b. `DllImportAttribute`
   c. `MarshalAsAttribute`
   d. `InteropServicesAttribute`
3. Select the type of wrapper class that enables you to interact with a COM object from your .NET application.
   a. Runtime callable wrapper (RCW)
   b. COM callable wrapper (CCW)
   c. Both RCW and CCW
   d. You have to create your own custom wrapper class to interact with a COM object.
4. Which one of the following command-line options can you use to sign your assembly during the import process?
   a. /keyfile
   b. /keycontainer
   c. /publickey
   d. None of the above
5. Which of the following attributes renders types that have this attribute set to false as invisible to COM?
   a. `ComVisibleAttribute`
   b. `ComUnregisterFunctionAttribute`
   c. `CoClassAttribute`
   d. `ClassInterfaceAttribute`

Review Questions

1. You have a COM type library that does not have a primary interop assembly. You want to use this in your .NET application. What is the easiest way to achieve this?
2. You have created a .NET application that you want your COM client to use. However, you want to restrict the types exposed by your .NET assembly to your COM client. How can you achieve this?

Case Scenarios

Scenario 11-1: Consuming Unmanaged DLL Functions

You must use the `CreateFont()` method from the GDI32.dll in your .NET application. Write code to use this unmanaged DLL function from your .NET application.

Scenario 11-2: Customizing COM Interoperability

Consider that you have a .NET assembly. This assembly contains a method named MethodA that accepts a Boolean parameter. You want to call MethodA from your COM client. When doing so, you want to control the interop marshaling to use a 1-byte integer to represent the Boolean parameter. How can you achieve this?

Workplace Ready

Choosing the Right Interop Service

.NET Framework allows you to seamlessly interoperate with your legacy COM components. You can call methods in your managed code from your COM clients. You can also call methods in your COM components from your .NET application. You can either use platform invoke or COM interop service to call unmanaged code from your .NET application.

You are the solution architect for XYZ Games, Inc. You have an existing COM type library that offers some excellent functions, which you want to use in your new .NET-based game. However, you want to control the data representation for your .NET application. Suggest an approach that you would take in this scenario.

LESSON 12 Configuring and Installing .NET Applications

OBJECTIVE DOMAIN MATRIX

TECHNOLOGY SKILL	OBJECTIVE DOMAIN	OBJECTIVE DOMAIN NUMBER
Configure .NET applications.	Embed configuration management functionality into a .NET Framework application.	3.1
Configure .NET applications.	Create a custom Microsoft Windows Installer for .NET components by using the System. Configuration.Install namespace, and configure .NET Framework applications by using configuration files, environment variables, and the .NET Framework configuration tool (Mscorcfg.msc).	3.2
Create custom installers.	Create a custom Microsoft Windows Installer for .NET components by using the System.Configuration.Install namespace, and configure .NET Framework applications by using configuration files, environment variables, and the .NET Framework configuration tool (Mscorcfg.msc).	3.2

KEY TERMS

application configuration file
code access security policy tool (Caspol.exe)
custom installers
machine configuration file
.NET Framework configuration tool (Mscorcfg.msc)
security configuration file

Configuring .NET Applications

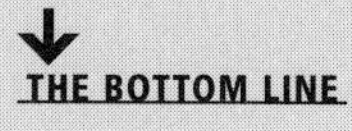

One of the main advantages of using .NET Framework is that the developers and administrators can easily monitor and manage the applications at runtime. Administrators can control and configure the protected resources that an application can access, versions of assemblies an application can use, and the locations of the remote applications and objects. Developers can use configuration files to modify the configuration settings without having to recompile the application.

Understanding Configuration Files

Configuration files are XML files that contain configuration settings for an application such as connection strings and assembly binding settings.

You can modify configuration files based on your requirements. Administrators use configuration files to set the policies that influence how the applications run on their network.

EXPLORING THE CONFIGURATION FILE FORMAT

The three types of configuration files that you can use to control a .NET application include:

- ***Machine configuration file.*** This configuration file contains settings that are common for all applications that run on a computer.
- ***Application configuration file.*** This configuration file contains settings that are specific to an application.
- ***Security configuration file.*** This configuration file contains settings that are related to a security policy or a code group hierarchy.

> **TAKE NOTE***
> An empty element has a start tag with a / before the closing > as in <myTag />. Such a tag need not have a separate end tag as in </myTag>.

The elements in these configuration files represent logical data structures that provide configuration information. Within a configuration file, you use tags to indicate the start and end of an element. For example, the `<appSettings>` element consists of `<appSettings>` *child elements* `</appSettings>`.

> **TAKE NOTE***
> The syntax in the configuration files is case sensitive.

You can use predefined attributes to specify configuration settings. These predefined attributes are name-value pairs inside an element's start tag. The following example specifies three attributes (`name`, `publicKeyToken`, and `culture`) for the `<assemblyIdentity>` element. These attributes indicate identity information for an assembly such as the name of the assembly, security token of the assembly, and the culture used by the assembly:

```
<assemblyIdentity name="MyAssembly" publicKeyToken="34b739ef0255d983"
culture="neutral" />
```

UNDERSTANDING MACHINE AND APPLICATION CONFIGURATION FILES

The machine configuration file consists of settings for the whole computer. That is, each computer has one machine.config file that contains machine-wide settings pertaining to all the .NET applications running on that computer. For example, imagine that your organization uses a single database and you want all your applications to use this database. You can create a connection string that specifies the location of your database to provide details on how to connect to your database. You can then place this connection string in the machine.config file, which avoids the presence of the same connection string settings in all the application configuration files. In addition, if there is a change in the location of your database, you only need to make changes in one location; all the applications will automatically refer to the new location.

Figure 12-1 depicts the configuration files that reside on a computer. Although every computer has a single machine.config file, each application running on that computer can have more than one configuration file associated with it. For example, Application 1 has two configuration files associated with it, Application 2 has a single configuration file, and Application 3 has three configuration files associated with it.

Figure 12-1

Machine and application configuration files

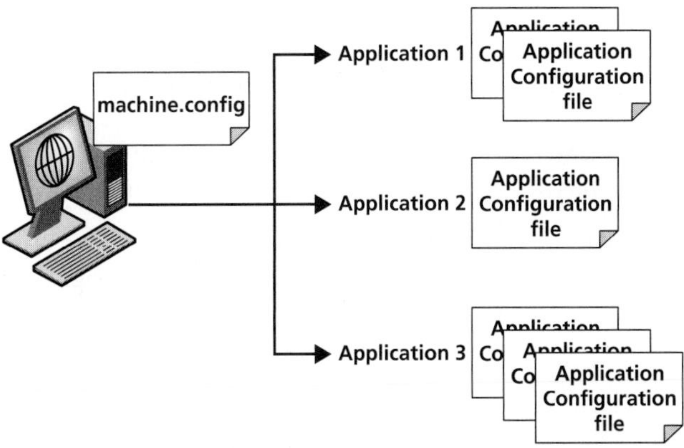

MORE INFORMATION
To learn more about machine configuration files, you can refer to the "Machine Configuration Files" section from the MSDN library.

The single machine.config file is located in the %runtime install path%\Config directory. You can use its configuration settings to configure machine-wide assembly binding, built-in remoting channels, and ASP .NET.

Application configuration files contain application-specific configuration settings that are readable by the Common Language Runtime (CLR) and your application. These settings include elements such as assembly binding policy and remoting objects. For example, the `<system.runtime.remoting>` element in the `<configuration>` section allows you to configure remote objects and applications.

The application's host forms the basis of the name and location of the application configuration file. The name of the configuration file is the name of the application with a .config extension; for example, the configuration file for an application called custApp.exe has the name custApp.exe.config.

As depicted in Figure 12-1, each application can have one or more application configuration files associated with it. For example, if you want two different parts of your application to have different configuration settings, then apart from these specific settings, you need to apply some common settings to both application parts. You can then create an application configuration file to contain the common settings and place it in the root directory. The application configuration files pertaining to the specific parts of the application can then be placed under the specific subdirectories under the root directory.

TAKE NOTE*
In Visual Studio projects, you must place the configuration file in the project directory and set its `Copy to Output Directory` property to `Copy always` or `Copy if newer`. Visual Studio automatically copies the file to the directory to compile the assembly.

MORE INFORMATION
To know more about application configuration files, you can refer to the "Application Configuration Files" section from the MSDN library.

UNDERSTANDING SECURITY CONFIGURATION FILES

Security configuration files store information about the code group hierarchy and the permission sets associated with a policy level. You must use the ***.NET Framework configuration tool (Mscorcfg.msc)*** or the Code access security policy tool (Caspol.exe) to modify the security policy. The use of these tools to modify the security policy ensures that policy changes do not affect the security configuration files.

Table 12-1 lists the locations of the security configuration files.

Table 12-1
Location of the security configuration files

SECURITY CONFIGURATION FILE	LOCATION
Enterprise policy	%runtime install path%\Config\Enterprisesec.config
Machine policy	%runtime install path%\Config\Security.config
User policy	%USERPROFILE%\Application data\Microsoft\CLR security config\vxx.xx\Security.config

Exploring the Configuration Namespace

The various elements of the configuration namespace enable you to programmatically access and manage the configuration data of your application.

The `System.Configuration` namespace contains various classes, interfaces, delegates, and enumerations to supply the programming model to manage configuration data.

Table 12-2 lists some of the classes in the `System.Configuration` namespace.

Table 12-2

Classes of the `System.Configuration` namespace

CLASS	DESCRIPTION
`Configuration`	Represents a configuration file applicable to a particular computer, application, or resource.
`ConfigurationElement`	Represents a configuration element (XML) within a configuration file, such as the machine.config file.
`ConfigurationElementCollection`	Represents a configuration element containing a collection of child elements.
`ConfigurationElementProperty`	Specifies the property of a configuration element.
`ConfigurationManager`	Provides access to configuration files for client applications.
`ConfigurationSection`	Represents a section within a configuration file.
`ConfigurationSectionCollection`	Represents a collection of related sections within a configuration file.
`ConfigurationSectionGroup`	Represents a group of related sections within a configuration file.
`ConfigurationSectionGroupCollection`	Represents a collection of `ConfigurationSectionGroup` objects.
`ConnectionStringSettings`	Represents a single connection string in the connection string settings section of the configuration file.
`ConnectionStringSettingsCollection`	Represents a collection of `ConnectionStringSettings` objects.
`ConnectionStringsSection`	Represents the connection string section in the configuration file.

Manipulating the Configuration File

Once you have created the configuration file for your application, you can use the functionalities provided by the `System.Configuration` namespace to read and manipulate the configuration file from your application easily.

You can use the `ConfigurationManager` class of the `System.Configuration` namespace to access machine, application, and user configuration files from a Windows application.

The two main programmatic manipulation operations that you can perform on your application's configuration file include:

- Accessing existing sections in the configuration file
- Defining new application configuration settings

ACCESSING EXISTING SETTINGS

You can use the properties of the `ConfigurationManager` class to access existing sections of your application's configuration file.

For example, you can use the `AppSettings` property of the `ConfigurationManager` class to read the elements of the application settings section. Note that the `Configuration.AppSettings` property gets the *AppSettingsSection* data for the current application's default configuration.

The following code sample shows you how to use the ConfigurationManager.AppSettings property to get the application settings section of a console application from the configuration file. The ReadAppSettingsFromConfigFile method gets the AppSettings section in the MyAppSettings object. MyAppSettings is an instance of the NameValueCollection class. If the MyAppSettings collection has any elements, the method displays the elements; else, it displays a message that the application settings section is not defined:

```
public static void ReadAppSettingsFromConfigFile()
{
   try
   {
      // Get the AppSettings section
      NameValueCollection MyAppSettings = ConfigurationManager.AppSettings;
// Get the elements of the AppSettings section
   Console.WriteLine("Reading application settings from the
application's Configuration file:");
      if (MyAppSettings.Count == 0)
   {
      Console.WriteLine("There are no settings defined under the
AppSettings section in your application's configuration file.");
   }
   else
   {
      // Loop through the appsettings collection to display each setting
      for (int i = 0; i < MyAppSettings.Count; i++)
      {
         Console.WriteLine("#{0} Key: {1} Value: {2}",i,
MyAppSettings.GetKey(i), MyAppSettings[i]);
       }
     }
   }
   catch (ConfigurationErrorsException e)
   {
      Console.WriteLine(e.ToString());
   }
}
```

ACCESSING CONNECTION STRINGS

Your application requires a provider to access a data source such as a SQL Server or Oracle database. Providers require connection information such as the name and location of the database to be able to connect to the database. Connection strings help you provide connection information to the provider in your application.

You can define connection strings in the machine or application configuration files. This allows you to change the location of your database without changing or recompiling your application code. You may define the connection string in the machine.config file if all your applications must use the same database. Alternatively, you can define the connection string in your application configuration file if the connection string is specific to your application database.

To read the connection string information from your application's configuration file, you can use the ConnectionStrings property of the ConfigurationManager class.

The following code sample shows how to use the ConfigurationManager.ConnectionStrings property to get the ConnectionStringsSection data from the configuration file of a console application. The method gets the connection-string section information in a ConnectionStringSettingsCollection object. The code checks for existence of connection string objects using the Count property of the ConnectionStringSettingsCollection object. If the object is not empty, then the code displays the elements in the configuration file, otherwise the code displays an appropriate message indicating that there are no connection strings defined in the configuration file. The code uses the ConnectionStringSettings class that represents a single, named connection string to read the individual connection string information from the ConnectionStringSettingsCollection object:

```
public static void ReadConnectionStrings()
{
      // Get the ConnectionStrings collection
   ConnectionStringSettingsCollection ConnectionInformation =
ConfigurationManager.ConnectionStrings;
        if (ConnectionInformation.Count != 0)
   {
      Console. WriteLine("Reading connection string information");
      // Get the individual connection string elements
      foreach (ConnectionStringSettings connection in
ConnectionInformation)
      {
        string name = connection.Name;
        string provider = connection.ProviderName;
        string connectionString = connection.ConnectionString;
        Console.WriteLine("Name:", name);
        Console.WriteLine("Connection string:", connectionString);
        Console.WriteLine("Provider:", provider);
   }
  }
  else
  {
      Console.WriteLine("No connection string is defined.");
  }
}
```

DEFINING NEW SETTINGS

Apart from accessing the existing sections in a configuration file, you can also define new application configuration settings at runtime. The following code sample demonstrates this action:

```
Configuration MyAppConfig = ConfigurationManager.OpenExeConfiguration
(ConfigurationUserLevel.None);
MyAppConfig.AppSettings.Settings.Add("SampleKey", "SampleValue");
// Saves the configuration file
MyAppConfig.Save(ConfigurationSaveMode.Modified);
```

This code adds new settings under the AppSettingsSection of an application's configuration file. The code uses the ConfigurationManager.OpenExeConfiguration method to open the configuration file for the current application as a Configuration object. Note that you must pass a type parameter, ConfigurationUserLevel, to the OpenExeConfiguration method. This ConfigurationUserLevel enumeration helps the runtime in determining the location of the configuration file being opened, depending on the level of the user. The previous example code passes a value of None to get the configuration object to apply to all users.

Using the obtained Configuration object, the previous code defines a new setting for the application and then finally saves the newly defined setting.

TAKE NOTE*

You can also read from the Machine.config file using the ConfigurationManager.OpenMachineConfiguration() method. However, when doing so, you should cast the corresponding configuration section that you would like to access to a class that is specific to that configuration section. This is because .NET provides unique classes for different sections in the machine.config file. For example, if you would like to access the <configProtectedData> section in the machine.config file, then you should use the ProtectedConfigurationSection class to access its elements.

Implementing Custom Configuration Sections

An application's configuration file can also contain custom configuration sections. You can access these custom sections in the application configuration file by creating custom classes.

You can create unique custom configuration sections in your application's configuration file by deriving an object of the ConfigurationSection class. Recall that the ConfigurationSection class represents a configuration section within a configuration file.

USING CONFIGURATIONSECTION CLASS

Consider the following sample configuration file that declares custom values as attributes. Note that the CustomSettings configuration section in the configuration file has a corresponding class declared for it. Consider the following configuration file:

```
<?xml version="1.0" encoding="utf-8"?>
<configuration>
   <configSections>
   <section name="CustomSettings" type="ConfigMyApp.
SampleCustomSection, ConfigMyApp"/>
   </configSections>
   <CustomSettings>
      <CurrentUser> Mary </CurrentUser>
   </CustomSettings>
</configuration>
```

Using the SampleCustomSection class defined next, you can declare properties for the CustomSettings section in the previously given configuration file. The runtime then automatically populates the properties, based on the data in the configuration file. The SampleCustomSection class derives from the ConfigurationSection class:

```
public class SampleCustomSection: ConfigurationSection
{
   public SampleCustomSection()
   {
   }
   // Declaratively define the currentuser element
   [ConfigurationProperty("CurrentUser", DefaultValue = "User",
IsRequired = true)]
   [StringValidator(MinLength = 1, MaxLength = 60)]
   // Define the get and set methods for the attribute
   public string LastUser
   {
      get
      {
         return (string)this["CurrentUser"];
      }
      set
      {
         this["CurrentUser"] = value;
      }
   }
}
```

You can also create custom sections in your application's configuration file by implementing the IConfigurationSectionHandler interface.

ACCESSING ELEMENTS OF A CUSTOM SECTION

The following code sample shows how to retrieve elements from a custom section. The code uses the `ConfigurationManager.GetSection()` method to retrieve the elements of the `CustomSettings` section of the configuration file discussed in the previous section:

```
class AccessCustomSection
{
    static void Main(string[] args)
    {
        SampleCustomSection settings = (SampleCustomSection)Configuration
Manager.GetSection("CustomSettings");
        Console.WriteLine(settings.CurrentUser);
    }
}
```

Using the Configuration Tool

The .NET Framework offers the .NET Framework configuration tool (Mscorcfg.msc) to help you manage the global assembly cache (GAC) and the security policies configured in your system.

The various activities that you can perform with the .NET Framework configuration tool include:

- Manage and configure assemblies in GAC
- Regulate code access security policy
- Control remoting services through the Microsoft Management Console (MMC)

You can start this tool by using one of the following options:

- Start menu
- Command line
- Microsoft Management Console

RUN THE CONFIGURATION TOOL FROM THE START MENU

Perform the following steps to execute Mscorcfg.msc from the Start menu:

1. Click Start, click Control Panel, and double click Administrative Tools.
2. Double click Microsoft .NET Framework `<version>` Configuration.

TAKE NOTE*

The configuration tool included in the .NET Framework 2.0 SDK is the latest version of the tool. The .NET Framework version 3.5 is built incrementally on the .NET Framework version 2.0. Therefore, you can use the configuration tool included with .NET Framework 2.0 SDK to manage .NET Framework version 3.5.

RUN THE CONFIGURATION TOOL FROM THE COMMAND LINE

Perform the following steps to execute the configuration tool from the command prompt:

1. Start the SDK command prompt.
2. Type **mscorcfg.msc** and press ENTER.

   This displays the user interface for the tool.

RUN THE CONFIGURATION TOOL FROM THE MICROSOFT MANAGEMENT CONSOLE

Perform the following steps to execute the configuration tool from the Microsoft Management Console:

1. Start the Microsoft Management Console by typing mmc at a command prompt.
2. Go to the File menu and click Add/Remove Snap-in (or press CTRL+M). This displays the Add/Remove Snap-in dialog box.
3. In the Add/Remove Snap-in dialog box, click Add. This displays the Add Standalone Snap-in dialog box.
4. In the Add Standalone Snap-in dialog box, select a version of the .NET Framework configuration tool, and then click Add.

TAKE NOTE*

To view applications configured earlier with this tool, you must expand the Applications node of the console tree. This displays the list of applications configured with this tool.

Some activities that you can perform in your applications by using the .NET Framework configuration tool include:

- Viewing applications that were configured earlier with this tool.
- Adding an application to configure with this tool.
- Viewing the properties of an application.
- Viewing the dependencies of an application's assembly.
- Configuring an assembly for an application.

ADD AN APPLICATION TO CONFIGURE WITH MSCORCFG.MSC

Perform the following steps to add an application to configure with the configuration tool:

1. Click the Applications node of the console tree, and then click the Add an Application to Configure link in the right pane. The tool displays the Configure an Application dialog box, which contains a list of managed applications that have run at least once on the current computer.
2. Select an application from the list.

   OR

   Click the Other button to navigate to an application that does not appear in the list.

   OR

   Navigate to a configuration file to add.
3. To configure the application, click the View the Application's Properties, View the Assembly Dependencies, Configure an Assembly, and Adjust Remoting Services links in the right pane.

CONFIGURE AN ASSEMBLY FOR AN APPLICATION

Perform the following steps to configure an assembly for an application:

TAKE NOTE*

If the application is not in the list, follow the steps to add an application to configure with this tool.

1. Expand the Applications node of the console tree, and click the name of the required application to configure the assembly.
2. Click the Configure an Assembly link in the right pane. The tool displays the View List of Configured Assemblies and Configure an Assembly links in the right pane.
3. Click the Configure an Assembly link. The tool displays the Configure an Assembly wizard.
4. Select an assembly from:

   The list of assemblies that the application uses.

   OR

   The list of assemblies in the cache.

OR

Manually enter the information for an assembly.

The tool displays a Properties window for the assembly to configure.

5. Select the Binding Policy tab to specify the binding redirections from a requested version to a new version.
6. Select the Codebases tab to specify the codebases for specific versions of the assembly.

Configuring the .NET Environment

The machine.config file stores settings configured during the deployment of .NET Framework. You can use this file along with the components of the .NET application to manage the versioning issues.

The configuration of the .NET environment involves:

- Configuring the runtime version that the .NET application should use.
- Configuring where the runtime should search for an assembly.
- Directing the runtime to use the DEVPATH environment variable when searching for assemblies.

CONFIGURING THE RUNTIME VERSION

The <supportedRuntime> element indicates the CLR versions that are supported by your application.

Two optional attributes, version and sku, represent string values that specify the version of the .NET Framework that this application supports and the SKU that runs the application.

The version attribute string must match the installation folder name for the specified version of the .NET Framework.

If you do not include the <supportedRuntime> element in the application configuration file, then the CLR assumes that the runtime version that builds the application is the only supported runtime. The CLR gets the version of runtime that builds the application from the application's assembly metadata file.

In situations where multiple versions of runtime are supported, the first element should specify the most desired runtime version and the last element should specify the least desired version.

The following example demonstrates how to specify supported runtime versions in a configuration file:

```
<configuration>
   <startup>
      <supportedRuntime version="v1.1.4322"/>
      <supportedRuntime version="v1.0.3705"/>
   </startup>
</configuration>
```

TAKE NOTE*

Additionally, you can use Mscorcfg.msc to specify either assembly locations or locations for the CLR to search for assemblies.

CONFIGURING THE LOCATION OF AN ASSEMBLY

You can use one of the following elements to specify the location of an assembly:

- <codeBase> element
- <probing> element

MORE INFORMATION
To understand how the runtime searches for an assembly, you can read the "How the Runtime Locates Assemblies" section from the MSDN library.

If you have changed your assembly to a different location, then you can use a configuration setting to redirect references made to that assembly. Only the machine configuration file or the publisher policy files that redirect an assembly can use the `<codeBase>` element. When the runtime determines the assembly version to use, it applies the code base setting from the file that decides the version. If there is no specific code base, the runtime probes for the assembly in the normal way.

The following example demonstrates how the `<codeBase>` element determines an assembly's location:

```
<configuration>
   <runtime>
      <assemblyBinding xmlns="urn:schemas-microsoft-com:asm.v1">
         <dependentAssembly>
            <assemblyIdentity name="sampAssembly"
publicKeyToken="75yz7ik27d1g36n7" culture="en-us"/>
            <codeBase version="3.5.0.0" href="http://www.mysite.com/
sampAssembly.dll"/>
         </dependentAssembly>
      </assemblyBinding>
   </runtime>
</configuration>
```

The `<codeBase>` element:

- Requires the `href` attribute
- Does not support version ranges
- Only the strong-named assemblies require the `version` attribute

TAKE NOTE*
The runtime uses probing to locate assemblies that do not have a code base.

You can use the `<probing>` element in the application configuration file to specify subdirectories that the runtime should search when locating an assembly, as shown in the following example:

```
<configuration>
   <runtime>
      <assemblyBinding xmlns="urn:schemas-microsoft-com:asm.v1">
         <probing privatePath="bin;bin1;bin2"/>
      </assemblyBinding>
   </runtime>
</configuration>
```

You can use the `privatePath` attribute to specify the directories that the runtime should search for assemblies. If the application is located at C:\Program Files\SampApp, the runtime will search for assemblies that do not specify a code base in C:\Program Files\SampApp\Bin, C:\Program Files\SampApp\Bin1, and C:\Program Files\SampApp\Bin2.

TAKE NOTE*
The directories specified in the `privatePath` attribute must be subdirectories of the application base directory.

CERTIFICATION READY?
Embed configuration management functionality into a .NET Framework application.
USD 3.1

CERTIFICATION READY?
Create a custom Microsoft Windows Installer for .NET components by using the `System.Configuration.Install` namespace, and configure .NET Framework applications by using configuration files, environment variables, and the .NET Framework configuration tool (Mscorcfg.msc).
USD 3.2

LOCATING ASSEMBLIES USING DEVPATH

You may have multiple applications that share an assembly. You may have to verify that the shared assembly functions properly with these applications when you are developing this assembly. You must place the assembly in the GAC repeatedly to verify proper functioning. Alternatively, you can create a DEVPATH environment variable. This environment variable specifies the build output directory for the assembly.

For example, consider a scenario where you are building a shared assembly called Shared Assembly and the output directory is C:\SharedAssembly\Debug. You can assign the path, C:\SharedAssembly\Debug, to the DEVPATH variable. In addition, you must specify the `<developmentMode>` element in the machine configuration file that informs the CLR to use DEVPATH to locate assemblies.

Now the runtime must locate the shared assembly. You can use the `<codeBase>` or `<probing>` elements in a configuration file to specify a private directory for resolving assembly references. You can also put the assembly in a subdirectory of the application directory.

The following example demonstrates how to make the runtime search for assemblies in directories specified by the DEVPATH environment variable:

```
<configuration>
   <runtime>
      <developmentMode developerInstallation="true"/>
   </runtime>
</configuration>
```

The default value of the `developerInstallation` attribute is false.

TAKE NOTE*

DEVPATH environment variable is an advanced feature, and you must use this feature only during the development cycle. The runtime always uses the first assembly it locates and does not check the versions on strong-named assemblies in the DEVPATH.

If you specify `<codeBase>`, `<probing>`, and DEVPATH, then DEVPATH takes priority over the other two. This is because the CLR first searches the configuration files to resolve the assembly location where the `developmentMode` element defined indicates the CLR to look at the DEVPATH variable to resolve the assembly.

■ Creating Custom Installers

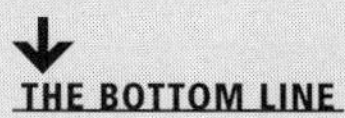

THE BOTTOM LINE

Once you build your application completely, you must create an installer to deploy the application in the client machine. You can create standard installer packages by creating a Visual Studio Installation project to deploy your application. However, you may have to perform application-specific actions during an installation. To achieve this, you can create ***custom installers***. The `System.Configuration.Install` namespace provides classes that you can use to perform application-specific tasks during installation.

Exploring the Install Namespace

You can write custom installers for custom components using the classes offered by the `System.Configuration.Install` namespace.

The `Installer` class is the base class of the `System.Configuration.Install` namespace for all custom installers in the .NET Framework.

Table 12-3 describes the classes of the `System.Configuration.Install` namespace.

Table 12-3

Classes of the `System.Configuration.Install` namespace

CLASS	DESCRIPTION
`AssemblyInstaller`	Loads an assembly and executes all the installers in it.
`ComponentInstaller`	Depicts an installer that copies component properties and uses them during installation.
`InstallContext`	Stores information about the current installation.
`Installer`	Offers a foundation for custom installations.
`InstallerCollection`	Stores a collection of installers to be executed during an installation.
`InstallEventArgs`	Provides data for various events like `BeforeInstall` and `AfterInstall`.
`InstallException`	Depicts the exception that is thrown when an error occurs during the commit, rollback, or uninstall phase of an installation.
`TransactedInstaller`	Defines an installer that either succeeds completely or fails and leaves the computer in its initial state.

TAKE NOTE*

The `Rollback` method facilitates the restoration of a failed installation. Alternatively, the `TransactedInstaller` class facilitates restoration of failed installations when multiple installers are associated with an assembly; that is, you can use this class when you have a series of installations that must be completed in a specific order as a single transaction unit.

Table 12-4 describes the `UninstallAction` enumeration of the `System.Configuration.Install` namespace. This enumeration specifies the actions that an installer should perform during an uninstallation process.

Table 12-4

`UninstallAction` enumeration settings

ENUMERATION VALUE	DESCRIPTION
`Remove`	Removes the resource created by the installer.
`NoAction`	Leaves the resource created by the installer as is.

You must create a custom installer to install an application on a computer.

CREATE A CUSTOM INSTALLER

Perform the following steps to create and use a custom installer:

1. Inherit the `Installer` class.
2. Override the `Install`, `Commit`, `Rollback`, and `Uninstall` methods.
3. Set the `RunInstaller` attribute of the derived class as true.
4. Place the derived class in the assembly along with the application to be installed.
5. Invoke the installer using the `InstallUtil.exe`.

The `Installers` property of the `Installer` class holds a collection of installers. The `Install`, `Commit`, `Rollback`, and `Uninstall` methods of the `Installer` class invoke the corresponding method of each installer from the collection of installers. These methods are not always called on the same instance of the `Installer`. So, for the derived class, it is not appropriate to save the state of a computer in an installer. You can use an `IDictionary` to store the state of a computer. When stored, the state is retained across calls and is passed to the `Install`, `Commit`, `Rollback`, and `Uninstall` methods.

The following example creates a custom installer using the `Installer` class:

- Set the `RunInstaller` attribute to true just before the class is defined in the next step:

```
[RunInstaller(true)]
```

- Create a class that inherits from `Installer`. Also, set the committed and committing event handlers for the installer:

```
public class CustomInstallerClass: Installer
{
  public CustomInstallerClass():base()
  {
    this.Committed += new InstallEventHandler(CustomInstaller_
Committed);
    this.Committing += new InstallEventHandler(CustomInstaller_
Committing);
  }
  // All the code in the next steps will come here
}
```

- Create the event handler methods for the `Committing` and the `Committed` events within the class:

```
private void CustomInstaller_Committing(object sender,
InstallEventArgs e)
{
  Console.WriteLine("This is the Committing Event.");
}
private void CustomInstaller_Committed(object sender,
InstallEventArgs e)
{
  Console.WriteLine("This is the Committed Event.");
}
```

- Override the `Install` method within the class itself:

```
public override void Install(IDictionary pastState)
{
  base.Install(pastState);
}
```

- Override the `Commit` method within the class itself:

```
public override void Commit(IDictionary pastState)
{
  base.Commit(pastState);
}
```

- Override the `Rollback` method within the class itself:

```
public override void Rollback(IDictionary pastState)
{
  base.Rollback(pastState);
}
public static void Main()
{
  Console.WriteLine("Usage:installutil.exe Installer.exe");
}
```

TAKE NOTE*

You can use the InstallUtil.exe to install assemblies as shown: `InstallUtil myassembly.exe`
To uninstall an assembly, you can use the tool as shown: `InstallUtil /u myassembly.exe`

Installing Assemblies

You can use the `AssemblyInstaller` class to load an assembly and execute all the embedded installers.

Assemblies can have multiple installers associated with them. One scenario in which you may use multiple installers in your assembly is when your assembly may be dependent on two other assemblies. That is, if the two assemblies on which your assembly is based must be installed before your assembly, then your assembly is associated with three installers that are installed in a sequence. Alternatively, your assembly can have multiple installers targeting different operating system editions such as the Web, server, client, or compact editions. Thus, if you have a generic application, you can create and associate multiple installers with that application to target different operating system editions or even platforms.

To install an assembly, you must first load the assembly and then invoke the installers associated with it. You can log the progress of installation during the assembly install. The example given here demonstrates the procedure to load an assembly and install it:

- Define the hash table for saving the past state:

  ```
  IDictionary pastState = new Hashtable();
  ```

- Set the `commandline` argument array for specifying a log file that records the progress of installation:

  ```
  string[] cmdline = new string[1] {"/LogFile=mylog.log"};
  ```

- Create an object of the `AssemblyInstaller` class by invoking the `Assembly Installer` constructor. The following code loads an assembly named customAssembly.exe and logs the errors in the log file specified by the `cmdline` object:

  ```
  AssemblyInstaller customAssemblyInstaller = new
  AssemblyInstaller("customAssembly.exe", cmdline);

  customAssemblyInstaller. UseNewContext = true;
  ```

- Use the `Install` and `Commit` methods for installing the `customAssembly.exe` assembly:

  ```
  customAssemblyInstaller.Install(pastState);
  customAssemblyInstaller.Commit(pastState);
  ```

CERTIFICATION READY?
Create a custom Microsoft Windows Installer for .NET components by using the `System.Configuration.Install` namespace, and configure .NET Framework applications by using configuration files, environment variables, and the .NET Framework configuration tool (Mscorcfg.msc).
USD 3.2

SKILL SUMMARY

This lesson described the concept of configuring .NET applications and creating a custom installer for the installation of an application.

Configuration files are XML files that include elements to configure settings. You can use tags to specify the start and end of an element in a configuration file. Machine, application, and security are the three types of configuration files.

The `System.Configuration` namespace contains several classes, interfaces, delegates, and enumerations to manage configuration data.

The .NET Framework configuration tool (Mscorcfg.msc) plays an important role in the configuration process. The configuration of the .NET environment includes specifying the supported runtime versions and redirecting the location of assemblies to specific paths.

You can create custom installers with the help of the classes in the `System.Configuration.Install` namespace. The `Installer` class is the base class of the `System.Configuration.Install` namespace for all custom installers in the .NET Framework. You can use this class to create a custom installer for your application by overriding the standard methods in that class. You can install an assembly using the `AssemblyInstaller` class.

For the certification examination:

- Understand the use of configuration files and various requirements to configure a .NET application.
- Know how to create custom installers to install .NET applications.

Knowledge Assessment

Matching

Match the following descriptions to the appropriate terms.

a. UninstallAction
b. DEVPATH
c. Machine configuration file
d. Security configuration file
e. Probing

_______ 1. Stores information about the code group hierarchy

_______ 2. Provides settings for the whole computer

_______ 3. Specifies subdirectories the runtime should search when locating an assembly

_______ 4. Specifies the actions an installer should perform during an uninstallation process

_______ 5. Specifies the build output directory for an assembly

True / False

Circle T if the statement is true or F if the statement is false.

T | F 1. The `ConfigurationElement` class specifies the property of a configuration element.

T | F 2. Application configuration files have the same full name of the application followed by .config as in myapp.exe.config.

T | F 3. The application calls the `Update` method of the configuration object to update an open configuration object.

T | F 4. You can create a custom configuration section handler using the `ConfigurationManager` class.

T | F 5. When you create a custom installer, you must not save the state of a computer for the derived class.

Fill in the Blank

Complete the following sentences by writing the correct word or words in the blanks provided.

1. There are ______ types of configuration files.
2. The ________ class provides access to configuration files for client applications.
3. The _________ class loads an assembly and executes all the embedded installers.
4. You can use an ___________ to store the state of a computer during installation.
5. The _________ class leaves the computer in its initial state when you are installing assemblies.

Multiple Choice

Circle the letter or letters that correspond to the best answer or answers.

1. Which configuration files contain configuration settings that are readable by the Common Language Runtime?
   a. Machine
   b. Application
   c. Security
   d. All of the above
2. Which class represents a configuration element within a configuration file?
   a. `ConfigurationElement`
   b. `ConfigurationElementCollection`
   c. `ConfigurationElementProperty`
   d. `Configuration`
3. Which of these methods are used for installing the assembly?
   a. `Commit`
   b. `Install`
   c. `Rollback`
   d. `InstallAs`
4. Which class provides data for events such as `BeforeInstall` and `AfterInstall`?
   a. `InstallContext`
   b. `ComponentInstaller`
   c. `InstallEventArgs`
   d. `TransactedInstaller`
5. Which element must you configure to specify the runtime versions supported by your assembly?
   a. `<supportedRuntime>`
   b. `<runtimeSupported>`
   c. `<supportedRuntimes>`
   d. `<runtimesSupported>`

Review Questions

1. You are the system administrator of a small organization where the members want to use a single database for all the three applications that they use. You may have to change the location of the database frequently according to your organization policy. As an administrator, you want to control the connectivity of the applications from a single place. How can you achieve this?
2. You are creating a custom installer. If the installation fails in between, you want to remove the files installed so far. How can you achieve this?

Case Scenarios

Scenario 12-1: Accessing Connection Strings

Consider that your application needs to access the connection string defined in the machine.config file. How can you do this?

Scenario 12-2: Installing an Assembly

Consider that you have created a .NET assembly. You want to load and install this assembly. Write code to achieve this.

Workplace Ready

Simplifying Configurations and Installations

Any application that you develop must be easily configurable and deployable if you want it to be used extensively. .NET offers separate namespaces to configure and create an installer for your application. You must leverage the classes in these namespaces to provide a custom deployment solution for your application.

You are the solution architect for XYZ Insurance, Inc. You have created an assembly that checks and installs automatic updates of an application that your organization uses. You have some settings that this assembly shares with other applications in your organization and few other settings that are specific to this assembly. You must design a configuration and deployment solution for your automatic update assembly so that the assembly is installable using a single.exe file. Suggest an approach that you would take in this scenario.

Appendix A
Microsoft .NET Framework Application Development Foundation: Exam 70-536

Objective Domain	Skill Number	Lesson Number
Develop applications that use system types and collections.		
Manage data in a .NET Framework application by using .NET Framework system types.	1.1	1, 2
Manage a group of associated data in a .NET Framework application by using collections.	1.2	2
Manage data in a .NET Framework application by using specialized collections.	1.3	2
Improve type safety and application performance in a .NET Framework application by using generic collections.	1.4	2
Implement .NET Framework interfaces to cause components to comply with standard contracts.	1.5	1
Control interactions between .NET Framework application components by using events and delegates.	1.6	1
Implement service processes, threading, and application domains in a .NET Framework application.		
Implement, install, and control a service.	2.1	6
Develop multi-threaded .NET Framework applications.	2.2	7
Create a unit of isolation for Common Language Runtime in a .NET Framework application by using application domains.	2.3	6
Embed configuration, diagnostic, management, and installation features into a .NET Framework application.		
Embed configuration management functionality into a .NET Framework application.	3.1	12
Create a custom Microsoft Windows Installer for .NET components by using the System.Configuration.Install namespace, and configure .NET Framework applications by using configuration files, environment variables, and the .NET Framework configuration tool (Mscorcfg.msc).	3.2	12
Manage an event log by using System.Diagnostics namespace.	3.3	8
Manage system processes and monitor the performance of a .NET Framework application by using the diagnostics functionality of the .NET Framework.	3.4	8

Objective Domain	Skill Number	Lesson Number
Debug and trace a .NET Framework application by using the System.Diagnostics namespace.	3.5	8
Embed management information and events into a .NET Framework application.	3.6	8
Implement serialization and input/output functionality in a .NET Framework application.		
Serialize or deserialize an object or an object graph by using runtime serialization techniques.	4.1	5
Control the serialization of an object into XML format by using the System.Xml.Serialization namespace.	4.2	5
Implement custom serialization formatting by using the Serialization Formatter classes.	4.3	5
Access files and folders by using the File System classes.	4.4	3
Manage byte streams by using Stream classes.	4.5	3
Manage the .NET Framework application data by using Reader and Writer classes.	4.6	3
Compress or decompress stream information in a .NET Framework application.	4.7	3
Improve the security of .NET Framework applications by using the .NET Framework security features.		
Implement code access security to improve the security of a .NET Framework application.	5.1	9
Implement access control by using the System.Security.AccessControl classes	5.2	9
Implement a custom authentication scheme by using the System.Security.Authentication classes	5.3	9
Encrypt, decrypt, and hash data by using the System.Security.Cryptography classes	5.4	9
Control permissions for resources by using the System.Security.Permission classes	5.5	9
Control code privileges by using the System.Security.Policy classes	5.6	9
Access and modify identity information by using the System.Security.Principal classes	5.7	9
Modify the code access security policy at the computer, user and enterprise level by using the code access security policy tool.	5.8	9
Implement interoperability, reflection, and mailing functionality in a .NET Framework application.		
Expose COM components to the .NET Framework and the .NET Framework components to COM.	6.1	11
Call unmanaged DLL functions in a .NET Framework application and control the marshaling of data in a .NET Framework application.	6.2	11

Objective Domain	Skill Number	Lesson Number
Create metadata, Microsoft Intermediate Language (MSIL), and a PE file by using the System.Reflection.Emit namespace.	6.3	7
Send electronic mail to a Simple Mail Transfer Protocol (SMTP) server for delivery from a .NET Framework application.	6.4	10
Implement globalization, drawing, and text manipulation functionality in a .NET Framework application.		
Format data based on culture information.	7.1	10
Enhance the user interface of a .NET Framework application by using the System.Drawing namespace.	7.2	4
Enhance the text handling capabilities of a .NET Framework application, and search, modify, and control text in a .NET Framework application by using regular expressions	7.3	10
Enhance the user interface of a .NET Framework application by using brushes, pens, colors, and fonts.	7.4	4
Enhance the user interface of a.NET Framework application by using graphics, images, bitmaps, and icons.	7.5	4
Enhance the user interface of a .NET Framework application by using shapes and sizes.	7.6	4

Index

A

O

P

T

X